W9-BCU-110

WITHDRAWN
FROM
COLLECTION

FORDHAM
UNIVERSITY
LIBRARIES

New Foundations of Ontology

A portrait of Gustav Bergmann at seventy, by Leola Bergmann

New Foundations of Ontology

Gustav Bergmann

Edited by William Heald

Foreword by Edwin B. Allaire

The University of Wisconsin Press

Fordham University
LIBRARY
AT
LINCOLN CENTER
New York, N. Y.

B
945
·B44N48
1992

The University of Wisconsin Press
114 North Murray Street
Madison, Wisconsin 53715

3 Henrietta Street
London WC2E 8LU, England

Copyright © 1992
The Board of Regents of the University of Wisconsin System
All rights reserved

5   4   3   2   1

Printed in the United States of America

Library of Congress Cataloging-in-Publication Data
Bergmann, Gustav, 1906–1987.
    New foundations of ontology / Gustav Bergmann ; edited by William
Heald ; foreword by Edwin Allaire.
    392 pp.   cm.
    Includes bibliographical references and index.
    ISBN 0-299-13130-0
    1. Ontology.   I. Heald, William Smith.   II. Title.
B945.B473N48   1991
111—dc20   91-31693

Fordham University
LIBRARY
AT
LINCOLN CENTER
New York, N. Y.

To Leola Bergmann, without whom this work would not have been possible

Contents

Foreword

During the last two decades of his life—from the publication of *Realism* in 1967 until his death in 1987—Gustav Bergmann published only five essays. One, "Diversity," his presidential address to the Western Division of the American Philosophical Association, appeared in 1968; the other four, between 1977 and 1981.

In those decades Bergmann worked as hard and as steadily as he ever had; and he was a hard worker indeed. In the twenty-five years prior to *Realism*, Bergmann published over a hundred essays, many of which are contained in four essay collections, and *Philosophy of Science*.

In his presidential address Bergmann made known his dissatisfaction with certain aspects of his ontology, in particular his assays of the facts expressed by universal and existential statements. (See "Generality and Existence," *Theoria*, 28, 1962.) He thus set about to rethink his system. *New Foundations of Ontology* is the result.

The manuscript seems to have been begun sometime in 1974 and completed in late 1975. Bergmann decided to delay its publication: he had reservations about the penultimate chapter, which deals with classes and arithmetic. He never returned to the manuscript per se. Instead, he led himself into the depths of set theory, a subject he had once known well. (Bergmann earned a PhD in mathematics and from 1928 to 1935 published eight papers in mathematics proper.)

Though absorbed by set theory, Bergmann continued to reflect on his new ontology and managed to publish three papers concerning it: "Sketch of an Ontological Inventory," *Journal of the British Society for Phenomenology*, 1979; "Notes on Ontology," *Nous*, 1981; and "Notes on the Ontology of Minds," *Midwest Studies in Philosophy*, 1981. As the first word of each title indicates, those papers merely hint at the new direction of his thought. Further, they are not informed by the systematics contained in the manuscript.

Beginning in 1980, I had a number of conversations with Bergmann about his work. By then, his reservations about the manuscript were severe; indeed, he never offered to let me see it. On occasion he contemplated destroying it; but he was persuaded to leave it amongst his papers.

In 1984, Bergmann and I had several long and difficult discussions about what he wanted done with his papers after his death. Though in good health at the time, Bergmann had decided not to publish again during his lifetime. His plan was to complete a long, independent essay on classes and the ontology of arithmetic; and I promised to publish it posthumously in a volume that was to include the three essays on his new ontology.

In fall 1985, Bergmann fell ill and did not work again. In summer 1986, I went through his papers and placed them in the University of Iowa Archives. The essay on classes was too incomplete to consider publishing; but I got my first look at the book manuscript and was immediately convinced that it should be published. With the encouragement and support of Leola Bergmann, Gustav's widow, I arranged to have William Heald edit the manuscript and prepare it for publication.

From the outset of his philosophical work, Bergmann was an ideal-language philosopher, a descendant of Russell and the early Wittgenstein; and, influenced by his early association with the positivists, he was an empiricist. The so-called Principle of Acquaintance was central to his thought.

Being an ideal-language philosopher meant for Bergmann that one had to design a formalism (a) the signs of which (i) stand for entities with which one is acquainted or with which one is presented and (ii) reflect the kinds or categories of entities required to solve the classical problems and (b) into which one could "translate" the unproblematic statements of the natural language, the logical relationships between them being preserved.

Bergmann's deepest conviction was that every true statement of the natural language expresses or states a fact which needs ontological analysis into either entities or other facts already analyzed. The analyses, which had to be integrated using a formalism, are needed in order to solve such classical problems as those of individuation and universals. The dominant problem in his early work was to develop a formalism that would bear the analytic-synthetic distinction, thereby solving the problem of necessity.

The ideal language is primarily a methodological device; but it forces one to be systematic and to face the consequences of having to use various types of signs in the formalism in order that the translation program succeed. If a kind of sign is needed then one is committed to there being a kind of entity and thus to showing that one is acquainted with it.

Of course, if one does not accept the Principle of Acquaintance one need not worry about whether or not instances of a kind of are experienced. But one who does not accept that or a similar principle is, for Bergmann, a *mere* formalist, someone who is not entitled to speak of kinds of entities, only of kinds of signs and of the properties of a formalism. Bergmann's disdain for the formalists intensified over the years and is particularly evident in "Sketch of an Ontological Inventory."

Bergmann's opposition to the formalists is embodied in two methodological principles: first, that the basic, undefined signs of the formalism must stand for simple entities and, second, that every feature of a formalism that does representational work indicates an ontological commitment. Both principles lead to grave difficulties.

Consider a formalism that has, amongst other kinds of signs, x type and f type signs. Two constants of the same type reflect that there are different entities; and since they are of the same type they reflect that the entities stood for are of the same category or kind. A simple sign is thus not really simple at all! Bergmann was aware of the difficulty early on but did not explore its ontological implications.

Consider a formalism that makes use of sentences of the form xRy. The difference between the facts reflected by 'aRb' and 'bRa' cannot be accounted for merely in terms of the signs and the form of sentence in which they occur. The order of the signs does representational work; but, not being a sign, it cannot be deemed to represent an entity. The early Bergmann ignored the difficulty or bided his time in addressing it.

Though *New Foundations* is structured so as to culminate in the ontological assay of classes, Bergmann's formalism is dictated by his attempt to solve the problem of order. And solve it he does, in a startling manner. He finds a way to assay order without the order of the signs in a sentence having significance. The solution is costly though. It forces Bergmann to give ontological status to *diads*, complexes of two entities which complexes are nonetheless not facts.

Bergmann minimizes the cost by showing that diads can be used to solve several problems; furthermore, the syntax of his ideal language is built on the notion of a diad. That puts the point somewhat inaccurately. In setting out his new ontology, Bergmann opts to talk in terms of canons regulating how entities can combine rather than in terms of formation rules regulating how signs can combine; and he opts to do so in order to stress that he is an ontologist, not a formalist.

New Foundations also addresses the problems caused by the simple signs of the formalism not being simple at all. Since no formalism that depends on formation rules can avoid using signs that harbor a complexity, Bergmann argues that he has unearthed a limit of ontological analysis. He does not leave the matter there, however. He tries to exhibit the manner in which one experiences the complexity of a "simple" entity. His conception of experience, however, is no longer the notion of acquaintance; it is now that of "phenomenological rock bottom." That notion, variously elaborated on, is used throughout and plays a conspicuous role in his new solution to the problem of necessity.

New Foundations is a difficult book. At several places Bergmann compares his present views with his earlier ones, thus assuming a familiarity with the latter. Also, his solutions to the classical problems, from those of perception of those of necessity and arithmetic, are complicated and reflected in a formalism the images or strings of which are unfamiliar. Also, his style is idiosyncratic. Finally, Bergmann does not display his formalism in a plain, well-structured, syntactical way; rather he lets it evolve as the needs require. The difficulties notwithstanding, Bergmann's final words on ontology are well worth the effort of working through, if only because they set an awesome standard for systematic ontology.

EDWIN B. ALLAIRE

Editor's Note

When Ed Allaire offered me the opportunity to edit Bergmann's last book-length manuscript I accepted enthusiastically, though I approached the task itself with trepidation. Most of Bergmann's colleagues and former students at Iowa and elsewhere knew that he had been working on a book, though almost no one knew the state and condition of this project. Indeed, a major preliminary part of my job was to determine whether or not there existed a document complete enough to merit publication, whether or not there was something to edit.

A first reading of the manuscript allayed many of my fears; it was not, as I had feared, a loose assemblage of notes or a disconnected assortment of outlines or monographs. Instead it was, as we had all hoped, a book, with a coherent, though difficult, pattern of reasoning leading from its first page to its last. It was clear that each of the manuscript's seven chapters or "Sections" played a vital role in securing this pattern and that nothing was really dispensable.

This is not to say that there weren't a number of editorial problems. The first four Sections had been cleanly typed, in triplicate. The fifth Section had also been cleanly typed, in duplicate. The symbols and formulae had already been neatly penned in on at least (and, usually, at most) one of the three triplicated pages of Sections I through III, but were entirely absent from Sections IV and V. After a search through the boxes of Bergmann's notes, I located a thick manila folder containing the roughly typed copies of Sections II through V in which the symbols were filled in (though not altogether neatly and legibly). I use these as a master to fill the blanks of the clean copies of Sections IV and V.

In many respects the most important, and in any case the longest, Section of the book is Section VI, the topic of which is classes. There was no cleanly typed version of this Section at all, but instead, three roughly typed versions, each in its own manila folder. There were a number of differences among these three versions, consisting largely of penciled-in marginal comments, added sheets with passages to be inserted, and slips of paper taped to the pages of the text that bore various comments or insertions. On one of these three folders was written the message, "This is my final copy—completed 2/26/75." The copy in this folder contained by far the largest number of marginal comments, taped-on slips, and alterations. One lengthy marginal comment, a note from Bergmann to himself expressing doubts about something he had claimed in the text, was dated "10/12/77." Although I was not able to decipher this note in its entirety, its first sentence was "This now seems dubious to me." This dated comment is important because, given Bergmann's customary practice of dating his manuscripts and/or the folders in which they were kept, it might signal the period of Bergmann's last active involvement with the manuscript. Among Bergmann's notes and papers I discovered evidence that he had begun work, apparently in 1977, on another book-length project, the first chapter of which was to be entitled "Classes" (the title of Section VI of the present manuscript). Bergmann's work on this latter project is too rough and unfinished to allow a judgment about whether he was dissatisfied with the ontology of classes presented in the present manuscript (henceforth *NFO*) or whether, on the contrary, he had thought of even more convincing reasons for affirming it. It is clear, however, that he found the topic of classes both extremely important and difficult.

In any case it was fairly clear that the "third copy" expresses Bergmann's finished convictions about the ontology of classes at the time that he was still actively involved with the *NFO* project and that it must stand as his last word on the matter regardless of whether it expresses his last thoughts.

There were two roughly typed copies of Section VII, located together in one manila folder that bore the Section's title and the information that the contents of the folder had been finished on "7/1/75." The two copies were identical and *not* different *versions*. In contrast with Section VI, there were virtually no marginal comments, and what minor additions and corrections there were seemed to be of no philosophical importance. Despite the fact that the apparent completion date of Section VII is five months later than that of Section VI the relative absence of marginal comments and corrections on the rough copies of the former indicates that Bergmann was reasonably satisfied with it, something that seems clearly not to have been the case with Section VI. This might seem surprising, because Section VII extends and completes the very difficult chain of reasoning that fills the last pages of Section VI and, as well, forges close links between this chain of reasoning and Bergmann's ontology as a whole. I believe that many readers will concur with my judgment that Section VII, which articulates Bergmann's convictions about the limits of ontology, expresses some of the most firmly held of his later opinions, and that much of the "innovative" changes detailed in earlier Sections are designed precisely to enable Bergmann to square ontological convictions reached in his earlier work with a more accurate conception of ontology itself.

Once Sections VI and VII had been retyped and the symbols and formulae filled in, I had a fairly clean and complete manuscript with which to work. This "work" consisted in part of the usual editorial tasks of checking for misspellings and errors in punctuation and grammar. By far the most difficult portion of my task was determining whether or not the symbols and logical formulae that I had filled in were "correct" or, at least, were as Bergmann intended them to be. This was more difficult than one might suppose, in part because Bergmann's handwriting was often nearly indecipherable. The symbols in the rough copies had no doubt been intended for Bergmann's eyes only and were to be transcribed by him once the Sections had been retyped. In Section VI it was especially obvious that the formulae on the rough copy, like many of the marginal comments, served as a kind of shorthand to remind Bergmann himself rather than as a guide to an editor or a typist. The arrow symbol, '→', was here sometimes used to represent material implication, while the dot symbol '·', was used to indicate both conjunction and set-theoretical product. Following the precedent Bergmann sets in the early sections, I replaced the arrow with the horseshoe, and the dot, where it was clearly intended to represent conjunction, with the ampersand. More problematic were those cases in which very long formulae contained either an insufficient amount of "punctuation" (parentheses, brackets, etc.) to remove ambiguities in the formulae and cases in which some of the connectives were missing. More difficult yet were those cases in which there were, to speak bluntly, mistakes. Sometimes it seemed clear to me that a given formula had a missing symbol or contained the wrong connective or quantifier. If I thought that these mistakes were straightforward and obvious ones, the sort of error that Bergmann himself would have quickly caught if or when he had gone carefully over the text himself, I didn't hesitate to correct them. On the other hand, if something appeared to me to be confused, or if it seemed to me to embody a *philosophical* or *logical* error, but otherwise conformed to the message of the surrounding text, I left it alone. Clearly this involved making a number of potentially controversial decisions, but at some point this is precisely what an editor must do.

Aside from the purely editorial difficulties involved with producing a clear and "accurate" transcription of symbols and formulae, something must be said, as a caveat, about the manner in which Bergmann uses logical symbols, a manner which may well be confusing even to those familiar with Bergman's earlier work and will without doubt be confusing to those unaccustomed to philosophizing in the style of *Principia Mathematica*.

Bergmann has always been a partisan, more or less enthusiastic, of the "ideal-language method," a way of doing ontology that relies heavily on artificial languages or schemata. The basic idea behind the method is that an ontological analysis, or "assay," of an "object" (broadly, an analysandum) is best conducted by transcribing a natural-language expression representing that object into an artificial language which "perspicuously" reflects the ontological structure of the object. The assay may, in effect, be "read off" from the IL expression. Bergmann still, in *NFO*, uses the method, and indeed might even be said to provide strong *ontological* grounds for the necessity of the method (see Section V).

In his earlier work Bergmann regarded the schema of the lower functional calculus, as developed by Russell in *Principia Mathematica*, as his ideal language. This is, in *NFO*, no longer the case. Here Bergmann has altered the *PM* schema to reinforce and emphasize the ontological "similarity" of the exemplification nexus, the connectives, and the quantifiers (in short, the "functions"), as well as to eradicate "variables," or variable-like signs, in the expressions representing general facts and classes.

There may be nothing wrong with this of course, but Bergmann often introduces these modifications, then lapses back into a more *PM*-like schema, or even a mixture of the two, without a clear announcement of what he is doing. For example, the general fact conventionally represented in *PM* by an expression like '$(x)f_1(x)$' is held by Bergmann to be more perspicuously represented by an expression such as '$\bigvee\langle a_1, \eta \langle f_1, a_1\rangle\rangle$'. Clearly this notational modification, however well justified and explained, is going to be very hard on the eyes when even slightly more complicated formulae are involved. Recognizing this, Bergmann uses, in these more difficult cases, "mixed" expressions such as '$\bigvee\langle a_1, f_1(a_1)\rangle$', or '$a_1)f(a_1)$', or $(a)f(a)$. In some cases he will use an expression such as '$(a)B(a)$' or even '$(a)B$' to stand in for any universally quantified formula, where '(a)' is playing the role of the *PM* universal quantifier '(x)', and '$B(a)$' (or 'B') represents *any* "propositional schema" in which 'x' has a free occurrence.

These procedures are usually easy enough to follow if one reads attentively, and in many cases the rapid shifting back and forth from one set of notational conventions to another makes brevity possible and understanding easier. Sometimes, however, it is confusing and a reader must be careful indeed if he or she wishes to grasp what Bergmann is saying.

Although the manuscript was, as I have said, a unified and integrated document, it was in certain respects incomplete. Throughout the book Bergmann refers to "Appendices," in which he presumably would deal in greater detail with certain issues and problems alluded to but not covered in the main body of the text. These appendices unfortunately were never completed and, for that matter, never really begun. I did discover a folder containing extremely rough handwritten notes and outline sketches for these appendices and, as well, equally rough notes for a preface to *NFO*. Given the condition of these notes, it would have been impossible to reconstruct either, so I did not try. It was tempting to rewrite the text so as to excise all the references to the appendices and would, in fact, have been relatively easy to do so. But I very much wanted to leave the text as I found it to whatever extent was possible, consistent with the demands of clarity. The only typed page in the folder containing these rough notes was a page stapled to its inside cover. On this page was a table of contents for *NFO* and also a list of the titles of the appendices. Without commenting further on the contents of the missing appendices, I reproduce these titles exactly as I found them on this page:

A. Dangling Principles and Philosophical Anthropology

B. Some Reflections on the Ontology of the Early Russell

C. Phenomenological Realism Revisited

D. The Meaning Nexus Revisited.

The precise nature of the views Bergmann intended to express in these appendices will have to remain a matter of conjecture.

It should in passing be mentioned that the rough notes for the intended preface to the manuscript bear the date "10/31/71," from which it is reasonable to conclude that this is approximately the beginning of the time of Bergmann's involvement with the project. In March of 1972 Bergmann was scheduled to read a paper at the Russell Centenary Conference at Indiana University; at very nearly the last moment Bergmann canceled. The paper, bearing the title "New Foundations of Ontology," was never published and never delivered. This paper, which I have read, contains many of the ideas that find a more extensive formulation in this manuscript. I read the paper before I discovered the folder containing the notes for the preface and appendices to the book and so naturally concluded that the book was an extension of the ideas first formulated in the paper. Since, however, the paper was apparently written after these notes, it may be more reasonable to conclude that the paper was to be the first public expression of ideas that Bergmann had already intended to cover more fully in a not yet written book. In any case, there are some significant differences between the paper and the book (see below), and it seems clear that Bergmann was dissatisfied with the paper as written and that the book project, though formulated before the composition of the paper, was in fact written with an eye to resolving the problems which Bergmann might have sensed in the paper.

A somewhat more significant shortcoming of the manuscript concerns apparent inconsistencies in the usage and even the definitions of some of the technical terms that Bergmann introduces. In Section IV Bergmann introduces the notion of a "primary class" and equates this notion with that of a "full-status" class, the latter notion being that of a class that is thinkable and so has full (nonderived) ontological status. But in Section VI, which enunciates Bergmann's more complete ontology of classes, we are told that primary classes, classes with a finite number of elements, are only *one* of the sorts of full-status classes, and that there are among these thinkable classes two more types, "secondary" classes and "tertiary" classes, which have respectively, to make a long story short, a denumerably infinite and an "indefinite" number of elements. Taken as it stands, this is simply a contradiction and, indeed, one that can be enormously confusing. Partly it is due to a change in usage; but it is also indicative, I think, of Bergmann's ambivalence toward infinite classes. On the one hand he wishes to grant full ontological status to only those determinates that can be construed as "producible" from a finite number of simples by a finite number of canonical "steps"; on the other hand he clearly does believe that if he does not grant full status to some sort of infinite classes, he cannot ground arithmetic. It is not going too far to say that much that is difficult and interesting in Section VI is a consequence of this ambivalence.

Again, when Bergmann introduces the extremely important notion of a "transparent" intention (in Section II) as an intention that is presented *with* its mode and then goes on to allow that there are acts with intentions that have no modes, it is clear that some other definition must be provided for this absolutely crucial concept. That the concept of transparency, or at least a proper definition of it, is both indispensable and problematic, may be gathered, I believe, from the unpublished and undelivered 1972 paper that gave its title to this book. In this paper Bergmann declared that all *things* (particulars and universals) have modes. There seems to be nothing at all to recommend this claim *except* that it would preserve the intelligibility of the above definition of 'transparency' in those cases in which a transparent intention has no mode; in this book Bergmann has wisely dropped the claim, leaving us, however, with the mystery of how to understand the concept of transparency. Bergmann does give us the metaphor of a transparent intention as one which is "illuminated," as it were, "from behind," but this is not altogether satisfying. There is a genuine tension here, one that cannot be quickly resolved by verbal housekeeping.

In these and a few other cases I have added footnotes in order to point out what may be jarring to a reader. I do not pretend to resolve the problems that these apparent terminological inconsistencies might conceal.

Another, much less significant mystery concerns a peculiar sequence of starred (arabic) numbers which appear throughout the text, from Section I through Section VII. The first, 1*, appears on page 47 and the last, 71*, appears on page 353. Each such starred number precedes a paragraph, and a few of these paragraphs are followed shortly thereafter by paragraphs that are preceded by a single (unnumbered) star. These numbers give the appearance of being convenient labels for those paragraphs that cover certain topics or contain certain arguments. Indeed, in several instances Bergmann does refer back to something presumably mentioned or discussed in a number-starred section, but this is not common; usually, if he wishes to refer to something he has discussed he uses page numbers. I have not been able to discern any significant division of topics demarcated by the starred numbers. I have not excised them, however, although this would not have been difficult. After all, there may well be some sort of pattern here, perhaps like Wittgenstein's numbering system in the *Tractatus*. Someone more acute than I may see what it is. (The reader should be aware that in two instances the number is repeated: 20* appears on both page 111 and page 114, and 50* appears on both page 236 and page 241.)

NFO is a difficult text, one that demands intensive study. It will not surrender its message easily to someone who merely reads it. Part of the reason for this is, in a sense, "stylistic": Bergmann's use of symbols, the manner in which he frames questions and pursues answers and emphasizes or deemphasizes issues may together constitute a real barrier to comprehension. Part of the reason is the very abstractness of the subject matter. Nothing can be done, nor can anything more be said, about either of these factors. Bergmann wrote the way he wrote, and ontology just is an abstract (and difficult) subject.

But something can and should be said by way of mitigating what will certainly seem to be a defect in the text in the eyes of those readers relatively unfamiliar with Bergmann's earlier work. *NFO* is very much an attempt to *consolidate* views that Bergmann held for many years. One will find herein no new, or even old, arguments for the existence of universals, bare particulars, or fundamental ties. Bergmann does not argue at all for his longstanding convictions that there are no substances (continuants), that the only distinction between generalizations that are laws of nature and those that are not is contextual, and that nonactual facts exist. These and many other views that would surely be considered controversial by most philosophers are simply not considered matters of contention in *NFO*. Instead, they are in the nature of assumptions or perhaps theorems that have already been established, that must be squared with each other in a systematic fashion and, perhaps more important, squared with what Bergmann now thinks is a more accurate and articulate conception of the scope and limits of ontology itself. Understanding this, and accepting that it is Bergmann's primary objective, will make comprehension and appreciation of this difficult and ambitious text easier than it might otherwise be.

The burdens of editing *NFO* were made considerably lighter by a number of people who lent me assistance. Ed Allaire, of the Philosophy Department of the University of Texas at Austin, and Panayot Butchvarov, of the Philosophy Department of the University of Iowa, who served as my advisors and consultants on the project, were generous with their time and efforts. Laird Addis, also of the University of Iowa Philosophy Department, read a first draft of my Introduction and made a large number of helpful suggestions. Phyllis Rooney and Evan Fales, again of the University of Iowa Philosophy Department, helped me interpret and understand some of the more difficult formulae in Sections IV and VI. I must also offer my thanks to Earl Rogers, Curator of Archives in the University of Iowa Special Collections Department, as well as the entire Special Collections staff. Joyce Kral, now an administrative assistant in the Business Office of the University of Iowa, graciously agreed to complete the typing of the manuscript she had begun typing many years before when she had been the Philosophy Department's secretary. Thanks are owed as well to Jan Kleinshmidt, the present secretary of the Philosophy Department, for her assistance in smoothing out my occasionally rough encounters with the Philosophy Department's word processors. The deepest debt of gratitude, however, is owed to Leola Bergmann, who gave me complete access to all of Bergmann's papers and notes, and indeed, even helped me decipher some of the more obscure marginal comments in Section VI. Without her enthusiastic support this book would probably never have been published.

Editor's Introduction

Editor's Introduction

Ontology, broadly conceived, involves proposal and defense of a system of categories, categories that correspond to the most general sorts of things there are, the most general kinds of existents. In addition to this or, indeed, as an essential part of it, the ontologist must provide a schematic description of the most general ways in which the existents that are members of these categories are related to each other, the ways they "go together" to compose the world. Bergmann's somewhat more narrow characterization—"Ontology accounts for everything there is in terms of simples"[1]—gives us a general picture of (I) the world for which he takes himself to be proposing a categorical system, (II) the basic shape of this system and, as well, (III) the fundamental strategy for defense of the system:

I. The world is the totality of existents that are composed of, or consist of, other, more nearly basic or fundamental existents. These other, more nearly basic, existents are, or may be, themselves composed of still other, still more nearly basic existents. Ultimately, however, all "composite" existents must have components that are not themselves composite, that themselves have no components; these are the "simples" of which all composite existents consist. There is no point at all in denying the largely metaphorical force of the terms "composite," "component," "consist," "basic," or "simple." One may think of composites and their simple components as analogous to spatial wholes and their parts.[2] One may think of composites as "objects

---

1. See below, p. 43.
2. See "The Limits of Ontological Analysis" in *The Ontological Turn*, ed. Moltke Gram and E. D. Klemke, University of Iowa Press, 1974, pp. 3–37. Butchvarov argues that ontological analysis in the atomistic style is based upon a systematic application of an analogy between existents and spatial wholes and parts; Butchvarov argues, moreover, that there are limitations to the utility of this analogy and that these limitations are evident at certain crucial junctures in the Bergmannian program. Not only are Butchvarov's arguments cogent but Bergmann clearly recognizes them to be so. Much of what Bergmann has to say in *NFO* is an acknowledgment of the limitations exposed by Butchvarov's criticisms. Bergmann by no means, however, abandons the atomistic approach he has always employed and to which he still sees no real alternative. While Butchvarov is very much on the mark in his evaluation of Bergmannian method, I believe there are other analogies and metaphors at work in Bergmann's work that are just

3

of higher order" that are "supported by" or "founded upon" their components. The simples of which composites ultimately consist may be thought of as "prior" to these composites, which are thus conceived of as "posterior" to their components. More dynamically, the simple components may be thought of as the "material" from which composites are "produced." The term "composite" itself perhaps suggests that simples are like "atoms" and the less nearly basic existents which they compose like "molecules." Either explicitly or implicitly Bergmann himself relies upon all of these analogies—spatial, temporal, physical, and chemical. In some ways this can become a problem, but it is almost certainly unavoidable. Any ontologist who concurs with the methodological slogan cited above must select some equally problematic set of terms to frame his conclusions, and it is surely an illusion to think that explicitly defined technical terms will obviate the need for metaphors. In what follows I will stick with the terms "composite," "compose," and "component," fully aware of the unexplicated analogical force they carry.

II. An ontologist must specify an exhaustive and exclusive schema of these componentless, or simple, existents, as well as a schema of the ways in which simples compose nonsimples. Clearly the most fundamental and important way that existents can be "related" to one another is by going together to compose another existent. For Bergmann, as for at least some other ontologists, relations, strictly speaking, are themselves existents that must in some way be connected to their relata in order to compose a relationship. It is this connection that is of special ontological importance rather than relations themselves.

III. An ontologist defends the categorical system which he proposes by showing that it allows us, starting from simples and the ways that simples can go together, to "recreate" or "build up" a world which contains those features and distinctions that belong to the pretheoretical (or at least prephilosophical) world of common sense. Another, roughly equivalent, way of stating this is to say that an ontologist *analyzes* various significant portions of the world of common sense *into* simples, where the "rules of decomposition," so to speak, are simply the reverse of the "principles of composition" governing the formation of nonsimples from simples. Bergmann himself sometimes uses the term "analysis" but seems to prefer the term "assay." The adequacy of an ontology, or categorical system, depends upon whether or

---

as problematic. The analogies of dependence and independence, and priority and posteriority, for example, are almost inextricably intertwined with Bergmann's conception of ontology and are perhaps as difficult to replace with a more literal set of terms.

not one can "ground" the various significant features and distinctions of the world "in" the existents available to a partisan of that system.

Even described in such a vague and incomplete fashion, the methodological program expressed by (I)–(III) shouldn't be unfamiliar. Avoiding the problematic phrase "logical atomism" for reasons that I hope will become obvious shortly, one may refer to this program as "atomistic realism," *atomistic* because it is an attempt to account for all the significant features of everything in terms of *simples, realism* for the slightly more subtle reason that it is an attempt to account for the features of existents in terms of other existents *in* those existents. If the ground of the features of an existent is *not in* that existent, the atomist is inclined to think, then the ground must be elsewhere, either in the mind of the person who perceives or conceives of the existent or, perhaps, in the patterns of discourse of those language-using persons who talk about the existent. In either of these cases, though, we are compelled to adopt an idealistic conception of the existent; at least to the extent that the problematic feature cannot be located outside of the persons who think or talk about the object, it becomes difficult to think of that object (or that object having that feature) as existing independently of the thought and discourse of those persons. Ultimately we are led to think of the object as a product of our thought or discourse, as something that we *make* by thinking and talking. It is no exaggeration to say that Gustav Bergmann has spent his philosophical career in the attempt to forestall such a conclusion, even of a limited sort (for example, that the logical form, though perhaps not the substance and content, of the world is a "contribution" of the human mind or language). It is important to emphasize this close intertwining of the realistic impulse and atomistic methodology in Bergmann's conception of first philosophy, for in this, his last extended ontological treatise, Bergmann displays a great deal of sensitivity to criticisms of atomistic metaphysics. Indeed, he as much as concedes that atomism *does* have "limits," that *not* everything *can* be accounted for in terms of simples. Accordingly, he has a great deal of difficulty maintaining the very extensive sort of realism that it is his hope to establish and defend. (I will briefly discuss this salvage attempt later.)

Although many ontologists are, or purport to be, realists, and although at least some of them are atomists, no other philosopher can match the passionate and focused energy Bergmann has devoted to the task of establishing a coherent and comprehensive atomistic realism. No one, therefore, can have a more legitimate claim to our attention when he describes the inevitable limitations of ontological analysis or proposes categorical schemata that are designed precisely to avoid the undesirable consequences of these limitations.

Categories and Canons

Bergmann's new ontology involves *three* categories of simples and *three* categories of nonsimples, or, equivalently as it turns out, three *ways* that members of the "most important" category of simples go together to compose nonsimples. The most important category of simple is that of "things," the major subsorts of which are particulars and universals. Universals themselves may be nonrelational properties of the first type such as red, green, or square; nonrelational properties of the second type such as color, shape, or pitch; relational-properties of the first type such as being-(spatially)contiguous-to and/or being-(temporarily)later-than; relational properties of the second type such as being-a-darker-color-than and being-a-higher-pitch-than. Bergmann is noncommittal about whether there are ternary or quaternary relations or relations that have even larger numbers of relata. He is also noncommital about whether there are universals of types still higher than those mentioned, though he does insist that the number of types is finite. He is completely silent about such issues as whether, say, loudness (as in the loudness of a tone) is a relational or a nonrelational property, believing, apparently, that these issues are "empirical" issues and are dialectically insignificant. Bergmann does insist that particulars are "bare"; that is, the properties that particulars have are "external" to the particulars and are not a part of the "nature" of the particulars. More surprisingly, perhaps, universals are also bare in this sense. This is an ontologically important issue to which I shall return later.

One of the most fundamental sorts of nonsimple is *atomic facts*. This-being-green (where "this" designates some particular), navy-blue-being-a-darker-color-than-yellow, this-being-to-the-left-of-that (where "this" and "that" designate particulars), and so on, are all atomic facts. Atomic facts themselves go together to form *molecular facts*, such as this-being-green-and-that-being-purple. Atomic and molecular facts are the most important and, in a clear sense, the most basic (though by no means the only) members of the first category of nonsimple: *facts*. What has always been more or less distinctive about Bergmann's conception of facts is his firm conviction that a fact is not merely a collection of the things "in" it; things do not "hang together like the links in a chain" but rather must be "tied together" by an entirely different sort of existent. In his earlier work Bergmann called these existents, appropriately, "ties" and characterized them as "subsistents." What distinguishes them from things and facts (formerly termed "existents," with the term "entity" being used as the most generic term to comprehend both existents and subsistents) is that they are, to speak again metaphorically, "unsaturated" or "dependent." It is this that allows them to ground the connection between the things in an atomic fact and the atomic (or other sorts of) facts in a molecular fact. Thus the subsistent "exemplification" ties a particular to a universal in an atomic fact while the subsistent "conjunction" ties two facts into a conjunctive molecular fact.

In *New Foundations of Ontology* this is not substantially changed, though now Bergmann refers, in his initial formulation, to existents such as exemplification and conjunction as "makers." Exemplification *makes* the atomic fact this-being-red out of the particular this and the universal red. Conjunction *makes* the molecular fact this-being-red-and-that-being-square out of the two atomic facts this-being-red and that-being-square. Makers are the second category of simple existent.

The *ways* in which things and makers go together to compose facts (Bergmann uses the term "produce" rather than "compose") are specified by "canons." That exemplification makes a fact (or, if you like, *can* make a fact) out of a particular and a universal (of the appropriate type) is, to use a phrase that Bergmann himself does not use, a canonical truth. That a single particular cannot exemplify a relation, that there is no such existent as a disjunction of a property and a fact, that a fact cannot exemplify a universal—these are all consequences of the *canons* which specify which makers can make which facts out of which (categorical) sorts of things and facts. Canons correspond more or less to the formation rules of an ontologically perspicuous language (an "ideal language" or IL). Just as formation rules specify which syntactical sorts of signs can be concatenated to form a well-formed string, canons specify which things of which categories "produce" facts.

It is an important feature of Bergmann's new system, however, that facts are not the only sorts of nonsimples produced from simples. This is one reason for refusing to characterize his new ontology as a form of logical atomism, at least if a logical atomist is someone who believes that the world is just the totality of *facts*.[3] The new category of nonsimple Bergmann calls "circumstances." The most important subcategory of circumstance is that of "diversities" or, synonymously, "diads." Red-being-diverse-from-square, this-being-red-being-diverse-from-everything-being-either-round-or-not-round, the-thought-that-this-

3. Even when Bergmann believed that the only category of nonsimple was that of facts he would still have probably rejected the label of "logical atomist." For the reasons, see his "The Revolt against Logical Atomism," reprinted in *Meaning and Existence*, University of Wisconsin Press, 1959, pp. 39–72.

is-green-being-diverse-from-this-being-green are all diversities or diads. Clearly the hyphenated locutions represent "possible"[4] objects of thought and, in some sense, knowledge; equally clearly each of them does, or may, represent something which has at least as much of a claim to be considered a "part" of the world as whatever is represented by locutions such as "this-being-red" (or "this is red") or "that-being-green-and-square" (or "that is green and square"). According to Bergmann, there is a significant difference between, say, this-being-green, on the one hand, and green-being-diverse-from-red, on the other. The fundamental difference is that the former involves a maker, the tie of exemplification, which grounds the connection between the particular designated by "this" and the universal green. There is no relation or connection or tie of diversity: green-being-diverse-from-red involves no other existents than green and red.

That there is a category of circumstances, nonsimple existents that require no makers to ground the togetherness of the things in them, is in itself an important departure from Bergmann's earlier ontological views. The conviction that the connection between things in a complex must be grounded in an existent distinct from these things ("complex" is Bergmann's generic term embracing facts and circumstances) sometimes found expression in the claim that "all connections are external." This claim is a more general and radical version of Russell's assertion that (at least some) relations are external. Russell's assertion was made in response to the idealists' construal of all relations as "internal," as, in other words, grounded in the *natures* of the related objects. The theoretical function of the doctrine of the internality of all relations is to initiate a chain of inferences that begins with the thesis that the nature of each apparently distinct object of thought and/or experience really includes the natures of all other objects and ends with the thesis that the world is a seamless undifferentiated whole, the "Absolute." To block this chain of inferences, Russell insisted that at least some relations are external to the relata that coexemplify them.

---

4. The sense of "possible" used here is difficult to explicate. It is not *logical* possibility, for Bergmann holds that complexes which are logically impossible are nevertheless thinkable. It is somewhat more accurate to understand this broad sense of possible in terms of well-formedness, though there are difficulties here as well: there are sentences that would clearly be ill formed in ordinary language (e.g., 'Green means this'.) that do more or less correspond to strings that would be well formed in Bergmann's IL and that do, therefore, express something "thinkable." Moreover, there are sentences that are clearly well formed by most ordinary standards (e.g., 'Conjunction is diverse from negation'.) that Bergmann holds to express what is in fact unthinkable. Perhaps it is best to understand a "possible object of thought" in a very vague way as what may come before the mind, where the modal term ('may') is explicated by Bergmann's ontology as a whole.

It is not much of an overstatement to say that Bergmann's entire (pre-*NFO*) atomistic realism is a systematic development of his rather enthusiastic acceptance of Russell's strategy. Bergmann's "principle" (for it seems to be as much this as an assertion or claim) of the externality of all connections is clearly much more radical than Russell's limited claim. Bergmann refuses to concede even that the properties of properties or relations between properties are, in the relevant sense, "internal" to those properties, a conclusion that Russell would probably not have accepted, regardless of his desire to undermine absolute idealism. A possibly bitter consequence of Bergmann's radical doctrine is that such facts as red-being-a-color and navy-blue-being-darker-than-yellow must be treated as straightforward atomic (and contingent) facts. Russell would most likely not have accepted this counterintuitive result, while Bergmann has apparently no difficulty at all in accepting it; indeed, whatever epistemological burdens such a view forces Bergmann to carry, it dovetails nicely with his conception of the bareness of *all* things.

Bergmann even takes Russell (and others) to task for failing to recognize that not only all relations but all connections are external. Not only, that is, are relations such as being-a-darker-color-than external to their relata, but the connection of a particular (or any thing) to one of its properties is external to the particular (or thing) and the property that it "has." In short, the tie of exemplification (or indeed any of the connectives that tie facts into molecular facts) is a distinct existent from those that it connects.

To claim, as Bergmann now does, that there is a category of non-simple that involves connections that are not gounded in connectors, that there are complexes that require no makers, marks a significant shift away from this pattern of reasoning. To be sure, it is perhaps not a real shift in opinion. Bergmann does not, for example, retract his claims that all relations are external or that the togetherness of things in a *fact* must be grounded in existents external to and distinct from those things. In his earlier work Bergmann may well have been to some extent guilty of simply fudging the issue of the status of diversities, claiming no more than that the diversity of, say, two things is "shown" by the diversity of the signs in the ideal language that stand for the things. It is clear that he now recognizes the vitiating circularity of this way of treating the issue; in order to know that a representational schema *is* the IL one must know that two distinct thing-names *are* the names of distinct things, and in order to know this one must know that the things *are* distinct. It is also clear that he is quite explicitly aware of the import of granting ontological status to circumstances. Although there are of course no internal *relations* (a notion that Bergmann still finds self-contradictory), there are internal *rela-tionships*. All circumstances (diversities are only one, though clearly the most important, subsort of circumstances) are internal relation-ships in precisely the sense that the togetherness of their terms is *not* grounded in a distinct relation, connection, or maker; rather, it is grounded in the "identity" of these terms, or, as Bergmann some-times puts it, their "being and nature."[5] For an ontologist to whom the notion of a "nature" is so distasteful that even his universals are bare to concede that there are complexes grounded in the nature of the constituents of the complexes is obviously a significant concession.

Bergmann calls the canons that regulate the composition (or pro-duction) of facts out of things and makers (or complexes and makers) "*(a)-canons*"; accordingly he often refers to facts themselves as "type-(a) existents." Those canons that regulate the composition (or production) of circumstances from their terms he calls "*(b)-canons*" and, therefore, circumstances themselves are often referred to as "type-(b) existents," or more simply, (b)-existents. Although facts and circumstances, (a)- and (b)-existents, are clearly the most fundamental sorts of nonsimple in Bergmann's ontology, they are, significantly, not the only sort of nonsimple. There is a still deeper reason for refusing to classify Bergmann as a logical atomist: there are nonsimples in Bergmann's world that are not complexes at all, that are neither facts nor circumstances, that are not representable by *sentential* strings. This third category of nonsimple is that of *classes*. The way in which the elements of a class go together to compose the class is quite differ-ent, Bergmann believes, from the way in which the constituents of a fact or circumstance compose the fact or circumstance. The canons that govern the production of a class from its simpler materials are called "*(c)-canons*" and classes themselves, accordingly, "(c)-existents."
The most fundamental, though not the only, sort of class is the finite class, namely, classes that have a finite number of elements. Such classes are called "primary classes." With certain important quantifications that will be described later, there are no restrictions on what sorts of existents can be the elements of a class. Not only is there no restriction on the *types* of *things* that can be elements of a class but there is no prohibition against classes whose elements are not things at all. That is, there may be classes whose elements are facts, others whose elements are circumstances, and still others whose elements are classes. Furthermore, there is no canonical prohibition against "mixed" classes, classes with elements from different categories. Thus

5. See below, p. 267.

there may be, in Bergmann's world, a class whose elements are: green, the fact that green is darker than white, the circumstance that blue is diverse from oval, and the class whose only elements are the particular *a* and the fact that *a* is blue. Such a class, of course, has a finite number of elements and is thus a primary class. Although there are also other sorts of classes, the important feature shared by all classes is that a class is the "weakest" sort of "togetherness" that existents may have that still deserves to be thought of as a genuine "unit." Classes are not as "structured" as either facts or circumstances but are, as it were, collections that are saved from being "mere collections" (which have no ontological status at all) by the fact that each of their members satisfies a "condition" (about which more later).

Bergmann metaphorically highlights the differences between facts, circumstances, and classes by saying that facts are "*made out of*" things (or "simpler" facts) by makers, circumstances are "*built out of*" the existents that are their terms, and a class is "*built on*" on the existents that specify the condition that must be satisfied by anything that is an element of the class. (Such existents are called selectors.) In line with the technical terminology explained earlier, the making of a fact is called an "*(a)-step,*" the building of a circumstance *out of* its terms is called a "*(b)-step,*" and the building of a class *on* its selector is called a "*(c)-step.*"

In themselves, of course, neither the metaphors nor the purely formal and abstract schema is likely to be very illuminating. It is the manuscript as a whole which is designed to unpack the metaphors and fill out the abstract schema, showing how existents from each of these categories are interrelated and how, together, they can be used to "account for everything." The important point to keep in mind for now is that (to focus on the simplest sort of examples) the *fact* of *this-being-green,* the *circumstance* of *this-being-diverse-from-green,* and the *class whose-only-elements-are-this-and-green* are categorically distinct ways that the two simple existents, *this* and *green,* can "go together" to compose a nonsimple existent. The challenge consists in showing that *any* nonsimple existent, however "complicated," can be understood as being of one (and of course *only* one) of these three types; in other words, it must be shown that all nonsimples, of which the world is the totality, can be construed as the product (in Bergmann's sense) of a (finite) sequence of (a)-, (b)-, and/or (c)-steps.

In order to comprehend the way in which Bergmann develops his categorical system to meet this challenge, we must focus sharply on the notion of a canon. The notion of a canon as "something which corresponds to a formation rule" (of the IL) is suggestive but far from clear. The best entering wedge in such a discussion must be the *state-ments* by means of which canons are expressed.

1.   If there is a particular, *a*, and if there is a nonrelational univer-sal of the first type, *f*, and if there is the maker, exemplification (of the appropriate type), then there is, eo ipso,[6] the (atomic) fact of *a* exemplifying *f*.

2.   If there is a particular, *a*, and another particular, *b*, then there is, eo ipso, the diad of *a* being diverse from *b*.

3.   If there is an existent that is a selector, *X*, then there is, eo ipso, the class it selects (i.e., the class whose elements are all and only those existents that satisfy the condition specified by the selec-tor *X*).

(This is not yet a fully satisfactory way of stating the schema for the canons regulating class formulation; a more complete statement must wait until the notion of a 'selector' is explained.)

The grammatical form of (1)–(3) *seems* obvious: each is a hypo-thetical proposition with an existential generalization as a consequent and an antecedent that is either a conjunction of two existential gen-eralizations, (1)–(2), or a single existential generalization, (3). This, however, is misleading. Bergmann makes it quite clear that the mean-ing of "there is" (or "existence") used in canon statements is *not* the same as that which is expressed by means of existential generaliza-tions. Existential generalizations are simply another species of *fact* and so are *made from* simples (or, at least, existents that are "simpler") by a maker in accord with a canon. The sort of existence mentioned in this canon, as in all other canons, is quite distinct from that sort of exis-tence which is, so to speak, "within" the product of the canon. In the ontologically relevant sense it is not the case that to be is to be the value of a variable.

Nor, it should be clear, is the locution "there is," as Bergmann uses it in a canon statement, synonymous with an ascription of "*actual* exis-tence," where this is the contrary of "merely *possible*" existence. In (1) above what is said is that *if* there is a particular and *if* there is a univer-sal (of the appropriate sort) and *if* there is exemplification (of the ap-propriate kind) *then* there exists the fact of the particular exemplify-

6. Bergmann rarely states the canons or canon schemata without using the locution 'eo ipso'. The purpose of this is, in the case of the (a)-canons, to stress again what Bergmann has long held: that "subsistent" ties (makers, functions) require no further tie to tie them to the existents they connect. In the case of the (b)- and (c)-canons the phrase emphasizes that no maker or function is required to make a circumstance or a class out of its "material." If the terms of a circumstance (say, a diversity) exist, then the circumstance exists, period. If the selector of a class exists, then the class exists, period.

ing the universal. A reader need not be overly critical to ask whether (1) should not be amended to include the more modest modal locution "might be" in its consequent. It is, however, an absolutely essential feature of Bergmann's ontology that this is *not* done. Even if the particular, *a*, does not actually exemplify the universal, *f*, the fact of *a*-exemplifying-*f* does *exist* in the sense of "existence" employed by canon statements.

This very wide and perhaps peculiar sense of "existence" cannot, Bergmann insists, be defined, but it is more or less clarified by a principle Bergmann calls the "Principle of Presentation" (henceforth, the PP): "Everything which exists is thinkable and vice-versa." The convertibility of *existence* and *thinkability* which this principle asserts is, to say the least, idiosyncratic; almost any nonspeculative philosopher would agree that whatever exists is thinkable (i.e., capable of being the object of thought or awareness), but few would concede that whatever is thinkable exists. For Bergmann, however, the controversial conversion is so strongly held that he calls the PP his "fundamental gambit."[7] It is the clear consequence of the PP that the canons should be read precisely as Bergmann expresses them, and thus that the fact of *a*-exemplifying-green *exists* even if *a* does not actually exemplify green.

Clearly, of course, such an odd use of the crucially important term "existence" is going to produce some intellectual discomfort, and this discomfort demands some sort of ontological remedy. Bergmann has such a remedy. Although *a*-exemplifying-green may not be an *actual* fact, it is, nevertheless, a *potential* fact. Or, to speak as Bergmann does, *a*-exemplifying-green is (assuming it is not an actual fact) "pervaded by the mode of potentiality." The two "modes," actuality and potentiality, are members (though not the only members) of the third category of simple existents: the "entities."[8]

Many metaphysicians are likely to think that granting ontological status to the modes, far from being a remedy for the discomfort caused by having granted ontological status to nonactual complexes, is even more outrageously excessive. But if one is an atomistic realist, or is at all capable of empathizing with his motives, then it is not at all difficult to feel the dialectical impulse behind both maneuvers. It is

7. See below, p. 61.
8. Bergmann uses the word 'member' to indicate the relation between an existent and a collection, reserving the word 'element' to indicate that between a determinate and the class to which it "belongs." Bergmann usually treats categories as collections, speaking of the members of the category rather than its elements. The members of some categories, however, may also be the elements of a class.

clear that there are actual complexes that have nonactual complexes as constituents; if one finds unintelligible the idea (or, perhaps, finds "uncomfortable the picture") of a whole, a composite, with nonexistent parts (components), then one may easily be driven to insist that, in some sense, even nonactual complexes must have existence.[9] Further, if the distinction between actual and potential complexes is a real distinction, a distinction that must be accounted for in terms of something that is "in" the complexes themselves (as opposed to something "in" the mind or "in" language), then it is more than reasonable to claim that it is the *modes* which ground this difference. And, of course, if a mode is "in" a complex, then the same pattern of reasoning that leads one to grant existence to nonactual facts leads one to grant existence to the modes themselves.

It is important to note that the way in which a mode is "in" a complex is quite different from the way in which, say, green is "in" two colored patches whose sameness of color its presence grounds, and also different from the way in which a fact is "in" another fact. Bergmann calls the way in which a mode is "in" a complex "pervasion." If the fact *a*-exemplifying-green is actual, then the mode actuality *pervades* it; if not, then the mode potentiality pervades it. But pervasion is not like exemplification, or constituency in a fact, or even like the very close "internal relationship" between the two terms of a diad. There can be no canon statement asserting that if there is a fact, *X,* and a mode, *Y,* then there is, say, the fact of *X*-being-pervaded-by-*Y.* This would clearly involve "iterating the modes."[10] We could, for example, ask whether *a*-exemplifying-green-being-pervaded-by-actuality is or is not pervaded by actuality. Treating the modes as straightforward properties whose composition with other existents could be regulated by canons would either generate a vicious infinite regress or, even if the regress is not vicious, populate the universe with an infinite number of existents even more bizarre than nonactual facts or modes (e.g., *a*-exemplifying-green-being-pervaded-by-actuality-being-pervaded-by-potentiality-being-pervaded-by . . .).

9. Bergmann's original motive for introducing potential facts and modes might be called "epistemological" (see "Realistic Postscript," in *Logic and Reality,* University of Wisconsin Press, 1964, pp. 302–40). Even in his later work Bergmann's chief motive was to provide an existing intention for each thought. This might not be an altogether persuasive reason for someone who has no trouble accepting the idea that some thoughts might not intend anything. Although the reasoning cited here is never overtly employed by Bergmann it does seem to be a pattern of reasoning that might be persuasive to an atomist, simply because he is an atomist, independently of whatever views he may have about epistemology or the philosophy of mind.

10. The phrase is Bergmann's. See below, p. 89.

So "close" is the connection between a complex and the mode that pervades it that Bergmann calls a complex-pervaded-by-its-mode a "Two-in-One," indicating thereby the very "low" ontological status, the "total dependence," of the modes.[11] Considered ontologically, as "composites" or "wholes," Two-in-Ones can hardly be considered as composites of distinct components at all; this is, after all, the point of the label "Two-in-One." Bergmann likens the connection between a mode and the complex it pervades, or, more generally, the connection between an *entity* and whatever other existent an entity is connected to, to the relationship between an Aristotelian-Thomistic substance and its nature or essence, a relationship Bergmann often describes as "hylomorphic composition."[12] This analogy will seem less strained if we shift our focus from complexes-pervaded-by-their-modes to the other sort of Two-in-One in Bergmann's taxonomy.

If we consider any particular or any universal, of whatever type or variety, in short, any *thing*, we can distinguish "in" it two features or aspects. The particular *a* for example, is both a *particular* and, as well, the very particular it is, distinct from all other particulars. The color green (a specific shade of green) is both a *nonrelational universal of the first type* and the very universal that it is, distinct from all others. These two aspects of each thing must be accounted for; and again, if we follow the pattern of reasoning that drives atomistic realism, they must be grounded by existents "in" the things. Bergmann accounts for these features by claiming that each thing is a kind of composite of two *entities*. One of them, called an "item," accounts for the individuality and distinctness of the thing of which it is a component; the other, called an "ultimate sort," accounts for the general formal type of the thing. Items are, as Bergmann sometimes says, the fundamental "matter" of the world, while ultimate sorts constitute its ultimate "form." Each thing is, thus, a hylomorphic composite of matter and form.

The general concept of a Two-in-One, applied as Bergmann applies it to complexes and things, is difficult and problematic. Each thing is presumably a simple existent, yet it is also, in another sense, a composite of two existents. Each complex is, of course, a complex, yet each also seems now to have a kind of simplicity, or at least unity, that

11. See below, p. 239.

12. Bergmann's doctrine of the Two-in-One is in large part a response to the criticisms of his atomistic realism formulated by John Peterson (*Realism and Logical Atomism*, University of Alabama Press, 1976). I suspect that the large amount of intellectual energy Bergmann expends trying to show that the forms of all nonsimples are thinkable is also a response to some of Peterson's charges.

transcends its complexity. Symptomatic of this is that each complex has its own mode; the mode which pervades a complex, and in this sense is "in" it, does not pervade (or may well not pervade), and thus is *not* "in", the complexes of which that complex is a constituent.

As in the case of complexes-pervaded-by-their-modes, so also in the case of things-being-of-their-ultimate-sorts: there can be no canons specifying which items go together with which ultimate sorts to produce which things. (I will not reproduce Bergmann's argument for this claim here.) One may thus say that hylomorphic composition is a kind of "extracanonical composition." It is tempting to say that the composition of items and ultimate sorts "into" things is "precanonical," and that the composition of a complex and its mode is "post-canonical" composition. The force of these metaphors is that unless things "already" exist (as the "result" of a "going together" of item and ultimate sort), there cannot "then" be the making of facts and the building of circumstances, and so on. And unless there "already" exist complexes (as a "result" of the canonical composition of things), there cannot be a pervasion of complexes by modes, for there would *be* no complexes for the modes to pervade. These are, of course, only metaphors, and potentially misleading ones at that. To point out that hylomorphic composition is noncanonical composition is simply another way of stressing the radical difference between things, facts, and even makers, on the one hand, and entities, on the other.

The crucial point to notice is that Bergmann's addition to his ontological inventory of those existents he calls "entities," as well as the notion of hylomorphic composition that necessarily accompanies this addition, marks yet another break with the interpretation and application of the general picture of atomistic realism reflected in his earlier ontologies. The connection between the two terms of a diad is such a "close" connection that there is no distinct existent, being-diverse-from, which grounds the existence of the diad. This in itself distinguishes diads from facts. But the connection between item and ultimate sort in a thing or between a complex and its mode is even closer than the "internal relationship" between the terms of a diad. A symptom of this is that, as Bergmann argues vigorously, there can be no sign in that IL that represents an entity; and a consequence of this is that there can be no sentential expression (well formed or not) that represents, say, green-being-a-universal or this-being-green-being-actual.[13] On the other hand, green-being-diverse-from-oval is as literally representable in such a language as this-being-blue. In spite of the

13. See below, pp. 331–33.

nonrepresentability of Two-in-Ones in an IL they are thinkable. We can be presented with a thing-being-of-its-ultimate-sort and in fact are presented with it *if* the thing in question is presented "in isolation," namely, if the thing is the sole intention of one of our mental acts. And we can, at least in certain sorts of cases, be presented with a complex-being-prevaded-by-its-mode. And because, by the Principle of Presentation, whatever is thinkable exists, it follows that Two-in-Ones, though not representable in an IL, do nevertheless exist.

The locution "Two-in-One" plays a methodological-rhetorical role as odd as the beings it designates. It does not refer to a *category* of existents on the same footing as those designated by the words "thing," "maker," "entity" (the three categories of simple existents), "fact," "circumstance," or "class" (the three categories of nonsimple existents). Rather, the division among existents signaled by the locution cuts across the system of categories: all *things* are Two-in-Ones (of one sort) as are all complexes (though of another sort). Classes are *not* Two-in-Ones of either sort for they are not pervaded by modes and are not *of* ultimate sorts. And, of course, neither entities nor makers are Two-in-Ones; such existents are completely without "matter" and thus could not in any sense be a composite of form and matter.

There is another important distinction that, like the concept of a Two-in-One, cuts across the schema of categories: the distinction between "determinates" and "nondeterminates." Things, facts, circumstances, and classes are all determinates; entities and makers are nondeterminates. One may, and Bergmann does, characterize determinates as being of "higher ontological status" (than nondeterminates), more "independent" and more "separable" (than nondeterminates). The ontological cash value of these metaphors, though, consists in the following features: (i) determinates are, while nondeterminates are not, the *terms of circumstances*, specifically of *diads;* (ii) determinates are, while nondeterminates are not, the *constituents* of complexes;[14] (iii) determinates are, while nondeterminates are not, in the range of bound variables, or, to speak concisely, determinates are *quantifiable;* and (iv) determinates are, while nondeterminates are not, *elements of classes.* Feature (i) Bergmann calls "the Minimal Restriction," meaning that given any two determinates, there also exists the diad whose

14. I will not bother to explicate Bergmann's new notion of constituency; it is quite technical (see p. 192). Basically, though, the idea is that a constituent of a complex (classes don't have constituents, though they may be constituents) is one of the determinates that is specified by a complete assay of that complex. This includes those *things* that are members of its *ultimate foundation* and, as well, the *facts, circumstances,* and *classes* that are members of its *intermediate foundations.*

terms these determinates are. What he has in mind here is that there is no canonical restriction on which two existents may serve as the terms of a diad, *as long as both are determinates.* This is to be contrasted with, say, the case of (a)-canons, the material for which must satisfy more stringent restrictions in addition to satisfying the minimal restriction. In order, for example, for a fact to be produced by the maker conjunction from other existents, these existents must be complexes (either facts or circumstances); a conjunctive fact cannot be produced from a thing and fact, a circumstance and a class, two classes, etc. A diad, on the other hand, is produced from any two of these existents without *further* restriction.

A consequence of the minimal restriction—and the other features (ii)–(iv) that jointly characterize the concept of a determinate—is that there are no such circumstances as actuality-being-diverse-from-potentiality, particularity-being-diverse-from-universality, or exemplification-being-diverse-from-conjunction. Nor could there be a class whose elements are, say, all and only the binary connectives. It is not a fact that there is more than one kind of exemplification or more than two binary connectives; because one cannot quantify over nondeterminates, one could not even say, literally, that there are two and only two modes, that negation is the only nonbinary connective. And because only determinates can be constituents, it follows that the makers that tie things (or complexes) into facts are not constituents of those facts, just as the entities that "enter into" hylomorphic composites are not constituents of those composites.

The upshot of the concept of a determinate carved out by the minimal restriction is that much that one might very naturally regard as expressible in propositions (or class expressions), indeed much that Bergmann himself does or has expressed by means of propositions (or class expressions), turns out not to be literally so expressible. The statement "conjunction is diverse from disjunction" represents nothing at all, and whatever knowledge it purports to express is either illusory or, perhaps, is *of* linguistic symbols. Those who are familiar with the spirit of Bergmann's work will recognize that this is not an insignificant claim, and the dilemma it presents, to which I will return later, is not at all easy to resolve. The problematic statements in question are, to be sure, not the sort that are usually made in the course of everyday life, not even by mathematicians; nevertheless, they do seem to express beliefs that form the core of our conception of the world, the very beliefs, in fact, that most interest the ontologist. It is, at the very least, odd for someone as committed to realism as Bergmann is to concede that these statements do not express beliefs at all, that they represent nothing; but it would be even stranger for him to allow that they do represent something, but that what they represent is certain features of language. In fact, as we will see, Bergmann surrenders neither to nihilism nor to linguisticism (or thinks he does not). Clearly, though, the consequences of the minimal restriction vis-à-vis Bergmann's treatment of these problematic and important statements require yet another departure from the basic strategy of atomistic realism.

The Standardization

One of the central features of the categorical system that Bergmann develops in *NFO* is "the standardization," a systematic reconstrual of the constituents and "production steps" that enter into the ontological structure of nonsimple existents. The standardization allows Bergmann to solve a number of ontological problems including that of providing a clear and unified portrait of the structure of even the most complicated sorts of nonsimples. The pretext for introducing the standardization is the need to ground the difference between such facts as *a*-being-to-the-left-of-*b* and *b*-being-to-the left-of-*a*. They are, in Bergmann's ontology, both atomic facts. Both have the particulars *a* and *b* and the relation being-to-the-left-of as constituents. Both, in addition, "involve" the same maker, binary relational exemplification of the first type.[15] They are obviously distinct facts, but there does not seem to be any thing or maker "in" them that could account for this distinctness. This is the problem of *order*.

Bergmann notes that many ontologists may be tempted to rest content with the fact that difference in order is often represented in language "in propria persona" by a difference in the order of signs, just as the diversity of existents is often represented by the diversity of signs that represent them. In neither case, however, is the representational convention an adequate ontological assay. Indeed, a perspicuous language may well represent diversity and order by, respectively, a diversity and order of signs, but the claim (or assumption) that a language *is* perspicuous must be, at least in part, based upon reality. We cannot claim that "two" things ought to be represented by two signs unless we "know" that they are diverse, that they are really two and not one. Similarly, if the order of signs is to be representa-

15. The use of the word "type" to describe exemplification(s) may be confusing. All I mean by saying that a nexus of exemplifications of the *first* type is that it connects particulars to universals of the first type (in a more straightforward and familiar sense of "type").

tionally significant, then the difference of order between "a is to the left of b" and "b is to the left of a" must be ontologically grounded. In short, we must find something "in" the facts represented by the two statements that accounts for their difference.

Bergmann solves the problem of order by introducing the notion of a "tuple," which is essentially a sort of diad.[16] A 2-tuple, for example, is a diad one term of which is itself a diad and the other term of which is one of the terms of this latter diad. Consider, for example, the diad whose terms are the particulars a and b. Bergmann represents this by the expression '(a, b)' (read: 'a is diverse from b', or, indifferently, 'b is diverse from a'). Given the relevant (b)-canon, if there exists this diad then there also exists, eo ipso, the diads, a-being-diverse-from-a-being-diverse-from-b and b-being-diverse-from-a-being-diverse-from-b. These two latter diads are represented, respectively, by the expressions '$(a, (a, b))$' and '$(b, (a, b))$' (which are in turn abbreviated by the expressions '$\langle a, b\rangle$' and '$\langle b, a\rangle$').

Bergmann now tells us that the two atomic facts a-being-to-the-left-of-b and b-being-to-the-left-of-a do, initial appearances to the contrary notwithstanding, have different constituents. One of them contains the 2-tuple $\langle a, b\rangle$ while the other contains the 2-tuple $\langle b, a\rangle$, and neither contains the other. In other words, in the sequence of steps by which the two facts are produced from the simples "in" them there is a different constituent (a 2-tuple) produced by a different step—though in each case the same *kind* of step, a (b)-step. The constituents of a-being-to-the-left-of-b are: a, b,being-to-the-left-of, and $\langle a, b\rangle$. The constituents of b-being-to-the-left-of-a are: a, b, being-to-the-left-of and $\langle b, a\rangle$. The maker, binary relational exemplification of the first type, is the same in each case.

The standardized assay of (asymmetric) relational atomic facts salvages the general methodological principle that differences between nonsimples must be accounted for by a difference of constituents. But Bergmann extends this approach to all facts, to (nearly) all circumstances, and even, in a peculiar sense, to all classes. The nonrelational atomic fact a-being-green is now assayed as consisting not only of a, green, and (nonrelational) exemplification but also of the diad whose terms are a and green. Schematically, what is conventionally represented by the string '$gr(a)$' is now to be represented by the string '$\eta(gr, a)$', where 'η' is the sign for the maker exemplification.[17] The

16. See below, pp. 121 ff.

17. Bergmann holds that there are several nexus of exemplification. The exemplification nexus which connects a particular and, say, the universal red (a specific shade of red) is a different function from the exemplification nexus which connects red

relational atomic fact *a*-being-to-the-left-of-*b*, conventionally represented by the string '$L(a, b)$', is now held to be more perspicuously represented by the string '$\eta(L, \langle a, b \rangle)$'. The molecular conjunctive fact conventionally represented by the string '$f(a) \ \& \ g(b)$' is now to be represented by the string '$\&(\eta(f, a), \eta(g, b))$'. And the material conditional conventionally represented by '$f(a) \supset g(b)$' is now to be represented by '$\supset(\eta(f, a), \eta(g,b))$'. All atomic facts and all molecular facts, with the single important exception of *negative* facts, are now ontologically understood to be the products of a maker and a diad (and if asymmetry—order—is a factor, that specific sort of diad called a tuple).

Once Bergmann introduces the idea of a standardized assay he alters his terminology to rid it of what he feels to be unduly anthropomorphic metaphors. Those existents he has been calling "makers" he now refers to as "functions." The diads which, according to the standardization, are the proximately simpler determinates that are transformed by a maker into a fact, are called "arguments" instead of the more anthropomorphic "material."[18] The facts themselves are to be thought of as "values" rather than as "products." Every fact *is* the value of a function (an exemplification, a connective, or, as we shall see, a quantifier) for an argument (which, except for the case of negation, is always a diad). The (a)-canons are to be reinterpreted in the light of these changes, for now each of them is understood as specifying the value of a function for an argument.

But the consequences of the standardization extend beyond the category of fact. In addition to diads there are two other sorts of circumstances, and thus two additional sorts of (b)-canons which regulate the production of these sorts of circumstances from their material. First, there are intentional connections (intentional nexūs) between thoughts and their intentions. Second, there are the connections between determinates and the classes of which they are the elements. Bergmann has always believed that the constituent in a mental state that accounts for its "directedness toward an object" is a nonrela-

---

and the universal color. Also, nonrelational exemplifications are different functions from relational exemplifications. Though Bergmann does not speak much about it, there are presumably different relational exemplifications for the different numbers of relata appropriate to the relations that these nexus connect to the relata. Thus, binary relational exemplification (of the "lowest" type) is a different function from ternary relational exemplification (of the same type). Strictly speaking, then, the signs for the exemplification function of the IL should have a subscript, indicating the "type" of exemplification, and also a superscript, indicating the "number" of the nexus. Usually Bergmann ignores these requirements unless it's necessary. I will too.

18. See below, p. 125.

tional universal that stands in a unique logical "relation" to the fact that is the intention of the mental state. This logical "relation" ("connection" is the word that Bergmann usually preferred) was seen as ontologically of the same category as the logical connectives. He still believes that the constituent of a mental state (or mental act) that accounts for the mental state's having the intention it has, the "thought," is such a universal, but he now believes there is no distinct existent which connects the thought to its intention. Instead, the intentional nexus is an "internal relationship" between the thought and the determinate which is that thought's intention, ontologically on a par with the internal relationship of diversity existing "between" any two determinates. The connection, in either case, is grounded solely in the *natures* of the connected existents.

The remaining type of circumstance, the elementhood, is similarly an internal relationship between a class and a determinate, or, indeed, even more broadly, any determinate and any other determinate. It is part of the nature of a class that all and only those determinates satisfying a certain condition are elements of the class, and it is part of the nature of any determinate whether or not it does satisfy this condition. Further, it is part of the nature of a determinate whether or not it is a class, and thus whether or not it *can actually* have other determinates as elements. This must be mentioned because elementhoods, like intentional nexūs and diads, are circumstances, and the only restriction on the terms of circumstances is that they be determinates. An ontological consequence of this tolerance is admission to the world of some very odd complexes: green-intending-this-being-to-the-left-of-that (i.e., determinates which are not thoughts intending other determinates), and green-being-an-element-of-blue (i.e., determinates being elements of other determinates which are not classes). Bergmann handles this "excess" in the same way he handles diads *both* of whose terms are the *same* determinate, namely, by claiming that the problematic complexes are pervaded by the mode of potentiality.

It is a defining characteristic of a circumstance that there is no distinct existent, a tie, connecting its terms; circumstances are complexes that are *not* the values of a function. Nevertheless, an ontologically perspicuous notation must allow us to reflect the difference between the sorts of circumstances being represented; otherwise we would be unable to distinguish between, say, an intentional nexus and an elementhood, or either of these and a diad. To resolve this problem Bergmann introduces the notion of a "diacritical expression," an expression that does not represent an existent but that draws our attention to ("shows" us) the sort of existent represented by the larger expression of which the diacritical expression is a part. The parentheses and comma '(. . . , . . .)' by means of which a diad is represented does not represent an existent, for there is no distinct existent being-diverse-from. If, however, the spaces flanking the comma are replaced by expressions representing determinates, then the parentheses and comma *show* us that the existent represented by the entire resulting expression is a diad. By contrast, the sign 'η', say, represents the function exemplification.

Bergmann introduces three more diacritical expressions, two of which are used to demarcate intentional nexus and elementhoods. 'M', which in Bergmann's earlier work was used to designate the intentional tie, is now a diacritical expression. '$\in$' is a diacritical expression used to indicate that an elementhood is being represented.

There is at least one very significant difference between diads, on the one hand, and the other two sorts of circumstances, on the other. For a diad, order is not a factor. That is, for example, *a*-being-diverse-from-*b* is not itself diverse from *b*-being-diverse-from-*a*. Even tuples, which ground order, are themselves indifferent to it. Thus, *a*-being-diverse-from-*a*-being-diverse-from-*b* is not itself diverse from *a*-being-diverse-from-*b*-being-diverse-from-*a*, though both are of course diverse from *b*-being-diverse-from-*a*-being-diverse-from-*b*. By contrast, order *is* obviously an important feature of intentional nexus and elementhoods. That a given thought intends a given fact, say, is quite different from that fact's intending that thought. Green-being-an-element-of-the-class-whose-only-elements-are-blue-and-green is an *actual* complex, while the-class-whose-only-elements-are-blue-and-green-being-an-element-of-green is merely *potential*.

Bergmann grounds these differences, just as he grounds differences of order in atomic and molecular facts—with tuples. If 'X' represents a thought and 'Y' the determinate which is its intention, then the circumstance of *X*-intending-*Y* is to be represented by the expression '$M\langle X, Y\rangle$'. In short, the circumstance has as constituents not only X and Y but also the 2-tuple $\langle X, Y\rangle$. If X were a determinate and Y a class, then the circumstance of *X*-being-an-element-of-*Y* is to be represented by the expression '$\in\langle X, Y\rangle$', indicating that the elementhood has as constituents not only X and Y but also the 2-tuple $\langle X, Y\rangle$.

In addition to atomic and molecular facts and the circumstances, there is one remaining sort of complex to discuss, the generality. For Bergmann neither existential generalizations nor universal generalizations are "reducible" to any other sort of fact; the former are not equivalent to (infinitely long) disjunctions, and the latter are not equivalent to (infinitely long) conjunctions. Both sorts of general fact are assayed precisely as the standardization demands: a general fact is a *value* of a *function* for an *argument*. The function is a quantifier, either universal or existential, and the argument is an appropriate sort of diad. This will require some explanation.

Facts such as those represented in natural language by such sentences as "something is red" or "everything green is square" are often conventionally represented in *PM*-like calculi by the following sorts of strings: '$(\exists x)(rd(x))$' and '$(x)(gr(x) \supset sq(x))$'. Bergmann believes that this mode of representation is unacceptable for the reason that there is no existent that is represented by the bound variables. Moreover, we can, he thinks, get by without variables; we don't, that is, have to treat them as diacritical expressions. Bergmann introduces some new symbolism and terminology. '$\bigvee$' represents the universal quantifier and '$\bigwedge$' represents the existential quantifier; they are both *functions*, ontologically on a par with exemplification and the connectives. The fact of something-being-red is now to be assayed as the value of the function $\bigwedge$ for the argument $\langle a, rd(a) \rangle$, where 'rd' stands for the color red and 'a' stands for an "arbitrarily" chosen particular. The general fact itself is represented by the string '$\bigwedge \langle a, rd(a) \rangle$'. The particular, a, is called the "target" of the generality, and the atomic fact, $rd(a)$, is its "scope." The slightly more complicated generality everything-being-square-if-it-is-green is now assayed as the value of function $\bigvee$ for the argument $\langle b, gr(b) \supset sq(b) \rangle$. The target is the particular b and the scope is the molecular fact, the material conditional $gr(b) \supset sq(b)$.

Obviously the target of a generality serves as the ontological counterpart of a variable, with the advantage, however, that, being a particular, it exists, and again, in being a particular, is of an ontological sort that has a clear and straightforward place in Bergmann's taxonomy of existents. Just as clearly, the scope may, to oversimplify somewhat, be any fact, or indeed any complex, of which the target is a constituent. Somewhat more controversially, he allows any *determinate* to be the target of a generality. In other words, one may quantify over things of any type and even over facts, circumstances, and classes. To be, to exist, is not the same as "being the value of a bound variable"; but being the value of a bound variable (or being capable of being one) *is* an essential part of what it is to be a specific sort of existent, namely, a determinate.

Several of the systematic implications of this new assay of generality must be pointed out. One of Bergmann's claims is that, to make a long story short, the target of a generality is, although of course a constituent of its scope, *not* a constituent of the generality itself. Thus, to take the first of our simple examples, the particular a is not a constituent of the general fact $\bigwedge\langle a, rd(a)\rangle$. This is not really a surprising assertion because, after all, a, or perhaps the sign 'a' which stands for it, is functioning as a variable and the identity of a variable, except in those special cases where the scope of a generality is itself a generality and we must avoid selecting a variable which is already therein bound, makes no difference to the identity of the entire generality. In conventional notation, for example, there would be no difference between the generalities represented by the two strings '$(x)(rd(x))$' and '$(y)(rd(y))$'. Similarly, it does not make any difference whether a or b or c or any other particular is "selected" as the target of the generality; the "resulting" fact is the same fact (as long as the one we select does not appear in the scope of the generality, either as the target of another generality or simply as a "free" particular).

There are, however, facts whose identity seems to be completely independent of the determinates the expressions for which might appear in the strings representing these facts. Consider, for example, the fact conventionally represented by the string '$(x)(f)(f(x) \vee {\sim}f(x))$'. If we remove the variables and use Bergmann's new notation, then the same fact is represented by the string '$\bigvee\langle a, \bigvee\langle rd, rd(a) \vee {\sim}rd(a)\rangle\rangle$'. It now becomes clear that neither a nor rd (i.e., the color red) is a constituent of the general fact represented by this string, and indeed, that this fact *has* no constituents as Bergmann is now using this term. Bergmann calls such complexes "limiting complexes."[19] Limiting complexes are the ontological counterparts of what in conventional notation are sentential strings in which only logical constants (and variables and the order in which they appear) are essential to the identity of the string.

That there are complexes with no constituents is, to say the least, a paradoxical feature of Bergmann's new ontology. After all, one is inclined to think that the idea of a complex, as it is employed by ontologists, just is the idea of something that has constituents. Bergmann himself would once, perhaps, have been tempted to say that such complexes have only subsistents as constituents. Now, however, he has committed himself to the view that only determinates can be (or have) constituents, so he could not allow that limiting complexes have only functions and ultimate sorts as constituents. Acceptance of constituentless complexes, it might be argued, is really a reflection of a shift of terminology: functions are "in" complexes in the sense that they must be specified in the assays of the complexes, but they are *not* "in" them in the quite different sense that they are constituents of

19. See below, p. 178.

them. Perhaps so. But behind this terminological shift one can sense the stresses and strains to which the whole-part analogy so fundamental to atomistic realism is subjected when pressed to cover all cases it must cover. (I will pick up this thread again later.)

With the extension of the standardization to cover general facts, Bergmann obtains an extremely elegant system for "constructing" virtually all complexes from simples. "Beginning" at the "level" of things (the temporal and spatial metaphors here are unavoidable), diads (and tuples) are produced from things by (b)-steps. Those diads whose terms are of the appropriate sorts are made into atomic facts by (a)-steps (exemplifications), and these are in turn made into molecular facts by further (a)-steps. At each successive "stage" of production, (b)-steps produce "new" diads, some of which, if they are of the appropriate sorts, are made into general facts by (a)-steps. These, in turn, can be made the terms of still further diads—(b)-steps—and also made the components of more complicated molecular and general facts, and so on.

Those diads that are *required* by the standardization for any (a)-step are called "standardization diads" and "order tuples."[20] Thus the diad (a, f) is required, by the standardization, for exemplification to make the atomic fact $\eta(a, f)$. The 2-tuple $\langle a, b \rangle$ is required, by the standardization, for exemplification to make the (asymmetric) relational atomic fact $\eta(L, \langle a, b \rangle)$. Not all of the complex components of molecular (and general) facts, however, are *atomic facts*. Diads, and other circumstances, are also complexes, and they may thus become the components of "higher order" facts. The statement "blue is diverse from green and oval is diverse from round" represents a conjunction of diads, neither one of which is a diad *required* by the standardization and neither one of which, therefore, is a standardization diad. On the other hand, the diad whose terms *are* these diads, $((bl, gr), (ov, rnd))$, *is* itself a standardization diad because the standardization *requires* the formation of such a diad for the function conjunction to make into the fact $\& ((bl, gr), (ov, rnd))$.

Generally speaking, circumstances may be negated, conjoined, disjoined, and made the scopes of generalities, just as facts may. The terminological, and ontological, point to keep in mind is that a complex is categorized *as a fact,* i.e., (a)-existent, or *as a circumstance,* i.e., (b)-existent, depending upon whether the *last* step in its production is an (a)-step or a (b)-step, respectively. A conjunction of diads is a fact; a diad whose terms are facts is a diad.

20. See below, p. 120-25.

Although we can, by using the procedure so far described, "reach" virtually all complexes by a finite sequence of (a)- and (b)-steps, we cannot reach them all. This is because many complexes have classes as constituents and the canons that govern class formation are neither (a)- nor (b)-canons. In order to grasp the outlines of the entire Bergmannian program, we must turn again to the subject of classes and the (c)-canons which govern their production from simples.

Classes

Bergmann's chapter on classes is the longest and most difficult of the entire book and it would be hard to do justice to it even in a lengthy monograph focused entirely upon that topic. Yet at least the outlines of Bergmann's assay of classes must be grasped if one is to have any hope of comprehending his ontology. The going-together of determinates in a class is an entirely distinct sort of (canonical) composition, one which Bergmann thinks of as the "weakest" kind that still deserves to be given ontological status. A class is not a mere collection of existents, for a collection is specified by a list, and whatever is specified by a mere list is entirely too devoid of structure to have the *unity* required of something that could be thought of as an existent, let alone as a determinate. On the other hand, classes are not designated by sentences and thus are, in a sense, less structured than either facts or circumstances. A class is thus "more" than a mere collection and "less" than a complex, ontologically speaking. Although classes are neither mere collections nor complexes they are related to both; it is accurate enough to say that a class is a collection of determinates each of which satisfies a certain condition, where satisfaction of a condition, of course, involves the actuality of some complex of which these determinates are constituents.

The problem is to find a place in one's categorical system for such existents, and to describe both how they are produced from simpler determinates and how they in turn may become components of more complicated determinates. Bergmann's handling of this task is, though extremely difficult to comprehend fully in all its details, quite ingenious, combining a conscientious effort to fit classes into the categorical system he has already developed and, as well, to extend this system to accommodate certain ambitious ontological plans. (I will mention these later.)

The basic sort of class is the "primary class." Any class with a finite number of elements, however "large," is a primary class. A very primitive example of such a class is the class whose only elements are *a* and

b (where a and b are particulars). Now if a class is a collection of determinates each of which satisfies a condition, then (at least one of) the conditions satisfied by a and b (and nothing else) is the condition being-the-same-as-a-or-(being the same as)-b. The question that must be answered is how satisfaction of this condition brings a and b together into a class.

In his earlier work Bergmann held that a class is a special sort of derived character that is exemplified by all and only the elements of the class; "coexemplification" of the character by the elements is what "unifies" them into a class. Thus the primary class which is serving as our paradigm might be (perspicuously) represented by the string '$\hat{x}((x = a) \vee (x = b))$'. Bergmann now professes dissatisfaction with this assay as well as the notational schema by means of which it is expressed. His fundamental reason is that he believes that there simply are no derived (complex) characters, special or otherwise. His new solution makes use of the standardization and takes its cue from his own handling of generalities. The string '$\hat{x}((x = a) \vee (x = b))$' does seem to involve the variable-like sign '$\hat{x}$' which does not, according to Bergmann, represent anything. Instead, he has us represent our paradigm class with the string '$\lambda\langle c, (c = a) \vee (c = b)\rangle$'. The sign '$\lambda$ is Bergmann's fourth (and last) diacritical expression, and like all diacritical expressions, does not represent anything; rather, it merely indicates the sort of existent represented by the larger expression of which it is a part. Thus 'λ' indicates that the larger expression of which it is a part represents a *class*. The 2-tuple to which it is prefixed specifies the condition that must be satisfied by any element of the class; Bergmann calls this 2-tuple the "selector" of the class.[21] The first term of the 2-tuple, c, is an "arbitrarily" selected determinate which obviously plays a role much like that of the target of a generality. The second term of the 2-tuple actually makes explicit the condition that must be satisfied by the elements of the class; clearly it is similar to the scope of a generality. The production of classes then, like the production of facts, necessarily involves a (b)-step which produces a diad. One important distinction between, say, the general fact, $\vee\langle a, rd(a)\rangle$ and the class $\lambda\langle c, (c = a) \vee (c = b)\rangle$ is that the former involves a function, $\vee$,

---

21. Strictly speaking the selector does not really "specify" the condition if by this one means that the sentence which represents the selector is a statement that a determinate is an element of a certain class if and only if it satisfies a condition. Instead, Bergmann claims that the condition which must be satisfied by an element of a class is 'encoded' in the selector of the class and can only be stated in a metalanguage. For the reasons, see pp. 290, 291.

and the latter does not; 'λ' is a diacritical expression and '$\vee$' is not, but rather represents an existent. Metaphorically, recall, facts are *made*, circumstances are *built out of* their terms, and classes are *built on* their selectors. The basic schema of the (c)-canons is: if a selector (namely, the appropriate sort of diad) exists, then eo ipso the class it selects exists. This type of production is a (c)-step.

The class $\lambda \langle c, (c = a) \vee (c = b) \rangle$ can now be seen as the product of a finite sequence of canonical steps.

1. The diads (c, a) and (c, b) are produced by (b)-steps from the things c, b, and a.

2. The facts $\sim(c, a)$ and $\sim(c, b)$ are produced by (a)-steps from the previously produced diads. [Note: for Bergmann '=' is a defined sign representing sameness; sameness is the negation of diversity. Thus '$(c = a)$' is definitionally equivalent to '$\sim(c, a)$'.]

3. The fact $(c = a) \vee (c = b)$ is produced from the previously produced facts by an (a)-step.

4. The diad $(c, (c = a) \vee (c = b))$ is produced by a (b)-step from the thing c and the previously produced fact.

5. The 2-tuple $\langle c, (c = a) \vee (c = b) \rangle$ is produced from the thing c and the previously produced diad by a (b)-step.

6. The class $\lambda \langle c, (c = a) \vee (c = b) \rangle$ is produced by a *(c)-step* from the previously produced 2-tuple.

Once obtained, classes can then become the components of further determinates, though it perhaps should be emphasized that the primary canonical connection of a class to other determinates must always be as the term of a circumstance, as, for example, the term of a diad or elementhood. Once a class is made the term of such a circumstance—by a (b)-step—then it can become the constituent of a fact, if the circumstance is made the material of an (a)-step. If our simple paradigm class is made the term of a diad, for example, and this diad is then negated, then the class is a constituent of the resulting negative fact. On the other hand, although classes may *be* constituents they do *not have* constituents. The constituency "relation" is, Bergmann maintains, transitive, so if X is a constituent of Y and Y a constituent of Z then X is a constituent of Z; the elementhood relation is of course nontransitive. In this sense classes, although "produced from simples," are more like things than complexes.

A class is a kind of "togetherness" of determinates, and it might seem odd that the determinates that are the elements of a class, those determinates whose togetherness the class *is*, are not construed as constituents of the class. One may be tempted to mitigate the oddness by pointing out that, although the elements of a class are not constituents of that class, they *are* constituents of the 2-tuple that is the selector of the class. Thus, in still another sense of "in," the elements of a class could be said to be in the class. This, however, would not be correct. It is correct that the elements of all *primary* classes are constituents of the selectors of those classes. But primary classes are not the only kind of classes, and one can not make a similar claim about the other sorts of classes.

In addition to primary classes, there are "secondary" and "tertiary" classes. Secondary classes are classes with a denumerably infinite number of elements. Bergmann also calls them "infinite recursive classes," indicating thereby the important role of recursion in generating the infinity of determinates that are the elements of such classes, and "Peano classes" or "P-classes," indicating thereby the theoretical role of these classes in the grounding of arithmetic. Following Russell and Frege, Bergmann holds that the concept of number is logically and ontologically derived from the concept of equinumerosity. If one takes this tack, then one obstacle that must be overcome is that of "obtaining" an infinite number of "objects" so that, for any numbers involved in mathematical "truths," there will be classes of objects for which these numbers *are* the numbers. Moreover, if one holds, as Bergmann does, that the truths of arithmetic are truths of logic, it would be preferable to obtain this infinity of objects without relying upon a clearly contingent assumption such as the axiom of infinity, for this would seem to undermine the logicist's conviction about the modal status of mathematical truths. It might be thought that in addition to the difficulties shared by all logicist ontologies of arithmetic Bergmann has an additional burden, for he must show not only that there exist the appropriate sorts of infinite classes to ground arithmetic but also that (and how) such classes can, like all other determinates, be produced from simples *by a finite number of* (canonical) *steps*.

Bergmann's approach to the problem follows more or less the same pattern established by his assay of primary classes. He shows how the *selectors* of infinite classes are produced. These selectors are again a certain kind of tuple, one term of which contains the "first" element of the class for which the tuple is the selector and the second term of which contains the "second" element of the class. The other components of the terms of the tuple (Bergmann calls them "iterators"), in conjunction with a "metalinguistic instruction," tell us how the third element of the class is "obtained" from the first and second, and then the fourth from the third and the second, and so on, ad infinitum. Without going into the formal details, which essentially involve recursive substitution, it can be seen that one can generate an infinite (and ordered) sequence of determinates, such as that consisting of the atomic fact $f(a)$, the disjunction of $f(a)$ and the atomic fact $g(b)$, the disjunction of the previous disjunction and $g(b)$, the disjunction of the previous disjunction and $g(b)$, and so on ad infinitum.[22] The facts that are the members of this sequence are, except for the first, analytically equivalent to each other of course, but for Bergmann analytically equivalent complexes are not necessarily the same complex; thus each member of the sequence so generated is numerically diverse from all the others. Moreover, the canons guarantee that if "two" facts exist, then the disjunction of those facts eo ipso exists. It follows that the class whose elements are *all* the members of this sequence is an infinite class. Further, although the canons are not themselves analytic facts (they are not facts at all, as it turns out), they are not contingent facts. And the criteria of sameness and difference that guarantee the diversity of all the analytically equivalent facts in the sequence *are,* Bergmann claims, themselves analytic. It seems to follow, then, that the existence of the infinite class does not not rest upon anything like the axiom of infinity.

The canon governing production of secondary classes is, schematically, exactly like that governing production of primary classes: if the selector exists, then the class eo ipso exists. But there is a significant difference between the selectors of primary and secondary classes aside from the obvious ones: The selector of a secondary class has only the first two elements of the class as constituents, while the selector of a primary class has all of its elements as constituents. So even in the weakened sense of "in" suggested above, one could not say that the elements of a class are in the class. A secondary class is a togetherness of determinates that are neither constituents of the class nor (except for the first two) constituents of the selector of the class. The benefit gained at the expense of whatever sense of paradox this may provoke is that secondary classes can now be seen as producible from simples in a finite number of canonical steps.

The most recondite sort of full-status class is the tertiary class. Although it is not easy to provide a definition of the term "tertiary class," it is easy enough to isolate the most important subsort of tertiary class and to describe its theoretical purpose. This is what Bergmann calls a "form class," a class the condition for being an element of which is that a determinate be of a certain logical form. Form classes, like tertiary classes generally, are of two sorts, nonrecursive and recursive. A nonrecursive form class would be, say, the class of all and only atomic

22. See below, p. 280.

facts.[23] Bergmann's example of a recursive form class is the class whose elements are all and only atomic facts, disjunctions of an atomic fact and an atomic fact, disjunctions of disjunctions of atomic facts and an atomic fact, and so on ad infinitum. The theoretical purpose of such classes is to ensure that all logical forms are ontologically grounded, or, in other words, that, for any nonsimple determinate, that determinate's being of a given logical form is itself a canonically producible determinate. The two above-mentioned paradigms of form classes are not themselves very significant, the former because a fact's being an atomic fact can be grounded without the class, as I will explain shortly. The latter is not important simply because logicians, or ontologists at any rate, are not usually interested in the logical form to which it "corresponds"; of more general interest would be, for example, the class of all molecular facts or the class of all determinates, both of which, *if* they could be formed, *would* be recursive form classes. (Again, I will explain shortly.)

Bergmann's assay of generality, recall, allows that one may quantify over things of all types and determinates of any category. This allows him to ground the logical forms of a great many determinates. To say that, for example, "this-being-green is a nonrelational atomic fact (of the lowest type)" is to say that "there is a particular and there is a nonrelational universal of the first type such that this-being-green is the same as the value of (the appropriate sort of) exemplification for the diad whose terms are this particular and this universal." To say that "this-being-red-or-that-being-oval is a disjunction of atomic facts" is to say that "there is an atomic fact and there is another atomic fact such that this-being-red-or-that-being-oval is the value of disjunction for the diad whose terms these atomic facts are." Although many logical forms may be grounded in this manner there are others that cannot, because they are "recursively infinite"; that a determinate is a molecular complex, for example, is such a form. In order to ground such forms, Bergmann claims, we must be able to assume the existence of certain recursively infinite form classes. To produce such classes requires producing their selectors. We may use the above-mentioned sorts of generalities to specify the conditions that must be satisfied in order for a determinate to be an element of the class for whose selector we are searching, embedding them in the appropriate "place" in a tuple to specify how all of the elements of the class may be "gener-

23. In order to make this a *nonrecursive* form class the number of types (of things) must be finite. Though Bergmann never really *argues* that the number of types must be finite he does insist upon it, giving as his reason, roughly, that unless the number of types is finite we could not think things we can in fact think.

ated" from those satisfying the condition. Consider, for example, Bergmann's paradigm of a recursive form class, the class whose elements are all atomic facts, all disjunctions of atomic facts, all disjunctions of an atomic fact with disjunctions of atomic facts, and so on. If we wish to produce the tuple from which by a (c)-step this class is produced, we will use the relevant generality (the one that grounds a fact's being an atomic fact) to specify the "first" *subclass* of the class whose selector we are producing, then another generality (the one that grounds a fact's being a disjunction of two atomic facts) to specify the "second" *subclass* of the class whose selector we are producing. Then we must arrange these conditions in a tuple in a manner that successfully "encodes" the "iteration step" by which all "subsequent" subclasses may be recursively generated from the first two. The class that is built on this selector is then the union of the classes in the sequence thus generated.

Following roughly the same sort of pattern Bergmann produces the selectors of form classes that are of a great deal more interest to him, though this, for reasons that must be at least briefly described, is a more difficult task. Bergmann accepts as an axiom the fact that no determinate can be either an element or constituent of itself, an element or constituent of a determinate that is one of its elements or constituents, and so on. He often calls this the "expanded Cantor condition." This implies that certain sorts of classes cannot be produced, that, in other words, not all conditions correspond to a class; to put it yet another way, not all apparent selectors really are selectors. Most fundamentally, of course, this applies to the class of all classes that have themselves as elements. But there are many others which would also violate the expanded Cantor axiom. We could not, for example, form the class of all determinates, for, because classes are determinates, this class would be a determinate and would thus be an element of itself. Thus the putative form class, the class of all and only determinates, cannot be formed. Similar sorts of difficulties attach to many other putative form classes, such as the class of all facts, the class of all circumstances, the class of all disjunctions, and so on. This is quite a problem, because the logical forms—being-a-fact, being-a-complex, being-a-disjunction, and so on—cannot be grounded except by means of form classes. To make a very long and intricate story very short, Bergmann concludes that he can ground these forms only if he "stratifies" his world, segmenting it into ontological "layers," for each of which one can produce certain problematic form classes but for all of which one cannot. Thus the first "layer" or "level" contains things, atomic facts, molecular facts whose components are atomic facts or molecular facts (whose components are atomic facts or . . . , etc.), or general facts whose target is a thing and whose scope is either an atomic fact or a molecular fact (whose components are atomic facts or . . . , etc.), or a general fact (whose target is a thing and whose scope . . . , etc.). Bergmann spends considerable effort producing the selector for the form class corresponding to the first level. Once he does so he can then produce the selectors for the classes corresponding to subsequent levels. The second level contains, for example, circumstances and classes whose terms and elements, respectively, are elements of the first level, and facts made out of these circumstances and classes. The third level contains those determinates produced out of determinates of the second level, and so on. The basic idea is that, although we cannot ground, for example, the completely general form of being-a-fact, we *can* ground the level-specific form, say, being-a-fact-of-the-second-level.

If all of this is successful, and one must concede that the formal complexities of the task make this assessment a formidable task in itself, then Bergmann has described a way of providing an ontological ground for any logical form that a determinate may have. Schematically, the production of the tertiary classes by means of which the solution is achieved proceeds in much the same manner as that of primary and secondary classes: a selector is produced by a finite sequence of canonical steps, the last one of which is a (b)-step (the selectors of *all* classes of whatever sort are diads, though those of primary and secondary classes are 2-tuples while those of tertiary classes, which involve a more complicated recursion pattern, are 3-tuples), and then, by a (c)-step, the class is "built on" the selector.

One may say that *diads are in everything* (nonsimple), from nonrelational atomic facts of the lowest type to tertiary classes of the most complicated sort. The underlined phrase is, in fact, not a bad slogan for concisely expressing the sweeping implications of the standardization: every nonsimple determinate is produced by a finite sequence of canonical steps at least one of which (and for everything but negative facts and diads themselves the penultimate step) is a (b)-step producing a diad. This is by no means simply a case of system-building, though admittedly there is something of the quest for theoretical elegance behind the standardization. It is, rather, a very natural expression of a conception of the world as a totality of *units* each of which is somehow "derived from" or "based upon" or "consists of" a *plurality*. In a fairly straightforward sense a diversity, a diad, is the most basic sort of unity that can be formed from a plurality, and a diversity whose terms are things (one could call them "atomic diads") the most basic sort of diversity. Bergmann's standardized schema of canons is by intention a way of displaying the most general ways that existents (or the determinates among them) are founded upon diversities; it provides a key for tracing any existent (or nonsimple determinate) back through the sequence of "foundings" until one reaches the simples that are its "ultimate foundation." Understood in this light, it is not at all odd or idiosyncratic to say that diads are in everything, rather, it is an appropriate, and perhaps even inevitable, consequence of the endeavor of the ontologist to describe the ways that plurality gives rise to unity in a world that manifestly contains both plurality and unity.

The Form of the World

Even if we remain within the realm of determinates canonically composed of determinates, it is clear that Bergmann's new ontology marks a significant departure from his own earlier interpretations of atomistic realism and indeed at many points seems to threaten the rhetoric, if not the substance, of atomistic realism itself. In granting ontological status to circumstances, Bergmann accepts the existence of internal relationships, connections grounded not in a tie distinct from the connected existents but rather in the "natures" of the connected existents. But not only is it not the case that all complexes are facts, it is also not the case that all nonsimples "produced from" things are complexes, for classes are not complexes. Even though classes have elements, and even though the elements of primary classes are constituents (note: not *terms*) of the diads which serve as their selectors, classes themselves have no constituents. If we remain within the category of facts, Bergmann's new and more restricted conception of constituency implies that those functions which have facts as values are not themselves constituents of these facts. If functions are existents that ground certain significant features of facts (and, of course, they are), then one may say that there are significant features of facts that are not grounded by existents that are "in" facts, at least "in" them in the sense of being constituents of them. Moreover, the notion of a "limiting complex" allowed by Bergmann's new assay of generality implies that there are facts with no constituents at all, a consequence that is at least surprising.

These innovations in Bergmann's new ontology range from terminological alterations which, it might be argued, are only of superficial importance (different senses in which one determinate can be "in" another) to changes that are clearly of more substantive significance (acceptance of connections grounded in the natures of the connected existents). Taken together, though, they graphically display the difficulty, perhaps the impossibility, of maintaining a simplistic version of the basic picture behind all forms of atomistic realism, a picture that would have us understand the world as a totality of complex *wholes* that consist of simple *parts*, of composites composed of non-composites.

But in any case we are not restricted to the canonical composition of determinates. Bergmann not only conceded but insists that there is much that cannot be grounded by canonical composites but must instead be grounded by Two-in-Ones, or hylomorphic composites. That a particular is a particular, or, more generally, that a thing is of its ultimate sort, can in no sense be a fact (or circumstance). That a given fact is pervaded by the mode of actuality cannot itself be a fact (or circumstance). Both, however, must be accounted for, because both are thinkable and thus in the appropriate sense exist. Bergmann's account of such "thinkables" in terms of hylomorphic composites is accompanied, to be sure, with the admission that these rather peculiar existents mark a "limit of ontological analysis." He might also have said that they mark the limits of atomistic realism.

But Two-in-Ones are, even if not canonical composites, at least composites of a sort; thus, whatever is grounded in them is still arguably "accounted for in terms of simples." We have already seen, however, indications that much that one may wish to include in the province of what is *known,* and that thus surely would be included in the realm of the *thinkable,* cannot be accounted for at all in an atomistic manner. Conjunction-being-diverse-from-negation is neither a fact nor a circumstance nor some sort of hylomorphic composite; it is literally nothing, because the minimal restriction prohibits nondeterminates from being the terms of diads. For closely allied reasons none of the following "pseudostatements" can really be taken as representing something thinkable:

a. There are three types of function: exemplification, connectives, and quantifiers.
b. The class of modes has fewer elements than the class of binary connectives.
c. There is more than one exemplification nexus.

For somewhat different reasons Bergmann holds that the following sentences are only pseudostatements:

d. Green is not a relation.
e. Being-to-the-left-of is not a particular.

It is sentences that purport to express the canons themselves, however, that are the most important sort of pseudostatement.

   f.   If there is a particular, a, and a nonrelational universal (of the
first type), f, then there is a diad, (a, f), whose terms they are.

   g.   If there is a diad whose terms are a particular, a, and a universal (of the first type), f, then, because there is the function of
exemplification, there is the atomic fact, $\eta(a, f)$.

   h.   If there is a 2-tuple whose first term is a determinate, X, and
whose second term is a disjunction of negated diads
(samenesses) each of which has X as one term but each of which
has different determinates, $Y, Z, \ldots$, as the other term, then
there exists the class, $\lambda\langle X, (X=Y) \vee (X=Z) \vee \ldots \rangle$, that has Y,
$Z, \ldots$ as elements.

Bergmann not only admits but argues insistently that (f)–(h) can no
more be taken as representing facts (or complexes) than can (a)–(e);
they do not even represent anything thinkable. Strictly speaking they
are mere strings of signs. One might be forgiven for finding this conclusion paradoxical, given the rather prominent role Bergmann gives
to the canons, not to mention the apparent conviction with which he
himself asserts (or assumes) what such sentences as (a)–(h) purport to
represent.

Bergmann does indeed address this paradox, and as one might expect, his treatment of it is quite ingenious, as of course it must be if it
is to meet his own high standards of success: he must show that the
illusion that (a)–(h) represent genuine realities is in fact an illusion
without, however, being any the less useful in establishing or expressing a "correct" ontology. His strategy, as one might also expect, is to
show that the illusion is engendered, in part, by language, or a misun-
derstanding of language. Uncharacteristically, perhaps, for a twen-
tieth-century philosopher, he wants to *deny* that such statements can
be understood as statements *about* language, either natural or artificial. On the other hand he wishes to deny that they are about the
world without at the same time precluding their usefulness for "correctly" describing the ontological structure of the world. This is
clearly a very narrow tightrope to walk, and the very terms of
Bergmann's solution to the problem presented to one attempting to
walk it would require much more explanation than can be presented
in an introduction which is already becoming too lengthy. But what
must be stressed is that we have here another, perhaps even deeper,
limitation to the program of ontological analysis. Clearly sentences
(a)–(h) have a prima facie claim to being considered intelligible state-

ments, statements each of which expresses something that is thinkable. When Bergmann argues that they do not express something thinkable, removing by decree (albeit a well-reasoned decree) what they purport to represent from the field of reality, then he is apparently conceding that *not* everything *can* be accounted for in terms of simples.

Although this is perhaps a paradoxical conclusion, it is not historically surprising. The author of the *Tractatus*, a text which certainly has as much right as any to be regarded as the bible of logical atomism, tells us the world is a totality of facts but that the *forms* of these facts are not themselves a part of the totality which comprises these facts. Bergmann has always found the latter of these sentiments as repugnant as he found, and still finds here, the former alluring. One of Wittgenstein's great failures, Bergmann has written, is his failure to recognize that "the form of the world is *in* the world,"[24] a slogan that he apparently interprets to mean that: (1) exemplification, the connectives, and the quantifiers have ontological status, are among the existents that compose the world, and (2) analytic complexes exist, or, if you like, analytic propositions represent facts. Bergmann still accepts both of these claims, though he has apparently concluded that the general issue of the world's form is more complicated than he had earlier believed. It is true that the ground of each nonsimple determinate's being of the logical form(s) that it is of *does* have an ontological ground that is itself a determinate. Bergmann expends an enormous amount of energy and ingenuity to make out this claim, and if he has been successful he has shown that, in at least this sense, the form of the world is indeed in the world; namely, every nonsimple canonical composite's being of a given logical form is itself a canonical composite.

As for analytic complexes, while it is true that these complexes themselves are canonical composites, the *ground* of a complex's *being analytic* is not itself a canonical composite. That a given complex is analytic does not depend *solely* upon its being of a given form (in which case the ground of its being analytic *would be* a canonical composite) but rather in its being of a logical form such that all complexes sharing that same form are pervaded by the mode of actuality. In short, the ground of analyticity is *hylomorphic* rather than canonical composition. Again, the ground of a *simple* determinate's being of *its* logical form, namely, its ultimate sort, is a hylomorphic composite. If a complex's being analytic and a thing's being of its ultimate sort can

24. See, especially, Gustav Bergmann, *Logic and Reality*, "The Glory and Misery of Ludwig Wittgenstein," University of Wisconsin Press, 1964, pp. 225–41.

be considered a part of the world's form—and it is very natural so to consider them—then grounding the aspects of the world's form in hylomorphic composites again allows Bergmann to make out the claim that the form of the world is in the world, though with a difference. Two-in-Ones cannot be construed as determinates and thus are not representable in the IL (at least *as* Two-in-Ones). These aspects of the world's form are thinkable, but not literally representable.

Turning now to our problematic pseudostatements, especially those that purport to represent canons, it is clear that all of them and, again, especially canon statements can easily be understood as statements which at least purport to describe the form of the world. To say that conjunction is diverse from negation *seems* to be a statement of a fact (or at least a circumstance) about these functions, a description of them. If one states that there are more binary connectives than modes, or that there is more than one nexus of exemplification, one certainly *appears* to be making a statement about these nondeterminates. That green is not a relation seems to be a description of the thing green. it is not at all unnatural to regard these statements as "descriptions" of the world's form, either in the sense that they are (apparently) about "formal existents" (Bergmann does in fact refer to nondeterminates as "forms") or, as in the last example, in the sense that they seem to be about the form of a thing.

Canon statements themselves may also very easily be regarded as descriptions of the form of the world, because they (purport to) specify the ways in which simple things (of certain specified "forms" or ultimate sorts) go together to compose complex (or nonsimple) existents and the ways in which these latter compose still more complex (or less simple) existents. In so doing they (purport to) describe the logical skeleton of the world, its ontological framework, its structure.

However successful one judges Bergmann's attempt to avoid both ontological linguisticism and ontological nihilism to be, his concession that the canons cannot be thought or (literally) represented surely constitutes at least a partial agreement with Wittgenstein: in a very important sense, though to be sure a sharply demarcated one, the form of the world is not in the world.

New Foundations of Ontology

I

Simples and Canons

What is ontology? Any formula or single paragraph one may design will neither help the beginner nor satisfy the initiated. Yet, picking such a formula and pointing out its shortcomings is an easy way of starting a lengthy ontological discourse which is selective and not meant for beginners.

"Ontology *accounts* for *everything there is* in terms of *simples.*" The formula, as good or, rather, as bad as any, suits my purpose. So I start with a string of comments drawing attention to some of its shortcomings.

Has any philosopher ever proposed an acceptable account of this sort? So far no one has; quite possibly, no one ever will. But that causes no trouble. The formula, not meant to proclaim an achievement, merely states a program. What then, one may ask, are the criteria of success? Eventually one must ask. But we would not get anywhere if we now pursued this track.

As philosophers often speak, 'to be there', 'to have *ontological status*', 'to *exist* (be an *existent*)', and 'to be an *entity*' are synonyms. That squanders four expressions on one meaning. Yet the ontologist must make so many distinctions that even if he plunders the tradition he is in danger of running out of words. And the fewer new ones one must coin the better. Thus I shall indulge habit and convenience only to the extent of spending the first three of these expressions on a single meaning.

Existence is univocal. So the tradition insists; and, of course, it is right. All that involves, though, however importantly for the sake of avoiding confusion, is a question of words. There are not two ways of having ontological status. (At this point, our speech habits being what they are, the second expression serves best.) Yet, the differences among some of the several existents (here the second expression proves most convenient) are very great indeed. I, for one, would not hesitate to call them momentous, or enormous. That, I submit, is a major source of the resistance serious ontology has always met. For these differences are much greater than most are prepared to face. If the traditional formula, existence being univocal, is misused to support this resistance, I demur. For the rest, let us agree to spend the first three expressions synonymously on that obvious univocal meaning while saving 'entity' for a more limited use, to be explained in due course, such that while every entity is of course an existent, not every existent will be an entity.

What is an account? What is a simple? As you may have gathered from the way the formula conjoins the two notions, an account is some sort of analysis that yields after a number of steps a *collection* of existents which are all "simple" in the sense that, if subjected to this sort of analysis, none of them yields anything further. Let us call this sort of analysis an *assay.* That, though, is merely a word. What does it stand for? Let α be an existent that is not simple. The first step of its assay will yield either a collection of existents, F_1, or, in the limiting case, a single existent, β, which is different from α. If each member of F_1 is simple, or if, in the limiting case, β is simple, the first step is also the last. If there is a second step, call the collection it yields F_2. In the limiting case, F_2 is the collection yielded by the first step of the assay of β. In all other cases, F_2 is the collection of all members of F_1 which are simples, and, in addition, all the members of the collections yielded by the first steps of the assays of all the members of F_1 which are not simples. And so on. *In this world, each of these collections, F_1, F_2, F_3, and so on, has a finite number of members; and one arrives after a finite number of steps at a collection, F_n, all of whose members are simples.* This collection I call the foundation of α, more fully, whenever it matters, the *ultimate foundation* of α, thus distinguishing it from the *intermediate foundations,* F_1, F_2, . . . , F_{n-1}.

The ultimate foundation of an existent is neither its assay nor of course the existent itself. To complete the assay one must specify how each of the intermediate foundations, F_i, as well as, eventually, how the existent itself is *produced* from some of the members of F_n. In this stepwise "reproduction" the order within some subsequences of steps is arbitrary; but that causes no difficulty. More importantly, there are in this world three ways of producing an existent from others. A nonsimple is either *made out of* others, or *built out of* others, or *built on* others.

Consider the four phrases: 'to be produced from', 'to be made out of', 'to be built out of', 'to be built on'. As they stand, they are but metaphors, all more or less patently anthropomorphic. That, though, if anything, is an advantage. For, being anthropomorphic, they are less likely to go unchallenged; and the unpacking by literal speech, within the limits of the humanly possible, of all metaphors, anthropomorphic, spatial, or otherwise, is nowhere more urgent, just as it is nowhere more difficult, than in ontology. 'Producing', here and occasionally later, merely serves as a generic expression for the three ways. Thus we need not bother with it. The unpacking, as complete as I can make it, of the other three metaphors is a very major part of this discourse as a whole. Yet, no matter how distant one's goal, if he wants to get there he must start walking. Nor can any one take more than one step at a time. My first step is to offer in a single paragraph two remarks about making; just enough to afford us a first glance at the schema that distinguishes the three ways from each other.

Making requires a *maker*. Human makers are out, of course. Nor may we go beyond the existents of the ontology. Hence, either the metaphor ought to be dropped or there are some very peculiar existents, such that their peculiarities justify setting them apart as an *ontological sort* and, except of course for the lacking humanity, calling them makers. In my world, whether old or new, there have long been such existents. Until now I have called them ties. Eventually both 'tie' and 'maker' will be discarded in favor of a word more convenient and less anthropomorphic than either. The makers of this world, whether old or new, are exemplification, the connectives, and the quantifiers; except that, while in the old world there was only one exemplification, there are now several.

Next the two remarks. Suppose, first, that the existent α is made out of three others, β, γ, δ, by the maker η. If so, then the first foundation of α is the collection whose four members are β, γ, δ, η. Generally, *if an existent is "made out of" others, the members of its first foundation are a single "maker" and the "material" out of which the latter makes the former.* Ask yourself, second, whether all makers are simples. There is of course the abstract possibility that some or even all of them are themselves products. This alternative, though, rather obviously, leads to a dead end. So we may safely discard it. *All makers are simples.* We are ready for the tripartite schema.

An existent is of *type (a)* if and only if it is *made* by a maker out of *some* others, each of a certain *ontological sort*.

An existent is of *type (b)* if and only if, provided *two* others are there, it is eo ipso there, without the need for a maker. Such an existent, which I shall eventually call a *circumstance*, is, as I shall speak, *built out of* the two others, which I shall eventually call its *terms*.

An existent is of *type (c)* if and only if, provided *one* other existent is there, it is eo ipso there, without the need for a maker or any other existent. The only existents of type (c) are *classes*. An entity which must be there for a class to be there, I shall eventually call a *selector*. All selectors are of a certain *ontological sort,* which is a subsort (or subtype) of existents (b).

This is the schema. Verbally, some similarities and differences among the types stand out. So I shall, in my second step, try to scratch at least the surface of what the words stand for by pointing out two striking differences. First, though, for an agreement about the words themselves. Let us suppress 'of the type' and speak of existents (a), (b), and (c), respectively. Let us next extend this nomenclature; calling a step leading from F_{i+1} to F_i, or, eventually, from F_1 to the existent under assay itself, a step (a), (b), or (c), depending on whether the producing involved is a making or a building-out-of or a building-on, respectively. Let us finally, whenever it it safe, suppress the adjective in 'ontological sort' and refer to the "sorts" which do not interest the ontologist either as kinds or by some other circumlocution.

One striking difference among the types is numerical: (c) involves a *single* existent; (b) involves *two.* In the illustration for (a) the maker η makes an existent out of three others, β, γ, δ; the formula speaks of *some,* with the actual number of existents as well as their respective sorts depending on the maker. The numerical difference, one versus two, between (c) and (b), will turn out to be one of the pivots of the overall dialectic. 'Some', on the other hand, is misleading. The formula is provisional; literally it is false. Except for the maker called negation each (a)-step will turn out to be several; all but the last of these are (b)-steps; only the last, making the existent (a) out of a single existent (b), is an (a)-step. This refinement will in due course be forced on us by the need to ground order. In the meantime, the provisional formulation will do. The new *assay of order,* together with that of *sameness,* from which it is inseparable, will be found in Section III. Both these assays are among the fundamental innovations.

Being a dog, or green, or a color, is to be of a kind but not of a sort. Particularity, being a fact, being a maker, are sorts. The difference that makes the difference I take to be familiar. More importantly, what grounds a sort? Every ontologist must sooner or later face the question; none can answer it while the questioner stands on one foot. In this world there are two ways of grounding sorts. Of one of them, and of the distinction between the two, more presently, still in this Section. Right now, having alerted you to the issue, I merely want to impress its importance on you by asking the same question in another way. With each sort goes a number of features such that, while existents of other sorts may have some of them, all those and only those which are of this sort have them all. What, then, grounds these features?

('Features' and 'connection', as used in this discourse, carry as such no ontological commitment.)

Another striking difference among (a), (b), and (c) concerns the sorts involved. The existent, or existents, out of which another is made, in case (a), or on which it is built, in case (c), must be of a certain sort or sorts. The formulae mention that, but, being merely parts of a schema, do of course not specify the sorts. The two existents out of which a third is built in case (b), on the other hand, do not seem to be subject to any restriction. This appearance is misleading. There is a restriction, which is another pivot of the overall dialectic. Yet it is so wide that it makes good sense not even to mention it in this first, rough sketch of the taxonomy. When we shall have to face it, we shall call it the *minimal restriction;* also because most philosophers deny all ontological status to the sorts it excludes. Among the sorts thus excluded are, very significantly, the makers. That is indeed one of the features that set them apart as a sort. Yet, as one would expect, there are other such features.

In my worlds there have always been classes. Yet the types (b) and (c) are new. Hence, unless I am again mistaken, much of what until now I have said about classes must be false. Specifically, as until recently I have assayed them, classes belonged to the category I called "derived entities," which from the new world has been expunged in that most important of all corrections which I felt as a liberation (p. 64). With the introduction of types (b) and (c), on the other hand, goes a whole cluster of innovations which in turn either require or at least suggest some corrections. Of these innovations three are "fundamental." One is the *new assay of classes* itself, which goes with (c). The other two are the new assays of sameness and diversity, already mentioned, which go with (b). All together, six fundamental innovations (p. 60) will be proposed in this discourse. Since this Section also serves as a preview, they will all be mentioned in it, together with two "major" ones.

1* Which features are fundamental, which "merely" major? There is no need to repeat what I have long propounded concerning the very nature of the ontological enterprise. Thus I merely remind you that an ontology is not a mere scatter of aphorisms, or, at best, of insights, but, rather, all contemptors of "systems" to the contrary notwithstanding, a dialectical structure, or system. That means, among other things, that all but a few of the features of an ontology rest on others, either by implication or by structural suggestion; and, second, that they all support each other by jointly grounding all the "required" distinctions. If one keeps that in mind, the answer to the question is immediate. A feature is fundamental if and only if it is one of the relatively few on which all others rest, while they themselves rest on no others, their only support being the actual "success" of the ontology. A feature is major if and only if relatively many rest either wholly or in part on it, while it rests immediately on some of the fundamental ones. That makes being major a matter of degree. But, then, what is "success"? and which are the distinctions the system is "required" to ground? The answers, not unrelated of course, are best left for another reminder, toward the end of the Section, when we shall be ready to turn to the phenomenological basis.

The existents usually called atomic and molecular facts are but one sort, or subtype, of existents (a). In the rest of this Section as well as in the next two, our main concern will be with this subtype of existents (a), although, if only in an auxiliary role, one of the three sorts of circumstances, or existents (b), will dominate Section III. The other two circumstances, however, will not be introduced until near the end. Classes, finally, which are the only existents (c), although they will have to be mentioned throughout, will not be assayed until Section VI. Why, then, start with the tripartite schema? It does provide a first glimpse of the whole. Previewing, though, if overdone, not only burdens the exposition but irritates the reader. So I explain next why I proceed this way.

As the words are used in this discourse, *a collection is literally nothing;* it has no ontological status whatsoever. Yet *classes obviously are there.* Accordingly, as I just felt bound to point out, they have always been in my world; only the assay now proposed for them is new. Again, as the words will be used, *a collection has members;* only *classes have elements.* Also, most importantly, unlike an element in a class, a member may "occur" in a *collection not just once but a finite number of times.* This dichotomy is another of the pivots on which the overall dialectic turns. Also, the ontological status of classes, or, as many now call them, sets, has long been at issue, not just among philosophers but also among the mathematical logicians, in this context often called axiomatic set theorists, who take an interest in ontology. Under the circumstances I could not possibly take the dichotomy for granted without at the very beginning introducing it and at least mentioning what it involves. This, I submit, is a very good reason for proceeding as I do.

For each class there is a collection such that the elements of the former are members of the latter, but not conversely. If the converse also held, there would almost certainly be no point in distinguishing between collections and classes. Thus there should be some limitations, and there are in fact two, in the direction from collections to classes. In other words, there is not for every collection a class such that the members of the former are the elements of the latter. The limitations, although otherwise very different from each other, are both very wide. It will pay to keep ourselves reminded of that by adapting an old use to a new situation. *Classes (I shall say) are arbitrary; collections, completely arbitrary.*

One of the limitations is really a small cluster of such. These, coming into play only for some infinite collections, the axiomatic set theorists have introduced in order to avoid the paradoxes, such as Russell's. Eventually, in Section VI, we shall have to take this cluster into account. Yet we shall never have to do anything about it, in the sense in which the mathematicians very ingeniously did very much indeed; nor of course could we; our job is merely to make ontological sense out of what they did.

The other limitation, which in the nature of things is our concern rather than the mathematicians', also applies to finite classes. The idea is, very simply, that some existents, or, rather, the existents of some sorts, cannot be elements of classes. These four sorts are on the one hand the makers and, on the other, three sorts of entities to which I shall soon generically refer as *entities,* with the word withheld from the univocal use in order to save it for this very purpose. About two of these three sorts of entities something will be done presently, still in this Section. The two modes, which are the only members of the third, will also have to be mentioned on this occasion, although virtually nothing will be done about them until the second Section, which, as you will see, they dominate.

We are ready for a second glimpse of the taxonomic pattern that will gradually emerge. The second limitation, on all classes, whether finite or infinite, coincides with the minimal restriction (p. 47). In other words, an existent is an element of classes (which are the existents (c)) if and only if it is a term of circumstances (which are the existents (b)). Still differently, *being an element of classes, being a term of circumstances, and fulfilling the minimal restriction are coextensive.* Why that is so, dialectically, we do not yet know, of course. Nor, therefore, can we as yet appreciate how deeply it cuts. One question, though, which may have occurred to you, is easily answered. Why is this limitation our concern rather than the mathematicians'? The answer is that, with one exception, none of the four sorts which the minimal restriction excludes even occurs in any of the ontologies any of these mathematicians has either proposed or embraced. The exception, with respect to the connectives and quantifiers, is Frege. Nor, to the best of my knowledge, has any ontology ever acknowledged all four, even though, as we shall presently see, two of them are direct descendants of Aristotle's matter and form.

2* *Obviously*, I said a while ago, there are classes. *Obviously*, I added, they are *arbitrary*, although not completely so. Why, in the midst of all the caution displayed, this double rashness? "The formulae of elementary arithmetic, such as '2 + 2 = 4', are about something in the world." If challenged, I could not defend this proposition directly but only indirectly, by inviting the challenger to consider the whole of my world (ontology), together with its phenomenological basis and its dialectic. Such a proposition I shall call a fundamental gambit. If this one is sound, the assay of what those formulae stand for must yield some existents. I know of no such assay, nor can I imagine one, except in terms of classes; hence the apparent rashness. It merely acknowledges an obvious adequacy criterion.

*'Classes are arbitrary'. Is this sentence obviously true because it is an implicit definition? I emphatically reject all *contextualisms*, linguistic or otherwise, of which such definitions, either outright or in some disguise, are the very essence. Yet we shall in Sections IV and VI encounter two features of my new world which are the sound core, small yet important, of contextualism. Or so at least I shall at the proper places take pains to argue; for each such core an ontology can recover, from the outside as it were, dialectically strengthens its case. But return to the sentence. Is it obvious because, without being an implicit definition, it states one of the several kinds of truths philosophers may or may not distinguish? We need not rashly commit ourselves. Eventually, I hope, I shall be able to accommodate what the sentence stands for in one of the categories of truths which by then I shall have distinguished. Right now I merely make sure that we are all talking about the same thing. For the "classes" the mathematicians handle and the ontologists worry about are all such that this sentence about them is true.

This will have to do right now for the two striking differences between (a), (b), and (c). A question that comes readily to mind brings out a third difference; so I conclude the line of thought by raising it. Take an existent and its ultimate foundation. Do they determine each other uniquely in both directions; downward, from the existent to the foundation, if I may so express myself, and upward, from the foundation to the existent? If not, is the connection unique in one direction, or perhaps in neither?

In case (b) we shall see, the two terms, which may or may not be simples, are uniquely determined by the circumstance, and conversely. In case (c), we shall also see, a selector determines "its" class uniquely; but each class is built, alternatively, on one of several selectors. For existents (a) the situation is more variegated. For nonrelational atomic facts and their negations, which are the simplest kind of molecular facts, the connection is unique in both directions. For all other molecular facts it is unique downward but not upward. A single collection is the basis of more than one such molecular fact. To see why that is so, consider what, with the conventional notation, '$f_1(a_1) \vee f_2(a_2)$' and '$f_1(a_2) \vee f_2(a_1)$' stand for. Consistent atomists deny that either expression stands for anything. Nonatomists must hold, as I do, that the existents for which they stand are two and not one. Yet, clearly, the ultimate foundation of either is the collection whose six members are the two particulars a_1 and a_2, the two universals f_1 and f_2, and the two makers called disjunction and exemplification, or more accurately, should it turn out that there are several exemplifications, the appropriate one. Beyond molecularity, when the quantifiers enter, downward uniqueness is also lost, even for generalities as simple as the two '$(x)f_1(x)$' and '$(\exists x)f_1(x)$' stand for in the conventional notation. In the limiting case, we shall see, alternative foundations need not even overlap, except for the makers among their members. That is indeed a crucial feature of the new *assay of generalities,* which is another of the six fundamental innovations. You will find it all later, in the second half of Section IV, where this assay will be proposed. Some comments, though, apparently just about a word, should help right now.

3* 'Constituent' and 'consist' go together. Until now I have used them both, the first quite regularly, the second occasionally, so that every member of each foundation of an existent was a "constituent" of it. This old use I now discard, not just because it lacks upward uniqueness; for, since among the old "constituents" there were also the makers, it seemed natural that, as in the case of the two disjunctions above, they would produce different results when "combining" the other constituents (of the ultimate foundation) in different ways. The reason for discarding the old use is, rather, that it lacks downward uniqueness, as comes out in the case of the generalities. To appreciate this reason, just consider how awkward it would be to speak of anything as consisting of alternative "constituents." Not that I ever consciously tried to avoid the awkwardness. Yet it may well be that the suggestion of downward uniqueness which the metaphor carries has until recently kept me from finding the assay of generality for which I have groped many years. So insidious, unless completely unpacked, are the metaphors in ontology.

*The old use I thus discard. Yet the word will not go to waste. In connection with the new assay of generality, a new use for 'constituent' will be proposed. Upon this new use, each existent will determine the collection of its constituents uniquely; being a constituent becomes downward transitive: and makers are no longer constituents. In view of the latter feature, makers no longer being constituents, since every existent (a) has one maker in its first foundation (and therefore at least one in its ultimate one), a foundation, whether intermediate or ultimate, of an existent (a), while of course a collection, is not a class. Nor is that the only reason why the new use is more convenient. It will also turn out that every (new) constituent will be an element of classes and a term of circumstances. Thus, being a constituent, being a term of circumstances, being an element of classes, and fulfilling the minimum condition will all four be coextensive. Nor is even that all.

*In due course we shall see that among all existents fulfilling the minimal condition, there are only two sorts that have no (new) constituents, namely, classes on the one hand, and, on the other, those existent—presently I shall again call them things—which are simples but not makers. With respect to this feature of having no (new) constituents, classes, which are the only existents (c), are thus more like things than existents (a) or (b), even though, being built on another existent, a class, unlike a thing, is not a simple. Nor, as one would expect, is that the only feature marking the distinction between things and classes on the one hand and all other existents satisfying the minimal condition on the other. Of all this in due course. But you sense already (I hope) that we are on the way toward a taxonomy that is pleasingly perspicuous, although much more complex than those afflicted with what they call a "sound sense of reality" are willing to accept. Just remember what was said about the enormous differences among the several sorts of existents. And remember, too, how the features of an ontology are supposed to support each other.

Suppose that r_1, a_1, a_2 are a relation and two particulars. If the relation is asymmetrical, the expression '$r_1(a_1, a_2)$' and '$r_1(a_2, a_1)$' stand, in the conventional notation, for two existents. What makes them two is of course the feature of the world called order. The conventional notation represents it by the order of marks on paper. That, clearly, is not an assay. Yet, even with the one you will find in Section III, the ultimate foundation of both $r_1(a_1, a_2)$ and $r_1(a_2, a_1)$ is the collection whose four members are r_1, a_1, a_2, and η; the latter being the appropriate exemplification. If so, then among the atomic facts the nonrelational ones are, as I just claimed, the only ones in one-one correspondence with their ultimate foundations. Similarly for the connectives. The noncommutative ones among them raise the problem of order. As it happens, though, nothing will be lost if in the rest of this Section and in the next we ignore this problem, or, what amounts to the same, if we limit our examples to nonrelational atomic facts, commutative connectives, and negation. Again, no harm will be done if in the rest of this Section and in the next two we suppress the adjective in 'appropriate exemplification', or, what amounts to the same, if we express ourselves as if there were still only one such maker in my world.

The members of an ultimate foundation are all simples. Hence, you will infer from what has just been said, r_1, a_1, a_2, and η are all simples. What, then, you will ask, are the simples of this world. A simple is either one of the "various" makers or one of the "several" members of each of the *ultimate sorts*. The ultimate sorts are particularity, nonrelational universality of the first type, nonrelational universality of the second type, binary relational universality of the first type, and so on. These *ontological* types correspond of course to the *logical* types of Russell's *Principia Mathematica (PM)*. Thus we may, whenever it is safe and convenient, use 'type' as a synonym for 'ultimate sort'. In a relaxed notation of the usual kind, the four types just mentioned may be put in correspondence with four kinds of variables, e.g., 'x', 'f', 'F', 'r'. A stricter notation, with or without variables, that can accommodate an infinite number of types uses a superscript built in the familiar manner out of '0', '(', ')', e.g., for the four just mentioned, '0', '(0)', '((0))', '(0, 0)'. *PM* does provide for an infinite number of (logical) types. In this world, we shall see, there can be only *a finite number of ultimate sorts* (ontological types); and there are in fact but few. Thus we need not bother with the superscript but shall instead, whenever necessary, speak of the appropriate ultimate sort. A *universal*, as I shall speak, quite traditionally, is a member of an ultimate sort that is not a particular. A simple that is either a particular or a universal I shall continue to call a *thing*. Hence, *a simple is either a maker or a thing*. The number of the "various" makers is rather small; on the number of the "several" members of each ultimate sort there is no limitation. But this merely numerical difference, characteristic as it may be, is not the one marked by the words 'various' and 'several'. Some features, things and makers share; that is why I call them both simples. With respect to some others they radically differ; and one of these differences, we shall see, goes rather nicely with the two words.

We are ready for the two major points I still want to make in this Section. Each introduces, and begins the examination of, an apparent difficulty. The first, inseparable from the very idea of an ontological schema, arises already, and perhaps most clearly, in the case of atomic facts, which although of course not simples are yet, in the familiar idiomatic sense, the "simplest" existents (a). The second difficulty arises when one inquires into the connection between a thing and "its" ultimate sort. Facing the first, one is brought face to face with the two modes, which are one of the three sorts I am now setting aside as entities (p. 56). To resolve the second, one must, I am now convinced, introduce the other two sorts of entities.

Let, in the familiar notation, 'a_i', 'f_2', 'F_k' stand for particulars and universals of the lowest (nonrelational) types, respectively; one for each subscript. Consider the collections whose three members are (1) a_i, f_2, η; (2) f_2, F_k, η; (3) a_i, F_k, η, respectively. Because of the sorts of the two things among its members, *none* of the collections (3) satisfies the first, or, as I shall also call it, the (a) part of the tripartite schema. *Some* of the collections (1) and (2) do. E.g., out of *some* collections of one particular and one universal of the first type, η makes an atomic fact. Out of some, but not out of each! Yet, if, as in ontology one must, we take the schema literally, as it stands, then it is one of the *canons* of part (a) that there is for *each* collection (1) or (2) an existent, which happens to be called an atomic fact, such that the maker among its three members makes it out of the other two as its "material." Yet, as one ordinarily speaks and thinks, the existent which by the canon ought to be there, sometimes is not there. That spots the difficulty, both obvious and familiar. Presently we shall address ourselves to it. It will pay if you let me first take care of a few preparations.

There are various makers; and, of course, a canon goes with each of them. As for (a), so for (b) and (c). So I shall, whenever necessary, distinguish among canons (a), (b), and (c). A more detailed examination of the differences among them will have to wait. The schema itself does not state all canons. Of course it doesn't. If it did, it wouldn't be merely a schema. To state them all, as accurately as our purposes require, and to clarify the ontological status they may or may not have are two major tasks of this discourse as a whole. In a sense, one may even think of them as the very heart of the matter. To grasp that as firmly as is possible at this point, consider that every canon, whether (a) or (b) or (c), amounts to this: *If a certain number of existents of certain sorts is there, then a further existent is eo ipso there.* Yet, one existent, whatever condition it may or may not fulfill, *is not* literally another (as it would have to be to trivialize canon (c)). Two existents *are not* literally a third; three, not a fourth; and so on. (That the number, as was mentioned (p. 46), will turn out to be always either one or two is at the moment just another detail; and the minimal restriction is of course a "condition.")

There are those, including myself, though of late to a diminishing extent, who philosophize by means of the diagrams called ideal languages. The canons correspond to the (metalinguistic) formation rules of this way of philosophizing. That is one good reason why, going out of my way to avoid 'rule', I use 'canon'. Another reason, equally good, is the blatant anthropomorphism of 'rule', which cannot be expunged from any ontological context. That is not to say that I shall in this discourse dodge the fundamental issues raised by (this variant of) the linguistic turn. Nor shall I ignore the crucial role real languages play in the ontology of mind. But I want to concentrate these matters in two places, in Sections V and VII, and as much as is possible keep them out of the rest. Yet I shall continue to do two things. On the one hand, I shall, wherever it is convenient, gradually and almost casually introduce some fragments of what I now believe is the ideal language. On the other hand, I shall avoid the extreme clumsiness and circumstantiality of the ideal pattern, which we shall come to understand are inevitable, by resorting, even while presenting it, to some fragments of the more relaxed notations, which are familiar.

Turn now to the difficulty I called obvious. Can one conquer it by replacing in the formula just italicized 'there is by 'there is or may be', so that it reads: If a certain number of existents of certain sorts is there, then a further existent either is or *may* be eo ipso there? In ontological discourse modal expressions merely mark a job still to be done. Eventually the modality must be grounded, either ad hoc, i.e., by an existent expressly provided for the purpose, or in a pattern of existents already available. For a pattern job atomic facts are too "simple." Thus we must look for another way out. In this world, the two modes, actuality and potentiality, provide it.

A mode is a very special sort of existent such that (in the example) the atomic fact is, as the canon requires, always there; in the mode of either actuality or potentiality, depending on whether, as one ordinarily speaks, it either is or is not there. How then, you will ask, does a mode "combine" with whatever it combines with? Why was it not counted among the members of the foundation of the atomic fact? Which features set these existents apart from all others? You will find many of the answers to these and similar questions in the next Section; the rest of them, in the rest of this discourse. A more general comment should help right now.

The modes have been in my world for quite some time, in order to provide intentions for all acts. But they did not do any other major job. Thus they were ad hoc, in the familiar pejorative sense, in which no sort of an ontology should be. Nor, for that matter, did I do much about them. By now, though, they are not only doing several other jobs but have become so pivotal in the overall dialectic that I cannot but count their new eminence as *another fundamental innovation.*

The several makers and the several members of each of the several ultimate sorts are the members of the respective subsorts of the sort whose members are the simples. Any two existents of any sort or subsort have something in common with each other but with nothing else. This something must be grounded, either in an existent expressly provided for the purpose or in a pattern of existents already available. What then grounds the several sorts? The questions clearly are several and so, therefore, are the answers. You will find them at the proper places throughout this discourse. The place for one, though, is here. What grounds the several ultimate sorts? Trying to answer, one runs into the other of the two difficulties mentioned. To resolve it one must, I now believe, introduce the other two sorts of entities.

Particularity is one; particulars there are many. As for particularity, so for all ultimate sorts. Green, blue, and the other colors, middle C, middle D, and the other pitches, though all of the same ultimate sort, are many. (Green and blue are also both color*s*; middle C and D, both pitche*s*. *C*olor and *P*itch, however, although each a single existent, are neither ultimate nor any other ontological sorts but two simples, of a different universality.) A simple, therefore, cannot *be* its ultimate sort; otherwise what is many would be one. Hence the last of the fundamental innovations. *A simple is a composite of two; one is an ultimate sort; the other, an item.* The latter is a mere "individuator." *Items and ultimate sorts are two sorts of entities.* An entity, therefore, is either an item or an ultimate sort or one of the two modes.

What holds the two components of a thing together? Another maker rather obviously would start a regress. Yet the matter is so important that we had better take a quick look at its first step. Each maker is subject to what I shall presently call a restriction. Hence, even if every ultimate sort were in a relevant sense "unique," the several items would all have to be of a sort. Here the second step of the regress begins.

What, then, I repeat, holds the item and the ultimate sort of a thing together? Nothing does. They are totally "inseparable" from, and "dependent" on, each other. (That these are but two metaphors will be acknowledged presently.) Nor, unlike all existents (a) and (b), does a thing have a mode. (Classes, we shall see, which are the only existents (c), go in this respect with things.) These are two good reasons, which we shall come to appreciate, for grouping all things, together with the makers, as simples. Notice, incidentally, that an assay of things, al-

though for good reasons called simples, as composites of two components, shows up the poverty of the formula as to what ontology is,
which I picked up as a starter. This, though, is neither here nor there.
The formula has served its purpose. Let me next say what burns on
my fingernails.

It does not take much learning to recognize in this "innovation" Aristotle's composition of a substance out of form and matter; or, rather,
in the manner of Aquinas, out of an essence and a bit of *materia signata,* with the former and the latter corresponding to an ultimate sort
and an item, respectively. Yet, grafted upon a world like mine, *this assay of things is surely a fundamental innovation,* if only because, in Butchvarov's felicitous phrase, it finally acknowledges *one limit of logical
atomism.* Let us agree to mark this limit by a word. Henceforth, whenever it serves a purpose, I shall call a thing a *Two-in-One.* The only
other Two-in-Ones, at the only other such limit, which we shall encounter in the next Section, involve, not surprisingly, the two modes.

Structurally, this graft of something very old and much tried upon
something new and untried is but the most conspicuous recovery of a
sound core.[1] Cores thus recovered not only often appear at a different
place in the structure; sometimes, as in this case, they also lie much
deeper. For this world of mine is still a world in which there are no
Aristotelian essences or natures (there are not even continuants in it),
either substantial or (whether Aristotelian or not) of, say, either gray,
or louder-than, or Color; while on the other hand, if for once 'essence' is substituted for 'ultimate sort', the several ultimate sorts, including particularity, are essences.

A series of comments will, I hope, flesh out what has been said so
far, about the last innovation as well as in the rest of the Section.

First. Unpacking a metaphor and grounding, either by an existent
or in a pattern, some feature or features, are often two sides of one
coin. 'Unique', 'separable', and 'independent' will eventually all be
grounded in patterns; just as the division of all simples into entities,
makers, and things will be justified by agreements and disagreements
with respect to some features. Makers, no doubt, are a sort. Which
features, then, set them apart? There is, we shall see, a sense in which
each maker but nothing else is "unique." (In a different sense, we shall
also see, all entities are also unique.) Moreover, degrees of "separability" will become available. And so on. Between things on the one
hand and all other simples, whether entities or makers, one difference

1. John Peterson has sensed the trend toward this step well before I was ready to take
it. See his "Bergmann's Hidden Essentialism," *Review of Metaphysics,* 22, 1969, 660–75.

stands out. A thing needs a tie (maker) to tie it to another or others. A tie needs no tie to tie it to what it ties. Nor is there anything that holds the item and the ultimate sort of a thing together. Similarly, we shall see, for the two modes.

Suppose, then, that this trichotomy is justified. That leaves makers and things as the only simples that are not entities. Henceforth, therefore, whenever there is no danger of confusion, as for the most part there won't be, I shall use 'simple' and 'thing' synonymously. Thus we can say that *an existent is either an entity, or a maker, or a thing, or a non-simple of one of the three types (a), (b), (c)*. Eventually, the last four of these categories will for very good reasons be collected into one. Then we shall be able to say that an existent is either an entity, or a maker, or an existent of this very broad category for which we shall borrow a rather suggestive name from the tradition.

Second. Participants in some recent discussions may wish to raise a question about particulars. If, like all other things, each particular turns out to be the composite of an ultimate sort and an item, are particulars still bare? The answer is part of a longish story. You will find it in Appendix A.[†] Now I merely say that, ironically, bareness has spread. *All things, particulars as well as universals, are bare.*

Third. The items are newcomers to my world. The ultimate sorts have long been there, much longer than the modes. Yet, as for the latter, I have until now done nothing, except for the bare recognition that they are needed, for the former. This neglect of the ultimate sorts (or, to put a better face on it, the almost complete absorption with the makers) is probably the reason why I lumped both ultimate sorts and makers as "subsistents." This classification was not "false." For the two categories do agree in some features. The new taxonomy, however, is more "accurate"; i.e., it is not only more detailed but also, or so at least I hope to show, more perspicuous.

Fourth. Ultimate sorts and universals share the one-many feature. Hence, some insist, the former are at best but a kind of the latter, and go on from there to argue that the former are redundant, that introducing them is inconsistent, or what have you. Also, either because their vision is so dim, or because they cannot brook the enormous differences among existents, or perhaps because they are wittingly or unwittingly committed to one of the classical ontologies, these critics fail to appreciate, even if it is pointed out to them, that there are other features, equally radical or deep-lying, and therefore of equal con-

[†]The "appendices" to which Bergmann refers here, and elsewhere throughout this book, were unfortunately never completed. For more about them and their possible contents see the Editor's Note, p. xvii.—WH

cern to the ontologist, in which ultimate sorts and universals differ.

What, in this new world, is the use of the old phrase 'one-many'? *The only mere individuators, one for each thing, are the items.* Every thing, on the other hand, enters into many (atomic) facts. E.g., exemplification makes out of one particular, say, a_1 and any f_j all the atomic facts, some actual, most potential, whose respective foundations are the three-member collections a_1, f_j, η. The two modes, the various ultimate sorts, and the various makers, all being unique, need no individuators. Yet each of them enters, in its own peculiar way, into many existents of the appropriate sort. E.g., exemplification and conjunction each make many facts. Particularity combines with each of many items into many particulars; and so on. ('Enter', as no doubt you noticed, I use for the moment neutrally.)

Fifth. At one point, you will remember, when establishing the most striking difference between universals and ultimate sorts, we refused to enter regress (p. 56). On this a critic may pounce. Why not, he asks, break that regress before it gets started by making the universals themselves, without makers, "inhere" in something. (The tradition provides him with a handy word; it almost always does.) Or, at the other end, why not take one more step instead of breaking off where I do? The answer is that *the difference is clearly felt.*

Such a difference is found in the *phenomenological basis.* The latter, although of course anthropocentric, is yet indispensable. As long as ontological discourse remains "pure," in the sense of not being anchored in this basis, it also remains futile. The metaphor of a "basis" not only expresses this but also suggests, correctly, that the dialectic, rather than probing it, is employed to erect the ontological structure upon it. The suggestion is made even more clearly by the metaphor of a "jumping-off place," provided only one realizes that while all ontological discourse must eventually attend to this side of the enterprise, it need not start from it. This Section, quite deliberately of course, was kept "pure." In the next the phenomenological basis will come to the fore. But let us right now take a look at the case in hand.

Is there a felt difference between the external property, as some call it, of being green and the internal one, as they also say, of being a property? Directly one cannot argue on either side. That is one reason, though to be sure not the only one, why at some place or places one must appeal to the phenomenological basis. All I can say, therefore, is that this particular difference pierces my eyes. So does the difference between being green and being a color, which I have long grounded in that between two ultimate sorts. Now, we shall see, "systematic pressure," i.e., in this case, what is needed to assay generalities, provides a welcome additional ground—welcome because it also grounds more deeply the felt difference between the a posteriori and the a priori within the synthetic—in the difference between green and Color on the one hand and an ultimate sort on the other (to me) stands out beyond doubt.

4* Which distinctions is an ontology "required" to ground? What is enough? What is the measure? The question was left pending when I first reminded you of what I have long propounded concerning the nature of the ontological enterprise (p. 47). Now we are ready for the answer. We need, first, a sufficiency of distinctions, neither more nor less, to ground all felt differences, to solve all philosophical problems, and to recover the sound core of all other positions. We must, second, be able to erect upon them a dialectical structure, or system, rather than, as it was put, a mere scatter of aphorisms or, at best, of insights. These are the required distinctions; this, however difficult to achieve, is the ultimate "success"; all the contemptors of "systems" and all the idolaters of a "sound sense of reality" to the contrary notwithstanding.

Sixth. I list in conclusion the six fundamental innovations, or, what amounts to the same, the new foundations: the assays of sameness, of order, of generality, and of classes; the Aristotelian-Thomistic graft; and the hugely expanded role of the two modes, actuality and potentiality. Of other innovations there are naturally quite a number. Some fill gaps or flesh out what has been there before, particularly in the assays of mind and of arithmetic. Some others correct mistakes. Of all this in due course. But the six bases have at least all been touched. The two "major" innovations I can now only mention. One is the new assay of, and the resulting additions to, what is *analytic*. The other is the new assay of the *meaning nexus*, i.e., of the connection between a thought and its intention. The latter, although a very important correction, is yet peculiarly self-contained or localized, if I may so express myself. Thus it is relegated to the last appendix.

II

Facts and Modes

Turn for the last time to that poor starter: ontology accounts for everything there is, and so on. What is everything? Should one perhaps invent a single existent, somehow to succor or support all others, call it exist*ence*, and say that whatever is thus succored or supported exists, and conversely? That plainly is a dead end. Nor is there a direct answer to the awkward question. It merely marks the spot for the "phenomenological turn." *Whatever can be intended exists.* This principle, of the existing intention, is of all fundamental gambits the one that has long engrossed me most. So I state it in two more ways. To be intended and to be presented are, as I speak, one and not two. Hence, second, *whatever can be presented exists.* This introduces a synonym that yields among other conveniences a handy label. I shall speak of the *Principle of Presentation.* Third, whatever can be thought, or, briefly, *whatever is thinkable exists.*

The Principle is intimately connected with the assay I have long ago proposed for the act. Specifically, the former sets a criterion of adequacy for the latter. Deep as that goes, the Principle lies still deeper. I, for one, would not without it know what it means for anything to exist. The assay of the act I shall not expound once more. But let me state the idea and remind you of some of the terms. An *act* is (the fact of) a particular exemplifying two universals, one a *species,* one a *thought.* Perceiving, believing, remembering, imagining, doubting, and so on, are species. A thought intends its intention. Let '$f_1(a)$', 'b', 'f_2', '*perc*' stand for an atomic fact and for the particular, the thought, and the species of an act of perceiving which intends this atomic fact, respectively. Then '$f_2(b) \cdot perc(b)$' stands for the act, '$f_2 \, M \, f_1(a)$' for the connection between the thought and its intention.

5* 'M' is taken from the first letter of 'means'. A thought means (intends) its intention. Until now, 'M' stood for a tie, which, although sui generis, was yet, if anything, more like a connective than a quantifier. Accordingly, such expressions as '$f_2 \, M \, f_1(a)$' stood for existents (a), or, as we shall soon call them, facts. Now they all stand for circumstances, or existents (b), of one of the three sorts. Accordingly, we shall see,

61

'*M*', like '=' and '∈', the traditional marks for sameness and ele-menthood, does not itself stand for anything. This new assay, men-tioned at the end of Section I, is one of the two major innovations. Yet, as was also mentioned, we may safely ignore it till the very end.

'Thinking', here and throughout this discourse, is used very broadly. That, though, is merely a way of words. We simply assign one use or meaning, broader than usual, to one word. To 'perceiving' and some other expressions for species we shall have to assign two mean-ings. Thus we shall play the familiar index game, distinguishing be-tween 'perceiving' and 'perceiving$_1$', 'imagining' and 'imagining$_1$', and so on, whenever there is danger of confusion. Of this more presently, in the second of the five comments which follow. The first gathers some preparatory remarks. The second, in order to forestall puzzle-ment, introduces in preview fashion some features of the newly fleshed out assay of minds, which will be proposed in Section V. The third distinguishes between the Principle of Presentation and what has been called a Principle of Acquaintance. The fourth eliminates the apparent modality in think*able*. The fifth and last, built on the fourth, is the opening move of the confrontation, continued through-out this Section, with a position I shall call absolutism.

First. (1) What can be intended exists. Whose intentions or intend-ings, yours or mine? The difference makes no difference. In this world the road to other minds does not wind through those passes. (2) Most of what exists never has been nor ever will be intended by anyone. Hence the modal expressions 'what can be presented', 'what can be intended', 'what is thinkable'. Of this more in the third com-ment. (3) How about the *un*thinkable? This is really two issues; one, in traditional words, as to whether and how the mind can think its own boundary; the other, as to what, if anything, lies beyond that bound-ary. About the latter, not being a "speculative" philosopher, I have nothing to say. Nor does it move me. The former is of a very different nature. Am I not at this very moment writing and, presumably, think-ing about the unthinkable? This issue, which of late has greatly vexed me, although not in its traditional form but, rather, in the style of the linguistic turn, as a clutch of questions about language and meta-language and about what can and cannot be said in either the one or the other, we shall face in the last Section. (4) When one intends some-thing, say, an atomic fact, he is presented not only with the intention as a whole but also with all the members of its ultimate foundation. As for the latter, so for all the members of all intermediate foundations, if any. If we agree to express this by saying that whenever a nonsimple is intended *explicitly,* all the entities thus involved are intended *im-*

plicitly, we shall save ourselves many cumbersome phrases with 'member of' and avoid misleading uses of 'in'.

Second. Sometimes I "perceive" a horse or a table. What is perceived is expressed by 'this is a horse' and 'this is a table', respectively. The "form" of these sentences is atomic. That may lead one to expect, first, that each of them stands for the intention of a single act; and, second, by the Principle of Presentation, that 'horse' and 'table' each stands for a universal. Yet in the new world there are no such universals. Nor, fortunately, upon the more detailed assay of conscious states, which will be proposed in Section V, is either of the two conscious states of "perceiving," either a horse or a table, a single act, but, rather, several simultaneous ones, with different intentions, none of which either explicitly or implicitly intends a universal called 'horse'. Such "perceiving," therefore, is not a species; and we do not, when "perceiving" a horse or a table, upon the new assay, intend a universal which in the new world is no longer there. That gives the idea of how we shall avoid contradicting the Principle of Presentation. The details can wait until Section V. For we shall not until then deal with apparent "intentions" so complex that they are not, upon the new, detailed assay of conscious states, the intentions of any act.

When "perceiving" the horse, one is "presented" with one, not with a temporal cross section of it, or with a sensory core presumably connected with a cross section, or what have you. Phenomenologically, nothing else will do. That is why for once, although of course between double quotes, I used 'presented'. Yet there still is in the new world a species quite properly called perceiving, since among the several acts of a "perceiving" there is always one with this species. Which of these two very different things shall we call 'perceiving', which 'perceiving$_1$'? We all say, in our studies as well as outside of them, that we perceive horses, tables, and so on. This way of words is so firmly entrenched that it would be awkward, even in an ontological discourse, to mark it by a subscript. Henceforth, therefore, when saying that someone *perceives* something, I shall mean that his conscious state is one of those whose assay yields several acts one of which is a *perceiving$_1$*.

6* For some purposes some philosophers sometimes replace our natural language, or a part of it, by an artificial schema, also called an improved language, because presumably it serves those purposes better than what it replaces. In our natural language there are many words and expressions, which in most improved languages are replaced by "defined" expressions. E.g., replace 'green' and 'square' by '*gr*' and '*sq*', respectively, and introduce into the familiar schema '*grsq*(*x*) as defined by '*gr*(*x*) & *sq*(*x*)'. That makes '*grsq*' a defined predi-

cate of the schema. Definitions being abbreviations, defined predicates are linguistic devices without any ontological import whatsoever.
So are definite descriptions and variables. *In the world, there is nothing
either a variable or a definite description or a defined predicate stands for.* In
the ideal language, therefore, whose only purpose it is to be ontologically completely perspicuous, or, rather, in what I now believe is
the ideal language, there are neither defined predicates, nor definite
descriptions, nor variables. That makes the ideal language, or, as I
would rather call it, the ideal schema, which will be proposed in the
last Section, psychologically all but unmanageable; ironically, perhaps, if one remembers all the nonsense that has been said about
these schemata, yet not surprisingly. Just imagine a language without
abbreviations, without definitions, and without anything to stand in
for the idiomatic equivalents of variables; and then imagine trying to
think in it!

 * Yet one may, without confusing words and things, claim, as until
recently I did, that the ideal schema contains all the predicates which,
as one says, are definable in it, and that each of these predicates (and
nothing else!) stands for one of the existents I call derived characters.
Onerous as the claim is, if one knows what he does, it is intelligible
and consistent with the idea of an ideal schema. The reasons why until
recently I made it are two. Phenomenologically, as I just repeated and
have long insisted, when one perceives a horse, he is "presented" with
one and not with anything else. What, then, does 'horse' stand for?
The only thing I could think of was a derived character. That the
word must stand for something I took for granted. That was the mistake which undid me. The other reason I had for hanging on to derived characters was not unlike the first. They were needed for still
another job which I did not then know how to do without them. Trying to make ontological sense out of what Russell had said about
classes, I assayed them as a special kind of derived characters. Or,
rather, preoccupied as I was with different issues, I uncritically took
for granted that this was the only way to ground classes. Now I know
(or so I hope) how to do both these jobs without that shadowy category. So I can now drop that onerous claim, which, as I have come to
understand, is the price I paid for having so long neglected the ontology of conscious states and of classes.[2]

 Third. There has of late been some discussion, also in print, of what

2. Concerning Russell's way, see also Appendix B. Reinhardt Grossmann, working
independently, has marshaled some very good arguments to the effect that derived
characters are redundant. See his "Russell's Paradox and Complex Properties," *Nous,* 6,
1972, 153–64.

has been called a *Principle of Acquaintance.* Some of this talk is a bit blurred. So let us make a distinction. *The Principles of Presentation and of Acquaintance are two and not one.* No act intending a universal, say, f_1, occurs in a life history unless there is a particular, say, a_1, such that $f_1(a_1)$ is also intended, either by this act or by a second act, either simultaneous with or preceding the first, that occurs in the same life history. As for f_1 and a_1, so mutatis mutandis for relations and the higher types. This is the Principle of Acquaintance. For the most part it has been stated "linguistically," as, deliberately, I now do not. However stated, it clearly is an anthropo*logical* principle; not, like the Principle of Presentation, the anthropo*centric* jumping-off place for all ontology. Or, with a twist, it is (a major part of) an adequacy criterion, anthropological in nature, which I have long accepted and still accept, for all assays of awareness. (For this use of 'anthropo*logical*' vs. 'anthropo*centric*' and 'anthropo*morphic*' as well as for the other major part of the criterion, see Appendix A. But notice that, as now stated, the Principle says nothing about the species of the acts it mentions. Hence, by the Principle of Presentation, when Hume wondered whether, if a shade were missing in the spectrum, we could imagine it, he raised a *further* anthropological question. That fits with the phenomenology in my "phenomenological realism." For the latter, see Appendix C.)

Fourth. Thought is inseparably intertwined with language, i.e., with the perceiving or imagining of words or strings of such, either auditorily, in outer or inner speech, as one says, or visually, of marks on paper either seen or remembered or imagined, or what have you. This is a phenomenological fact, or group of facts. In Section V I shall argue that these facts have an ontological counterpart in the crucial role which perceivings$_1$ and imaginings$_1$ of words play in the assay of all conscious states, except in some cases of perception and imagination. If for the time being you accept that on faith, you will see that even a mistake, such as the one I made, of ontologizing words the wrong way, may yet, however dimly, reflect the way how in an ontology things do hang together in patterns; thus encouraging us, at least in retrospect, to persist in the arduous search for the right way. Be that as it may, that counterpart of the phenomenological facts, as I called it, being an ontological assay, remains for ever controversial. Not so, however, those facts. And they are all we need to answer the question that will not wait. *What can and what cannot be thought?*

Words we can arbitrarily string together. Sometimes, having made such a string, we cannot, no matter how hard we try, find a thought that goes with it in the way just pointed out. If there were such a thought, or conscious state, the intentions of "its" acts would, by the Principle of Presentation, exist. Since there is none, what the string purports to stand for is unthinkable; thus, by the same princple, it does not exist. That shows how I use 'unthinkable'.

What is in fact unthinkable? Some nonsense strings, such as 'green two as', provide examples that do not particularly interest us. Those that do, of several very different kinds, are all at the phenomenological rock bottom. (1) 'green is red', with 'is' standing for exemplification, is of one such kind; (2) 'green is a relation', of another. The taxonomy of these several kinds and the account of how they fit into the ontological schematism are an important part of the job ahead. In the meantime the two examples will do. How, then, about (1) and (2)? Is what they purport to go with really unthinkable? Since that is rock bottom, one cannot directly argue the case. What strengthening, if any, it needs will come from the relevant parts of the dialectic.

7* String (1), purporting to stand for what, if it existed, would violate a canon, itself violates what the syntacticists call a formation rule. Green being a property and not a relation has been said to show itself; and that is presumably why it cannot be said. What "shows itself" and what "cannot be said," the "formation rules" and what "cannot be thought"; formulae in which these phrases occur have long been with us; some for half a century. Many of them, I believe, are not sufficiently accurate; some are ambiguous; some, outright mistaken. Thus it will be prudent to avoid both the phrases and the formulae, except of course 'thinkable', which will be used only with the meaning just specified, until the last Section, where I shall try to prune the excesses of, while at the same time doing justice to, the linguistic turn.

Fifth. What we can and what we cannot think, in the sense specified, is a matter of fact. And facts, according to some, no matter how non-controversial or even rock bottom, are yet "merely" facts, or empirical, or synthetic, in the sense in which some claim that what they call analytic is not; just as, with a further distinction on which I have long insisted and in a new way still insist, what is categorial is not "merely" analytic. Yet I shall try to accommodate this threefold distinction within a dialectical structure whose phenomenological basis is "merely" factual. Does one who proceeds in this way commit the fallacy of *a minori maius?* To charge that he does is to be blind to the need for that indispensable jumping-off place which is not only inevitably anthropocentric but also, as we now come to appreciate, "merely" factual. Such critics, therefore, set for themselves and for others a goal neither attainable nor reasonable. To me it does not even make sense. What I shall try to do, *if otherwise successful,* is all that need be done and all that can be done. So I call those blind seers *absolutists;* the position they take, *absolutism.* Notice, finally, that all this does not contradict but, rather, supplements and illuminates what has been said in the last Section, when we considered introducing the modal phrase 'is or may be' into the schema for all canons, namely, that in ontological discourse a modal phrase merely marks a job still to be done. For, indeed, once we have taken off from the anthropocentric basis and are airborne, as it were, in ontology, are not the accommodation within the dialectical structure just envisaged and the complete unpacking of those phrases one and the same?

Just as one of the two universals of an act is a thought, whatever its species may be, so every species, whether a believing or a remembering or a perceiving, and so on, is a thinking. Thus the Principle of Presentation adds to the realm of existents not only the intentions of false beliefs, nonveridical memories, and erroneous perceptions, whether the error be qualitative or, as one says, existential; but also those of entertainings, doubtings, imaginings, and whatever other species a fully developed ontology of conscious states requires. For, as consistently we must, we hold to be unthinkable only what cannot be intended under any species. This vast addition must be balanced. That is where the modes come in. If, however, they can do that for one species, they can do it for all. Thus we may stay with one.

Consider a belief. Depending on whether it is either true or false, its intention is either actual or potential. That is how the two modes, *actuality* and *potentiality,* secure the Principle of Presentation. This is one of the jobs they are supposed to do. Consider, too, that even if, as I shall argue, they are existents, they cannot possibly on *all* occasions be presented to us. Otherwise one who believes something falsely could not hold the belief. For what he in fact does believe would be presented to him as something potential; which, roughly speaking, in this world amounts to his being presented with his belief being false. Similarly, how could one doubt what in fact is actual if it were presented to him as something actual?

Are there really two existents to ground the modes? When, under the pressure of structural needs, I first claimed long ago that they existed, I added, however reluctantly, that they are *never* presented to us. Such "speculation" will not do. Having once indulged in it, I feel only more keenly the obligation, now that I claim they are *sometimes* presented, to argue their case as painstakingly as I can. To this argument, which is the main task of the Section, I now turn.

If the modes are only sometimes presented to us, which are these occasions? When presented, what do they look like and feel like?

Surely, whatever they are, if there is a case for them, they must be very familiar to us, even if so far they have not been ontologized at all, or perhaps only very differently. But to close in on a feature in this manner is only the first, phenomenological step. If an ontologist wants to ground what he has thus singled out in one or several existents, he must, in the second, dialectical step, locate this existent, or existents, in the taxonomy of his world and fit it, or them, into its schematism. E.g., I shall argue that the two modes are entities, that like items or ultimate sorts, which are the only other kinds of entities, they too "combine" with something else into Two-in-Ones, so that there neither is nor could be a tie to make One out of the Two. How, then, it may immediately occur to you, about those "somethings" the modes "combine" with? Aren't they a further sort of entity? We shall see. All this is in the future. I mention it mainly in order to give a body of meaning to that convenient phrase, "the taxonomy and the schematism of an ontology." For the rest, we are not yet ready for the first step. Some further phenomenological preparations are necessary. ('Combine' appears above between double quotes because another expression I shall propose will keep reminding us of the characteristic difference between the two kinds of "combining," both without ties, into the two kinds of Two-in-Ones; one those which we called things; the other those we shall eventually call "complexes.")

8* An existent is not acceptable unless it pays its way by either grounding or helping to ground what, although presented, cannot be grounded without it. What job or jobs, then, do the modes do? (And it better be more than just one; such internal economy or mutual support, we know, is the very essence of "system.") About this third step we may in the case of the modes be more relaxed. Not only do we already know that in this world they ground all intentions; we shall, as the pattern unfolds, encounter several assays for which they are needed. Remember that in view of these additional tasks the modes perform, I counted their hugely enlarged role, which they could of course not play unless they were at least sometimes presented to us, among the six fundamental innovations.

Are there facts? Are there classes? Are there makers? Are there simples? In Section I I took it for granted. Of course I did. Otherwise there would not have been anything to talk about. Yet at certain points I held back. The reason for the restraint should now be obvious. As long as the discourse was kept "pure," the inevitable appeal to the presented, or, as one says, to the given, had to be kept out. Now we are ready for these bits of phenomenology. The first two of the four questions above belong together. Let me first turn to them, then to the third.

9* Are there simples? A word at least should be said about the fourth question. Recall once more: ontology accounts for everything there is in terms of simples. I, for one, have no other notion of the enterprise. If, as I believe, there is no other notion, intelligible, articulate, and worthwhile, then, if there are no simples, there is no such thing as ontology. It does not follow that there are any. Ontology's latest foes, very acutely from where I stand, insist that there are none. We know that there are some only from the witness of the given. What one must do, mentally, if I may so put it, in order to establish that an existent is simple is not this time string words together but, rather, start on a series of conscious states that fulfills certain conditions. The existent under examination will be simple if and only if it is (explicitly or implicitly) intended in the first and in the last of these states. What these conditions are I need not expound once more. I rather add a distinction, also to serve as a caution. The conditions that make a series of conscious states an "introspective analysis" on the one hand and those which jointly are the adequacy criterion for the assay of a conscious state are two very different things. A very major one among the latter is (as we know) the Principle of Acquaintance. But there is no other, either major or minor, requiring that what an assay yields can also be reached by introspection. Or does anyone with a minimum of phenomenological sensitivity hold that a conscious state of perceiving a horse can be "introspectively analyzed" into the conjunction of a "sensing" and a believing? Notice that, so unpacked, "being a simple" is neither a property nor an ultimate sort nor anything else that must be grounded specifically. As for "simple," so in this respect for "existent," and for nothing else. How fitting! Notice, too, that in this paragraph things, being Two-in-Ones of simples sensu stricto, are not, as often elsewhere, called simples.

Sometimes I am presented with a fact and a class. Suppose they are (1) $f_1(a_1)$ and (2) $\{f_1, a_1\}$. Is that all one can say? Fortunately it is not. At some point talk must stop. Nor, once the phenomenological appeal has been made, can the point be too far away. Here, though, there is one more step; fortunately, as I said; for otherwise a critic could ask an embarrassing question. Why (he might challenge me) should I put any stock in your claim to be presented with either this or that or anything else, if what you are presented with may, upon your own terms, be potential and therefore, upon mine, be nothing at all? I answer as follows: As it happens, I am presented not only with facts, such as f_1a_1, but also, either on the same or perhaps on another occasion, with such existents as (3) $f_1(a_1)$-being-an-atomic-fact, and this third existent, of a very different sort, if presented at all, is presented to me with its mode, which is actuality. As for (1) and (3), so for (4) $\{f_1, a_1\}$-being-a-class (i.e., more naturally, without the conventional notation, sometimes one is presented with f_1 and a_1 forming a class). Moreover, one is sometimes also presented with such existents as (5) $\{f_1, a_1\}$-being-diverse-from-$f_1(a_1)$ (i.e., more conveniently this time: $\{f_1, a_1\} \neq f_1(a_1)$); and these, too, if presented at all, are presented with their mode, which again is actuality. That gives the critic pause. Let me use it for four comments, to make sure I haven't overshot the mark.

First. When an intention is presented with its mode, I shall say that it is *transparent*.[†] (3), (4), and (5), the only examples we have so far, are such that, first, their mode is actuality, and, second, if presented at all, they are presented with their mode; which I shall express by saying that the mode of these existents is *immediately available*. Neither is necessarily so. For one, what is presented with the mode of potentiality is also transparent—as nonexistent, as the critic from whom we last heard, though of course not I, would say. For another, what is presented without its mode may "become" transparent by being presented with its mode to a subsequent act. This is indeed the point of all deductive reasoning from transparent premises. The mode of such intentions I shall call *accessible*. Those of many other existents, which do have one, is not even accessible. The mode of (1), for instance, or, for that matter, that of any atomic fact, we shall see, is not. Immediately available, accessible, not accessible—to us! Transparence is an anthropo*centric* notion. What, then, we must ask, either is, or may become, transparent (to us)? The answer involves almost everything this discourse is about. For its completion, therefore, you will have to wait until close to the end. In this Section I take only the first step. But, again, a word of caution should provide a sense of direction. Do not rush to the conclusion that everything transparent has a mode. Consider (6) green-being-a-property and (7) louder-than-being-a-relation. Unless the image is deliberately chosen to deceive, as of course it isn't, it doesn't make phenomenological sense to deny, as of course I don't, that (3), (4), (5), (6), and (7) are all equally transparent. Yet, we shall see, (6) and (7), unlike (3), (4) and (5), although transparent, have no mode. Thereby, too, as we shall at least begin to understand in this Section, dialectically hangs very much.

[†] That this definition is problematic should soon be obvious, for Bergmann will allow that a single thing may be the sole intention of an act of "grasping"; he will claim that if a thing is thus "explicitly intended" then the intention of the act by which it is "grasped" is transparent. Clearly, though, a thing does not have a mode. Perhaps the definition given here of transparency was formulated at the time that Bergmann composed the unpublished and undelivered paper whose title this book now bears, for in that paper Bergmann *did* espouse the odd claim that every thing has a mode. See Editor's Note, p. xviii–WH.

The image of transparence is too beautiful to have been caught out of the air. As soon as it is unpacked, you will recognize it as a non-theological variant of Augustinian illumination.

Second. Let us take stock so we may see how little has as yet been done. Notice, first of all, that even though you may have guessed what the two features I call the modes are, officially, if I may so put it, I have not yet closed in on them. Nor can I, until we are done, phenomenologically, as well as dialectically, not only with $f_1(a_1)$, $\{f_1, a_1\}$, and the tie that presumably ties the elements (not: members, as of a collection!) of the latter into the former, but also with negation and at least one binary connective. Notice, next, how much of the little that has been said is as yet mere assertion, very unconventional and therefore doubly in need of support. Just consider (3) and (4). Are there such existents as $f_1(a_1)$-being-an-atomic-fact? If there are, how shall we assay them? As for (3) and (4), so for (5), (6), (7). At this point I just want you to realize that eventually all these questions will have to be answered. In Section IV they will face us again. But only in the last two Sections shall I try to answer them as completely as I can. Once again, though, a comment right now might make you more willing to stay the course. Just as 'horse' stands for nothing even though in each case someone asserts truly 'this is a horse', there is a very complex (actual) existent by virtue of which his assertion is true, so one may consistently hold both that, say, (3) is an existent and that 'atomic fact' stands for nothing. For this, the difference between the two cases, (3) being transparent while this-being-a-horse is not, makes no difference; fortunately, again, for an ontology that must ontologize every word or phrase is as trivial as it is absurd. Only, one must not let his "sound sense of reality" lure him into the ontological desert. On the other hand, just think for a moment how many more jobs anything but trivial I have set myself if I am to make a case, as of course I shall try, for what has just been asserted, as yet without support, in connection with (3), (4), (5), (6), and (7).

(I need no reminder that all these interruptions and asides, prospective and, as we shall advance, also retrospective, do not make for easy reading. But, then, no matter how perspicuous when once grasped, the pattern I have undertaken to unfold is very complex; so complex indeed that I wouldn't know how to proceed without such lighting of the patch and lightening of the burden.)

Third. Permit me, in this Section and in what later relates to it, a rather special use of 'theoretical-practical', which (I trust) needs no explanation. Theoretically, by providing for the modes of some existents being presented, I have gone as far as, taking my way, one *can*, although not of course as far as, if one takes the absolutists' way, according to them one *must*, in "anchoring" or "securing" what is there. This you already sense: and it will soon be out in the open. Whether that is as far as practically one *may* go will depend on how much or how little he claims to be transparent, either immediately available or at least "in principle" accessible. The smaller one's claim, the more plausible it is that practically he will not be confounded. My claim, you will see, is very small indeed, and therefore very "safe." (The reasons for the qualification, this time, of 'accessible' by 'in principle' will have to wait until later.)

Fourth. An absolutist who has read this far will point out how non-committal 'anchoring', 'securing', and 'safe' are, and will express the suspicion that at critical points I use these words because they are noncommittal. Then, using his words, he will go on to say that in my devious way I just claimed to "know" that there is this fact and that class; in the traditional sense of 'knowing', in which one can only "know" what is "true" and, according to some, must, when knowing it, also know that he knows it, or be "certain" of it as well as of his knowing it, and so on. He is right, of course. His suspicion is justified. Yet surely you see already that the very point, now and for some time to come, is to avoid his words. Eventually I shall arrange a confrontation. Of course I shall. First, though, we must finish these preparations; then close in on the two modes phenomenologically and insert them into the taxonomy and the schematism dialectically; attend to whatever pertains to these jobs; and, while doing all this, proceed so conservatively that the absolutist will not be able to shake our case on practical grounds. So I turn next to the last of the four preparatory questions. Are there makers?

To be presented, explicitly, with (1) $f_1(a_1)$ is to be presented, implicitly, with f_1, a_1, and a tie tying the latter two into the former. This is the claim. 'Tie' and 'tying' were used earlier; now, provisionally, I use 'maker' and 'making'. The words by which they will be replaced in Section III are not only free from the anthropomorphism of either 'tying' or 'making' but also more suited structurally. But let us agree right now to replace the conventional '$f_1(a_1)$' by '$\eta(f_1, a_1)$'. The idea behind the change, beyond the convenience it will immediately afford us, is that a tie, *being an existent but not an entity*, should in the schema that is ontologically completely perspicuous be represented by an expression. In the schema that will be proposed in Section VII, '$\eta(f_1, a_1)$' does stand for (1). But one cannot argue this cogently without making the case, which will have to wait for Sections III and IV, that '(,)' is a *diacritical* mark.

9* *Diacritical* I call marks of the ideal schema which stand for nothing. There are, as we shall see, all together four such marks: the parentheses; one each for elementhood ('$\in$') and the meaning nexus ('M'), i.e., for two of the three sorts of circumstances; one for the "connection" of a class with its "selector," as, roughly, 'λ' in '$\lambda(x|(x = \alpha) \vee (x = \beta))$'. (I say roughly because in the ideal schema there are no variables.) Conversely, as you may have inferred from the phrase just italicized, there are in the ideal schema no marks to represent the three sorts of entities; items, ultimate sorts, and modes. Eventually, all this will make excellent sense. Nor, of course, if it didn't would the schema be ideal.

10* More accurately, as we shall see, every class of this world has an indefinite number of selectors. Thus one cannot accurately speak of "its" selector. But the difference here makes no difference.

The claim just entered is really two, viz., that one is on this occasion presented (a) with an existent, η, called a *tie*, and (b) with this existent *tying* two others, a_1 and f_1, into a further existent, $\eta(a_1, f_1)$. It will pay if, before undertaking to support (a) and (b) directly, we take time out to do three other things. I shall reject a counterclaim; attend to what naturally goes with it; and start streamlining our as yet rather clumsy terminology.

Some may have held that every existent is either a thing (*Urelement*) or a class. Some, even more extremely, hold now that all existents are classes. A critic sympathetic to such views might challenge me as follows. Suppose, he says, if only for the sake of the argument, that there are the three existent a_1, f_1, η, as you call them; why, then, is not what you call the fact in the case the class whose elements are these three? That spots the counterclaim: (c') One is (on this occasion) presented with the class whose elements are a_1, f_1, η.

There "is" of course, without any ontological status and therefore not presented to anyone, the collection whose three members are a_1, f_1, η. One is not, however, either on this or on any other occasion, presented with a class one of whose elements is η. Nor can I think such a class. Hence, by the Principle of Presentation, there is none to be presented. As for η, so for all other ties; as for all ties, so for all entities. At this point I appeal to the given. Once such an appeal is made, phenomenological rock bottom, where all direct argument ends, cannot be very far. Some such appeals, though, can be supported indirectly, either by showing how they gibe with others or dialectically. This particular appeal, rather fortunately, I would say, since, if I may so express myself, it is negative, can be supported in both ways.

Remember some of the propositions that have been stated, in pre-

view fashion and without any support whatsoever, for the sole purpose of providing us with a glimpse of the pattern which will emerge,
in the "pure" discourse of Section I. The existents which are (A) elements of classes are all those and only those which are (B) terms of
circumstances as well as all those and only those which are, with a new
use of an old word, (C) constituents. These existents, which were also
said to satisfy the (D) minimal restriction, are the members of four
sorts, being either things or existents (a), (b), (c). To say the same differently, the only existents not satisfying the minimal restriction are
all the items, the various ties and ultimate sorts, and the two modes.
(C) we can as yet safely ignore; (D) is merely a suggestive label. But we
are by now ready, although only in preview fashion, to provide dialectical support for the equivalence of (A) and (B), and thereby also,
although of course again only in this fashion, for rejecting the counterclaim (c').

(1) Something being diverse from something will turn out to be one
of the three sorts of circumstances. Something being the same as (not
diverse from) something, being made by negation out of a circumstance, is, as I shall presently propose we speak, a fact. Yet surely we
could not think these facts, $(\alpha = \beta)$, if we could not think those circumstances $(\alpha \neq \beta)$. (2) The existents $\alpha = \beta$ and $\alpha \neq \beta$, one actual, one
potential, as the case may be, are the ground of the sameness and the
diversity of α and β. (If the sameness is actual, there are in the ideal
schema not two expressions, for which in this very relaxed notation 'α'
and 'β' stand in, but only one.) If, however, either α or β does not
fulfill (D), then, by the Principle of Presentation, there are no such
circumstances. For we cannot think that, say, conjunction is the same
as exemplification, or that negation is the same as green. This, by the
way, is the sense in which in due course all ties and all entities will be
called "unique." That is, if I may for once so express myself, suggestively rather than accurately, the "sameness" or "difference" of
these sorts needs no ground. All this is the burden of Section III. In
Section VI it will be argued what even without argument is plausible,
to say the least, namely, first, that one cannot think a class without
thinking one of its selectors; and, second, that if there were that
would-be class, which the critic suggests I mistake for the fact, "its"
selector would be "either being the same as a_1 or being the same as f_1
or being the same as η." Hence, in view of the last clause, the one which
is italicized, since by (2) there is no such class, one could not possibly
be presented with it, either on this or on any other occasion. That
much for the dialectical support. Let us turn to phenomenology.

To say that an existent is independent (dependent) is to say that it can be intended explicitly (only implicitly), i.e., to repeat, that it can (cannot) by itself be the intention of an act (p. 62). That makes the claim that an existent either is or is not independent, phenomenological; and the feature itself, independence or dependence, as the case may be, anthropocentric. Yet, such a (phenomenological) feature very strongly and, I believe, very convincingly supports an ontology provided only the existents which have it are all those and only those which are the members of certain (ontological) sorts. Nor, conversely, would a feature, of whatever kind, such that some but not all members of a sort have it, interest the ontologist. The dependence-independence feature does provide such general support. Hence, in particular, since no one will deny that whatever does not satisfy the minimum condition is dependent, the feature supports also the rejection of (c'). I put it that strongly because the issue, if I understand it at all, is not whether these existents of my world, if they are there, are dependent, but, rather, whether they are there at all. (Another anthropocentric feature is the key to the new assay of analyticity, which is one of the two major innovations. This line of thought will start in Section IV.)

Suppose, then, that all existents not satisfying the minimal restriction are dependent. Are all others independent? In this world they are. We have uncovered a very major bifurcation. So I repeat for the sake of emphasis. *The existents not satisfying the minimal restriction are all dependent. Those satisfying it are, with one qualification, all independent.* The qualification, together with what else can be said in this context, is better left to one of those digressions which (I hope) lighten the burden by lighting the long path ahead.

11* The existents satisfying the minimal restriction are either things; or existents (a), which presently we shall call facts; or existents (b), which we called circumstances; or existents (c), which are the classes. That one can intend either this-being-green or green-being-diverse-from-red without intending anything else I take to be obvious. That facts and circumstances are independent we may thus safely take for granted. That leaves things and classes. Neither of these two sorts has either modes or constituents. Neither is a simple in the strict sense. Yet classes (each of which is an independent existent (c)), being built on selectors, are not even simples in the broad sense in which things, being Aristotelian-Thomistic composites of an item and an ultimate sort, are simple. For another, subtle difference, turn to (4) $\{f_1, a_1\}$-being-a-class, or, more naturally and as I would rather put it, (4') f_1-and-a_1-forming-a-class, on p. 69, on the one hand, and to (6) green-being-a-property, on p. 70, on the other. Both are, if presented

at all, presented transparently. Nothing else, I insisted, makes phenomenological sense. Similarly, as I shall soon insist, nothing, unless
intended explicitly, is presented transparently. What, then, are the intentions of acts such as (4′) and (6)? Or, rather, how shall we assay
them? Here is the subtle difference. (6), it will be argued, still in this
Section, is the one thing itself, i.e., the composite of an ultimate sort
and an item. Things are thus literally independent. Not so for (4′).
Its assay does not yield the class and nothing else; although only for
two structurally obvious and therefore "natural" reasons, which, if I
may so express myself, strengthen rather than weaken the import of
the proposed bifurcation; namely, *first,* because there is no ultimate
sort "class" that could be presented to us, as one of the various ultimate
sorts is presented to us, whenever we transparently intend a thing and
nothing else; and because, *second,* as has already been mentioned, one
cannot think a class at all, whether explicitly or implicitly, without
thinking one of its selectors. Under the circumstances, we shall see,
the assay of (4′) provides a structural equivalent for classes being independent although, literally, they are not. This is the qualification I
had in mind. The assay of (4′) itself will of course have to wait until
the last two Sections. But make right now a note of something else.

* A certain feature of the old world is gone. The formula was that
"all awareness is propositional." What that meant was that every intention is a fact. In the new world this is no longer so. An intention is
either a fact or a circumstance or, whenever a thing's ultimate sort is
transparently presented to us, the thing itself. Yet it is still true that in
a natural language every intention is expressed by a sentence; which
just goes to show that the earlier assays, if any, of what a sentence may
stand for were not accurate enough. Or, if you insist, it shows that my
old schema was not yet the ideal language.

Now for adapting our terminology to the great bifurcation at least
provisionally established. Let us first make official a use that has already cropped up. *To be a fact and to be an existent (a) is one and the same.*
That is, to repeat, a fact is an existent which the one maker among the
members of its first foundation makes out of the other or others.
Then we can say that an existent is either a fact or a circumstance or a
class or a thing; or that it is either a maker or one of the three sorts of
entity. *All members of the second quartet, i.e., the several items, the two modes,
and the various ultimate sorts and makers, are dependent. The members of the
first quartet, i.e., all facts, circumstances, classes, and things, are independent.*
(That ignores the "natural" qualification for classes, which in this context is irrelevant.) This is the great bifurcation. Although no doubt
ontologically significant, since it coincides with the division of the

eight categories into two quartets, it is yet, as here introduced, directly (and not just indirectly, as is everything) grounded on a phenomenological feature. But we can do better than that. *The existents of the independent quartet are all those and only those which are produced out of items by ultimate sorts either with or without makers.* (The last clause, 'without makers', acknowledges the peculiarity of canons (b) and (c).) This is purely ontological characterization. I propose that we mark it by putting an old term to a new use. A *determinate* is either a fact, or a circumstance, or a class, or a thing. Then we can say, whenever it suffices for the purpose at hand, as often it does, that an *existent is either a determinate, or a maker, or an entity.* And, just to remind you, *to be a determinate and to fulfill the minimal restriction is one and the same.* As you see, our terminology is getting less clumsy.

Two brief remarks will round this out. First. Less accurately, yet more emphatically, as some philosophers may want to put it, in traditional terms, a determinate, being produced out of matter, is a One, or a This. 'Matter' I shall leave alone; my business is with items, which correspond to *materia signata*. 'Form' I shall eventually so unpack that, in one of its several ontological uses, ultimate sorts and makers are forms. Second. By way of comparison, in case that helps, in my old world there were things, facts, classes; there were, lumped together in the single category of "subsistents," the various ties and ultimate sorts; and there were also, although never presented, the two modes. But there were as yet no circumstances and no items. Thus there were two terzets, rather than, as now, two quartets.

Return now to the main line of thought. The two claims (a) and (b) on p. 73 still wait for direct support. (b) merely needs unpacking of that most pungently anthropomorphic facet of the metaphor, the "activity" of tying or "making" by the tie or maker. So let us start on (a).

Concerning (a). In view of what we have learned while rejecting the counterclaim (c'), the issue is no longer whether we are presented with the existents under examination we call facts but only how to assay them. Specifically, when (explicitly) presented with $f_1(a_1)$, are we (implicitly) presented not only with f_1 and a_1 but also with a third existent, the one I call the tie of exemplification. (1) I, for one, am on all such occasions presented not only with the two things but also with their "togetherness." (2) I am not on these occasions (either explicitly or implicitly) presented with the class, say $\{f_1, a_1\}$, of which these things are the only elements. (3) Nor, on those occasions on which I am (explicitly) presented with that class, is the "togetherness," if that be the word, of its two elements that of the fact. (1), (2), and (3) are the phenomenological rock bottom on which I take my stand. Hence, by the Principle of Presentation, the "togetherness" exists. But what sort of existent is it? More elaborately, as I put it when describing the second, dialectical step of each proper ontologization, where does it fit into the taxonomy and the schematism? There are three alternatives, or, as one says, abstract possibilities.

(α) The togetherness and the fact are one and not two. If they were, how would one know $f_1(a_1)$, $f_2(a_2)$, $f_2(a_1)$, and so on, from each other? (The conventional notation is used, as before, in order to avoid the prejudicial 'η'.) The mere question disposes of the alternative. (β) The togetherness of each fact is different from that of every other. A notation that does justice to such existents must write '$\eta_{f_1 a_1}$', '$\eta_{f_1 a_2}$', '$\eta_{f_2 a_1}$', and so on. Ironically, it thereby also reveals the fatal flaw. The double subscript represents the alleged "uniqueness." Yet the Greek letter on the line remains indispensable. Otherwise the first two alternatives—which, incidentally, are opposite extremes—would merge into one. Negatively, that disposes of the alternative. Positively, we see, ex-emplification, if it exists, has the one-many feature. That points the way to the third alternative, the one I propose. (γ) *Exemplification is an existent with five features, all of which it shares with all other ties but with nothing else.*

Specifically, for one, a tie is a simple in the strict sense. For another, it has the one-many feature. Third, it does not satisfy the minimal restriction, or, equivalently, it is dependent. And, just to mention once more the two metaphors, still to be unpacked, for a fourth and a fifth feature, a tie is (in two senses of the term) "unique"; and it shares with all other ties but with nothing else a certain degree of "separability." That ties have the one-many feature does not, except for the purblind, make them universals (p. 58). And they also share this feature with the ultimate sorts and the modes among the entities. For the only mere individuators of this world, and, by virtue of being that, the only existents out of which, either singly or severally, a determinate (i.e., more emphatically, a One or This) can be produced, are the items.

The "togetherness" of $f_1(a_1)$, $f_2(a_2)$, and so on, are one and not many. That is merely another way of stating the familiar feature. Yet it spots a premiss for an additional argument, in support not only of η but, more generally, of there being ties. Since this argument requires by now only a slight anticipation which causes no trouble, and since it fits in here very well, I present it next.

So far we have considered only nonrelational atomic facts of the lowest type. From relational ones, which involve order, we must stay away until Section III. But suppose now that there are, as in my world there long have been, at least two sorts of nonrelational atomic facts, such as (8) *a*-is-green and (9) green-is-a-Color; i.e., as conventionally one writes and speaks, with variables, of the sorts '$f(x)$' and '$F(f)$', respectively. Are the ties, between the particular and the color on the one hand and the color and Color on the other, one or two? One *may reasonably plead* on phenomenological grounds that the togetherness of (9) is tighter, or closer, or more intimate—more inseparable, one might want to add, had the word not already been reserved for another job—than that in (8). If so, the ontologist must ask what is the ground of the "felt difference"? One abstract possibility is to ground it in the differences among the types of the things involved; particularity and universality [(0)] in (8), universality[(0)] and universality[((0))] in (9). Phenomenologically that is at most second best. The difference, if any, resides in the tie, or, should there be none, in whatever else, if anything, holds the two things together, rather than in (the types of) the latter. Yet we need not quibble. This gambit, we shall see later, fails on purely dialectical grounds. Thus, disregarding it now, we are left with only the tie to carry the ontological burden. The way out, therefore, if there is that difference, is to admit two ties of exemplification, or, more generally, as many as are required by the number of types, which, as we shall also see, is small in fact and finite in principle. That spots the additional dialectical reason for ontologizing (the several) exemplification(s). Nor is that all of it. As for exemplification, so *a fortiori* for the several ties called conjunction, disjunction, and so on, as well as the two new ones, which will make their first appearance in Section IV, when the two kinds of generalities, corresponding to 'all' and 'some', respectively, will be assayed. For, again, if the substitution instances of '$\alpha \lor \beta$', '$\alpha \& \beta$', '$\alpha \equiv \beta$', and so on stand for something, as in Frege's, Husserl's, and my worlds they do, and if '$\lor$', '$\&$', '$\equiv$', and so on stood for nothing, what would the differences among the instances of the same substitution be grounded in?

How about the contrast to which I just called attention by italicizing 'one may reasonably plead' and 'a fortiori'? A fortiori, as it happens, is too weak. Phenomenologically, the distinction between any two connectives is unchallengeable. Only that between two exemplifications is perhaps merely a shade, a nuance. Does that undermine our trust in what is in fact unchallengeable? I do not see why it should. Why shouldn't the hard, luminous core at the center trail off into shades and nuances at the periphery? Even so, two comments, to stave off confusion, are in order.

Negatively, phenomenologists, in a very broad sense that comprehends moralists, artists, and critics, do, and should, strain for shades and nuances. Yet, however valuable this pursuit of theirs may be, it does not, upon my conception of ontology, yield anything relevant to the latter. Positively, the penumbra over some of the area where phenomenology and dialectic meet gives a freedom sometimes badly needed, of which the case in hand is as good an example as any. If there were only one exemplification instead of several, the new assay of the generalities would, as we shall see, collapse. Yet this assay is one of the very foundations on which the new world rests. Naturally, therefore, there are several exemplifications among its ties. Yet I feel no urge to plead for that plurality on phenomenological grounds; I would much rather offer additional dialectical support. With two (or more) exemplifications, the "felt difference" between the synthetic a priori and a posteriori in (9) and (8), respectively, is grounded in the difference between two (or more) ties and therefore, in an obvious sense, more directly and also more deeply than it was in the old world. But, again, this does not mean that the old analysis was mistaken. It merely means that the new one greatly adds to its strength. (Such, if I may be tiresome, are the perils and the rewards, the discipline and the delights, of "system.")

Concerning (*b*), having refuted (c′) and established (a) by itself, we may safely reconsider the original claim as a whole, before it was split into (a) and (b). To be presented with (1) $f_1(a_1)$ and to be presented with (1′) f_1, a_1, and η, the latter ty*ing* the two things into (1), are one and the same. That was the claim, as originally worded (p. 72). Now I reword it as follows. (w) *(1) and (1′) are one and the same.* The shift thus brought about, from the presentation to the presented, is justified by the Principle of Presentation. Add to (w) what is already established, viz., that (b′) there is nothing, class or otherwise, for which '{f_1, a_1, η}' could stand, and (b″) that η depends (in this case) on these two things while neither of them depends on it, and you will have unpacked (b), i.e., the claim that we are presented with a tie ty*ing* something (or a maker mak*ing* something out of something). Clearly, nothing more needs to be done about (b). Here an astute critic interrupts. What you just did (he tells me) does not unpack, positively, as it were, the "participial" part or facet of the metaphor; it merely sloughs off, negatively, what, being irredeemably anthropomorphic, cannot and need not be unpacked. The observation is well taken; so well indeed that at the proper place we shall build on it what is anything but merely "negative." This place, not surprisingly, will be in Section III, when we shall get rid of both 'tie' and 'maker', replacing them with a word as free from all anthropomorphism as any "abstract" term of a human language, where all such terms, as it has been put, very aptly, are but one vast graveyard of metaphors, often buried in the decent obscurity of roots from a dead language.

Let us take stock. The main burden of the Section is to ontologize the two modes. In order to do that, one must first ontologize at least one (sort of atomic) fact as well as negation and at least one binary connective. So far only the assay of (1) $f_1(a_1)$ has been established; and that took quite some time. The remaining two preparatory tasks can be dispatched much more quickly.

Consider (8) not-$f_1(a_1)$. (I avoid '~' because it may seem more prejudicial.) Two questions arise. First, is (8) sometimes explicitly presented to us? If it is, then, by the Principle of Presentation, it exists. Second, supposing that it exists, what is its assay? More specifically, how shall we assay the obvious excess, if I may so put it, of (8) over (1)? The answer to the first question, as clear to me as sunlight at noon, is Yes. All one need do about it, therefore, and all I shall do, is to show dialectically and "negatively" that the two reasons some believe they have for denying our ever being presented with (8) are bad reasons. Of one I shall show that now. The other I shall merely mention. The demonstration that it, too, is a bad reason will have to wait. In reply to the second question I shall not just restate the old assay but also support it dialectically; and since this is a "positive" job, I shall do it first.

Nothing cannot be thought. More specifically and less aphoristically, whatever we may say when speaking idiomatically, without ontological commitment, we are never literally presented with the "absence" of anything. The case in hand is at the root of the matter. When presented with (8), one is not literally presented with the absence of f_1 but, rather, with the "nontogetherness, in the way in which they are together in $f_1(a_1)$, of f_1 and a_1." As for this pair of togetherness and nontogetherness, with respect to (this) exemplification, so for all other such pairs, one for each tie. Thus, once more we are face to face with the one-many feature. Hence, since the only things involved in both (8) and (1) are f_1 and a_1, and since all makers share the one-many feature, the only plausible way of ontologizing the excess of (8) over (1) is by a maker, called *negation* (~), which in this case makes (8) out of (1). Three comments will round that out.

First. Every maker goes with a restriction. If one judges from what has just been said, it may seem that both what negation "works on" and what it makes out of it are facts. As will gradually transpire, the restriction is less narrow. Everything negation can "work on" has a mode; and conversely. *Second.* As a tie among ties, negation, being monadic, is an oddity. 'Maker' avoids at least the verbal awkwardness. In Section III we shall see that with a "standardization" which is indispensable, since without it order resists ontologization, all makers "work on" a single determinate. *Third.* How does the argument that we are never presented with an "absence" spread from the root of the matter to "everything"? Suppose someone expresses what on a certain occasion he is presented with by asserting: 'There is no (colored) spot on this (white) surface'. What an ontologist holds the man to be presented with depends on how he, the ontologist, assays what the sentence stands for. In my world, whether old or new, with all detail that is irrelevant suppressed, it stands for '$\sim(\exists x)[\ldots]$'. And in the new world the two quantifiers will turn out (in Section IV) to be two ties. That shows how, recursively, the claim spreads. But perhaps it should be added, if only in order to counteract the baneful effect of that most misleading phrase, 'knowledge by description', that, irrespective of whether or not there is one and only one particular (call it, in case there is one, a_1) such that $f_1(a_1)$ is actual, one does not, when intending $(\exists x)f_1(x)$, implicitly intend a_1; nor, of course, does one intend it explicitly.

I, for one, am sometimes directly aware of an act of mine which is a "perceiving" of the negation of an atomic fact, say, (8). Thus "I cannot doubt" that there are such acts and therefore, by the Principle of Presentation, such facts. The double quotes around 'perceive' are a challenge to those who wear the blinders of what I call the *cluster view*. Upon this view, or doctrine, and the inaccurate notion of introspection associated with it, every awareness "is" nothing but a conjunction of atomic facts, say, $f_1(a_1)$ & $f_2(a_2)$ & $f_3(a_3)$ & $f_4(a_4)$; f_1, f_2, f_3, f_4 being such characters as green, hot, middle C, and perhaps some further ones, but certainly not those, of which upon this view there are none, which I call thoughts. Consider now that (8) is not atomic and you will see that we have already come upon one bad reason. Or, perhaps better, we have unearthed one structural root of the resistance. Wittingly or unwittingly, those who either doubt or outright deny our ever being presented with (8) in exactly the same way in which we are presented with (1) are, I believe, under the spell of the cluster view. That this view is false is obvious. The question is how it ever came to hold sway. Historically, I believe, it is the greatest single liability of the succession whose first modern culmination was Hume. (Concerning the use of 'doubt' in the phrase above, see presently, still in this Section.)

12* In the more liberal versions of the doctrine some of the facts in the cluster may be relational. Some versions, on the other hand, are marred by a blur; all of them have still another grave defect. Some think of the clusters as "mental" and call the particulars of them, the characters of which I gave examples, and those of which I spoke without giving examples as further ones, "sensa," "sensory qualities," and "affective qualities," respectively. In the case of some others, one cannot be sure whether what they speak about is always "mental," or always "nonmental," or sometimes the one, sometimes the other. This is the blur. One version, avoiding it at the price of absurdity, holds that the particulars at least are "neutral." The defect is due to the circumstance that as the doctrine's fortunes rose, those of the act fell. Hence the double quotes around 'is' in the preceding paragraph. That is, to spell it out, all the assay of any awareness ever yields supposedly is a cluster. Nor is that the full extent of the devastation. For, as the doctrine conquers, nominalism triumphs. Thus the cluster is not really a conjunction of facts but, rather, a conglomeration, I do not know of what sort, of I know not what. It is perhaps a class of perfect particulars?

The other bad reason, the one I can now only mention, for either doubting or outright denying that there are these acts and these facts, has a sound core, which a critic, who for the sake of the argument is willing to use 'present' and 'assay' as I do, might state as follows. The difference between the two awarenesses in which we are presented with (1) and (8), respectively, is that while the assay of the latter yields (images, visual, or auditory, or kinesthetic, of) words, that of the former does not, or at least need not. As you will see in Section V, I agree with this core or premiss. But you will also see that it does not imply the critic's negative conclusion concerning (8) (and all nonatomic facts).

13* Still another reason for that negativism, which has its root in the nominalism associated with the doctrine, I state only most succinctly. If, "looking at a yellow spot in front of me," I claim to "perceive" that it is not red, an articulate nominalist will tell me that while there is, among the things in front of me to look at, a perfect particular "associated" with yellow, there is, except by chance in some cases, none associated with red. That locates his trouble. Yet there is none; provided you hold with me, first, that what I perceive is a fact; and, second, concerning the universal of it, that it need not by the Principle of Acquaintance (p. 65) be exemplified by "a particular in front of me to look at."

That will do for negation. The connectives, happily, will not detain us at all. For, like negation, I have ontologized them long ago; and what has just been added to the case or the former mutatis mutandis also holds for the latter. Order, though, I repeat, is as yet beyond our grasp. So we must stick with the symmetrical connectives, and, or, and so on.

Have the two modes been singled out so clearly that, irrespective of whatever ontological status they may or may not have, you are phenomenologically already familiar with them? Or, as it was put, have we closed in on them? Yes and No. Yes; because some examples have already been given, if only passingly, in order to keep the exposition going; and, also, because on that occasion (p. 69) a suggestive word was thrown in. No; because so far the word, however suggestive, is but a metaphor; and, also, because each of those examples is one of three very special kinds to which one cannot usefully attend until after the modes have been properly ontologized by means of the two standard examples I am about to add to our little store. The three kinds, by the way, were represented by (3) $f_1(a_1)$-being-an-atomic-fact, (5) $f_1(a_1) = \{f_1, a_1\}$, and (6) green-being-a-property. The kind (6) represents will be examined soon, still in this Section; the other two will have to wait longer. The word is 'transparent', of course; its key use such that whenever a determinate is presented with its mode, it is said to be *transparent*, or, synonymously, to be presented transparently as either actual or potential. (3), (5), and (6), by the way, are all three transparently actual.

The two examples now added are (9) $f_1(a_1) \vee \sim f_1(a_1)$ and (10) $\sim(f_1(a_1) \vee \sim f_1(a_1))$ or, abbreviated, α_1, and $\sim\alpha_1$; the modes of the former and the latter being actuality and potentiality, respectively. The determinates (9) and (10) are a sentential tautology and its negation. That, to be sure, is not controversial (except, perhaps, the ontological use of the familiar words; this, though, is at issue throughout the discourse). Upon the view of some, including myself, (9), therefore, is *analytic* (and (10) is *contradictory*); analyticity being a very rich and important notion of ontology. Is there such a notion? That nowadays is again controversial. Thus it should help if, like a surgeon who puts a clamp on a vein so that he may operate in a clean field, I temporarily staunch the controversy. Whether or not the notion of analyticity I shall in due course propose is in fact as rich and as important as I shall argue; whether in particular it is or is not anthropocentric; what its extension is; and in particular, which, if any, of the three special kinds fall under it, are four further questions, such that the answers to them do not matter for the ontologization of the modes, and which, therefore, until their turn comes, you may safely ignore.

What matters here is one thing only. Now that these five examples, with the modes I claim for them, are all available, any likely reader of this discourse who reflects on them for a moment will know very well what a mode is; so well indeed that, if he is an absolutist waiting for the promised confrontation, he can no longer restrain his impatience. So we had better let a critic of this persuasion have his say. I know only too well (he tells me) that yours is but another attempt at ontologizing truth and falsehood, and, therefore, all details apart, as absurd as Frege's, who, I take it, was the last to try this sort of thing. Is the critic right? The answer, again, is Yes and No. Yes; because, as I, too, believe, for reasons which will at least be touched, my new world is indeed in the succession starting with Augustine, if not perhaps with Plato, that leads over Malebranche to Frege and, however obscurely, Meinong. No; because, I am tempted to remind the critic, *le bon Dieu est dans le détail*. Less sententiously, I offer four preliminary observations. (1) In this world, whether old or new, truth or falsehood, as the case may be, is primarily a feature of thoughts, and only derivatively of certain acts, e.g., believings, as well as of assertions and, in schemata that are context-free, of sentences, but never of what a thought intends. (2) In the new world, rather significantly in this context, 'true' and 'false', purporting to stand for what I used to call derived characters, do not literally stand for anything. (3) To think of what I ontologize as actuality and potentiality, which thus in this world are not nothing, as truth and falsehood is absurd indeed and has been a source of great trouble. (4) Frege's T and F are two odd things and therefore determinates. (His world is 'saturated'.) A mode, on the other hand, is not a determinate of any sort. Nor is it a tie but, rather, an entity. But the triad determinate-tie-entity establishes in this world a sort of hierarchy among what has ontological status. Thus the two modes are on its lowest level; while Frege's T and F, transplanted into this world, would be on its highest.

But I must not allow myself to be carried away. These four observations are part and parcel of the argument on my side in the eventual confrontation with the absolutist critic. Yet, if I persisted, I would hurt my case. For how could one make it as thoroughly as it must be made unless he has first properly ontologized the modes? This, therefore, is the job we must do next. Even so, what has been said is said; thus we might just as well first get all the good out of it which we now can. The critic and I want to talk about the same thing. Yet it is very difficult to do that unless one talks either as he does, which is the traditional way, or in my way, which is anything but traditional, and which therefore, as I just insisted, I should have an opportunity to develop first. Thus it will help if for a little while we borrow a word on which we can easily agree without prejudice to either side, since it is taken from the strand of the tradition most alien to both of us. We shall eventually confront each other over the "warranty of beliefs."

If a sentence is true its denial is false and conversely. This connection is fundamental among words. Ontologically, that among the three existents, actuality, potentiality, and negation, is just as fundamental; so fundamental indeed that one cannot do justice to it dialectically unless he starts from the phenomenological rock bottom. But we shall merely save words without losing or distorting anything if for the time being we limit ourselves among determinates to things and facts, thus continuing to ignore classes and circumstances.

The modes of α_1 and $\sim\alpha_1$ are immediately available. That, roughly, was the claim we must now polish. Disregarding whatever other conditions, if any, must be satisfied, either of the two, α_1 and $\sim\alpha_1$, is transparent if and only if it is explicitly intended. That is why they make such handy examples. As a necessary condition, though, the qualification holds throughout. *Unless explicitly intended, no existent is transparent.* That this is another appeal to the witness of the given needs by now no pointing out. Something else does. This is the first time you see at work that "conservatism," as I called it, which makes the eventual warranty of the modes presented as strong as practically it must be. The appeal, being phenomenological, must of course stand on its own feet. Yet it is reassuring to see how it dovetails with the dialectical need. As for supporting it in a way an appeal may properly be supported, I simply restate it as a psychologist might. An existent's mode, he might say, cannot be "noticed" unless one "pays attention" to the existent.

The bulk of the facts presented to us, including all atomic ones, neither is nor ever becomes transparent; i.e., synonymously, their modes are in principle inaccessible. The conservatism of so sweeping a limitation stands out. The issue is whether, given the "strength" of many of our beliefs, it is even plausible. Thus I had better not delay answering two questions which immediately arise.

First. If the modes of all these facts are in principle inaccessible to us, why should we "suppose" that each has one? The right answer is to admit first that this is indeed an *extrapolation* and then to add four remarks. (1) There is all the difference in the world between an extrapolation and a *speculation,* in the sense in which in the old world, where they were on no occasion presented, the modes themselves were still speculative. (2) The limitation this extrapolation balances is an- thropo*logical.* (3) To the extent this discourse as a whole succeeds, the extrapolation is successful. (4) There is another case of this sort. In my world, whether old or new, one is never presented with a particular not simultaneous with the particular of the act intending it (see Appendix A). Yet we successfully suppose, by extrapolation, that there are such particulars.

Second. In several of the ontologies from which I have learned much, a very high degree of warranty, if not perhaps the highest, is associated with direct awareness. Paradigmatically, what a direct awareness intends is an act simultaneous with it, i.e., a conjunction of two atomic facts, e.g., "*b* being a perceiving and *b* being a thought-that-$f_1(a_1)$," i.e., as before (p. 61), $perc(b)$ & $f_2(b)$, or, abbreviated, β_1 & β_2. For what follows pick either β_1 or β_2; call that very high degree of warranty "indubitability"; consider that, say, β_1 being an atomic fact, its mode, like that of all atomic facts, is supposed to be in principle inaccessible, and you will see that I have two jobs cut out for myself. I must, first, ontologically ground "indubitability"; and I must, second, close in on a still higher warranty that covers, say, α_1 and $\sim\alpha_1$, but neither β_1 nor β_2. While directly aware of, say, β_1, I can indeed not doubt that *b* is a perceiving; yet I can imagine, negatively, that it is not, as well as, positively, that it is an entertaining or, perhaps, itself either an imagining or a doubting. Hence, and more generally, while *one cannot be directly aware of something and simultaneously doubt it, one can yet simultaneously think its negation*. Thus I provide, in the new world, the first, phenomenological step of—or, perhaps better, the appeal required for—the ontologization of the anthropo*centric* feature which I, too, shall henceforth call *indubitability*. The second, dialectical step is implicit in what follows.

   When presented with α_1 and its mode, actuality, one cannot simultaneously also think, i.e., be presented with, under whatever species, $\sim\alpha_1$, except with its mode, which is potentiality. As for α_1, so mutatis mutandis for $\sim\alpha_1$. Of course this is a further appeal to the given. To me, thus articulated, it is as compelling as any. It is also, among the several appeals in these passages, the one closest to the dialectical heart of the matter. So I shall sometimes more concisely speak of the *Unthinkability of the Negation*.

   The Unthinkability of the Negation is one of four phenomenological data, if I may so call them, which involve the modes and are most immediately relevant to their dialectic. Thus, if we wanted to, we could already start on the latter. But it will simplify the exposition if, before doing that, we gather the other three. First, though, let me spell out a bit of dialectic already secured. Just compare the two italicized sentences in the last two paragraphs and you will see that what was called the second job is already done. *Under the same circumstances, unthinkability of the negation of a fact clearly is a higher degree of warranty for it than its "mere" indubitability.*

   14* The phenomenological material here introduced is one thing. The assays of the conscious states, or awareness, that go with it, is quite another thing. What needs to be said about these and quite a few other assays is all gathered in Section V. But you may be put off by some things that were said. So I add three remarks to make you more willing to wait for this particular denouement. (1) Properly assayed, all the conscious states here mentioned turn out to be not just single acts but conjunctions of several simultaneous ones. In the old world that was slurred over. (2) In several of the ontologies from which I have learned much, the intentions of all direct awarenesses either are all "sense data," or, at least, have sense data among them. In my old world these fictions still have a precarious place, although only from inertia and because there were as yet no sufficiently articulate assays of conscious states rather than from any systematic need. From the new world, we shall also see in Section V, sense data have been ejected. Thus we need not worry what has become of their traditional indubitability. (Sense data, as you see, join the derived characters as the other victims of the purge. That, though, is the extent of it.) (3) It may help you to be reminded of what is not again expounded in this discourse, viz., that in strict parlance 'direct awareness' is the name of a species, coordinate with 'perceiving', 'believing', 'doubting', and so on, or, more precisely, as was already mentioned, of 'perceiving$_1$', 'believing$_1$', 'doubting$_1$', and so on. Thus it does not, or at least not primarily, name a kind of act, although, whenever there is no danger of confusion, one may, as I just did, call an act with this species a direct awareness, just as one calls those with another species, say, believing, believing$s$. Notice, too, that I just called a conscious state an awareness. So used, 'awareness' does of course not stand for a species.

If a sentential tautology is "simple" enough, its mode, actuality, may upon presentation be immediately available to me. If it is too "complex" for that, then, schematically speaking yet without loss of anything here essential, the following may happen. The presentation is followed by a series of acts that (1) the intention of the first is an immediately transparent tautology, (2) the intention of each would be transparent to us if the intentions of the preceding ones, which we still remember, were transparent, and (3) the intention of the last is the tautology originally presented without being transparent. The individual differences affecting this partial schema of the phenomenology of making deductive inferences we can ignore. The connection in (2), being causal and a matter of anthropological fact, is of no special concern to us. Nor need we here concern ourselves with the role, causal or otherwise, which images of words or even of the marks of an artificial schema may or may not play in the coming about of such series. One question, though, must be asked and answered now: Can anything be transparent to an act of remembering? By the witness of what is given to me, the answer is No. That dovetails with the need for being as conservative as is practically required. For memory is notoriously "fallible" in all contexts. So, therefore, is the making of deductive inferences! As for remembering, so for all other species except believing. *The only species with which a fact is ever transparently presented is belief.* Call this datum the "Limitation to Belief." Now, however, we must face another question. What in fact does one remember when seeming to remember a mode? We stand at the rim of what seems a gaping hole in our road. Yet it will pay if we postpone the answer until we have come upon another such hole.

Suppose one is presented with the actuality of γ_1. If so, is he also presented with the "actuality of γ_1 being actual"? Correspondingly, in case γ_2 happens to be potential, can anyone ever be presented with the "potentiality of γ_2 being actual"? Similarly, is one ever presented with the "actuality (or potentiality) of a fact being potential"? I answer that in either case the words between the double quotes do not stand for anything I can think. That makes this a third datum. Call it the "Unthinkability of the Iterated Mode." With a view toward what follows, I support it, in a manner in which it may properly be supported, by asking two questions. Is something's being clear and distinct itself clear and distinct? Is something being illuminated for us (in Augustinian fashion) itself illuminated? (Metaphorically, as was pointed out earlier (p. 71), the step from illumination to transparence is not great.)

Can one ever be presented with the "negation of a fact being actual (potential)"? Once more, the words between double quotes do not stand for anything I can think. Thus we have come upon the fourth datum. Call it the "Unthinkability of the Negated Mode." I support it, again properly, by drawing attention to a distinction. The Unthinkability of the Negation, i.e., the circumstance that, while transparently presented with a fact, we cannot think its negation except in the opposite mode, is one thing. The Unthinkability of the Negated Mode is another thing. If the two were one—except of course for the obvious condition of simultaneous presentation for the first—the suspicions, which some of you may still harbor, that the modes are nothing but assertion and denial ontologized, or, perhaps, that potentiality is nothing but negation, gratuitously ontologized for the second time, would indeed be justified. Nor is it just a matter of noncommutativity, since, by the Principle of Presentation, what cannot be thought does not exist.

The three unthinkabilities, if I may so express myself, of the Negation, the Negated Mode, and the Interated Mode, respectively, and the Limitation to Belief; these four, then, are the four data closest to the dialectical heart of the modes. The Limitation to Belief very sweepingly restricts their accessibility in principle. The other three merely "exclude" from presentation what is not there to be presented. It is nevertheless fair to say that they are all four very conservative.

We are ready to collect the five major pieces of the dialectic, to examine them, and to fit them into a pattern.

First. The ontologization of the modes first suggested itself, in the pure discourse of Section I, in connection with the canons. Let us again speak of materials for, and the product of, a maker and call the materials appropriate if they satisfy the restriction that goes with the maker. Given a maker and materials appropriate to it, we must say either that there may or may not be the product, or, as we preferred, for good reasons which need no rehearsing, that there is the product with the mode of either actuality or potentiality. Thus, if a fact's being either actual or potential, as the case may be, were itself either actual or potential, we would have started on a pointless regress—even within pure discourse, irrespective of the Unthinkability of the Iterated Mode. *Second.* Obviously there are no such existents as the negation of a thing or a class. Equivalently, there is nothing either '$\sim a_1$' or '$a_1 \vee f_1$' or '$f_1 \& f_2$' or '$\sim\{a_1, a_2\}$' stand for. If you keep that in mind while considering, first, the Unthinkability of the Negated Mode, and, second, that, speculation apart, what cannot be thought does not exist, you will see that a fact's being either actual or potential, as the case may be, is in this respect like a thing. *Third.* We suppose, by extrapolation, that each fact is either actual or potential but never both. *Fourth.* A fact, say, γ_1, being tied to its mode by a maker is equivalent to γ_1's being actual or potential, as the case may be, being itself a fact, say, γ_2. But if γ_2 is a fact, so is $\sim\gamma_2$. That does not jibe with the Unthinkability of the Negated Mode. *Fifth.* Remember that a thing is a Two-in-One. That means, first, that it is a "combination" of an ultimate sort and an item; and, second, that, just as it has no mode, there is no maker to hold together the two "components" of these Aristotelian-Thomistic "composites," in the sense in which, *as one may want to say,* exemplification holds together the particular and the universal in a (nonrelational) atomic fact.

15* Three remarks will help to make the pattern stand out. (1) 'As one may want to say' was italicized because such hold*ing* together is just as unnecessarily and irremediably anthropomorphic as the mak*ing* we rejected (p. 80). The chaster and safer formula is provided by the schema for canons: If the maker and the material appropriate for it are there, so is the product. But no harm comes, as long as one knows what he is doing, from using the suggestive phrase when it helps the exposition. (2) An existent is appropriate material for a connective if and only if it has a mode. Equivalently, that is the restriction which goes with each of them. Still differently, as will be spelled out in Section IV, that is their very nature. Facts have modes. As for facts, so, as we shall see in due course, for circumstances. The quartet of determinates thus divides into two pairs. Facts and circumstances have modes; things and classes don't. The former two we shall eventually call "complexes." But notice that, as we agreed to speak, the product of a maker is always a fact. Thereby, as we shall also see, hangs a division of all facts into two levels. (3) Perhaps it will occur to you that what the job just started and to be finished in Section IV amounts to is the "ontologization of the truth tables." As an aphorism that will do. Taken literally or even structurally it is most misleading. Actuality and potentiality "are" neither truth nor falsehood, either Fregean or otherwise. (See also the confrontation below.)

Return to the five items above. If one examines them separately and then tries to fit them together, the structural suggestion that emerges is irresistible and inescapable. *The combination of a fact and its mode is a Two-in-One, which itself has no mode; nor are the two existents thus combined held together by anything.* In this respect things and "moded facts," if for the moment I may so call them, are the two sorts of Two-in-Ones, marking the two limits of (logical) atomism. In other respects they differ. As a first step toward exploring the differences, consider the way I have spoken and still speak. A Two-in-One that is a thing I called a composite; the two existents it combines, its components. All together, that makes, for one sort of Two-in-Ones, three existents, the two components and the composite. 'Combine' and 'combination', on the other hand, have been used neutrally, in a way that does not, in the case of the second sort, commit us to a third existent, in addition to the fact and its mode. (The price paid for this convenience is that momentary barbarism, 'moded fact'.)

Let us again move from the given through the anthropocentric to the dialectical. Consider two acts. The first transparently intends a fact; i.e., as for the moment we speak, it intends a moded fact. The second explicitly intends a thing. To such an act the thing being a composite of a certain item and a certain ultimate sort is transparent. To deny that, or, even worse, to deny that there are such acts, does not make good phenomenological sense (p. 70, p. 71). The urgent questions they may raise in your mind, particularly if you consider that things have no modes, I beg leave to postpone for a short while. At the moment I merely want you to notice that in the intention of the first act the fact and its mode are as "close" to each other as are the item and the ultimate sort in that of the second. This use of 'close' is of course purely phenomenological. The more formal notions, we know, are separability and dependence. The former, which can be handled in pure discourse, will again have to wait. With respect to the latter, which is anthropocentric, there is an important difference.

One is never presented with an item without being presented with *its* ultimate sort as well as (explicitly and transparently) with the thing whose two components they are; just as, conversely, one is never presented with an ultimate sort without being presented with *an* item such that, and so on. One is never presented with a mode without being presented (explicitly and transparently) with the combination of it and (what ordinarily we call) a fact; but not by any means conversely. Thus, while the dependence of items and ultimate sorts on each other is mutual, that of modes on facts is one-sided. Call this the *first difference* between the two sorts of Two-in-Ones. It is but one aspect of the limited accessibility of the modes, which in turn is one of the most distinctive features of this world.

When transparently presented with a fact, we are not, as in the case of a thing, presented with a third existent, that stands to its mode as an item stands to its ultimate sort. Call this the *second difference*. One may try, of course, to postulate, or, as I would rather say, to introduce "speculatively" such thirds which are never presented to us. This speculation, we shall see on a later occasion, leads to disaster.

Let γ_1 and γ_2 be two facts. Since there are, in addition to them, the three makers called negation, conjunction, and disjunction, there are also, by the three relevant canons, the facts $\sim\gamma_1$, $\sim\gamma_2$, γ_1 & γ_2, $\gamma_1 \vee \gamma_2$. Each of these facts, materials as well as products, has a mode; none of them, being all facts, has the one-many feature. The two modes have it; as, we remember, do makers, ultimate sorts, and the things called universals, but nothing else. Suppose now that γ_1 & γ_2 is potential. Clearly it does not make sense to say that, γ_1 and γ_2 being there, since & is also there, so is potentiality. For the latter would be there, combined with some other fact, even if neither γ_1 nor γ_2 were. All one can reasonably say, therefore, is that a connective, while not a maker of modes, is a mediator of them, i.e., that, depending on its own nature and the modes of the materials, it determines the modes of its products. How, then, an astute critic might ask, about exemplification, whose materials have no mode, while the product does. Should we say that at this level the modes supervene or emerge? If I were in search of metaphors, that is indeed what I would say, adding, with a word from the tradition, that, not by chance, at this level "contingency" emerges. As to the *third* difference between the two limits of atomism all this amounts to, notice that if a thing were made, as of course it is not, by a maker, it would be a third, made out of its item and ultimate sort; while in the case of a fact, which actually is made, its mode supervenes as a second.

In the light of these three differences, jointly with the five points made earlier, the proposed assay is dialectically inescapable. A "moded fact" is a combination of a "fact" and its mode and of nothing else; or, as I shall put it, with the metaphor unpacked in advance, *a Two-in-One of the second sort is a fact pervaded by its mode.* The contrast, thus, is between *pervasion* of a determinate by one entity, on the one hand, and *composition* of two-entities into a determinate, on the other. Very conveniently, this manner of speaking permits us to drop 'moded fact' and to use 'fact' as every one else does, merely adding the anthropological comment that, in the manner by now familiar, our access to their modes is subject to rather sweeping limitations.

How about green-not-being-a-property (universal$^{(0)}$) and green-being-a-relation (universal$^{(0, 0)}$)? You will say that surely we know both these things,[†] and have no patience with two new appeals, the Unthinkability of the Negated Ultimate Sort and of the Different Ultimate Sort, respectively, according to which we cannot literally think either. If I tried to support these appeals now, the exposition would bog down. But I promise that in Section V I shall smooth out the seeming roughness in a manner that will remind you of how the "fallibility" of making deductive inferences was accounted for (p. 89). So I hope you will read on. If you do, you will, and should, expect me to answer two questions. Do these two new "data" fit with, and thereby support, the nucleus, which has already emerged, of the system we hope to build? Supposing they fit, do they also provide cues for what may, or perhaps must, be added to that nucleus? Let us see.

If green-being-a-property and green-not-being-a-property were both (literally) thinkable, they would both be facts, or perhaps circumstances, the first actual, the second potential. If so, then things would not be Two-in-Ones. Thus the Unthinkability of the Negated Sort and the proposed assay of things as Two-in-Ones support each other. Similarly for the Unthinkability of the Different Sort. If green (f_1)

[†]Bergmann should be taken as saying here, I believe, that 'surely we know the falsehood of both the statements contained in the previous sentence', for clearly we could not "know", even in a loose and ordinary sense, that green is *not* a property or that it *is* a relation. If anything, we "know," again in the loose ordinary sense, just the opposite: that green *is* a property and that green is *not* a relation. Nor, on the other hand, should Bergmann be interpreted as saying that 'surely we know the *modes* of the complexes represented by the statements in the previous sentence, namely, potentiality', for Bergmann's whole point here is that these statements are only pseudostatements: they do not represent complexes at all.—WH

being a particular were potential, green being red (f_2) would by the relevant canon be a potential fact. Thus there would be a potential and presumably thinkable fact, $\eta(f_1, f_2)$, that "violates" a canon. But it is still another incontestable datum that *what would, if it existed, violate a canon does not exist* (and cannot be thought). When the canons were first introduced, the discourse was still pure. Thus, naturally, this particular datum was then not mentioned. So I state it now, on the first occasion that arises, without further ado. That much for the confirmations, now for the cues.

Consider that the intention of one of those special acts, being a thing, has no mode. What, then, is the source of its transparence? For the second time, it seems, we stand at the rim of a gaping hole in the road. Yet there is one way out, or around. The source, or to speak as usually, the ground of the transparence is in the act, and therefore, broadly speaking, in its species. I say broadly speaking because that still leaves an alternative. The ground may be either a species all its own—the absolutist would call it "knowing"—or a third character which the particular of the act exemplifies, in addition to its species and thought. "Choosing" the second alternative and borrowing a word from Brentano, I call that character *evidence*. But there is still another choice. Is the species of these special acts sui generis or is it believing? This time I "choose" the first alternative, call the new species *grasping*. Thus, speaking succinctly, yet I trust without danger of confusion, since being evident is upon this assay a character of the act's particular rather than of the act itself, *when one intends transparently that, say, green is a property, his act is a grasping and is evident.*

The absolutist interrupts, asking me whether there are in this world of mine any graspings that are not evident. I readily admit that there are none. This further increases his suspicion that the two "choices" I just made are specious. So he remarks that, although I do not realize it, the only motive for them is my stubborn aversion to both the word and the thing, his use of 'knowing' and what he claims it stands for. I ask him to bear with me until I have brought one more ship into port, which I assure him won't take long; then I shall be ready for the confrontation.

Recall the other gaping hole. What does one remember, e.g., in deductive reasoning from transparent premisses, when seeming to remember the mode of a fact? An answer has become available. What he remembers is an act of his own, which is—or, as one would ordinarily say, was—a believing and evident. That not only grounds what must be grounded, fitting it phenomenologically very well into the penumbra (p. 80) of this region; it also is as conservative as we must be by not extending the highest warranty beyond "the presented mode of the moment" and at the same time allowing for the ubiquity of human error. Thus, not only have both gaps been bridged, but a considerable increment to the gradually emerging system has been secured. I, naturally, am encouraged. The absolutist, however, interrupts again. Do you claim, then, he asked me, that, using 'knowing' and 'true' as I do, you know that an act is evident if and only if one of two conditions is fulfilled, viz., that it is either an act of believing to which, as you say, a fact or circumstance is presented transparently; or that it is what you call a grasping, such that what it intends is true. I acknowledge that to face his question is as good a way as any of starting the confrontation, and promise that I shall do just that if he will permit me, as a preface to it, five comments and, after them, a disgression into structural history.

(1) Elsewhere I have argued at great length, and I still believe, that virtually everything Brentano has said about what he calls evidence is wrong. Yet, in spite of this fundamental disgreement, every thorough student of his work will recognize *some* structural similarities about what he and I have to say about error and the privileged position of the "presented mode of the moment." Thus I do want to acknowledge that, far from just borrowing a word from him, I have, however subtly and indirectly, learned very much from his errors. Nor is that unusual in philosophy, either in my case or, I take it, that of others. I, for instance, first learned many very important things from G. E. Moore, which, had I only known enough, I could have learned from Brentano, or Meinong, or the early Husserl, although I was even then, and still am, convinced that much of what he believed is false. And I have probably never learned more from Russell, or through Russell, than during the last years, after I had at long last ceased to take for granted what he taught about classes, numbers, and some related topics. (See Appendix B.) (2) You may wonder why I wrote '$\sim a_1$' and '$\sim f_1$' rather than, say, '$\sim \phi_1 i_1$' and '$\sim \phi_2 i_1$', with the 'ϕ' and 'i' standing for ultimate sorts and items, respectively. The reason is that, as has already been mentioned, there are in the ideal language no expressions for the entities. Remember, too, that the two unthinkabilities for things were stated in terms of the latter, rather than of their items. (3) Could evidence be a second-type property, riding piggyback, as Broad might say, on a species? If it were, believing sometimes would, and sometimes would not, be evident (exemplify evidence), which is just as absurd as green sometimes being, and sometimes not being, a color. Granted that, couldn't it be that, while believing being evident is a fact as "timeless" as green being a color, this fact sometimes is, and some-

times isn't, presented to us? A brief reflection will show you that the move is counterstructural. (4) Unless there is the penumbra, there is no "choice" in phenomenology, which in turn limits the "choices" in ontology. (Standardization, which we shall encounter in Section III, is a thing all its own and not really a choice.) Prima facie, therefore, the critic's suspicion of the two "choices" I made was not unreasonable. There is a penumbra in this region. That, enough, is beside the point. The point is, rather, that dialectically the choices make no difference. I might just as well have ontologized this region by proposing, instead of an evident believing for the one case and an evident grasping for the other, a single new species of "knowing" for both. There are only two good reasons for not doing that. For one, avoiding any technical use of 'knowing' does facilitate the exposition of my views, or, as the absolutist would have it, of my aversions. For another, as the critic himself has pointed out earlier, when one is conscious of a grasping it is always evident. The overwhelming majority of beliefs, on the other hand, is not. The replacement, in these very special acts, of believing by a new species, the one called grasping, reminds us of this differ-ence. (5) Are a transparent fact and the same fact not transparent one intention or two? If it were not for the principle, of which we shall hear more later, that each thought has exactly one intention, the ques-tion would be moot. With evidence now available, the issue, such as it is, can be defused by putting the matter as follows. The intention is the same in both cases; but the acts are not just numerically different; for one is, and one is not, evident. Whatever roughness seems to re-main after that has been pointed out is the proper manifestation of the same peculiarity of the two entities called modes which suggests thinking of them as "pervaders."

16* Where, *if anywhere*, did the tradition put the warranty? *Basically* there are three possibilities. It is either (a) in the intention, or (b) in the act, or (c) in both. When Augustine speaks of illumination, he puts it in the intention. Structurally, the intervention of a divine Third, to do the illuminating for us, is but a theological metaphor. Male-branche, when insisting that we see all ideas in God, merely varies the metaphor. The most lucid and, as often happens, also the most ex-treme proponent of (b) is Brentano. His evidence, in this one respect like mine, is in the act. From there his commitment to knowing in the absolute sense leads him to the extreme thesis that no act can know anything but itself. This story need not be retold. Frege is the most extreme recent protagonist of (a). The view this discourse propounds falls of course under (c). Where, though, shall we put Descartes? His warranty is clearness and distinctness. That is obvious. What is clear and distinct is an idea. That, too, is obvious (as well as, for the purpose at hand, sufficiently accurate). But where is the idea? In the act or in the intention? Descartes' idea is a Third. Nor does an ideas's being clear and distinct warrant its own existence, which is taken for granted, but that of what it purports to "represent." With Descartes, for all his towering greatness, the misery of representationalism begins. This is another story that need not be retold. Just notice that, if it is true, his warranty couldn't possibly fall under either (a) or (b) or (c). That is why I italicized 'basically'. For representationalism, however hardy, is but an aberration. 'If anywhere' has been italicized because there are also those who put the warranty exclusively into what they call coherence. Neither my critic, I take it, nor surely I, feel the urge to examine once more that strand of the tradition, most alien to both of us, from one of whose later figures we agreed to borrow 'warranty'. But see what will be said in later Sections about contextualism.

17* Critics speak of the grammar of metaphors. That of mine is now an open book. Imagine a hollow sphere of thick, frosted glass with a source of light in its center. The light *pervades* the space inside the sphere. Depending on circumstances, it also *illuminates* the outside. Whenever it does, the glass is *transparent*.

Now I finally face the absolutist. What you want me to claim, I tell him, or, rather, what you think I must claim lest my case collapses, is that I know, in your strong sense of 'knowing', the principle by which *an act (of belief) is evident if and only if its intention is presented with its mode.* From where you stand, I must make this claim. From where I stand, I need not and must not. The "principle" is one of those, such as, e.g., that every fact has exactly one mode or that there are past and future particulars, which in Appendix A will be called "contingent." These principles have in this world no warranty ontologically grounded. That is the heart of the matter. Everything is clear and out in the open. Theoretically, therefore, using 'theoretical' and 'practical' as before (p. 71), I cannot and need not say more. Practically, provided that you "know," in your way, the types of things and (the instances of the) sentential tautologies, you will have to suspend judgment until the list of existents which I claim we sometimes intend with evidence is complete.

The critic generously waives the practical half. But he feels let down. He expected something much more massive. Yet it was all over so quickly. Appreciating as I do his generosity, I shall try to temper his disappointment by four concluding remarks. The first takes care of a technicality. The second and the third each reexamines critically a formula with which I had contented myself before introducing actuality, potentiality, and the (mental) character evidence or being-evident; the first two earlier, the third only recently. For, as I now see, all three are needed to recover completely the sound core of what haunts the absolutist. The fourth, starting from a proposition which (I think) every articulate absolutist must be prepared to defend, brings out an intriguing corollary of our basic disagreement.

When the absolutist first drew our attention to the above principle he spoke of what is grasped as "true." The reason I ignored these special cases is not only the awkwardness, in any case, of using 'true' when wanting to say of an intention that (as we ordinarily speak) it exists, or (as I here speak) that it exists in the mode of actuality; but the even greater awkwardness due to the intentions of these special acts being things and not facts. The point need not, I trust, be spelled out again.

"The task is not to find what is certain but, rather, what philosophers have meant by 'certain'." This is one of the two old formulae. Positively, it was meant to reject absolutism. Still positively, it makes a meta-philosophical point. We must dissolve, not to be sure the philosophical problems, but what has been called the philosophical uses. Negatively, I did not then push the analysis beyond the ontological characterization of the two sorts of existents some of which most absolutists have claimed we "know"; i.e., in the first place, what is in the classical sense analytic or, as one also says, a logical truth; and, in the second place, what is synthetic a priori. (In this discourse I shall eventually propose a broader notion of analyticity, upon which the modes not only of the logical truths but also of some others are accessible to us, although never the modes of those called synthetic a priori. This is one of the few things on which I have never changed my mind; although, as has already been mentioned, the synthetic a priori will in this discourse be grounded more deeply.) Still negatively, this use of 'certain' sells the issue short. For, obviously, anything reasonably so called is in the act and thus obviously cannot provide the kind of warranty the absolutist craves for the act's intention. To make that very clear is, I believe, one of the strengths of the assay, long ago proposed, of the knowledge situation. For there is, upon this assay, first, the act, say $f_1(b)$ & *bel*(b) & *certain*(b); there is, second, its intention, say, γ_1; and there is, third, $f_1 \, M \, \gamma_1$, which in the old as well as in the new world is analytic and whose mode in the new is accessible to us. Of that more later. Now I merely want you to appreciate the gulf, unbridgeable by any ontologically grounded warranty, which upon this assay separates the mental character certainty from the actuality, or, if you insist on speaking the other way, from the existence of γ_1.

"The nature of truth is correspondence; its criterion, coherence." This is the other old formula. In a world with modes its first half must be reworded as follows. A thought is either true or false depending on whether the fact it intends is either actual or potential. The only question which remains is what, if anything, 'true' and 'false' stand for. In this world, whether old or new, the answer starts from the proper adaptation of the Artistotelian definition: '$T(f)$' for '$(\exists p)[f \, M \, p \, \& \, p]$', and '$F(f)$' for '$(\exists p)[f \, M \, p \, \& \sim p]$'. (That ignores for the time being the weighty issue of quantification over propositional variables.) In the new world, 'T' and 'F', being defined, stand for nothing. That surely helps; also because, by contrast with the modes, it discourages a familiar misuse of the two adjectives. In philosophical discourse we must not say such things as that a thought is true (false) if and only if the fact it intends is true (false), instead of saying, correctly, that the thought is true (false) if and only if the fact it intends is actual (potential). Turn to the second half. Here the question is how, in a world where the modes of most facts are not accessible to us, we manage to assign truth values to the thoughts intending them. The answer is that this assignment, theoretically although of course not practically forever tentative, proceeds, deductively, from what (at the moment) we cannot doubt, in conjunction with some beliefs intending generalities (laws of nature) which (at the moment) are more or less certain, by means of logical truths whose modes are accessible to us. That defeats the objection, fatal to the radical coherence views, that there is nothing for the assignment to start from. The answer itself is of course merely schematic. Nor, reasonably, could it be anything else. Even so, the choice of words, 'criterion' and 'coherence', was perhaps more confusing than enlightening.

One not only sometimes knows something, but, when knowing it, he sometimes also knows that he knows it. That, I believe, is the proposition all absolutists must defend. Call the intentions of the two acts involved γ_1 and γ_2, respectively. I agree with the absolutist that the regress they initiate, $\gamma_1, \gamma_2, \gamma_3, \ldots$, is harmless. This I have argued on earlier occasions and shall consider again, more carefully, I hope, when assaying some of our conscious states. Two other points bring out our basic disagreement. (1) γ_1 may or may not be analytic; γ_2, however, either upon the classical or upon the new, broader notion of analyticity, never is. But, then, why should it be? Perhaps I was overimpressed with this feature and thus kept from doing earlier what can, and therefore must, be done in order to recover completely the sound core of absolutism by means of the three new existents. (2) Suppose that the act intending γ_1 is evident. How then about γ_2? In this world, either old or new, γ_2 is a conjunction of atomic facts intended by a direct awareness. What is thus intended is indubitable (p. 87) but not evident. That permits us to epitomize the basic disagreement very neatly. The absolutist sometimes knows that he (now) knows something. I "merely" cannot doubt that something is (now) evident to me.

III
Diversity and Order

Let a_1, a_2, a_3, a_4, f_1, f_2, f_3, f_4 be eight things, of the two types (ultimate sorts) the letters conventionally indicate. Since they are there and exemplification is also there, so, by the single canon relevant in all four cases, are the facts $f_1(a_1)$, $f_2(a_2)$, $f_3(a_3)$, $f_4(a_4)$. Again, since these are there and conjunction as well as disjunction are also there, so, by the two relevant canons, are a fifth and a sixth fact, viz., $f_1(a_1)$ & $f_2(a_2)$ (briefly: γ_1) and $f_3(a_3) \vee f_4(a_4)$ (briefly: γ_2). That much the canons secure. But how do we know that, say, γ_1 and γ_2 are two and not one? Commonsensically, the question is rhetorical. Yet it is an opening wedge for two ontological ones. (1) Is there in the world we are building something that secures γ_1 and γ_2 being two and not one, in the sense in which the three relevant canons secure that the six facts are all there? (2) Supposing this something is there, is it ever presented to us? The first question immediately suggests a third. (3) Do the two relevant canons which severally secure that γ_1 and γ_2 are there, jointly also secure their being two and not one? To ask (3) is to answer it. They don't. That determines the answer to (1). There must be something to do the job. In the more formal language of ontological discourse, *there is an existent that grounds the diversity of* γ_1 *and* γ_2. To close in on it, we turn to phenomenology. Another appeal to the given is in order. Let α and β stand for any two determinates. *Sometimes I am explicitly presented with* α-*being-diverse-from-*β. Hence, by the Principle of Presentation, α-*being-diverse-from-*β, or equivalently and in many contexts less clumsily, the *diversity-of-*α-*and-*β, is an independent existent. Call it δ. That answers (2). Even an idiomatic reply to the idiomatic opening wedge now seems safe. If we want to "know" whether γ_1 and γ_2 are two and not one, we must "look for" the appropriate diversity. But then I may be asked: What, if anything, do you "see" when, looking for that diversity, you do not find it? I postpone answering for a short while. Yet the question serves a purpose right now. It reminds us that all we have achieved so far is a phenomenological toehold; at best the whole, more likely than not merely a part, of the first of the two steps of every proper ontologization. A second reminder, worthwhile for its own sake, will reinforce the first. None of the above uses of 'knowing', either with or without double quotes, prejudges in any way whether a presented diversity is ever transparent, nor, in case some or even all are, whether, like sentential tautologies or things, respectively, they do or do not have modes. These are but two of the several issues we must face before we may confidently bestow ontological status on the new candidate.

I interrupt for a reassurance, a caution, and an anticipation. Just as the relevant canons secure that γ_1 and γ_2 are there, so (I said) δ secures (grounds) their being two and not one. What, then, an alert reader will ask, grounds a canon. A canon must indeed have a ground. What it is we shall see later, still in this Section. That is the reassurance. 'γ_1-being-diverse-from-γ_2' quite appropriately—quite literally, one is tempted to say—stands for δ. It does not follow that a sentence stating a canon would with the same appropriateness stand for what grounds the latter. That is the caution. Being independent and somehow, we do as yet not know how, produced out of existents, *a diversity is a determinate* (p. 77). Hence, if it is neither a thing nor a fact nor a class, it must belong to one of the three subsorts of circumstances.

Next for two remarks. Obvious as they are, they should help you to catch the drift.

First. As for γ_1 and γ_2, so for any conjunction and disjunction made out of (at most) four atomic facts. Commonsensically, again, we know that. Ontologically, therefore, we expect, or ought to expect, that there is something like a canon, which secures the existence of the appropriate diversities. I say "something like a canon" and propose to call this existent a *criterion*, because I do not want to use either 'canon' or 'rule'. 'Rule' has no literal meaning outside of human affairs. Thus, considering the way many philosophers now use it, I would rather avoid it. 'Canon' I want to avoid because, as we shall see, the ground of a criterion is something very different from that of a canon.

Second. As for γ_1 and γ_2, so for any two of the four atomic facts of the paradigm. There is a diversity grounding their being two and not one. We are working our way downward, as it were; recursively, as we shall eventually say. Again, therefore, as for any two of these facts, so for any two of the eight things. If any diversity is ever presented to us, so surely is that between two things, say, green and red, or, even more strikingly, green and louder-than. The only question, if any, in the case of things, is whether there is a criterion, such as, say, that two things are diverse if and only if either their items or their ultimate sorts or both are diverse. If so, how about existents grounding the "diversity" of items and ultimate sorts? Clearly, we stand at the threshold of an infinite regress. That is a warning to heed. We must not rush into anything. As we shall see, continuing to use 'criterion' so that a criterion has ontological status, the criteria there are all regulate the diversity, or lack of such, not of simples, but of what is produced out of simples. Or, with a twist that might help as long as you realize that it is purely verbal, every diversity of things is its own "criterion." All this will become much clearer as we shall see how it fits with everything else.

Among philosophers, the awkwardness of using 'one' and 'two' in connection with 'same' and either 'diverse' or 'different' is notorious. It is also inevitable. Phrases such as 'two and not one' and 'one and not two' serve to relieve it. We shall (I think) live even more comfortably with it if you will permit me to speak and write sometimes in a certain way. Instead of saying that two determinates are diverse, I shall say, occasionally, that they are a *Two* and not a *One,* or even more exuberantly, a Platonic Two and not a Platonic One. The capital letter, either alone or together with the exuberant adjective, will keep it before our minds that the two words do not stand for the integers 1 and 2. (Nor, we shall see, do they stand for a one-class and a two-class, or pair, respectively.)

If there is something that grounds two determinates being a Two and not a One, is there also a ground for every single determinate being a One and not a Two? The question seems odd. Have we really gained comfort rather than a smoke screen for either vacuity or nonsense? If you remember what was said about alternative bases in Section I (p. 51), the question will no longer seem odd.

Among the makers there are not only the connectives but also the two quantifiers for which, roughly speaking, 'all' and 'some' stand. These two, as now assayed, make out of different material (alternative bases) the same product. For the assays themselves and, of course, the arguments in support of them, you will have to wait until Section IV. If, however, you will in the meantime give me credit for them, you will, to say the least, find credible the one thing that matters now. There is nothing in the canons for the quantifiers that secures the product either makes out of alternative bases being a One. For such, very credibly indeed, as in the case of the connectives, is the way of all canons. Dialectically, we find ourselves in the same situation as before. Phenomenologically, the support required again comes forth. *Sometimes I am presented with a determinate being a One.* So I call such a determinate a "sameness" and make the gambit. *For each determinate there is another, which grounds its being a One.* (I speak of a gambit because the ontologization has barely begun.)

Are "diversities" and "samenesses" two new sorts of determinates? Upon my "choice," there is only one. In particular, I choose diversity, call it a *diad,* and make sameness out of it by negation. Explicitly, *a diad is a determinate which has a mode such that, in the case of a Two, say, α and β, "its" diad, α-being-diverse-from-β, is actual, while in the case of a One, say, α, "its" diad, α-being-diverse-from-α, is potential.* A diad, then, most crucially, has a mode. Also, *diads are sometimes transparent.* If this claim can be made good, it will secure one of the pivots of the system. So I shall in due course support it, as carefully as one must and as well as I can, by all the arguments, phenomenological as well as dialectical, which I can marshal.

Terminologically, you notice, 'diversity' and 'sameness' have become expendable, although we may of course for convenience' sake continue to use them whenever there is no danger of confusion. That is why in the last paragraph I put them between double quotes.

18* A "choice" in ontology is always problematic (p. 94). How, then, about the one I just made from the alternative of either (a) one or (b) two new sorts? Linguistically, (a) corresponds to introducing into a schema (1) 'α-being-the-same-as-β', as an abbreviation for (2) 'α-not-being-diverse-from-β'. In an ideal schema, or language, there are no abbreviations. Hence, in the ideal language for (a) there is (3) 'α-being-diverse-from-β', but not, of course, either (1) or (4) 'α-not-being-the-same-as-β'; while in the ideal language for (b) there are (1) and (3) but of course neither (2) nor (4). With this linguistic pattern in mind, a critic, remembering a certain view I have long held, challenges my choice. There are (he claims) at least two good reasons why I cannot justify it. *First,* he points out, there are in what I call the new world no derived existents. Hence, if one chooses diversity over sameness, as I did, then, by the linguistic pattern, 'diverse' would stand for something and 'same' wouldn't, while if one chooses sameness over diversity, 'same' would and 'diverse' wouldn't. Such arbitrariness seems excessive. Thus, he concludes, somewhere something has gone wrong. *Second,* he adds, the obvious way out of this difficulty is to make (1) and (2) stand for a single existent; and, of course, as for (1) and (2), so for (3) and (4). This way, though, he insists, is not open to me, since, idiosyncratically, I hold that, say, $\sim(\gamma_1 \,\&\, \gamma_2)$ and $\sim\gamma_4 \lor \sim\gamma_2$, although analytically equivalent, yet are two and not one. Thus, he concludes, I have no choice but am implicitly committed to (b). I answer as follows. Your *first* argument overshoots the mark. What you say would be a good reason if 'same' and 'diverse' stood (or purported to stand) for relations; one simple, one (in the old world) derived. But you will soon see that, as the relevant existents are assayed in the new world, neither, upon either choice, stands for a relation nor anything else. Your *second* reason is impressive; I do still hold the view that to be analytically equivalent and to be One are two and not one. Thus the structural suggestion to "choose" (b) is not to be trifled with. All I can say in favor of my choice is that, while it saves not only breath and ink but also a tail of existents doing no real job, the difference between (a) and (b) makes no difference. Even so, your point is worth making. But notice, too, that I introduced it by starting, as I usually do not, from a linguistic pattern. Why in this case that is the proper approach and how its propriety is connected with there being a choice we shall come to understand in Section V.

For each determinate there is another, its diad, i.e., its being diverse from itself, which is potential; for any two determinates, there is a third, their diad, which is actual. Provisionally, at least, the formula ontologizes the new sort. How does it fit with what has already emerged of the pattern?

To be explicitly presented with an atomic fact, say, $\eta(f_1, a_1)$, is to be implicitly presented with the two determinates involved and, as a third, the tie of exemplification. Are diads in this respect like facts? We may safely limit ourselves to actual diads; since what in this respect holds for them holds a fortiori for those which are potential. Take then the diad of α and β; call the two determinates its *terms;* write for it '(α, β)'; and ask again. Is one, when explicitly presented with (α, β), implicitly presented with its terms only or also with a third existent, either a tie or whatever else it may be? By the uncontestable witness of the given, there is no third. The difference in feel, or look, between (α, β) in general, or, for that matter, (f_1, a_1) in particular, on the one hand, and $\eta(f_1, a_1)$, on the other, is as striking as any. With a metaphor we have outgrown, the togetherness grounded in a tie is something very different from, and much closer as well as more specific than, the "togetherness," if that be the word, of the terms of a diad. Let us try other formulations. (α, β) needs no other ground than α and β themselves and their each being what they are; or, as I shall also say, a diad needs no other ground than the "identities" of its terms. Still differently, α and β being there, (α, β) *is eo ipso there.* Once this feature is firmly grasped, another immediately strikes us. *The mode of a diad depends only on the identities of its terms but not at all on the modes, if any, of the latter.* This will turn out to be another pivotal feature of the system. (Notice, too, how well it agrees with our thinking of the two modes as pervaders on which the ties don't operate.)

The Latin tag eo ipso helps by bringing out the contrast to the need for makers in the case of facts. Later on, it will help us in a different way. Remember now where it was first used. An existent, it read there

(p. 45), is of type (b) if and only if, provided the members of its base are there, it is eo ipso there, although there is no maker among them. Finally we have come upon existents of this type. *Diads are one of the three subsorts of type (b).* The others are the element nexus, usually called class membership, $(\alpha \in \beta)$, and the meaning nexus $(\alpha\ M\ \beta)$. They, too, we shall see when in due course encountering them, are determinates, have modes, and share the two pivotal features. Until then, the exposition will gain if we continue to ignore them. But let us right now drop 'existent (b)' and replace it by 'circumstance'. *A circumstance, then, is either a diad or an element nexus or a meaning nexus.* And, to repeat, *every circumstance has a mode. The latter is (sometimes) transparent and determined only by the identities of the terms rather than by their modes, if any.*

Some philosophers speak of *internal relations.* Let me use a paradigm to sketch what I consider the most viable explication of this classical notion. Suppose that α and β are *a* middle *c* and *a* middle *e*, respectively. The interval between them, or, perhaps, if the philosopher is a consistent nominalist, this instance of the interval, is said to be an internal relation. Negatively, I take it, this means that (5) 'being-a-third-higher-than' does not stand for anything, since, positively, what it signifies is grounded in the identities of α and β. Whether it also means, positively, that (6) 'α-being-by-a-third-higher-than-β' stands for an existent, which one might call an internal relation*ship,* since, α and β being there, it is eo ipso also there, I am not prepared to say. Probably it doesn't. Even so, the structural similarity between internal relationships and circumstances is unmistakable. Thus, since I value continuity with the tradition, I point it out, even though I, for one, find the use of 'relation' and its cognates for anything but non-unary universals rather confusing. Nor must one overlook the momentous differences. In my world, after all, (5) and (6) have long stood, and still stand, for a relational thing and a fact.

19* Since we are on the topic, how about "internal properties"? Some philosophers, I believe, think of the ultimate sorts as such properties. Thus, if there were full-fledged facts in their worlds, they would, or consistently should, think of, say, 'atomic fact' and 'conjunction' as internal properties. In this world, that is very different. The ultimate sorts, being existents, surely are not internal in the sense in which the classical internal relations are. 'Atomic fact', on the other hand, and the names of the other "syntactical properties," as so misleadingly they are often called, being definable, do not stand for anything. Thus one may think of them as signifying "internal properties." And, of course, as for the "defined syntactical properties," so for the "defined syntactical relations," such as, say, 'being the subject of a non-relational atomic fact'. (All this, though, is merely an anticipation.)

So far the formula I called provisional has not fared badly. Yet one couldn't say that we have completed the systematic ontologization of the new sort. So I propose to do three more things. First, I shall offer a series of five comments of various kinds. Next I shall probe the claim already made concerning the accessibility of the modes of diads. Third and last, I shall explore how things stand with respect to the minimal restriction which the terms of each circumstance must satisfy.

First. Facts and circumstances are the two sorts which have modes. That was mentioned before. Now, if I may so put it, it's official. The feature, shared by these two of the quartet of determinates and by nothing else, is no doubt very significant, if only because, as we already know, although perhaps not yet officially, it is also the restriction that goes with all connectives and with nothing else. So let us acknowledge the importance of this feature by introducing officially a new term. *A complex is either a fact or a circumstance.* A determinate, then, is either a complex or a thing or a class. (Things are, in the broader sense, simples. Classes, although not even in the broader sense simples, share yet with things the two features of having no modes and no constituents. Thus our way of speaking will not put too much of a strain on the idiomatic dichotomy 'complex-simple'.)

Second. (1) Many philosophers use 'identical', 'same', and their respective cognates synonymously. Since I never do, I put the first word on another job. For what Russell mistakes for sameness, I shall, the few times it will be mentioned, use 'RL-identity', for 'Russell-Leibniz identity', or in symbols, '$\underline{RL}$'. (2) In the relaxed schemata which we often use, (7') '$\alpha \neq \beta$' and (8') '$\alpha = \beta$' stand for 'α-being-diverse-from-β' and 'α-not-being-diverse-from-β', respectively. Yet '=' stands for nothing. In the ideal schema, therefore, where every nondiacritical expression stands for something, we write (7) '(α, β)' and (8) '$\sim(\alpha, \beta)$.' How, then, about the parentheses and the comma? Do they stand for anything? 'α' and 'β,' in the very relaxed notation of this passage, are of course but stand-ins for expressions which stand for existents. But if these latter are there, the diad is eo ipso there. The parentheses, therefore, are not expressions but merely diacritical marks directing our attention to the diad. Would juxtaposition do as well? To see why it doesn't, consider that $(\alpha, (\beta, \gamma))$ and $((\alpha, \beta), \gamma)$ are two and not one. The comma, finally, is an abbreviation for two diacritical pairs of parentheses, as in '((. . .) (. . .))', so that we are always sure where one expression ends and the other begins. That leaves two questions. How about the order of the expressions for the terms in that for the diad? Are the parentheses in '$\eta(f_1, a_1)$' what consistently they ought to be, viz., the diacritical marks of a diad? We shall not have to wait long for the answers. And, of course, as now for '=,' so later on for '∈' and 'M'.

Third. The ontology of sameness and diversity is so fundamental that we ought to take notice of the two key contributions to it, by Russell and the early Wittgenstein, among the recent ones. A more detailed examination of Russell's assay is best left to Appendix B, which provides the context required. One point, though, which is very familiar and can stand on its own, particularly if put linguistically, belongs here. Upon Russell's assay, unless 'α' and 'β' stand for things of the same ultimate sort (type), '$\alpha = \beta$' is ill formed. Yet arbitrariness, within the minimal restriction, is of the essence of diversity. Thus, even in a world of many-sorted things, let alone one like mine, in which there are also three other sorts of determinates, his assay must be inadequate. Nor does it help that his assay of sameness and diversity structurally implies his famous restriction of classes to elements which are all things and all of the same type. For, again, as already mentioned (p. 49), arbitrariness, within the minimal restriction, is of the essence of classes. The gist of *Wittgenstein's* contribution, or what I take it to be, I state, in order to avoid problems of exegesis, in my own words. Whenever one utters (an instance of) either '$\alpha = \alpha$' or '$\alpha \neq \beta$', language either has gone on holiday or, at best, clarifies itself. Just look, and, depending on whether there is one or two, use one mark or two. Exactly, I reply, so would everyone else when constructing an ideal language. I just acknowledged that by writing once '$\alpha = \alpha$', once '$\alpha \neq \beta$.' Yet, if one has to look first, there must be something to look at. For two reasons, both rather subtle, this was not seen. First, when proceeding as told, we *represent sameness and diversity by themselves.* They appear in the language in propria persona. Second, whenever we are (explicitly) presented with a diad, its mode is accessible to us, and in this sense, "shows itself." Of the errors associated with this use of 'showing itself', more later, in the last Section. The error, or, if you please, the danger associated with the first reason pierces the eye. For, is it not a first step toward replacing the world by language if one "concludes" from something appearing in propria persona in the latter that it doesn't there stand for anything in the former? If, on the other hand, Wittgenstein merely meant to assert that '=' by itself does not stand for anything, then, of course, I concur.

Fourth. Some philosophers, including I believe Quine, hold that something exists if and only if there is an "identity criterion" for it. In this world, all determinates and only determinates can support, i.e.,

be terms of, diads. Thus, since these philosophers do not grant ontological status to anything but to some sorts of determinates, there
is here, qualified by this fundamental disagreement, a measure of
agreement.

Fifth. Are diads, potential and actual, but one-classes and pairs,
thinly disguised? In this world, they are not. A diad has a mode, a
class does not. A class can only be a term of a circumstance. So, of
course, can a diad; but it also makes suitable material for the connectives. Granted that eventually you will show all that, a critic challenges
me at this point, do you not multiply entities beyond necessity? Every
ontologist is subject to the discipline of Occam's razor. This time I
plead in his court: no more guilty than others. Even in the "universes"
of the axiomatic set theorists, which are the most jejune ontologies I
know of, so jejune indeed that I hesitate to call them "worlds," there
are the corresponding ontologizations, or, as they would rather call it,
"postulations." For one, to "postulate," in addition to α, the diad (α, α)
is neither more nor less gratuitous, or, if you prefer putting it negatively, neither less nor more commonsensical, than to "postulate," in
addition to each determinate, the class of which it is the only element. Yet the only one among these thinkers who avoids that postulation is Quine, although only at the price, which leaves me utterly
confounded, of "identifying" in these cases the "internal relations" of
elementhood and nondiversity. (The reason I am confounded is that,
no matter how ingenious it may be mathematically, ontologically this
use of 'identification' is to me obscure.) For another, the set theorist
must, as Quine does, at a minimum "postulate" pairs. Correspondingly, though not of course identically, I "postulate" the diads. I need
not, however, and I do not, as we shall see, postulate the null class,
which, by the way, is anything but commonsensical.

That much for the first step in the systematic ontologization of the
new sort. Let us take the next. A diad was to be "sometimes" transparent. That is not good enough. What can be said, more accurately,
about the accessibility of the mode of a diad?

The only presentations of modes we have so far encountered are of
tautologies and, as I shall not always add, contradictions. These have
negations. So do diads. Structurally, therefore, one is led to expect
that tautologies and diads share the feature we called the Unthinkability of the Negation. More strongly, even, being presented with the
mode of a complex, be it fact or circumstance, on the one hand, and
while being presented with it, being unable to think its negation except with the opposite mode, ought to be equivalent. Take, then, the
diad whose terms are a shade of green and a shade of red. If its mode

is accessible at all, it is, whenever the diad is presented, immediately available. That we may safely take for granted. Thus we are in this case ready for the question. Can one, while (explicitly) presented with these shades being diverse, think that they are the same without being presented with the potentiality of that circumstance? My answer is No; my appeal, to the given. Directly that is the end of the road. Indirectly, and therefore properly, one can, and I shall, again support the appeal; first by meeting what seems to be a phenomenological challenge; then by considering the cases in which the mode is not immediately available.

The challenger invites us to consider two shades, not of two colors but of one, which are so close that even if one strains and peers, one cannot be sure whether they are one or two. Then he asks me whether I am familiar with what the psychologists call threshold phenomena. I answer, or, rather, start my answer as follows. In every single act of the series of acts, which is this straining and peering with often uncertain issue, one is indeed transparently presented with a diad of shades either actual or potential. These diads, however, vary from act to act, and they may all be diverse from the one which is "really" there. The challenger, quite properly, inquires into this use of 'real'. But he accepts, as I hope you will, my referring him to Appendix C.

If two complexes are sufficiently complicated, the mode of their diad is not immediately available. With an innocuous metaphor, no one can see it at a glance, even if his "criteria of sameness and difference" are as strict, or narrow, as mine; i.e., so narrow that complexes which are "merely" analytically equivalent are a Two; $f_1(a_1)$ & $f_2(a_2)$, for instance, upon these criteria not being the same as anything but $f_1(a_1)$ & $f_2(a_2)$ and, in particular, diverse from $\sim(\sim f_1(a_1) \vee \sim f_2(a_2))$. Yet, even in these complicated cases, the mode is not only accessible in principle but can be reached, like that of a sentential tautology, recursively, as one says, or decidably, in a finite number of steps, each involving a single criterion. The complication, such as it is, consists merely in these steps being too many to be comprehended at a single glance. The criteria themselves, except for the quantifiers, of which more in Section IV, all seem so "trivial" that the ontological gap which cannot be filled without granting them some ontological status has been overlooked. E.g., no diad is the same as a conjunction, or a negation, or any determinate of any other "kind." Again, the diads (α, β) and (γ, δ) are the same if and only if either $\alpha = \gamma$ and $\beta = \delta$ or $\alpha = \delta$ and $\beta = \gamma$. Again, as for (α, β), so for $(\alpha \vee \beta)$; and so on. The two features securing the decidability are, first, that each complex is produced in a finite number of steps from a finite ultimate base; and, second, the number of "kinds" of steps is finite and in fact rather small; one for each of the various connectives and quantifiers; three others to arrive at each of the three sorts of circumstances from their terms; and one more, from a selector to its class. Thus the claim already entered can be clarified and strengthened. *The mode of a diad is either immediately available or recursively accessible.* Lest you be puzzled, I hurry to add that if the terms are both classes, this holds only for those which, roughly speaking, the intuitionists admit. That, though, will do; all other classes have a very peculiar and merely derivative ontological status all their own. For they are, or so at least I shall argue, merely the denizens of what will be called an axiomatic extension. These matters, though, must, and safely may, wait until Section VI. Let us now take a quick glance at a pont where a bit of mutual support of the several features in the pattern is about to emerge.

(1) The mode of a diad is either immediately available or recursively accessible. Also, the mode of a diad is determined only by the identities of its terms but not by their modes, if any. (As for diads, so for all circumstances.) (2) The mode of an atomic fact is in principle inaccessible; it is also the product of a maker. But the mode of a (first-level, sentential) tautology is either immediately available or, as everyone knows, recursively accessible. Such a tautology is of course also the product of a maker. Yet its mode is not, on the familiar combinatorial grounds, determined by the modes of the atomic facts out of which it is made. If you compare (1) and (2), you will see the concurrence.

20* A tautology, as the term is used in this discourse, ontologically and also more broadly than usual, is not just a first-level sentential one but any complex that is, upon the new explication of the notion still to be proposed, analytic. Yet the generalization holds. The mode of an analytic complex is at least in principle, though of course not always recursively, accessible; and it does either not at all, or, if I may borrow Quine's phrase for an ontological use, only vacuously depend on the modes of its constituents.

We are ready for the third and last step in the ontologization of the new sort. Diads are supposed to be circumstances; a term of a circumstance, by the minimal restriction, must be a determinate. How, then, in this respect, about the terms of diads? That is the question we must explore. It will be best if I first baldly state my case; proceed to turn away an obvious phenomenological objection; and only then attend to the dialectic of the matter, which, as we shall see, is double-pronged.

The terms of a diad must indeed be determinates. Or, equivalently, there is no diad, either actual or potential, to support ontologically the "sameness" or "diversity," as the case may be, of one or two nondeterminates, or, for that matter, of one determinate and one nondeterminate. Hence, by the Principle of Presentation, we cannot *literally* think or intend what we could think if these diads were there to be intended. This is the stand I take. The objection is obvious indeed.

I "know," an objector very reasonably tells me, such things as particularity-being-diverse-from-exemplification, negation-being-diverse-from-black, and so on; or, to speak as you do, I am transparently presented with them. Quite so, I reply, yet I have a way out; the cue to it, as you probably guessed, is the word italicized. We cannot "literally" think, etc. The predicament is (structurally) the same as the one in which I found myself twice before; once when there was talk about perceiving a horse; once when the two unthinkabilities of the Diverse and the Negated Ultimate Sort were introduced. Prima facie the objector was right then, just as he is right now. My only way out is to argue that, upon the new, more detailed assay of conscious states, our "perceiving" horses, in the first case, and "believing," to all appearances with evidence, such things as, in the second case, green-not-being-a-relation, or, as now, particularity-being-diverse-from-exemplification, is compatible with there not being in this world anything either 'horse' or 'green-not-being-a-relation' or 'particularity-being-diverse-from-exemplification' could stand for and which, therefore, we could either perceive$_1$ or believe$_1$. But again, as before, if I tried to make this argument now, the exposition would bog down. Thus I merely renew the promise, which I then made, that you will find this argument in Section V, where it belongs. Having read on, you must have accepted this promise the first time. Thus, hoping that my credit is not yet exhausted, I turn to the dialectic. First, though, for a word.

The nondeterminates are either items or ultimate sorts or modes or makers; the latter being the only existents among them which are not "merely" entities. Yet it will pay if for once we sunder this grouping and oppose the items, which are the only individuators of this world, to the three *forms* (makers, ultimate sorts, and modes), which share with each other (and with the things that are universals) the one-many feature. 'Form' has been used in so many ways in the tradition that one more use, clearly specified in a special context, should not add to the confusion. A form, then, in this sense, is a nondeterminate that has the one-many feature.

On the one hand, all nondeterminates are so "weak" that they are not "separable" from what they combine with, as they would have to be in order to support a diad. This is one prong of the dialectic. On the other hand, they are so "strong" that, being "unique," their being diverse from every other existent needs no ontological support; the three forms because they are so "luminous," the items because their very nature is to be individuators. That is the other prong. 'Separable' and 'unique' will be unpacked on this occasion, a job long overdue. 'Weak' and 'strong' are merely the rhetoric of the moment. The luminosity metaphor, for what it is worth, together with its twin, opacity, will be located within the literal.

An existent, then, we may henceforth suppose, on the strength of the Principle of Presentation and of the argument promised for Section V, is a term of diads if and only if it is a determinate. (As for diads, so for the other two sorts of circumstances, as we shall see in due course.) Significant progress has thus been made toward establishing, rather than merely asserting, the importance of distinguishing between determinates and nondeterminates. Thus encouraged, let us take time out for still another purely ontological distinction that contributes to making this division between the two quartets the major bifurcation.

Facts and circumstances are of many, many subsorts. But they are all terms of circumstances as well as elements of classes; they all have modes; and the connectives as well as the quantifiers, i.e., all makers except the exemplifications, make further facts out of them. The connection between things and the exemplifications is especially close. The latter are among all the makers the only ones that combine the former into what we call atomic facts. Classes, finally, are not materials for any makers. Yet, like things, they are elements of classes and terms of circumstances; just as, like things, they have no modes. These are the main similarities and differences among the four sorts of determinates. Two have modes; two don't; and they differ in the makers whose materials they are. The feature they share is the variety of complexes into which they enter as well as the variety of ways of entering. The feature is worth a label. Determinates, I shall henceforth say, are *separable*. The three sorts of entities do not have so wide a range of association. Each item combines with one and only one ultimate sort. An ultimate sort combines only with items. The modes combine, rather widely, with both facts and circumstances. Yet, decisively, no entity requires a maker to combine with whatever it combines with; just as neither of the two sorts of Two-in-Ones into which they combine, either the Aristotelian-Thomistic composites we call things or the moded complexes, has itself a mode. Henceforth I shall refer to these features by calling all entities *totally inseparable*. The makers fall in between. A maker or tie, to be sure, needs no tie to tie it to what it ties. That is indeed their very essence. Yet it ties only determinates into others. Nor does it pervade what it ties but rather attaches itself to it from without. Also, decisively, what a maker makes has a mode. Henceforth I shall refer to these features, which are also the main reason for distinguishing the makers from the entities, by saying that a maker, while neither separable nor totally inseparable, is yet *inseparable*. (The attaching metaphor, in view of what has already been said about mak*ing* and of what will be said at the end of this Section, will do no harm.)

There are thus three "degrees" of separability. *An existent is either separable, or inseparable, or totally inseparable.* Determinates are separable; makers, inseparable; entities, totally inseparable. The bifurcation runs between what is separable on the one hand and what is either inseparable or totally inseparable on the other.

20 * As the two words are used in this discourse, independence, unlike separability, is an anthropocentric notion. Yet it, too, admits of a tripartition which correlates not uninterestingly with that of separability. Nondeterminates obviously cannot be intended explicitly. Facts and circumstances, equally obviously, can be so intended under several species. (The special position of direct awareness, of which more in Section V, is here beside the point.) Things, on the other hand, cannot be intended explicitly unless with the species of grasping. For classes, as already mentioned (p. 76), there is a certain qualification. Thus, if you please, *nondeterminates are dependent; things and classes, independent; complexes, totally independent.* This time, the bifurcation runs between what is either totally independent or independent on the one hand and what is dependent on the other. No doubt, the pattern is jelling.

That much for one prong of the dialectic. The nondeterminates are too weak to support diads. Turn to the other prong. They are so strong that, being unique, their being diverse from everything else needs no other ground but themselves. 'Unique', so used, is merely a label for the feature. *An existent is unique if and only if it is not a term of diads.* To be unique in this sense and not to satisfy the minimal restriction are thus equivalent. That takes care of the word. How about the thing? Why should all nondeterminates be "unique?" I offer four comments, the first three about the forms, the last about the items.

21 * Not surprisingly, to be sure, even though here beside the point, what is not a term of a diad is not a term of any circumstance, and conversely. For another use of 'unique', see Section IV.

First. A mode, whenever presented, stands out. So do the makers and the ultimate sorts implicit in whatever is explicitly presented, either with or, as is most often the case, without its mode. They stand out, for instance, in an atomic fact, say, α_1, whose mode is never presented; also because α_1 having the structural feature of being-an-atomic-fact becomes readily transparent and because its having this feature depends on the ultimate sorts and the maker but not on the items implicitly presented with α_1. What thus stands out I call *luminous*. For a mode, if presented, transparency and luminosity are one. Makers and ultimate sorts, whenever presented, always implicitly, of course, are luminous.

22* What I just called a structural feature is often called a form or, even, a formal property. Don't let these different uses of 'form' confuse you. While the entities exist, although, as already mentioned, there are in the ideal schema no expressions for them, such phrases as 'atomic fact' are merely abbreviations which stand for nothing.

Second. If two forms were one, the world would be so radically different that we couldn't think it. Conversely, worlds with the "same" forms as ours are the only ones which, if they existed and we existed in them, we could think. That adds to the flavor of "uniqueness." To connect it with the familiar, consider a schema with expressions for the "same" ultimate sorts and exemplifications as those of our world but such that, if its expressions stood for the existents of a world, the latter would, as one says, be three-valued. Notice, first, that with an ontology like mine, there would be three modes in that world. Consider next what I take to be obvious, viz., that we could, if it existed and we existed in it, think the atomic facts of that world but neither its modes nor its molecular facts. (Such schemata or calculi may nevertheless be of some use, not only as one would expect in mathematical logic but also, as at this very point, occasionally and by indirection in ontology.)

Third. We can think what such expressions as '$(\exists x) \ldots$' and '$(\exists f) \ldots$' stand for. This is not to say that, when intending them, we intend, in case the complexes they stand for are actual, any of the things by virtue of which the complexes are actual. On that I insisted before, when deploring Russell's misleading phrase 'knowledge by description'. Say, then, for the moment, that on these occasions we think *about* those things. One can think about things; but *one cannot think about either forms or items.* For there is *of course* no quantification over nondeterminates. This 'of course', which comes so naturally, even in a world like mine, in which, we shall see, there is quantification not only over things and classes but also, most unorthodoxly, under certain circumstances over complexes, adds another flavor to the "uniqueness."

Fourth. The only jobs of items is individuation. They are, with an exuberant metaphor, nothing but the anchors, or the incarnation, of Oneness and Twoness in matter. That makes nonsense—in the strong sense in which the nonsensical is unthinkable and not just unimaginable like, say, green being a pitch—out of the claim that two items being one or one being two is thinkable. As for any two items, so a fortiori for an item and anything else. But let us listen to a critic. You distinguish, he tells me, between (9) green-being-the-same-as-louder-than, on the one hand, and what (10) 'universality$^{(0)}$-being-the-same-as-universality$^{(0,0)}$' purports to stand for and (11) the "sameness of the two items in the case" on the other; holding that the latter two, not being there, cannot be thought at all, while, on the other hand, (9), though it can of course not be imagined, can yet be thought, if only with the immediately available mode of potentiality. If one considers that the two things are in the familiar way composites of the four entities, one may well wonder whether that is not one distinction too many. I reply as follows. The distinction is subtle indeed. Yet, as it seems you appreciate, I must insist on it. Phenomenologically, I can always fall back on the argument, to be presented in Section V, which (I promised) in some cases accounts for the evidence, to all appearances, of what isn't even there. Ontologically, though, I shall try to do a bit better, at least indirectly, by placing this distinction into the tradition. An important strand of the latter is not inaptly summarized by a formula: Form is intelligible, matter is not. 'Form' in the tradition means several things. In this discourse at this point it may mean at least two, either what has just been called a form or what has just been called a structural feature. 'Form', therefore, I do not tamper with. Matter, in this discourse, is items and nothing else. So I replace 'intelligible' and its negation by 'luminous' and its opposite, 'opaque'; then rewrite the formula; *forms are luminous; items are opaque.* How, then, about the "opacity" of items? An item, beyond grounding a One or This, is merely an I-know-not-what. All items, including those of universals, are bare (Appendix A). The step, if any, from a bare I-know-not-what to something opaque is small indeed. In a thing, on the other hand, which, although not a complex, is yet a composite of a form and item, both sensu stricto simple, the luminosity of the former is dimmed by the opacity of the latter. That is why (9) can at least be thought, while (10) and (11) cannot. The former because of the luminosity of the two forms, the latter because two items, unless diverse from each other, are nothing at all.

Order, upon the assay about to be proposed, is grounded in diads. In a world of both things and facts this is the only way of grounding it.

More cautiously, I can think of no other. But, then, as far as I know, for such a world, in which there are not only things and classes but also facts, the need for grounding order has not even been seen. Or so I claim. The claim is blunt and bold. If it can be made good, the dialectical support which the two assays, of diversity and of order, lend each other is impressive indeed. For, on the one hand, if there were no diads, there wouldn't be anything to ground order in; on the other, since there are diads, the gap which has not been seen can finally be filled.

After a fashion, although as will transpire after a fashion only, the axiomatic set theorists in their universes, which are either single-sorted "worlds" of classes only or two-sorted ones, in the style of Zermelo, of things (*Urelemente*) and classes, have grounded order. The first who did it, more than fifty years ago, were Wiener and Kuratowski. With Bernays, in the thirties, the mathematical machinery they had invented became common property of all mathematicians. This machinery I take over. The only change I propose is ontological. This, you will see on reflection, is as it ought to be. Just as we cannot and need not either do, or redo, or add to what only the mathematicians can do, so we must not expect them to do the ontologist's job. Since this particular bit of machinery is very simple and very familiar, I shall first, without any machinery, make two general comments, of the sort which is the ontologist's business, and then, in a third comment, with a bare minimum of Russell's machinery, indicate why I didn't credit him with having filled the gap.

First. The mathematicians ground order in classes. They, of course, don't use 'ground'; but that does not bother. More specifically, they ground order in pair classes, or, briefly, pairs, i.e., in classes with two elements. I replace classes by diads. That is the only change. Pairs versus diads; unless the difference is ontologically as momentous as I claim, I am making a mountain out of a molehill. What then is it, mountain or molehill? In a world of classes only, or of classes and things but without facts, in which, however miraculously, from where I stand, classes do have an ontological ground, the difference makes indeed no difference. In a world of facts, however, order appears at two places long *before* classes do. The *first* time it appears in relational atomic facts, such as this-being-later-than-that, this-being-between-that-and-that-other, and so on, which are in the conventional notation expressed by '$r_1^2(a_1, a_2)$', '$r_1^3(a_1, a_2, a_3)$', and so on. For the *second* time it appears in such molecular facts as $\alpha_1 \supset \alpha_2$. As you read on, though, you will see that while my case is strengthened by this second appearance, it yet does not depend on it. Since the ontological status of atomic facts is less controversial than that of all others, this seems worth calling attention to.

"Before," "first," "second"; what is the import of these temporal metaphors? In a world of things and atomic facts but without connectives and quantifiers, there would not be the order which makes the difference between $\alpha_1 \supset \alpha_2$ and $\alpha_2 \supset \alpha_1$. Yet there would be the difference, grounded in order and nothing else, between $r_1^2(a_1, a_2)$ and $r_1^2(\alpha_2, \alpha_1)$; there would be the several canons, corresponding to (and as we shall see grounded in) the several exemplifications; these canons, like all canons, would require supplementation by criteria of sameness and difference; and the latter in turn would have to be grounded in diads, or, if there isn't even negation, in samenesses and diversities. Thus, even in this rudimentary world, there would have to be the diads which suffice to ground the order in its relational facts. Classes, on the other hand, we shall see, may be added to a world otherwise like ours but without classes. More succinctly, our world is so "layered" that after its things diads come first, classes come last. This is the reason, structural, if you please, or even "stylistic," if you insist, why the order in relational atomic facts cannot be adequately grounded in classes. The mutually corroborating dialectical support will have to wait for the assay of classes in Section VI. The idea, I trust, is clear and simple. The reason, one may plausibly speculate, why this gap has so far not been noticed, or at least a reason or a cause, is that there are few ontologies, if any, with full-fledged facts.

Second. Looking at the expressions '$r_1^2(a_1, a_2)$' and '$r_1^2(a_2, a_1)$', one is struck by a feature order shares with diversity. The two existents for which the two expressions stand differ in the order of the two things a_1 and a_2, and in nothing else. Once a_1 is the latter, or the louder, or the brighter of the two; once a_2 is. As for the existents, so for the expressions. They differ in the (linear) order of the two expressions which stand for the two things and in nothing else. Once 'a_1' precedes 'a_2'; once the latter precedes the former. *In natural languages as well as in artificial schemata, order, like sameness and diversity, sometimes appears in propria persona.* If firmly grasped, this communality helps, dialectically as well as by shedding light on the tradition. The pivotal role of, and the uniquely close connection between, the assays of diversity and of order is one of the few novel ideas in this discourse. The communality lends dialectical support to this idea. The common feature, one may plausibly speculate, is the reason, or at least a reason or a cause, why neither diversity nor order has as yet been properly grounded. Thus the communality helps us to understand the tradition.

One cannot firmly grasp what he does not understand accurately.

Why, then, in the formula above the qualification, "sometimes"? With the conspicuous exception of the generalities, of which more in the next Section, there is, in the ideal schema which I shall eventually propose, for each existent only one expression, if any. Nor, accordingly, are there descriptions. In this schema sameness, properly ontologized, is not only represented by such expressions as, say, '(α_1, α_1)'; it also always appears, with the above-mentioned exception, in propria persona, as in this very expression. In natural languages, however, and in the conventional schemata which are indispensable to the mathematicians and sometimes also aid the ontologist, there are, indispensably because of the limitations of our minds, definite descriptions and, therefore, also such expressions as 'Peter is (the same as) the son of John', which latter requires the qualification in the case of sameness and diversity. Order appears in natural languages both in propria persona and by means of the passive voice, not to mention such auxiliaries as 'the latter', 'the former', and the numerals. The qualification calls attention to the blur due to this redundancy. In the conventional schemata, which have no passive voice, order always appears in propria persona, not only in the case of the connectives but also whenever, as one says, there is in the schema a primitive (undefined) relational predicate sign purporting to stand for a (binary) relation which is not symmetrical. As far as the connectives are concerned, it might be held, that is irrelevant, since they can all be "defined" in terms of a single symmetrical one. From where I stand, as you have long sensed and as in the next Section I shall argue, this "linguistic" play is without ontological merit. In the case of the relations, there is not even a prima facie defense. Yet, as the mathematicians "axiomatize" it, '$\in$', which appears in the conventional notations for what in my world is the circumstance of elementhood, stands for just such a relation. Its asymmetry, i.e., to put it our way, $\alpha \in \beta$ and $\beta \in \alpha$ never being both actual, is "secured" by "axioms." Its nonsymmetry, however, or, rather, the nonsymmetry of what it stands for, has no other ground but the notation itself. Or, with a twist, the mathematicians' way of "grounding" order in their "universes" presupposes order on a "deeper" level. That is why I said that they ground order "only after a fashion." Or, if you please, they ground it "relatively." We, having undertaken to ground it "absolutely," shall build the nonsymmetry of elementhood and of the meaning nexus, which are the two sorts of circumstances not themselves diads, on diads. Accordingly, in the ideal schema, each expression for one of these two sorts of circumstances will contain an expression for a diad.

The one "linguistic" point which remains is that, as we shall see, we can get rid of the linear order in, say '(α_1, β_1)', which if I am right "ought" to be an excess feature of the ideal notation, provided only we are prepared to abandon the conventional linearity of our script. That, too, is dialectical support.

Third. In *Principia Mathematica* order is "introduced"—one cannot be sure whether only among classes or also into atomic facts—by means of such expressions as '$[\hat{x}\hat{y}((x = a_1)$ & $(y = a_2))](u, v)$', called ordered pairs, which are taken to be predicate expressions in the same sense in which in this work '$r_1^2(u, v)$' is such an expression. The gist is that, by notational arrangement, the sentential expression resulting from substituting 'a_1' and 'a_2' for 'u' and 'v', respectively, is analytic, while that resulting from substituting them for 'v' and 'u', respectively, is contradictory. Specifically, this is so because 'x' and 'u' precede 'y' and 'v' in the prefix, '$\hat{x}\hat{y}$', and in the suffix, '(u, v)', respectively. If you change the order in either, but not in both, you pick the other ordered pair. Thus the order in the existents Russell called relations *in extenso* rests on the order of marks on paper and on nothing else. The only gain, if that be the word, is that the gap is papered over by an unnecessarily complicated notation. That is why I didn't credit Russell with a contribution to the ontology of order. Wiener and Kuratowski sensed that and thus were led to their "relative" ontologization. (This, to be sure, is not the only thing that is wrong with Russell's ordered pairs. But it belongs here and can stand by itself. The rest you will find in Appendix B.)

Now, most concisely, for the machinery. The mathematicians take the two classes for which (9) '$\{\alpha_1, \{\alpha_1, \alpha_2\}\}$' and (10) '$\{\alpha_2, \{\alpha_1, \alpha_2\}\}$' stand; abbreviate these expressions by (11) '$\langle\alpha_1, \alpha_2\rangle$' and (12) '$\langle\alpha_2, \alpha_1\rangle$', respectively; then show that $\langle\alpha_1, \alpha_2\rangle$ and $\langle\alpha_2, \alpha_1\rangle$ have all the features they might want to call "formal," of the two "ordered pairs" based on α_1 and α_2, such as, say, $\langle\alpha_1, \alpha_2\rangle = \langle\alpha_2, \alpha_1\rangle \equiv . \alpha_1 = \alpha_2$. Finally, by an easy iteration, they introduce ordered triples and, generally, *n-tuples,* e.g., $\langle\alpha_1, \alpha_2, \alpha_3\rangle$ and $\langle\alpha_1, \alpha_2, \ldots, \alpha_n\rangle$. "Formally" that does the trick. We, as announced, replace the pairs by diads; call the resulting determinates, which are not "ordered pairs," *2-tuples;* write accordingly (9') '$(\alpha_1, (\alpha_1, \alpha_2))$' and (10') '$(\alpha_2, (\alpha_1, \alpha_2))$', again abbreviated by (11) and (12), for the two 3-tuples based on α_1 and α_2; and start the iteration from there. "Formally," with the help of the sameness criteria, that again does the trick. In ontology, though, there are no tricks. Nor is this use of 'formal' unproblematic. So we shall have to face an obvious double question. Is, say, $\langle\alpha_1, \alpha_2\rangle$ "literally" an order; and, whether or not it is, how does it manage to ground the order in, say, $r_1^2(a_1, a_2)$? It will help if, before answering, we prepare the ground, taking our cue from another question, concerning a possible fragment of the ideal schema, which arose earlier but was left unanswered.

22* As you see, I use the old abbreviations, '$\langle \alpha_1, \alpha_2 \rangle$', and so on, for the new existents. When it comes to words, though, while 'tuple' is kept, 'pair' and 'ordered pair' are scrupulously avoided; for these two neither could nor, I think, should be taken off their present jobs. Practically, it will almost always be easy to avoid the clumsy '2-tuple' by simply writing the symbols with the corners. Which of the two, $\langle \alpha_1, \alpha_2 \rangle$ and $\langle \alpha_2, \alpha_1 \rangle$, we "associate" with the order in which, as we say, α_1 comes first, is a matter of convention, and, as far as the iteration is concerned, of convenience.

At one point we presumably anticipated the ideal schema by writing (13) '$\eta(f_1, a_1)$' for what is conventionally expressed by '$f_1(a_1)$'. At a later point we wrote, with the same anticipation, (14) '(f_1, a_1)' for the diad whose terms are f_1 and a_1. In the ideal schema the same expression stands in all contexts for the same entity. Hence the question that was left unanswered: Does '(f_1, a_1)' also stand for the diad in (13)? The answer, for which we are now ready, is Yes. If you want to arrive at it, "look" at the fact no longer as the product which a binary maker, suggestively called a tie, makes out of the two determinates f_1 and a_1, but, rather, as what a monadic maker makes out of a single determinate which is the diad whose terms are f_1 and a_1. Moreover, if you keep "looking" this way, $r_1^2(a_1, a_2)$, $r_1^3(a_1, a_2, a_3)$, $\alpha_1 \supset \alpha_2, \alpha_2 \supset \alpha_1$, and so on, "become," respectively, $\eta(r_1^2, \langle \alpha_1, \alpha_2 \rangle)$, $\eta(r_1^3, \langle \alpha_1, \alpha_2, \alpha_3 \rangle)$, $\supset \langle \alpha_1, \alpha_2 \rangle, \supset \langle \alpha_2, \alpha_1 \rangle$, and so on. Whether or not the exemplifications involved are one or several is irrelevant for the business in hand. So ignore the issue. We have, it seems, ontologized order in all atomic and molecular facts; which, *if it can be consolidated,* is a big gain.

"Looking at something as something else," or, even more blatantly, so that it "becomes" something else, is in ontology as nasty a trick as any. At best, it is a metaphor. Thus we are back where we started. Is, say, $\langle \alpha_1, \alpha_2 \rangle$ "literally" an order; and, whether or not it is, how does it manage to ground the order in, say, α_1-being-later-than-α_2? As a moment's reflection will show you, to answer this double question and to come clean on the "looking" trick are one and the same. So far we have merely focused the issue.

Order undoubtedly must be grounded. As presented to us, most fundamentally in relational atomic facts, it is neither a thing nor a fact but something about (at least) two things involved in a fact, as a_1 and a_2 are involved in a_1-being-later-than-a_2. Nor is it a single nondeterminate, either maker or ultimate sort. All this, too, is beyond doubt. Hence, unless it be a category all its own, which does not even make sense to me, order can only be a circumstance. Thus our hand is forced. I yield and ground order in tuples. If you accept this "standardization," you cannot but also accept the two others, of all connectives and exemplifications as monadic and of the materials of all of them, except negation, as diads. (The exception is necessary, not because negation works on things, which we know it doesn't, but because facts and two of the three sorts of circumstances, on all of which it does work, are not diads. This in turn fits well with the special position of negation due to its intimate connection with the modes.) Ontologically all this is quite smooth. Phenomenologically, there seems to be a problem. As presented, order has neither the "looks" nor the "feel" of the determinate which presumably grounds it. One who foolishly denies that asks for trouble. I would rather insist on it myself; come clean by offering three nonphenomenological "justifications," one negative, two positive, of the "standardization" proposed; and thus consolidate the important gain.

When explicitly presented with the binary relational facts, we are implicitly presented with five existents; e.g., the three things, a_1, a_2, and r_1^2; a maker presumably ternary yet, as we are now keenly aware, wholly innocent of order; and the "order" itself, still to be properly ontologized. In the standardization there are again, in addition to the fact, five existents; the same three things, a monadic maker, and one of the 2-tuples based on the two particulars among the things. Thing for thing; maker for maker; order for "order", i.e., more explicitly, for the "order" presented and still to be properly ontologized, one of the 2-tuples based on the two things "ordered." In an obvious sense, though not literally, of course, nothing has been added, nothing has been suppressed. Literally, there is no change except the minimal one made necessary by the only available way of grounding order. Call this the negative justification.

Sometimes we are presented with 2-tuples, 3-tuples, and so on. How far we can ascend this ladder does not matter for the business in hand. Nor does the difference, which therefore I ignore, between intending something or thinking it literally, on the one hand, and being aware of it, on the other. The point is, rather, that although, phenomenologically speaking, we are not, when presented with the fact, also presented with the diad or diads which the standardization "puts into it," we are yet sometimes presented with diads; even, if we make the effort, with these very diads. In this crucial sense, *the standardization is not speculative.* This is a positive justification. (A tuple, if the reminder be needed, is a sort of diad.)

The mode of an atomic fact is in principle not accessible to us. Such a fact, therefore, is never transparent. Yet the order in it, if presented at all, is "transparent"; i.e., it has the phenomenological feature which, in the case of, say, $f_1(a_1) \lor \sim f_1(a_1)$, we accounted for by the presented actuality of the tautology. You recognize immediately the new phenomenological claim. Should you believe that this claim for a new case (not: sort!) of "transparence" needs support, just ask yourself whether you can think that Mary-loving-Peter and Peter-loving-Mary are one and not two. If, as I do, you eventually find the claim as compelling as any, then you ought to know how to account for the feature. The standardization, rather remarkably, shows us how to do that in three easy steps. (1) The mode of a diad, we saw, is either immediately available or recursively accessible. (2) A tuple is a diad whose one term is a determinate, while the other is a diad of which this very determinate is a term. Hence, by one of the sameness criteria, whose modes (we shall see) are themselves (at least) recursively available, we are either immediately or recursively presented with the actuality of all tuples which are presented to us. (3) Hence we may reasonably account for the "transparence" of the order in the non-transparently presented fact by the actuality of the diad which the standardization "puts into it."

23* 'Standardization' stands here for a methodological notion, or, as one says, more solemnly, for a metaphilosophical one. That is why I avoided 'argument', using 'justification' instead. But we not only *standardize;* we already did, and shall soon again, *extrapolate* and refuse to *speculate;* eventually we shall even *extend* our ontology, adding what will be called a frontal and a vertical extension. All these are methodological notions. Nor, at first sight, are they wholly unrelated. What, then, are the similarities and the differences among them? Since they all are methodological notions, there is no rush. We can only gain by postponing the answer till close to the very end. Yet I thought attention ought to be called to the question.

As far as relational atomic facts are concerned, one more gain ought to be registered. The standardization removes an irritation that has chafed me for decades. Some philosophers construct the calculus, which they hope to make their ideal schema, as the logicians construct theirs, syntactically; or they borrow one from the logicians; the difference makes no difference. Next they take an expression in it, of the kind the logicians call primitive or undefined predicate constants, and make it stand for a relational character, say 'lt' for later-than. Then they proceed to define its "converse," '$\breve{lt}$', by writing '$\breve{lt}(x, y)$' for '$lt(y, x)$', and make '$\breve{lt}$' stand for earlier-than. Why, someone is bound to ask, go this way and not the other way, starting from a primitive '*ear*', define '*eăr*', and make the former and the latter stand for earlier-than and later-than, respectively. For their purposes, the logicians will tell him, correctly, the difference makes no difference. In ontology there is a complication. The philosophers I have in mind all hold, either explicitly or implicitly, that a primitive predicate sign of the ideal schema stands for an existent. For defined predicate signs, however, there are three alternatives. (a) One may hold that every predicate sign, whether defined or undefined, stands for an existent, and that all these existents have the same ontological status. The only reasons that have ever been given for this alternative are bad reasons. Of that more in Appendix B. (b) One may hold, as unhappily I did for a long time, that both simple and "derived" characters, represented by the undefined and the defined predicate signs of the ideal schema, respectively, exist, but that the ontological status of the former is higher than that of the latter. (c) One may hold, as I now do, that while in ideal languages there are no defined expressions, those which occur in other schemata do not literally stand for anything. Only the left sides of (the substitution instances of) their definitions as a whole stand, by a special stipulation about words and about nothing else, for what the right sides stand for. In case (c), depending on which way you go, either later-than exists and earlier-than doesn't, or conversely. In case (b), again depending on which way you go, the ontological status of either the one or the other will be higher. Which way, then, should one go? Either choice seems utterly arbitrary. That spots the irritation which has long chafed me. What, then, you will ask, do I propose to do about the "converse." In my new world, I answer, where all characters are simple, there is for each relational character (not: for each relational predicate sign!) exactly one other such that, first, (15) $(r)(\exists s)(x)(y)[r(xy) \equiv s(yx)]$ & U with 'U' abbreviating the uniqueness clause; and, second, the actuality of (15) and of all its instances is immediately available to us. Notice, first, that I have doubled the number of (binary) relational characters. Where others have one, I have a pair. Notice, second, that I did not mention either words or definitions. You may of course continue to call each member of such a pair the converse of the other. This, though, is merely a convenient locution. The irritation has been removed. Three comments will add perspective.

First. Is (15) really transparent? Clearly, this is still another phenomenological claim. Equally clearly to, it speaks for itself. Dialectically and in anticipation, as we shall explicate the notion of analyticity in Section V, (15) will turn out to be analytic. Yet it is not analytic in the narrower, classical sense. For in ontology "substitution" is the replacement, not of an expression by an expression, but of an existent by an existent. Thus a "derived character," being literally nothing, cannot be the "guaranteed substitution instance" that would make (15) analytic. *Second*, not surprisingly and, to some perhaps, reassuringly, (15) corresponds to the axiom B6 in Goedel's celebrated axiomatization of set theory. B7 and B8 provide for the n-ary relations with $n > 2$. *Third.* Are a-being-the-same-as-b and a-not-being-diverse-from-b two or one? We decided to count them as one (p. 104). Are a-being-earlier-than-b and b-being-later-than-a one or two? I just insisted that they are two. If they are two, then, in either case, the two are analytically equivalent. That is a similarity. In the first case, there are one or two circumstances, with 'same' and 'diverse' upon either choice standing for nothing. In the second case there are, upon either choice, two facts, and, depending on the choice, either one or two universals. That is a difference.

I take it, then, that the standardization has been justified. If so, order in atomic and molecular facts has been properly ontologized. The gain is great. Yet there is more in the offing. The two basic ideas were the diads and the tuples. Making use of them, one can also properly ontologize the quantifiers, which are monadic to begin with. Thus the road is free. We could next systematically examine the connectives and the ontological issues they raise, proceed to ontologize the quantifiers and do the same systematic job for them. But we have reached a plateau; so we had better first look about. More literally, we need not wait for these development in order to undertake another examination, which will but for one anticipation be as close and as complete as we shall ever be able to make it, of the fundamental category of fact. To this task, as delicate as it is difficult, I now turn.

The maker, or perhaps the making, is a "relation" between the material and the product. Call this the thesis of *relationism;* those who assert it, *relationists*. Relationism, I am about to argue, leads to disaster. The making metaphor is not only anthropomorphic, it also suggests relationism. From the contexts that concern us the anthropomorphism is easily expunged. Once he has got rid of it, the relationist need not distinguish between the making and the maker. The relationist suggestion, or temptation, is not so easily disposed of. He makes a book. You make a tool. She makes a print. 'Making' is a transitive verb. If we want to do battle with relationism, we had better free ourselves from this grammatical insinuation by dropping the metaphor and adopting the last terminological change, which has been long overdue.

What I called a maker, I now call a *function*. What I called its material or materials, I now call its *argument*. What I called its product, I now call its *value* for this argument. *All functions are monadic. Their arguments are all single determinates. To be a value of a function and to be a fact are one and the same.*

Let us next agree on a notation of convenience. Occasionally, I shall write 'ϕ_i' for a function, 'arg_2' for an argument satisfying the restriction that goes with ϕ_i, '(ϕ_i, arg_i),' for the value of ϕ_i for arg_i. Nor shall I hesitate to write '(ϕ_i, α_k)' as long as it is clear from the context that α_k satisfies the restriction which goes with ϕ_i. But I shall never write a special symbol such as, say, 'v_1', instead of the two expressions for a function and a determinate inside a parenthesis, in order to indicate that it stands for a value.

Remember now the two kinds of canons, (a) and (b), and the use we made of 'eo ipso' (p. 105). For any two determinates, α_1 and α_2, there are without any restriction three circumstances, one for each of the three canons (b). But, again, nothing will be lost if we ignore the two sorts of circumstances (and canons) we have as yet not encountered. Then one can also say, as we did, that if α_1 and α_2 are there, the diad (α_1, α_2) is eo ipso there. So used the tag meant: without a maker and without restrictions. The schema for all canons (a), simplified by the standardization, reads as follows. If the determinate α_1 is there and satisfies the restriction that goes with ϕ_1, then the fact (ϕ_1, α_1) is eo ipso there. Now combine the two formulae. *If the first and the second are there, then the third is eo ipso there; in case the first and the second are both determinates, without any restriction; in case they are a determinate and a function, if and only if the former satisfies the restriction that goes with the latter; in the first case the third is a circumstance, in the second it is a fact.* So used, more broadly, the Latin tag means that everything needed for the third to be there has been specified. (That in this context 'first' and 'second' do not mark an order we understand already, vary accurately.)

Remember next a double assertion which was made earlier in this Section (p. 102). A canon (a) has a specific ground; but its ground is neither a fact nor a circumstance for which its statement might stand. The negative half I then took and still take to be evident. Even so, in the last Section it will be "proved." The positive half we are now ready to make good by specifying the ground. I restate part of the above formula with a slight variation. *If arg_1 is there, then, since ϕ_1 is there, the fact (ϕ_1, arg_1) is eo ipso there; if α_1 does not fulfill the restriction which goes with ϕ_1, then even though ϕ_1 is there, there is no fact;* i.e., ϕ_1 has no value for α_1 as argument. Reflecting on this while keeping in mind that a canon is essentially a restriction, you will see that *every function is the* *ontological ground of its canon;* or, if you would rather put it this way, every function is the ground of the restriction that goes with it.

Loose and fragmentary as it is, our notation of convenience may yet reflect the ideal schema, where '(ϕ_i, α_k)' would be well formed or ill formed, depending on whether α_k does or doesn't satisfy the restriction that goes with ϕ_i; and where (disregarding the generalities) there is only one expression, if any, for each existent. Notice, too, for later reference, that if our functions were what the classical mathematicians called by that name, they would be *partially defined.* For that is what they call one of their functions of it doesn't "coordinate" something to everything in their universe of the moment.

At this point a tempter who has waited in the wings steps forth and offers two observations.

I, too, *he begins,* shall consider a first, a second, and a third, and shall speak of them, with your permission, I hope, although against your advice, as the argument arg_1, the function ϕ_1, and the value v_1. I, though, unlike you, am a relationist; thus I assay ϕ_1 as a "relation" and write '$\phi_1(v_1, arg_1)$'; for I believe that there must be a connection between the argument and the value. This is indeed the heart of my position. But I would like to add some remarks which should meet two objections which I am sure you will raise. (a) ϕ_1 is not a relational universal. If it were, I would not only fall into the most blatant regress but ignore a phenomenological difference which, like you, I clearly feel. Nor is 'ϕ_1', which stands for something, like '=' or '∈', which (I agree) stand for nothing. Rather, ϕ_1 is what I call an "internal relation." These existents share two features with relational universals. They have the one-many feature; and the mode of, say, $\phi_1(\alpha_1, \alpha_2)$ depends on the identities of α_1 and α_2 and on nothing else, just as the mode of, say, $r_1^2(a_1, a_2)$ depends on the identities of a_1 and a_2 and on nothing else. On the other hand, there is no restriction (or, to be completely accurate, there is only the minimal restriction) on α_1 and α_2, which is reminiscent of circumstances. Otherwise ϕ_1 would be like binary exemplification before you standardized it monadically. As you see, internal relations do belong to a category all its own. (b) Your second objection, I suppose, concerns order. I meet it by standardizing $\phi_1(\alpha_i, \beta_i)$ into $\phi_1\langle \alpha_i, \beta_i \rangle$. For I need not and do not exclude diads from my world.

Nor do I, *the tempter continues,* confuse the connection I propose with the mak*ing* you disposed of much earlier (p. 80), when you claimed that when explicitly presented with v_1 we are implicitly presented with arg_1, ϕ_1, and nothing else. (I adapt your original claim to the standardization.) Phenomenologically, that may or may not be so.

But surely you do not think that, ontologically, v_1 *is arg*$_1$ and ϕ_1. Perhaps you believe that v_1 *is* ϕ_1 clinging to *arg*$_1$. If so, what grounds the clinging?

I reply as follows.

Concerning your first observation. There is no connection. That is the heart of my position. More precisely, there is no connection grounded either, as you believe, in ϕ_1 or in something else. That is the import of *eo ipso!* You may keep the word, of course. Then the "connection" becomes what the canon says it is: the third is there if and only if the first and second are there. Put differently, *the identity of a fact, or, with the traditional words, its being and its nature, is completely exhausted by its being the determinate which is there if and only if the argument and the function are there.*

Is the new category to which you claim ϕ_1 belongs needed or even viable? I do not think it is either. That, though, is beside the point. I shall merely argue that if ϕ_1 belongs to it, you are in trouble. (a) You started with three and end up with four. For surely the internal relation*ship* $\phi_1\langle v_1, arg_1\rangle$ is not nothing. What then does the connecting, ϕ_1 or the fourth? Since you claim that ϕ_1 does it, the fourth causes you an *embarras de richesses.* Nor is that all. What connects ϕ_1 with $\langle v_1, arg_1\rangle$? If they do not need a connection, then the supposed gap you set out to fill has reappeared. If they need one, you are started on a regress. Moreover, considering the categorial difference between ϕ_1 and $\langle v_1, arg_1\rangle$, you are, from where I stand, faced with the absurdity, or something very close to the absurdity, of a tie tying a tie to what it ties. Perhaps you remember this old formula of mine. (b) Holding, as you do, that $\phi_1\langle v_1, arg_1\rangle$ is actual by virtue of the identities of v_1 and arg_1, you are, again from where I stand, caught in a circle. For, as I just said in my way and now repeat in yours, the identity of v_1 is completely exhausted by $\phi_1\langle v_1, arg_1\rangle$ being actual. Do you then have some other access to the identity of v_1? Is it perhaps presented to you, as a thing is, as a composite of an item and an ultimate form?

Concerning your second observation. If you remember that separability is an ontological notion, you will see that the "clinging," which you believe needs a specific ground, is already accounted for by argument and function being separable and inseparable, respectively. 'Clinging', though, is a pretty word; so I shall borrow it and occasionally use it, after having surrounded it with double quotes, in order to indicate that it carries no specific ontological commitment. For the rest, I can only repeat, the fact is neither the collection, nor the class, nor the "sum," nor anything else "of" the first and the second, but rather, the third which is eo ipso there if and only if the first and the second are there. Or, with a twist, the nature of the fact is completely exhausted by the first satisfying the restriction which goes with the second and by the second being inseparable from the first. That is the key to the category of fact. Otherwise it wouldn't be what it is.

The tempter withdraws. We, though, had better complete the examination by doing two more things. Let us first inquire into the structural reasons why anyone should be tempted; and let us conclude by trying to find out what we can learn from the contributions which some of the modern masters have made to these arduous and recondite studies.

Reism is the thesis that all existents are things. Its hold on the tradition is a matter of record. The natural bend of our minds, it would seem, is reistic. Nor therefore is it unreasonable to suppose that even those philosophers who tried to make a place for the category of fact in their ontologies were all more or less prisoners of reism. In other words, to conform the images, it always was and still is very difficult not to think of facts as if they were would-be things, each with an item and an ultimate form.

Consider now once more that simplest of all facts, $\eta(f_1, a_1)$. Suppose, contrary to fact, that when explicitly presented with it, one is implicitly presented with the monadic function clinging to the diad. The supposition simplifies but does not falsify. The reason it doesn't is that when explicitly presented with the diad (f_1, a_1) one is implicitly presented with two things, each a composite of an item and a form (ultimate sort), but never with a third item and a third form, presumably of the diad itself. In this crucial respect all complexes, i.e., all determinates not things, are alike. They are not composites of an item and an ultimate sort. As for the supposed presentation, so for the real one. When explicitly presented with the fact, one is implicitly presented with the two things, each a composite of an item and an ultimate sort, but never with a third item and a third ultimate sort, presumably of the fact. About the inaccessibility of the "third item" there is no question. There is one about that of the "third form." But the first half alone suffices for much of the case. So I let the second go for awhile.

The prisoner of reism has at this point only one way out. He will hold that the argument with the function clinging to it, which is presented, represents the hidden thing, v_1. *Presented, represented, hidden;* the words are chosen advisedly. Substances are hidden; this is a perennial strand of the tradition. What is represented is hidden; representationalism has been a blight for the last four centuries. The reistic temptation is reinforced by those of substantialism and representationalism.

The relationism comes in rather ironically, or even tragically, as one inclines to say when under the pressure of a historical situation or of an intellectual pattern a man's strength causes his downfall. Our tempter is not a reist in the classical sense. His things, like mine, are particulars and universals, including relational ones. That is his strength. He falls down when he assays the function as a "relation" between the presented (ϕ_1, arg_1) and the hidden (v_1). Others have faltered; others have erred; we all do. Why is his fall so shattering; his cause, beyond hope?

There are degrees of "hiddenness." In some ontologies, including this one, we are never presented with particulars either past or future nor, of course, with the acts of others. Yet, prudently managed, these existents can be accommodated. The relationists' hidden things, however, are unthinkable; or, what amounts to the same, they are purely speculative, which is the highest degree of hiddenness; and the penalties for speculation are severe. The reason these would-be things are speculative is that *we cannot think a "form," be it ultimate sort or function, that has not been presented to us.* This is a new phenomenological claim. As far as I am concerned, it needs no support. I merely suggest that this limitation on the "forms" of our world is the price we pay for their luminosity (p. 115).

At this point the question we let go for a while reappears. Isn't being an atomic fact of that simplest kind an ultimate sort (S_1), and are we not sometimes not just presented, but even transparently presented, with $\eta(a_1, f_1)$-being-S_1? The answer is that we are and that there is yet no such existent as S_1. The only "ultimate sorts" that exist are those of things. The resolution of the apparent paradox hinges on the distinction between intending something and being aware of something (p. 207) on the one hand and on the place language has in the assay of our awarenesses on the other. Thus it will have to wait for Section V. (This is the anticipation which was mentioned at the start (p. 112) of this line of thought.)

In my new world there is still another temptation. The modes, being sometimes presented, are no longer speculative. Extrapolation is not speculation. Yet the mode of a circumstance, which does not involve "making," is always accessible, at least recursively, while that of a value, unless there is some sort of combinatorial balance, either as in the tautologies or in some other vacuous (p. 111) way, is in principle unaccessible. The details of that can wait until we come to analyticity. You see already how the tempter may lead us on. The mode is hidden, hence the making is hidden; the making is hidden, hence its product is hidden. I have wrestled with this temptation for quite some time.

There are three notions of function. One, of classical mathematics, is in philosophy associated with the name of Russell. The second is Frege's. The third, of this discourse, is seminally Meinong's. Call them, for the convenience of the moment, R-functions, F-functions, M-functions.

Let 'Peter', 'Paul', and '*a* father of' stand for two particulars and a (binary) relation. Suppose that Peter is the father of Paul. The only determinates involved in this fact are the three things. Accordingly, neither (16) '*the* father of' nor (17) '*the* father of Paul' occurs in the ideal schema. In other schemata, including those modeled after *Principia Mathematica*, (16) is a *Russell-function;* (17), a definite description. *Russell-functions do not literally stand for anything; nor do definite descriptions.* The traditional issues and the traditional machinery concerning (16) and (17) are thus linguistic rather than ontological. The functions of the modern mathematician do exist. For what he now calls a function or, with the Russellian phrase, a relation in extenso is a class (f_1) of ordered pairs, $\{ \ldots \langle y_i, x_i \rangle \ldots \}$, such that $x_i = x_k \supset . \; y_i = y_k$. The associated definite descriptions, $f`\bar{x}$, succeed and yield $\bar{y}$ if and only if $\langle \bar{y}, \bar{x} \rangle$ is an element of $f_1$. The associated R-function $(f`)$ is therefore, like all such functions, partially defined (p. 127). The mathematicians, however, usually "extend" it by "assigning" the same conventional "value" to all "arguments" for which the description fails. Zero, for instance, may be assigned as a son to John. In mathematics that does no harm. Given the nature of the human mind, it is even inevitable. For just as we cannot think and talk without definite descriptions, so the mathematicians cannot write and think without many notational devices, of which this is one. But beware of those who would uncritically transfer it to ontology. For an M-function, for instance, it amounts to "violating" the restriction that goes with the function. Its result in the mind, therefore, if there were any, would be an unthinkable thought; its result on paper is an ill-formed expression.

Frege is a relationist. An F-function not only "clings" to its argument; it also "points at" its value, i.e., at one of the two odd things, T and F. These two, unlike the modes, which are subentities[†] pervading complexes which exist, are particular things, which "preexist." In Frege's words, the F-function green projects Peter on, say, T. But T would exist even if this particular argument and this particular function didn't; which is what I express by saying that it preexists. *This clinging to the argument at one end, and this pointing at what preexists at the other, make Frege-functions irreducibly relational.* Structurally this is the deepest

---

[†] The modes are, in fact, *entities*, as Bergmann is now using this term. They might well be called "subdeterminates," however, to indicate their "lower" ontological status.—WH

root of two of the most striking features of his ontology. (1) If green (T, Peter), then, as we know, the description 'the greening of Peter' does not literally stand for anything, although in many schemata it is allowed to "stand in" for what according to Frege is 'T' (not: T). So does 'the blueing of Mary' and the 'yellowing of John'. Hence the doctrine that sameness is a relation between names. (2) What 'Peter is green' commonsensically stands for does not depend on whether for the argument Peter the function green points at F or T. Hence the bifurcation of meaning and reference and the doctrine of the double semantic tie. This is not to deny that the problems of intentionality are another root, which goes deep indeed, of this doctrine and that bifurcation. Yet, in a world without minds these problems would disappear, while the two structural suggestions just pointed out would still be there. That shows why the relationist root is the deepest.

Frege's saturated-unsaturated corresponds to our separable-inseparable; except that, unlike his dichotomy, ours does not put universals, which are things, and connectives, which are M-functions, into the same category. Again, unlike his dichotomy, ours is not ad hoc but triply rooted in the schematism. What is separable can support a diad, and conversely. What is separable can be an element of a class, and conversely. This we already saw or at least heard. What is separable can be quantified over, and conversely. This we shall see in the next Section.

Meinong's basic dichotomy runs between the foundations and what they found. In his words, if the foundations are there, the "object of higher order," which they found, is necessarily there. In my words, if the former are there, the latter is eo ipso there. Unhappily, Meinong is also an extreme reist and nominalist. Thus he holds that if this particular middle C and that particular middle G are there, then a third "perfect particular," namely, the fifth between them, is also there. Naturally, there are many gaps in such an ontology. Yet seminally, I like to think, he had the idea of the schema for all canons. That is why, in tribute to the ceaseless meanderings of his profound and subtle mind, I speak of *Meinong-functions*.

Wittgenstein's insistence that a sentence is not a "name" fits very well; not because, if the complex it stands for is potential, there is nothing to be "named," but because, irrespective of their mode, complexes cannot in the ideal schema be represented by simple signs. Again, the image of f_1 and a_1 hanging together in the fact as two links hang together in a chain fits the idea that there must be an end to specifically grounded "connections." Unfortunately, from where I stand, the author of the *Tractatus* chose the wrong links. What hangs thus together in the simplest fact are not, symmetrically, two separable things but, asymmetrically, a separable diad and a function that is inseparable from it. Or so I have long argued. Let me in conclusion dialectically strengthen my argument by making the best case I can think of, outside of phenomenological and systematic considerations, for Wittgenstein's choice. Ignore order and the nonatomic, stay with the nonrelational atomic, which is after all the least controversial. There is the abstract possibility that, say, a_1 and f_1 determine, in addition to three circumstances, eo ipso also a quasi-circumstance, which would be the fact. I say quasi-circumstance because, although there would be no function, there would be, corresponding to the ultimate sorts involved, a set of restrictions. E.g., there would be a quasi-circumstance for a_1 and f_1 and one for F_1; but there would be none for either a_1 and a_2, or F_1 and a_1, or f_1 and f_2. What, then, would ground these restrictions?[3]

3. For an argument that even the linguistic approach reveals the need for grounding them, see E. B. Allaire, "Types and Formation Rules: A Note on Tractatus 3.334," *Analysis,* 21, 1960, 14–16.

IV

Functions and Analyticity

A function is either a connective or a quantifier.[†] The latter we have so far managed to avoid. Some ontological features of the former, which had to be introduced, were taken for granted. What is taken for granted at one point must be made good later. Now we are ready for that. In this Section I propose to assay the functions, first the connectives, then the quantifiers. But let us first of all catch our breath while looking around in order to find out how far we have come and how best to proceed. Three remarks will serve as signposts. The first two are merely reminders of what is very familiar; the third anticipates once more, although with a new urgency, what will be done in the next Section concerning the connection between thought and language.

First. Some complexes are analytic. Analyticity is in this world an ontological feature of great import. What then is the ground of a complex being analytic? The assays of analyticity and of the functions are so closely connected that they are virtually inseparable. Thus their expositions will be intertwined in this Section. To remind you quickly of the connection, permit me for once a use of 'truth' which I otherwise scrupulously avoid. If one calls an actual complex a "truth," one can say that *many* analytical complexes are "combinatorial truths," with the "combining" all being done by functions. Notice the 'many'. In the old world it would have been 'all'. An example will justify the apparent weakening. Let α_1 and β_1 be two things; 'α' and 'β', two variables. (1) $\alpha_1 \neq \beta_1$, we shall see, is analytic; yet '$\alpha_1 \neq \alpha_1$', which stands for a contradiction, is a substitution instance of '$\alpha \neq \beta$'. Thus (1) is not, in the familiar sense, a combinatorial truth. The weakening is merely apparent because, while what is analytic in the old world is analytic in the new, the converse does not hold. $\gamma_1 \in \gamma_2$, for instance, will turn out to be either analytic or contradictory for any two determinates,

---

[†] This is not quite correct as stated. A function is either a connective, a quantifier, or an *exemplification* nexus.—WH

depending on whether γ_1 is or is not an element of γ_2. (The contradictory is merely the negation of the analytic. Thus no harm will come to us if for the most part we ignore it.)

Second. Analytic complexes, or perhaps the expressions standing for them, are often called "formal truths." That spots the connection, virtually inseparable, between the notions of analyticity and of form. *If a complex is analytic, so is every other with which it shares its relevant form.* What, then, the ontologist immediately asks, grounds a complex being of a certain form. This is a big question; so big indeed that much of the answer will have to wait until we come to the last two Sections of this discourse. Presently we shall at least face the question; later on in this Section we shall take one important step toward answering it; right now I shall merely clear away some underbrush.

A. *Non*ontologically speaking, what is a form; and what, in particular, a relevant form? Let α_1, α_2, α_3 be three atomic facts and consider (2) $((\alpha_1 \supset \alpha_2) \ \& \ (\alpha_1 \supset \alpha_3)) \lor \sim((\alpha_1 \supset \alpha_2) \ \& \ (\alpha_1 \supset \alpha_3))$. (a) (2) is a disjunction. (b) (2) is the disjunction of a complex and its negation. (c) (2) is the disjunction of a complex and its negation, such that the complex is a conjunction. (d) first repeats (c), then adds the clause that each term of the conjunction is a conditional. (e) adds to (d) that the two conditionals have the same antecedent. (f) adds to (e) that the terms of the conditionals are all atomic facts. (g), finally, adds to which sorts of atomic facts α_1, α_2, and α_3 belong, and which, if any, among the things they involve are the same. Each of these seven statements specifies a form. Each of these forms is more specific than the one preceding it in the order from (a) to (g); in the sense that every complex which has (or: is of) one of them, has all the preceding ones. Also, they are all forms of (2). One complex, unless it is either an atomic fact or a circumstance whose terms are either things or classes, has more than one form. (b) is in this series from (a) to (g) the first form such that every complex sharing it with (2) is, like (2), analytic. That makes (b) the relevant form of (2).

B. 'Form' has been used earlier. The functions, the ultimate sorts, and the modes have been called forms. The present use is different. Thus we must distinguish. Call the existents just mentioned forms$_1$; say that each of the statements (a) to (g) above specifies a form$_2$. 'Form$_1$' will not be used often in what follows. So we shall save ink and breath if we agree that where there is no danger of confusion, 'form' will stand for 'form$_2$'.

C. Forms$_1$ are existents of the sort called entities.[†] This we know.

[†] More accurately, entities are among those existents which are forms$_1$—WH

Forms$_2$ are literally nothing; only a complex being of a certain form has a ground. This has already been mentioned. Why then has the same word been used? The reason is again familiar. Whatever the right answer to the big question, as I called it, and no matter how unorthodox the one I shall propose will be, every one knows that, with one obvious exception, the functions and the ultimate sorts, which are forms$_1$, and the way they "hang together" in a complex, are the very skeleton of the latter's form$_2$. The exceptions are of course the three forms shared by all the members of one of the three sorts of circumstances, respectively.

24* (a) Since there are no forms, it is inaccurate, and therefore potentially dangerous, to speak, succinctly, of the assay or ground of a form, or of form, rather than, accurately, of the assay, or ground, of something having a certain form. Yet I shall, when there is no danger of confusion, often speak succinctly rather than accurately. (b) 'Structural feature' and 'formal feature' will later on serve as convenient synonyms of 'form'. For we shall have to attend to features which are in all respects like forms, except that they are either contextual or nonunary (relational). In the first case, 'contextual feature' versus 'formal feature' will provide a useful contrast. In the second case 'formal feature' will avoid the awkwardness of either having to speak of the form of tuples or calling something nonunary a form. (As you see, I am going out of my way to avoid calling anything that is not a thing either a property or a relation.) (c) Classes, unlike things, have no form$_1$. That is why the qualification (p. 76) to the effect that, unlike things, classes are not literally independent, was necessary. But, again, classes are unlike complexes and like things in that, like the latter, they have no form$_2$. Yet they can be "formally" characterized by a contextual feature; and so, we shall see, can things. That is why the qualification makes no dent in the schematism. It merely reflects the complete "formlessness" of classes, which is part of their very special nature.

Third. Consider such words as 'not', 'or', 'all', and 'some'. In the schemata, whether merely improved or claimed to be ideal, which some philosophers employ, these words "correspond" to certain marks (or expressions), which in turn stand accurately for the functions. The "correspondence" between the marks and the words, however, is approximate at best; more often than not it takes all sorts of maneuvers to establish it. That is one of the reasons why many have long held and still hold that those schemata are of no use in philosophy. This issue I shall not reargue. Rather, I want to call attention to a case where the lack of "correspondence" between the words, on the one hand, and the marks of the schema I shall eventually propose, on the other, is at first sight so blatant that, unless something radical is done about it, the ontology which goes with the schema would be left without any phenomenological plausibility whatsoever. The connectives cause no trouble. In the case of the two quantifiers, however, the "maneuver" required amounts to no less than the new assay of conscious states, which will fill the whole of Section V. Thus I must once more ask you to be patient. Without the support, phenomenological and otherwise, which it will receive in the next Section, much of what will be done in this one would remain "pure."

The signposts have been planted. What can we read off them? The assays of the functions and of analyticity are virtually inseparable. So are those of analyticity and of form. The two pairs have an element in common. Hence, the assays of the functions, of analyticity, and of form are all three inseparable from each other. Yet most of the answer to the big question, as I called it, concerning form, will have to wait for the sixth and seventh Sections. Again, what will be done in this Section about the quantifiers cannot, as was just pointed out, stand by itself without the fifth Section. Nor is that all. Remember (3) 'green is not a relation' and (4) 'or is diverse from not'. It *seems* that we know very well what these sentences purport to stand for. Yet, since they stand for nothing, we can *in fact* not think (intend) "it." That is so characteristic a feature of this world that we had better agree upon a succinct way of referring to it. I shall speak of the *discrepancy, the excess,* and the *limits of thought.* The latter separates what can be thought (and therefore in this world exists) from the excess. In some cases, such as (3) and (4), the discrepancy between what we seem to intend and what in fact we intend is not so large that the gap could not be bridged, phenomenologically as well as otherwise. This, you remember, is one of the things I promised to do in Section V. Once it is done, the gap is no longer disturbing. But there are other cases. As soon as we shall get down to brass tacks, the very first step toward an assay of the functions and of analyticity will lead us to a gap that is unbridgeable. Or, with a twist, the excess of the ontology of logic over its phenomenology is in this world very large and of a very striking nature. One who sees that clearly cannot but be disturbed. For he finds himself—prematurely, as it were—faced with the question which, in an obvious sense, is the biggest of all. Just remember the image of the ladder that must be thrown away. Mathematical logic may be left to the mathematicians. But does not what goes for the ontology of logic also go for all of ontology; and if it does, is not all ontological talk excess? I am still determined to ignore this question until the very end. That is why I said "prematurely."

We have looked around. Where, then, do we stand and how shall we proceed?

The features of an ontology are all in various ways linked with each other. If they weren't, they couldn't, as they must, dialectically support each other. Yet, broadly speaking, there are different degrees of closeness, or interdependence, or what have you; and these differences produce clusters. (I use 'closeness' rather than 'inseparability' because of the technical meaning we gave to the latter.) If you keep that in mind while looking back on the first three Sections and reflecting on what we just read off the signposts, you will easily gather where we stand. We are at the halfway point of this discourse. The first three Sections are the first half; the remaining four, including this one, are the second. Look first backward, then forward, and you will see why. The first Section introduces some of the sorts; states the tripartite schema of the canons; takes the first steps toward exploring the former and elaborating the latter. The rest is all promises and anticipations. Some of these are made good in the second Section, or there is at least movement in this direction; but there are also new promises and new anticipations. As the second Section stands to the first, so the third stands to the first two. At the end of that Section, though, a certain closure is achieved. There are, to be sure, still many promises unfulfilled, many questions left without answer. Otherwise there would not be a second half. The last thread left hanging in the first half will not be tied up until we come to the last Appendix. Yet a cluster has emerged. The main links between the canons, the modes, and the diads are established. In the taxonomy there are still three empty slots, one for the classes, one for each of the two sorts of circumstances which are not diads. Nor of course could that be otherwise; for these are three of the topics in the second half. Yet the taxnomic pattern is by now reasonably clear; and there is already much solid support for it. The issues taken up in the second half will produce a second cluster. To convince you of that was the main purpose of this longish introduction. If you are convinced, you will (I hope) not disapprove of the way I shall proceed. Although in command of the first cluster, we must yet begin anew. Just as the first Section is an introduction to the whole, so this one is an introduction to the second half. Thus there will be more promises and anticipations in this Section than in any of the following ones. The outline of a new ontology of conscious states in the fifth Section is an indispensable intermezzo.

But the sixth Section will stand to the fourth as the second stands to the first; and so on, down to the last Appendix. Let us then finally start.

I present first a division among complexes, then a schema for analyticity. The division, though not urgent, is yet convenient to have on hand from the outset. The schema, as far as it goes, can, like that for the canons, stand by itself; although, as in the case of that first schema, its complexity and its import are much greater than the bare statement reveals. Thus, while not merely an anticipation or a promise, it is yet in style.

A circumstance is either a diversity, or an element nexus, or a meaning nexus. In the usual relaxed notation, with variables, which I shall continue to employ unless a fragment of the eventual ideal schema is being introduced, (5) '$\alpha \neq \beta$' and (6) '$\alpha \in \beta$' stand for the first two of these three sorts. For the meaning nexus I shall continue to write (7) '$\alpha \, M \, \beta$'.

25* The correction that makes 'M' a diacritical mark, like '$\neq$' and '$\in$', can (I repeat) wait until the last Appendix. But it may help to recall that, since circumstances are not subject to any restriction, except the minimal one, to the effect that both terms must be determinates, (5) will remain well formed if expressions for a thing, or a fact, or a class, or a circumstance, and so on are substituted for the variables; just as (6) will be well formed even if the substituend for β does not stand for a class, although in this case what (6) stands for will of course be potential. A class, by the way, until we come to Section VI, is always what will there be called a "primary" class, i.e., roughly, one of those denumerable classes which the intuitionists among the logicians admit; although in this world, unlike theirs, there are also the classes which the nonintuitionists admit. The ontological status of these "secondary" classes, however, is wholly derivative and sui generis, not unlike, except for one major feature, that of electrons, or of neutrons.†

The proposed division among complexes is a dichotomy. A complex is of either the first or the second level; or, synonymously, it is either a complex-I or a complex-II. *Every circumstance is a complex-II. A complex is a complex-I if and only if, except for the required standardization and order steps, each step, from its ultimate foundation up to the complex itself, is an (a)-step,* i.e., a making, either by an exemplification or a connec-

---

† Bergmann will later abandon this terminology. In Section VI the term 'primary class' will designate *finite* classes, while the term 'secondary class' will designate denumerably *infinite* classes. Both these sorts of classes, and in addition another sort, tertiary classes, are "full-status" classes; that is, their ontological status is *not* merely "derivative."—WH

tive or a quantifier, not either a building-out-of or a building-on. Take, e.g., $\eta(f_1, a_1)$. The three members of its ultimate foundation are f_1, a_1, η. The first step, a (b)-step building (f_1, a_1) out of f_1 and a_1, thus leading to the collection whose members are (f_1, a_1) and η, is a standardization step. The second step, which is also the last, is an (a)-step corresponding to an exemplification. Again, an order step is a finite number of successive (b)-steps, each corresponding to the building of a diad out of its terms. E.g., if α_1 and α_2 are two complexes, then the two steps building first (α_1, α_2) out of α_1 and α_2, then $(\alpha_1, (\alpha_1, \alpha_2))$ out of (α_1, α_2) and α_1, lead from the intermediate foundation of (8) $\supset \langle \alpha_1, \alpha_2 \rangle$, whose members are α_1 *twice*, α_2, and $\supset$, to the collection whose two members are $(\alpha_1, (\alpha_1, \alpha_2))$ and $\supset$, from which latter (8) is reached by a single (a)-step.

26* Some reminders and anticipations should help. (1) '$\langle \alpha_1, \alpha_2 \rangle$' abbreviates '$(\alpha_1, (\alpha_1, \alpha_2))$'. See p. 120. (2) Notice the underscored 'twice'. So far not much has been made of this feature of many foundations. Yet it has been stipulated at the very beginning (p. 48) that a member of a collection may "occur" in it a finite number of times. (3) At an earlier occasion (p. 121) the standardization and order steps were "absorbed" into the others. Now we must be more explicit. (4) If a complex has an intermediate foundation, F, such that all of its members are either connectives or circumstances, then the complex is a *pure* complex-II, and, in particular, a *molecular* one relative to F. E.g., (9) $(\alpha_1 \in \alpha_2) \vee (\alpha_3 = \alpha_4)$ is pure, while $(\alpha_1 \in \alpha_2) \vee f_1(a_1)$ is mixed. In case there is a quantifier among the members of F, the complex is no longer molecular and a certain qualification concerning the determinates of F has to be added. This will become clear as soon as we shall have assayed the quantifiers. But the idea is the same; and all we shall ever need in this discourse is the idea. *A complex-II is thus either pure or mixed.* (5) The second level is easily stratified. (9) for instance will belong to the first stratum if and only if α_1, α_2, α_3, and α_4 are all either things or complexes-I; it will belong to the second stratum if and only if at least one of them belongs to the first stratum and the others are all either things or complexes-I; and so on. Eventually you will see, although we shall make no use of it, that this stratification introduces another one, among the primary classes of this world, which corresponds to an initial segment of Zermelo's cumulative types, provided only all things and complexes-I are counted as *Urelemente*.

A determinate is analytic if and only if its mode, actuality, and that of its negation, potentiality, are both (either immediately available or either recursively or at least in principle) accessible to us. Only complexes have negations; obviously, therefore, only facts and circumstances can be analytic. Postpone for a while consideration of the less obvious clause in parentheses. Note instead that, thus explicated, analyticity is an anthropocentric feature. For, surely, whether the mode of a certain complex is or is not accessible to us is a matter of anthropology. Yet (I claimed) analyticity is an ontological feature of great import. If you wonder whether that is a contradiction, remember the case of independence (p. 114). What we can or can't explicitly intend is a matter of anthropology. But we found that an existent is independent if and only if it is a determinate; and being that is an ontological feature, although, of course, like all such features, only within the unbreachable confines set to us by the need for a phenomenological jumping-off place. This equivalence, or correspondence, or whatever one may want to call it, between the two notions, the ontological one of being a determinate and the anthropocentric one of being independent, makes the latter ontologically significant. The thing to do, therefore, is to search for an ontological condition, or characterization, that fits all those and only those complexes which are analytic. And, of course, I shall try to make this case. More precisely, I shall argue that there are several sorts such that a complex is analytic if and only if it is of one of them. There is even a feature shared by all these sorts. That, though, is better left until near the end; otherwise I might lapse into aphorisms. Something else can, and should, be done now. If analyticity is a notion of great ontological import, we had better pick a word and agree on a use of it that makes it stand to 'analytic' as 'determinate' stands to 'independent'. Using 'tautology' as before, ontologically and more broadly than most, I shall say that *a complex is a tautology if and only if it is of one of the sorts whose members jointly exhaust the analytic.* (The last sentence, together with the first of this paragraph, is the promised "schema" of the analytic.)

The several sorts of tautology will be distinguished by prefixes. A *p-tautology*, for instance, is a complex such that the expression standing for it in most schemata is a so-called "sentential tautology." Everyone knows what makes a complex a p-tautology. Yet there is some point in stating the matter for once ontologically, in terms of complexes and their modes, rather than linguistically, in terms of expressions and their truth or falsehood. An actual complex, α_1, is a p-tautology if and only if it has an (intermediate) foundation, F, such that all its members are either complexes, say n, or connectives, and if a further condition is met. To each such α_1 belongs, in a familiar sense, a form. Every other complex of this form may be "obtained" from α_1 by "substituting" in it for each of the complexes of F another complex. The condition is that each complex of this form be actual, irrespective of which of the α^n combinatorially possible distributions the modes of the complexes substituted for those of α_1 belong to. Of course. But, then, this merely gets us back to form. Or, with a twist, we are back at the second signpost. So you will once more ask the big question. What grounds a form? If you will be patient a bit longer, the urgency of the question, when eventually I shall at least face it, will be even greater.

As the p-tautologies correspond to the sentential calculus, so the complexes I shall call *q-tautologies* correspond to the functional calculus, although not, as we shall see, to the first-order one only. Jointly these two sorts exhaust what I take to be the classical notion of analyticity, which is narrower than the one here presented. For in this world there are some further sorts the modes of whose members are accessible to us; such as, among others, the complexes grounding the fundamental features of classes. Remember, too, that in this world the diversity of things is transparent. Thus by the schema it is analytic. As for things, so, I shall argue, for all determinates. Even more strongly and more broadly, as this second half will unfold, so will the arguments to the effect that *the modes of all circumstances are not only in principle but recursively available to us.* This is indeed one of the pivots of the overall dialectic; also, though not only, because it supports, and is supported by, an equally remarkable companion feature: *the members of the "new" sorts, beyond the classical notion of analyticity, are all of the second level (or mixed).*

I interrupt for three comments. (1) Just as a complex may have more than one form, it may also have more than one foundation that fulfills the combinatorial condition. The least explicit of the forms which correspond to these latter foundations is the one we called relevant. That makes the foundation to which it corresponds the "relevant foundation." (2) α_1' is, as one says, "obtained" from α_1 by "substitut*ing* in the latter β_1' for β_1 if and only if $\alpha_1, \beta_1, \beta_1', \alpha_1'$, in this order, have a certain quaternary formal feature; or, equivalently, if and only if $\langle \alpha_1, \beta_1, \beta_1', \alpha_1' \rangle$ is of a certain form. Of this later, when we come to the quantifiers. Until then I beg leave to speak of substitution naively and even anthropomorphically, as if by "doing" something one "obtained" a certain result. For right now we have our hands full as it is. (3) The prefix in 'q-tautology' is of course the initial of 'quantifier'. 'p' is taken from 'proposition' because the initial of 'connective' will be needed as the most suggestive prefix for the class tautologies.

Why is the mode of a p-tautology accessible to us? *That* it is, is an anthropological fact. Facts, even if, like this one, so fundamental that they are better set aside as "principles," are yet contingent. The con-

tingent has no reasons, only causes. Causes do not concern the ontologist. Yet he must, whenever he appeals to a "contingent principle,"
show that it makes sense. That is, he must show how it fits dialectically
with his ontology. To do that expeditiously in the case at hand, suppose that the complexes in the relevant foundation of our example,
α_1, are all atomic facts, say, $\gamma_1, \gamma_2, \ldots, \gamma_n$. The modes of the latter,
we know, are not accessible to us. For, with an image that should be
safe after the catharsis at the end of the last Section, all making is hidden from us. Also, as it was put earlier, contingency arises at the level
of the atomic. How, then, could the mode of α_1 be presented to us
unless it does not depend on the modes of the γ_i? Why, on the other
hand, shouldn't it be presented to us, *provided only we know how each
connective mediates between the modes of its (nonstandardized) arguments and
that of its value for these arguments?*

27* (a) I just said "mediate" rather than "determine," because, as
we saw, the connectives do not operate on the Two-in-Ones into which
a fact and its mode combine but, rather, on the former. As for facts,
so for circumstances. This is, after all, the import of the pervading
metaphor. (b) Circumstances are not made but built out of their
terms. Again, as we saw in the case of the diads, the mode of a circumstance does not depend on the modes of its terms but only on their
identities. If you put that together with the recent anticipation that
the modes of all circumstances are accessible to us, you will (I trust)
get a first glimpse of, or sense for, the patterns that will emerge.

Are we ready for an orderly examination of the connectives? Let us
try. Are these alleged existents really there? That is of course the first
question of all. Yet, having nothing to add to the arguments for the
affirmative I have made for quite some time, I shall not reopen the
case, even though, as far as I know, only Frege and Husserl have
taken this position. Later on, at a place where it fits, I shall show why a
certain reason, which I believe was given by the author of the *Tractatus,* for there being no existents of this sort is not a good reason. But
I do not feel like starting with a negative point. Suppose, then, that
there is at least one connective. If so, how many are there? Presently I
shall try to answer. First, though, for something more fundamental;
so fundamental indeed that, almost immediately blocked, we shall be
virtually forced to face the big question about forms. (Notice that, as
before, I say "face," not "answer." The complete answer, I repeat, or
at least an answer as complete as I can make it, will not be in before
the very end.)

With each function there goes a restriction. The restriction on all
connectives is the same. *A determinate is an argument of a connective if*

and only if it has a mode. Thus it is either a circumstance or a fact. All products of connectives being facts (or, synonymously, values), *all connectives are mediators of modes.* Within this community, each connective is *uniquely* characterized by the way it mediates. The negations of what is actual are potential, and conversely. The values of conjunction are actual if and only if both arguments are actual. And so on. *Loosely* speaking, this is but the ontological version of the truth tables. Since order has been taken care of, we might just as well stay with the symmetrical examples. Nor will anything be lost if we limit ourselves to the first level. And I have already stopped repeating that the arguments here spoken of in the plural are not yet standardized into a single diad or tuple.

Pick an example and look *closely* at an accurate statement of what has just been said loosely. Let α_1 and α_2 be atomic and consider (10) 'If (α_1 is actual) and (α_2 is actual), then (α_1 & α_2 is actual); if either α_1 or α_2 or both are potential, then α_1 & α_2 is potential'. Since the mode of the atomic is not accessible to us, how do we come to "know" what (10) purports to stand for? Searching for an answer, one soon discovers that it takes at least two steps. The first is easy; the second gets us into trouble. If the three facts for which the three clauses in parentheses stand are either analytic or contradictory, their modes are accessible to us. In such cases, therefore, we may have been presented with the four combinatorially possible distributions of modes. The rest, I would have no difficulty admitting, is *extrapolation.* This way the easy step. Remember next the Unthinkability of the Iterated Mode (p. 84). Unless we jettison this phenomenological datum, as of course we must not and shall not, none of the three clauses in (10) stands for what has a mode. Hence, by the restriction that governs all connectives, (10) itself stands for nothing. It belongs to the excess. The discrepancy is stunning. Even worse, the scandal spreads. Turn to the proviso underscored at the end of the paragraph preceding 27* on p. 143, and you will see that while a p-tautology may indeed be transparent and thus, by the first part of the schema, analytic, one cannnot even think, let alone "know," what, by the second part of the schema, makes it a tautology. As for the p-tautologies so of course for all others. In this respect and in some others, the former merely serve as a paradigm. The source of the trouble, here as well as in cases which have nothing to do with analyticity, is that what has no mode is not an argument of connectives.

Is then everything the logicians tell us excess? Do they merely talk about geometrical designs? Or, perhaps a bit more satisfactorily, the modes of geometrical complexes, unlike those of arithmetical ones, being inaccessible, do they merely talk of arithmetical "modes" obtained by Goedelization? But, then, what would these be the modes of? Things are not quite that bad. Yet, even for the p-tautologies, although for them the gap is much narrower than for the q-tautologies, it is much wider than for such cases as, say, green-not-being-a-relation (p. 93). We have come upon one of those disturbing cases that bring one up against the very limits of human thought. Even so, I repeat, I shall not until the last Section try to come to terms with all discrepancies. In the meantime we shall, as we go along, bridge the gaps that can be bridged and make an inventory of those which can't. But it may help you to get one of the major trends of this discourse if something else is pointed out right now. The logicians put such statements as (10) into what they call a syntactical metalanguage. For their purposes that is the proper way out. The ontologist, for his, may not throw away the ladder before he must; if only because, unless the line is drawn exactly, it cannot be adequately rationalized.

(TF) "A complex β_2 is a tautology if and only if not only it but all complexes sharing its (relevant) form are actual." Blocked as we are on the notion of tautology, we cannot but wonder about that of form and about how much, if anything, of (TF) can be salvaged. Does the line perhaps run between these two notions? If (11) β_2-being-a-tautology and (12) β_2-being-of-a-certain-form were one and not two, there wouldn't be any place for it to run between them; we would again be blocked; and all of (TF) would be excess. As it happens, there is some hope. Whatever else they may or may not be, *(11) and (12) are two and not one.* Just consider that, supposing β_2 to be a p-tautology, it is one, as we saw, not by virtue of its form alone but, rather, by virtue of its form in conjunction with the ways in which the connectives making it mediate the modes. (Confirmation by indirection comes from the many-valued calculi.) As for p-tautologies so for q-tautologies as well as most of those on the second level. Such exceptions as, say, $\alpha_1 \neq \alpha_2$ will, as we shall encounter them, be obvious. Also, with the notion of tautology providing the required link, *to be analytic and to be of a certain form are two and not one.* This, though, does not imply that something-being-of-a-certain-form is a sort of existent. If it is, however, then some such existents, unlike faraway stars or events of the distant past, surely are sometimes presented to us. If they are, are their modes even accessible? If so, what is the degree of their accessibility? Are some or all of them either sometimes or always immediately available, or recursively accessible, and so on? It is time we start paying attention to these "degrees." First, though, we must once again touch phenomenological rock bottom.

Let 'β_1' stand for '$\eta(f_1, a_1)$'; 'β_2' for '$\eta(f_1, a_1) \vee \sim\eta(f_1, a_1)$'. β_1 is an atomic fact of a certain sort, call it the first (At_1). β_2 shares its form ($DNAt_1$) with all disjunctions of a fact of the sort At_1 and its negation. (In the case of β_2, as in most others, one should either speak of *a* form or single out the relevant one. But, to repeat, when it does no harm, I shall in this respect be succinct rather than accurate.) Let, without as yet any ontological commitment, 'δ_1' and 'δ_2' stand for "$At_1(\beta_1)$' and '$DNAt_1(\beta_2)$'; i.e., for β_1 and β_2 being respectively of these forms. Not only are the modes of δ_1 and δ_2 accessible to us; even more strongly, if presented at all, δ_1 and δ_2 are transparent. The mode of β_1, on the other hand, is in principle inaccessible. Is β_2, when presented, always transparent? If so, that is neither here nor there; for, surely, the modes of many tautologies, although not immediately available, are yet accessible. An intention, whether or not it is, or becomes, transparent, remains one and the same. The difference is in the act. A complex, we saw, is transparent if and only if the particular of the act intending it exemplifies not only the species of believing but also the character of being evident. Not so for a complex and its (being of a certain) form. β_1 and δ_1 are two and not one. Just consider that while the mode of β_1 is in principle inaccessible, that of δ_1 is immediately available. As for β_1 and δ_1, so for β_2 and δ_2, and, in general, for all complexes and their forms.

(a) *A complex and its being of a certain form are two and not one.* (b) *For some complexes, their being (or not being) of a certain form is sometimes presented to us; and, if presented at all, is transparent.* These are the two appeals to the given made in the last paragraph. Only the parenthetical clause goes a bit further. Presently I shall claim, and eventually argue for, much more. (c) *For every complex, its being (or not being) of a certain form is recursively accessible and, if presented at all, transparent.* This, though, is the big story. Let us stick with (a) and (b). Since they are appeals to the given, I shall, as usual, not support them directly but only indirectly; this time by attending to the task they set us. But stop first long enough to appreciate how much light, if it can be made good, (c) throws on the pattern. The connection between the three notions of analyticity, of tautology, and of form is close indeed. Yet, while something being analytic and something being a tautology belong both to the excess, something being of a certain form not only is thinkable but its mode is recursively accessible.

What does β_1-being-of-the-form-At_1 consist in? The answer is obvious. It consists in there being a particular and a (nonrelational) universal (of the first type), such that β_1 is (the same as) the value of η for these two things. In symbols, less obviously, (13a) '$At_1(\alpha)$' is an abbreviation for (13) '$(\exists x)(\exists f)(\alpha = \eta(f, x))$'. Less obviously, I said, because it goes beyond the conventional notation in that, first, '=' stands for the new notion of sameness, and, second, the new variable, 'α', since it occurs only as the term of a circumstance, ranges over (the expressions for) all determinates.

(13a) being an abbreviation has three consequences which, very plausibly, to say the least, hold for all forms. *First.* 'At_1' stands for nothing. Only the substitution instances of (13a) stand for what the corresponding "right sides" of this definition stand for—in a schema which, by the very fact that it contains them, is no longer ideal. *Second.* Since the variable in (13) ranges over all determinates, the result of any admissible substitution for it is well formed, although what it stands for is of course potential for anything but an atomic fact of the first sort. $At_1(a_1)$, for instance, is potential. Thus a difference as fundamental as any between ultimate sorts (which are forms$_1$) and forms (i.e., forms$_2$) is finally established. 'Green-being-a-relation' and 'a-not-being-a-particular' stand for nothing. $At_1(\beta_2)$ and $\sim At_1(\beta_1)$ are complexes pervaded by potentiality. Incidentally, as soon as the new assay of generalization is proposed in the second part of this Section, we shall see that while the substance of the limitation of the ranges of the two quantifiers in (13) is of course maintained, its form will yet be significantly different. *Third.* Remember what we said earlier (p. 63). Although we perceive (not: perceive$_1$!) this-being-a-horse, 'horse' yet may not, and as I undertake to argue in the next Section, in fact does not, stand for anything. The situation and, essentially, the argument are the same for forms. One may be conscious of (or: aware of) the "left side" of a definition, such as (13a), without being aware of the "right side" that goes with it. (The double quotes will warn you that I speak succinctly rather than accurately.) That, we shall see, is the idea. E.g., we are with immediate evidence aware of $subst\langle f_1(a_1), a_1, b_1, f_1(b_1)\rangle$ without plausibly being aware of the "right side," rather long-ish as we shall see, that goes with it.

That much for δ_1. What can we learn from δ_2? Or, rather, since the latter is more elaborate than the immediate purpose requires, what can we learn from something being of the form (*Disj*) which β_2 shares with all disjunctions? Proceeding as before, one would want to write (14a) '$Disj(\alpha)$' as an abbreviation for (14) '$(\exists \beta)(\exists \gamma)(\alpha = \beta \vee \gamma)$'. Yet something new gives pause. Quantification in (14) is not, as usual and still in (13), over (expressions for two types of) things but, rather, over (expressions for) complexes. Are there such quantifications? In this world, most unconventionally, *provided only a certain condition is fulfilled*, there are. Or so at least I shall argue in due course. This is indeed the one important step toward answering the big question about form, which I promised to take in this Section, but it will light the path ahead and greatly facilitate the exposition if we try now to acquire some notion of what more will have to be done after that step has been taken.

28* Notice that, since '$\beta \lor \gamma$' is well formed if the expressions substituted stand for either facts or circumstances but not if they stand for either things or classes, the quantifications in (14) range over the former, but not over the latter, of these two pairs in the quartet of determinates. And, *of course*, there is no quantification over anything but determinates. Of all this later in this Section. The condition mentioned above is, all details apart, that the scopes of the quantifiers be II-complexes. Thus, rather than blurring the schematism, this condition makes it stand out by adding to the import of the level division.

Being molecular of the first level is to be of a certain sort; call it molecularity (*Mol*). '*Mol*' stands again for nothing; '*Mol*(α)' is again an abbreviation, i.e., as one says, the left side of a definition. But there is also something new. Molecularity is said to be a recursive notion. Yet literally it is not. To see what I am driving at, consider how the syntacticist—or metalinguist, as I shall also call him—goes about laying down what he calls the formation rules of a sentential calculus (with constants). First, he selects a series of shapes, presumably denumerably infinite, say, 'p_1', 'p_2', . . . , then specifies individually two more shapes, say (—) and '.'. Next he singles out some finite strings of shapes, to be called sentences, such that (a) every 'p_i' is a sentence; (b) if α and β are sentences, so are $\bar{\alpha}$, $\bar{\beta}$, $\alpha \cdot \beta$; (c) nothing else is a sentence. As is apparent from the absence of single quotes around the Greek letters, he uses them, as we do not, metalinguistically; the two individually specified shapes he uses, as one says, automatically. (a), (b), and (c) allow for each finite string the decision whether it is a sentence. Because of this feature the formation rules are said to be recursive. Literally, though, recursiveness is a number-theoretical feature. A class of integers, for instance, by Church's famous hypothesis, has this feature if and only if one can for every integer decide whether it is an element of the class. That accounts for the use of 'recursive' in both contexts. Yet the syntacticist, when he uses the term, literally talks about integers and, say, classes of integers, which he has obtained by Goedelization of a calculus. In this discourse, when claiming that all forms (and formal features) are recursive, I shall speak as everyone else does, yet mean and claim something else. In the case of *Mol*, for instance, the claim is that there is a class, μ_1, that has four features. (1) μ_1 is of the sort—eventually I shall call it primary—

whose members are the only classes we can intend and, therefore, also the only ones which in this world enjoy full ontological status. (2) A complex (not: an integer!) is molecular if and only if it is an element of μ_1; thus (15a) '$Mol(\alpha)$' may be introduced as an abbreviation for (15a) '$\alpha \in \mu_1$'. (3) For every class of this sort, μ_k, and for every determinate, α_i, it is *decidable* whether the circumstance $\alpha_i \in \mu_k$ is actual or potential. (4) These special classes, of the sort I shall eventually call iterative, which correspond to the forms, have a feature that structurally corresponds to the recursiveness of the classes of integers the syntacticist speak about. A more detailed statement of this fourfold claim and the reasons that will be adduced in support of it will have to wait for the last two Sections. 'Decidable', as used where it was just italicized, is synonymous with 'recursively accessible'. To understand what either expression means, we must acquaint ourselves with the notion of a *Cartesian progression.*

Nothing will be lost for what we are about if, ignoring inference from premises, we limit ourselves to what has been called demonstration. A demonstration is a series of n expressions, each standing for a tautology, say, $t_1, t_2, \ldots, t_n$, connected in a way we need not rehearse; t_n being the one which is demonstrated. A Cartesian progression is a succession of conscious states, $M_1, M_2, \ldots, M_n$, in one mind such that (a) M_i is an awareness of evidentialy believing t_i; (b) the modes of either the first or the first few of the t-series are immediately available; and (c) the modes of all the other t_is become transparent as, and because, M_i succeeds M_{i-1}. Such a series I call a progression because what proceeds, or spreads, in it from the first to the last link is transparence; and I call it Cartesian because the transparence of this world corresponds to the clearness and distinctness of Descartes' (p. 96).

We are ready for an unpacking long overdue. A complex of a certain sort is decidable, or synonymously, *its mode is recursively accessible, if and only if, provided it is a tautology, its mode becomes transparent in the last link of a Cartesian progression, such that we can learn how to cause this progression to occur in our mind for every member of the sort.*

Four comments will round this out. (1) Unlike the expressions of a language, either natural or improved or claimed to be ideal, the shapes and strings of shapes of a calculus do not stand for anything. That is why at the beginning of the next to the last paragraph I spoke of expressions. Unless one holds fast to this distinction, he is in danger of confusing (mathematical) logic and ontology. (2) The way the matter is usually put by the logicians, what is said to be decidable is the sort. The way it is put here suits the purposes of this discourse, which is not about logic but rather, if only in part, about its phenomenology and ontology. (3) As it actually occurs, a Cartesian progression is more often than not interspersed with awareness of imaginings$_1$ and perceivings$_1$; either of sentences of a language either natural or improved; or of strings of shapes of a calculus, together with all sorts of sentences "about" these strings including some of those the metalinguists call derivation rules. Without such support, many, if not most, Cartesian progressions would not occur. Close as it is, this dependence of thought on language is yet merely causal, or, if you please, *external.* The occurrence of one awareness causes the occurrence of another. But even a single awareness, as has already been anticipated more than once and will soon be argued, unless it is either a perceiving or an imagining, is one, viz., an awareness, by virtue of there being, among its several acts, at least one which is either a perceiving$_1$ or an imagining$_1$ of words. This is an *internal,* or, if you please, an ontological dependence. (4) Derivation rules are about calculi. 'If this and that are both theorems, so is that other'; that is their pattern. Transposed from calculi to the world, they become "derivation rules" and the pattern turns into 'If (this is actual) and (that is actual), then (that other is actual)'. Hence, since the parenthetical clauses cannot be arguments of connectives, all "derivation rules" belong to the excess. Schematically, every transition from one link in a Cartesian progression to the next corresponds to such a "rule." Thus the claim that, at least in principle although not of course recursively, the modes of all tautologies are accessible to us cannot but rest, in part, on a phenomenological appeal to the effect that certain transitions "convey" transparence. (The logicians' use of 'rule', which for once I followed, does no harm. Outside of logic, though, I quarantined the word between double quotes. See also p. 102.)

That much for now about form. Supposing it stands up, what does it amount to? I offer two points. Each states not only a reason why what has been said and eventually, if only in outline, will be done is important but also the limit of what can be done and, therefore, of its importance.

When one is presented with $\beta_1 \lor \sim\beta_1$, not only its mode but also that of its being of the form $DNAt_1$ is immediately available. That makes the example unsuitable as a paradigm for an important feature. Suppose, then, that in the case of β_3 it takes, schematically speaking, two Cartesian progressions to reach first its mode and then its being of its (relevant) form. I say "schematically speaking" because in fact the two progressions often intermingle. The feature is that, after by a third progression it has become transparent that another complex, β_4, is of the same form, it takes only one transition to reach the mode of β_4. That does not mean that a complex being analytic or its being a tautology can be retrieved from the excess. But, then, is it not just because they are irretrievable that the feature is important? This is the first point.

That the forms of p- and q-tautologies are what in this discourse they are said to be is, *non*ontologically speaking, an old story. But it is neither an old story nor obvious nor unimportant that a complex being of a certain form is grounded in a further complex, whose form is in turn thus grounded; and that, therefore, we can intend this further complex and need not, or not yet, when trying to think about it, think instead about the shapes of a calculus. But then, again, neither of those two strategic notions, being analytic and being a tautology, can be retrieved from the excess. That is why I just said "not yet." This is the second point.

We are ready to resume the examination of the connectives which was interrupted when it had barely got under way. A comment about a "connection" between the connectives and form will provide the transition.

Whenever a connective is implicitly presented, any instance of one or more of a small number of tautological schemata "regulating" it becomes, with its mode, immediately available. Suppose, for instance, that when explicitly presented with β_5, one is implicitly presented with negation. If so, then from whatever cause β_6 and β_7 may have come to mind, and irrespective of whether they are implicitly presented with β_5, such tautologies as, say, (15) $\beta_6 \equiv \sim \sim \beta_6$ and (16) $(\beta_6 \vee \beta_7) \equiv (\sim\beta_6 \supset \beta_7)$ become with their modes immediately available. As for negation, so for all connectives. For disjunction, for instance, it may again be (16), or perhaps (17) $\beta_6 \vee \sim\beta_6$, or something else. Which, if any, and if some, how many of these tautologies are in fact presented on such an occasion makes no difference. The point is, rather, that some must, with their modes, be immediately available on each such occasion. For, if they were not, we would not, as the new contextualists say, know what the words 'not', 'or', and so on meant. I, of course, when talking ontology, would not say that, but merely state the feature the way I just did. Stating it their way is merely my way of pointing out that the feature is one of the two which, as anticipated, recover the sound core of contextualism.

A thread left dangling can now be tied up. Each collection of tautological schemata that goes in the way just specified with a connective, goes in this way only, with this connective and with no other. That unpacks the secondary sense of 'unique' in which every connective is unique (p. 114).

29* (a) As for the connectives, so for the quantifiers with respect to both these contextual features. But I shall not return to the matter. (b) Uniqueness in the other sense of the term, which is more important and which therefore by implication I just called primary, is, you remember, a feature shared by all nondeterminates. None of them can be a term of a circumstance. (c) When talking about tautological schemata, as for brevity's sake I did, one talks of course the language of the syntacticist; just as saying that these tautologies "regulate" the connectives has the flavor of the new contextualism. That is why 'regulate' was quarantined. If you need convincing on this score, just expand the verb into 'regulate the use of'. (d) The other feature, recovering the other part of the sound core of contextualism, is one of classes. So we shall not encounter it until Section VI. (e) A Contextualist critic, who prefers to deal with sentences rather than complexes, may point out that just as 'this is green or this is not green' regulates the use of 'or' and 'not', so 'nothing is both green and red' regulates that of 'green' and 'red'. Thus, he concludes, all these words are "contextually regulated." He adds, for good measure, that the distinction between the analytic and the synthetic a priori, of which so much is made in this world, is precarious at best and quite probably untenable; for it rests on nothing more solid than the difference, alleged to be clearly felt, between two complexes such that, while the negation of the one cannot even be thought, that of the other cannot be imagined. I readily admit, not only that this difference is indeed the phenomenological ground of that distinction, but also that, if you throw it away, this world collapses. But so, I believe does much, if not most, of ontology.

How many connectives are there? A logician willing to suppose, if only for the sake of the argument, that there are some, will tell us that one will do, and offer us a choice between neither-nor and not-both. The ontologist knows that any situation in which he seems free to "choose" what exists is rather peculiar. But let us for a little while ignore this wrinkle and, for convenience' sake, indulge in a fiction. Our friend (I imagine) tells us that (without choice) negation and disjunction will do. His reason is familiar. All other "connectives" can be defined in terms of these two. (So used, between double quotes, 'connective' refers to the words which may or may not stand for the putative existents.) As long as he speaks about a calculus, or, rather, about trivial isomorphisms among some calculi, he is right, of course. But he goes further. Why, he asks me, if you suppose that '~' and '∨' stand each for one existent, should not all other "connectives" be introduced into your ideal language, through abbreviations, e.g., '$\alpha_1 \supset \alpha_2$' for '$\sim\alpha_1 \vee \alpha_2$'; '$\alpha_1 \mathbin{\&} \alpha_2$' for '$\sim(\sim\alpha_1 \vee \alpha_2)$'; and so on; so that upon your own view they would all, with those two exceptions, stand for nothing. Then he reminds me that I undertake to justify in the next Section exactly this sort of reasoning in the case of 'horse'.

I first reply, then propose my own answer, as follows: The reminder is in order. 'Horse', since it occurs only in abbreviations, stands indeed for nothing. Nor, therefore, is there any intention for which—except pleonastically in a language no longer ideal—an expression containing 'horse' could stand. The case of the connectives, however, is different. On the one hand, as already claimed, $\alpha_1 \vee \alpha_2$, $\alpha_1 \mathbin{\&} \alpha_2$, $\alpha_1 \supset \alpha_2$, and so on can all be intended. On the other hand, as will be claimed and argued in the next Section, even if α_1 and α_2 are atomic, we could not be aware of $\alpha_1 \vee \alpha_2$, $\alpha_1 \mathbin{\&} \alpha_2$, $\alpha_1 \supset \alpha_2$, and so on unless there is among the acts of the respective awareness one which implicitly intends the words 'or', 'and', 'if-then', and so on; or, in case we do not, as one says, think in English, the words, *if any*, which correspond to them in whatever language we happen to think in. I say "if any" because, clearly, which and how many words of this kind a language has is an anthropological accident. In this respect—call it epistemological, if you like, since it involves the assay of awareness—all connectives are in the same boat. How, then, could the ontologist choose among the ten combinatorially possible binary connectives? The answer I propose avoids the unacceptable choice. *There are, in addition to negation, ten binary connectives.* To be sure, this is an "extrapolation," arrived at dialectically rather than on phenomenological grounds. I am also sure it is harmless. Yet it raises some questions. To these, with your permission, I shall presently attend. First, though, since this is the place where it fits, I shall try to show why a certain reason for there being no connectives is not a good reason (p. 143).

30* There are among the sixteen combinatorially possible binary truth tables four pairs such that the difference within each pair is accounted for by the order in the standardized argument. $\supset\langle\alpha_1, \alpha_2\rangle$ and $\supset\langle\alpha_2, \alpha_1\rangle$, for instance, correspond to one such pair. Yet there is of course only one conditional. Taking that into account and putting aside tautology and contradiction, of which more presently, one arrives at the number ten.

The argument starts from a comparison of the "connectives" with "defined predicate expressions," such as 'p_1', 'p_2', 'p_3', respectively introduced by '$p_1(x)$' for '$gr(x) \supset sq(x)$', '$p_2(x)$' for '$red(x) \mathbin{\&} rd(x)$', '$p_3(x)$'

for '$p_1(x) \lor p_2(x)$'; with 'gr', 'sq', 'red', 'rd' standing for the four characters green, square, red, and round, whose existence, since they are "simple," is taken for granted. Such expressions, the argument observes, can only be introduced in a certain order. P_1, for instance, presumably cannot be defined in terms of p_2 and p_3. Whether or not that is so in this case, the situation in general certainly is different from that of the "connectives," where one can start a definitional hierarchy that reaches them all from either '$/$', or '$\downarrow$', or '$\sim$' and '$\lor$', or '$\sim$' and '$\&$', and so on. From this difference, or contrast, the argument concludes that there are no connectives; i.e., to spell it out once more, that no "connective" stands for anything.

This argument has two flaws. First, it implicitly presupposes that defined predicate expressions do stand for something. Thus it embraces the untenable view, which it took me so long to reject, that there are "defined characters." For, otherwise, what is the point of the contrast? The second flaw is, if anything, even more fatal. Suppose (18a) '$\alpha_1 \& \alpha_2$' abbreviates (18) '$\sim(\sim\alpha_1 \lor \sim\alpha_2)$'. (18) either does or does not purport to stand for something. If it doesn't, we are dealing with a calculus and nothing relevant to the issue at hand can be said. If (18) does purport to stand for something, what is that "something"? α_1 and α_2 presumably are two atomic facts whose existence is taken for granted. Yet, if the "connectives" in (18) stand for nothing, how does (18) itself manage to stand for anything? And how, if it did, would whatever it stands for manage to be different from what any other molecular expression in 'α_1', 'α_2', '$\sim$', '$\lor$' consistently would have to stand for? Or do they perhaps all stand for the pair class whose elements are α_1 and α_2? Such are the woes of the position, often called atomism, which holds that atomic facts are the only ones that exist.

There are, then, by an extrapolation both inevitable and harmless, at least eleven connectives, viz., the ten binary ones and negation. I say "at least" because two questions immediately arise. How about the binary tautology and contradiction? How about ternary, quaternary, and, in general, n-nary connectives? You may, if you wish, ontologize the binary "tautology" and "contradition." All I can say is that, since I do not see what job they would do, by Occam's rule, I don't. The second question is a bit more interesting.

Let 'δ_1', 'δ_2', 'δ_3' abbreviate

$$'(\alpha_1 \lor \alpha_2) \lor \alpha_3',\ '(\alpha_1 \lor \alpha_3) \lor \alpha_2',\ '(\alpha_2 \lor \alpha_3) \lor \alpha_1,$$

respectively; α_1, α_2, α_3 being complexes of any sort. (19a) $\delta_1 \equiv \delta_2$, (19b) $\delta_2 \equiv \delta_3$, (19c) $\delta_3 \equiv \delta_1$ are tautological equivalences whose modes are recursively, if not perhaps immediately, accessible. For those who do not distinguish between the sameness and the tautological equivalence of complexes, δ_1, δ_2, and δ_3 are one and not either two or three. In this world $(\gamma_1 \vee \gamma_2) = (\gamma_3 \vee \gamma_4)$ if and only if either $(\gamma_1 = \gamma_3)$ & $(\gamma_2 = \gamma_4)$ or $(\gamma_1 = \gamma_4)$ & $(\gamma_2 = \gamma_3)$. This is one of the obvious sameness criteria, of which more later. Hence, by another such criterion, (20a) $\delta_1 \neq \delta_2$, (20b) $\delta_2 \neq \delta_3$, (20c) $\delta_3 \neq \delta_1$. One who considers that a roughness, or an inconvenience, will argue that if a ternary "disjunction" turned these diversities into samenesses, there would be a good reason for ontologizing this particular ternary "connective" and therefore, if only for consistency's sake, all other combinatorially possible ones. Suppose there is such a disjunction $(\vee^3)$. However inconvenient one thinks the inconvenience is, a brief reflection will show him that $\vee^3$ does not do the trick. If one abandons the new assay of order, the world collapses and there is nothing more to be said. If one does not abandon it, the three "arguments" of $\vee^3$ must be standardized into a single one. That makes $\vee^3((\alpha_1, \alpha_2), \alpha_3)$, $\vee^3((\alpha_1, \alpha_3), \alpha_2)$, and $\vee^3 ((\alpha_2, \alpha_3), \alpha_1)$ three equally likely candidates for the value of $\vee^3$ for the nonstandardized argument. Yet, by a sameness criterion just appealed to, the single arguments above are three and not either two or one. Hence, if the inconvenience is to disappear, an additional set of sameness criteria, which is just as inconvenient, will be needed. As for the ternary "connectives," so for the quaternary ones, and so on. We conclude that what seemed at first sight a good reason is in fact not a good reason for ontologizing any "connective" beyond the eleven. Nor can I think of any other good reason. There is, however, a very good reason, of the sort I am tempted to call dialectically decisive, for not ontologizing any of them. Those eleven are the minimum required to reach iteratively what is needed. If one went beyond them, one could not consistently stop at any n. Thus there would be an infinite number of connectives. And in this case, we shall see in due course, certain indispensable recursions could not get started.

There are two more things to be done about the connectives. Then we shall be ready for the quantifiers.

Is every p-tautology analytic? Equivalently, is the mode of every p-tautology at least in principle accessible to us? Since the (ontological) characterization of these complexes ((TF) on p. 145) makes no reference to accessibility (which is an epistemological notion), we must, by the very schema of analyticity, take three steps. We first select a *base*, i.e., a number of forms such that each member of each of them is a p-tautology of which we claim that its mode is immediately available to us. This claim is of course an appeal to the given. Next we specify a number of transitions of which we claim, by another such appeal, that they are Cartesian. And we must, third, convince ourselves as well as we may that each p-tautology can at least in principle be reached from that base by a Cartesian chain with no other transitions than those specified. Familiar as the pattern is, if only in its syntactical version, it is yet worthwhile stating it once ontologically also, because of the three comments it suggests. (a) The selection of the base in the first step corresponds to the syntacticist's proceeding by primitive schemata rather than sentences. The "derivation rule" corresponding to the one kind of Cartesian transition needed for the p-tautologies is of course a modifed rule of detachment: 'If α and $\alpha \supset \beta$ are tautologies, so is β'. This rule is one thing. The tautologies of the form $[\alpha \ \& \ (\alpha \supset \beta)] \supset \beta$ are quite another thing. Such rules, we know already, belong to the excess (p. 137); and they have no ground. Nor, therefore, is the class of all tautologies of this particular form the ground of this particular rule. Yet it makes sense to say that if there were not this class, the transitions of this particular kind would not be Cartesian. (b) The syntacticist, who gets along with a single "connective," can also do with a single primitive schema. The ontologist, on the other hand, if he insists on the eleven connectives, also needs a sufficiency of primitive tautologies, such as, e.g., $\alpha_1 \ \& \ \alpha_2 \equiv \sim(\sim\alpha_1 \lor \sim\alpha_2)$, in order to secure what the syntacticist achieves by definitional schemata, such as, e.g., $\alpha_1 \ \& \ \alpha_2$ for $\sim(\sim\alpha_1 \lor \sim\alpha_2)$. Thus, since the ontologist for his purposes (as we saw) needs all these connectives, he selects a base which the syntacticist would reject as reundant. That, too, illuminates the difference between the two enterprises. (c) Since the lower functional calculus, although not decidable, is yet upon the usual criterion complete, each of "its" tautologies, i.e., each complex selected by this criterion, can in principle be reached by a Cartesian chain. Or, if you please, our conviction that this is so is as strong as our trust in the ontological status of the classes in the completeness proof. Among the complexes corresponding to the second-order calculus, and therefore also to "arithmetic," the same result is, as Henkin has shown, achieved by his criterion, which we shall see is the only one that makes ontological sense. (Yet there remains the ineluctable Goedelian incompleteness; hence the quotes around 'arithmetic'.)

How close can we come to the truth tables? Take any two determinates, call them T and F; select n complexes; build the 2^n classes of 2-tuples, each of one of the complexes first and either T or F second, such that each of these classes corresponds to one of the possible distributions of truth values. Then one can recursively assign the appropriate distribution to every complex which is molecular relative to those n. Everything is finite and recursive. The classes are all among those which we can intend. This is no longer so for the classes mentioned in the characterization of the q-tautologies. For this characterization, as we shall see and as of course you expect, is but a modification of the classical validity criterion. Thus the ontological status of most of these classes is merely derivative. ('Recursive', here and elsewhere if nothing is said, is used in the sense specified on p. 148.)

The assay of the connectives, we saw, is inseparable from the characterization of the p-tautologies; and this ontological characterization "corresponds" to the syntacticist's validity criterion for the sentential calculus. As for the connectives, so for the quantifiers. Their assay is inseparable from the characterization of the sort we call for this very reason the q-tautologies; and the (ontological) characterization of this sort "corresponds" to the (syntactical) validity criterion of *a* functional calculus. There is thus again the issue, or the issues, of the "correspondence" between the two criteria, one ontological, one syntactical, and its limitations. The latter will again turn out to coincide with the very limits of thought. This, though, is no longer surprising. Nor, therefore, should any harm come to us if henceforth I suppress the double quotes around 'correspond' and its derivatives. In the first round, concerned with the connectives, we were virtually forced to start by articulating, in the simplest case, the nature and the problems of any such correspondence. In this second round, concerned with the quantifiers, since we already possess those general ideas, we need not rush the matter.

Notice the indefinite article just underscored: *a* functional calculus. Since there are several calculi that go by this name, which of them, if any, corresponds to the assay of the quantifiers about to be proposed? Equivalently, which, if any, of these calculi is a fragment of the ideal language eventually to be proposed? There is the lower or first-order calculus, now often called quantification theory. There are the first-order calculus with identity, the second-order calculus, also called the enlarged first-order calculus; and the calculus of *PM,* or, more cautiously, of the most viable reading of it, which is a higher functional calculus with an infinite number of types and the appropriate primitive sentences of extensionality. The new assay of the quantifiers corresponds to none of these familiar or standard calculi. Whence, negatively, the discrepancy? What, positively, is the "new" calculus like? More realistically, since, not being a logician, I shall not actually construct but merely sketch it, what are the differences and similarities between it and the standard calculi which reflect what concerns the ontologist? The complete answer could only come by way of conclusion, when it will have become obvious and thus no longer be useful.

But it will (I hope) help if, before presenting the new assay, I assemble, and comment on, some of the materials for the answer. Since they precede the new assay, these comments cannot but be rather general. They are also, more than anything else, dialectical and even, although only in a structural sense, historical. Keep in mind, then, that they are not offered as conclusions but merely as an introduction to the second half of this Section.

In the world of this discourse, the distinction, or perhaps better because more strongly, the contrast between properties and classes is stark. (A) Properties are stratified; classes are not. (B) Classes, by their very nature, are extensional; properties, by their very nature, are not. (C) Classes "generate" others in a way properties do not. These are the distinctions at the root of all others. Presently we shall look at them. First for a word about words. Standardized, $r_1(a_1, b_1)$ becomes $r_1\langle a_1, b_1 \rangle$. As for r_1, so for all relational universals. In this sense, every universal of whatever ultimate sort (Russellian type) is a property; the corresponding classes, corresponding to Russell's "relation *in extenso*," are classes of tuples. Sometimes, as right now, it is convenient to speak this way.

(A) In the world of the early Russell, or, as I shall also call it, the *PM*-world, there are not only particulars and properties, but the latter are stratified into a number, in principle infinite, of types. There are also, or at least so he thought, facts and classes. The latter, crucially for the matters in hand, were also stratified. For his assay of classes, however futile ontologically it may be, is such that the stratification spreads from the properties to the classes. When it comes to intellectual motives, though, the spread, every one knows, was in the other direction. For he also thought that unless classes are stratified, one cannot avoid his famous paradox. Thus he stratified properties in order to avoid unstratified classes. What he actually achieved, I submit, is quite different from what he thought he did even with the benefit of doubt more than due to one who not only broke so much new ground but also changed the very face of some old issues: a property of the *PM*-world and the class coextensive with it are one and not two. Thus there are in that world only particulars and, *if only after a fashion*, classes as well as circumstances, the latter being mistaken for facts.

30* Take what in the world of this discourse is a fact, say, green-being-a-color ($Col(gr)$). In the *PM*-world it becomes $\hat{gr} \in \hat{Col}$, which in our world is a circumstance of the sort we listed second; '$\hat{gr}$' and '$\hat{Col}$' stand of course for the appropriate classes. '$\in$', to be sure, in either world stands for nothing. In this world, though, we shall see, that makes sense; while in the *PM*-world rather obviously, at least from where I stand, it doesn't. For the only clear-cut existents of that world are determinates; the only simple determinates are the particulars; and classes, although in both worlds in some respects like things, are not simples in either. That is why 'if only after a fashion' is underscored. For support of the diagnosis, here and below, see Appendix B, on the ontology of the early Russell.

A. Russell and the mathematical logicians (axiomatic set theorists) all wanted to answer certain questions about classes. Yet the roads they took toward the goal they shared were radically different. Russell, again with the benefit of doubt, syntactically constructed a calculus, to be interpreted as an ideal language, such that a part of it reflected his assay of classes. The logicians searched for, and found, axiomatic systems each of which achieves four things. It gets rid not only of the paradoxes but also of the flaws which, inevitably, marred Russell's pioneering effort. It provides axiomatic foundations for all the classes of mathematics. Its "classes" are all "particulars" and conversely. Its classes are not stratified. Nor are these just mathematical achievements. *Potentially* they are of great ontological import in two respects. For one, as has been argued in Section I, classes are indeed arbitrary in a sense that makes it repugnant for elementhood to depend on any stratification among determinates. For another, as will be argued in Section VI, one cannot ground all the classes of mathematics without making use of the axiomatists' results. Who, then, is right, Russell or the axiomatists? One cannot answer without bringing in two more points.

First. As long as an axiomatic system remains uninterpreted it is about nothing; ontologically, therefore, it is nothing. Scientists interpret such systems into the world. Then they are about something, although not thereby ontologically significant. The only way in which the "entities" of such a system may, derivatively or secondarily, acquire some ontological standing is for an ontologist to interpret them into the calculus which he proposes as his ideal language. That is why the two roads, Russell's and the axiomatists', differ so radically. On the other hand, though, one cannot ground all the classes of mathematics without giving them in this way at least some secondary, or derivative, ontological standing. The arguments for all this can and must wait. For the pattern I am now weaving we need only the assertion. You see why in the preceding paragraph 'potential' has been underscored and why 'particular' and 'class', as in this paragraph 'entity', have been quarantined between double quotes.

Second. The set theorists who are also ontologists, most eminently among them Quine, make their system the ideal language; with neither '=' nor '∈' (which I think is right) nor the expressions for the functions (which I think is wrong) standing for anything. (They of course wouldn't put it this way, for reasons which, from where they stand, are very good reasons. Do I then take more liberty than I should? If you think that I do, you ought to give up all attempts to compare ontologies.) Thus we are presented with a world all of whose existents are classes, or perhaps, although not in Quine's case, either classes or particulars.

We are ready to balance the accounts. On the one side, there is a world of particulars and, at least putatively, of facts and classes; the latter, unnecessarily and rather unfelicitously, stratified. Yet there is also Russell's monumental ontological achievement of having been the first who saw that there are relational as well as higher-type properties and that they are all stratified. On the other side, there is a world, if that be the word, of classes only. But there are also, if only potentially, the two major ontological achievements of having shown that classes need not be stratified and of having provided the apparatus needed to ground them all. This discourse tries to have the best of both these worlds. *For this is a third world, of stratified properties and nonstratified classes.* E.g., a thing, a fact, a circumstance, and a class can all be elements of the same class. More cautiously, this is the goal. Having failed so often, the most I dare hope is that this time I am merely fumbling, making only mistakes that are mathematical and of the kind an ontologist who has the required skills could correct without tearing down the whole structure. But is this not one more reason for holding out the trail of this dialectical reconciliation?

B. Two classes are one if and only if every element of the one is also an element of the other, and conversely. For every property there is a class such that a determinate *actually* has the property if and only if it *actually* is an element of the class. In this sense, every property determines one and only one class, or "its" class, but not conversely. Given a class, there may be either no property, or exactly one property, or any number of them, either finite or infinite, that determine it. More concisely: *Classes by their very nature are extensional; properties by their very nature are not.* Is this formula, call it (*F*), just common sense? If so, why the conspicuous, almost provocative qualification: by their very nature?

Remember what has been said in Section I (p. 49) about another formula, to the effect that classes are arbitrary. The formula, I claimed, is common sense, rather than an implicit definition, because an ontologist's world of which, *in his style*, it isn't a feature is not the world philosophers have talked and worried about. Put differently, the formula is simply an adequacy criterion. As for that formula, so for (F). Why, then, the new qualification: in this style? Consider the class of all green things. In the style of this world, the mode of this-being-green is in principle inaccessible to us. How, then, can we know that there is a class coextensive with green? Even more forbiddingly, as we shall see, one cannot in this world intend a class, β, unless the mode of $\alpha \in \beta$ is for every determinate α at least recursively accessible to us. That accounts for the new qualification as well as for the underscoring of 'actually' in the preceding paragraph.

There is a difference between the two halves of (F). Classes-being-extensional is, in the style of this world, a complex whose actuality is immediately presented to us. In the case of classes that accounts for the almost provocative qualification: by their very nature. The case of properties is strikingly different. In this ontology there are only "simple" properties. In some others there are also "derived" ones; either implicitly or, as until recently in mine, explicitly. Use, then, for the moment, the two adjectives which in this ontology are redundant; and ask yourself whether in the world (not: ontology!) in which we all live there are two "simple" properties that are coextensive. The answer is No. Yet I can think (intend) both, that there are and that there are not, two coextensive properties, without the mode of either complex being accessible to me. That makes the nonextensionality of the properties of our world one of its contingent principles. By their very nature, properties are nonextensional. Notice, too, that this particular contingent principle, being about a world either with or without man, has not the slightest anthropological tinge.

(C) Given two classes, say, of all red things and of all square things, there are "in general" also the classes of all things red or square, both red and square, red and not square, and so on, which either single, or jointly, or together with still other classes these two "generate." Not so for properties. There is no property of being red or square, none of being both red and square, and so on. That unpacks the formula: *Classes generate others in a way properties do not.* What makes the difference is of course the suppression, in ontology, of all "derived characters."

31* (a) I just said "in general" because there is in this world no empty class nor the class of all classes nor that of all determinates. Ontologically, I shall argue, no matter how convenient certain notations may be, the notion of an "empty class" is an absurdity. The other two, of the class of all classes and of that of all determinates, lead immediately to the notion of a class being its own element, which, as I shall also argue, is in itself, irrespective of the contradictions it engenders, an ontological absurdity. (b) To appreciate the import of (C), consider the issue, or problem, of impredicativity, which so preoccupied Russell and still occasionally occupies some logicians. If there are no derived properties, then there is for properties no such problem. In the case of classes, say, in the case of *PM*, what Russell took to be an "impredicative definition" of a class may be read as a definite description that cannot fail of what, with or without this description, is there. Thus, again, *ontologically there is no problem of impredicativity*. Yet, for all I know, there may be some such problem in some calculi serving some nonontological purpose.

Return now to the main line of thought, where we left it before starting on (A). The new assay of the quantifiers corresponds to a functional calculus. What is this calculus like? In which respects, if any, is it new? Even a partial and preliminary answer will give us the sense of direction we need for tackling the assay itself. (A), (B), and (C) have laid the ground for such an answer.

Since the properties of this world are stratified and include some higher types, the new calculus cannot be either the lower functional calculus or the second-order calculus (i.e., the lower functional calculus enlarged by quantification over its predicates). Nor, on the other hand, can it be a higher functional calculus, if by that one means, as I do, one of stratified classes; either overtly or, as in the *PM* case, covertly. For in such a calculus the number of types cannot but be infinite, while in this world it is finite. Thus the new calculus can at most be an initial segment, or fragment, of a higher calculus. Presently I shall answer. Let us first inquire what difference, if any, the difference between a finite and infinite number of types (i.e., just to remind ourselves, of ultimate sorts) makes ontologically.

(a) If, as I claim, the number of types in this world is not only finite but rather small, how many are there? Four, or seventeen, or one hundred and twenty? As long as it is finite, the number is a matter of fact that does not concern us. This is one of the several respects in which the ontologist merely constructs schemata. In the case at hand, all he can do and all he need do is to show that while there are some higher types, a finite and rather small number of them will do. Having attempted to show that on two earlier occasions[4] and having nothing to add, I shall not try again. Unhappily, these attempts still work with derived characters; but that blemish can be removed. As far as I know, no other answer has ever been put forth except the two ex-

---

4. *Logic and Reality*, University of Wisconsin Press, 1964, pp. 272–301; *Realism: A Critique of Brantano and Meinong*, University of Wisconsin Press, 1967, chapter 5.

treme ones, of the nominalists who admit only particularity and of those who, in addition to particularity, admit only one nonrelational and a few relational types whose members all exemplify particulars. (b) A critic demurs, "As long as it is finite, you say, the number of types, being a mere matter of fact, does not concern you. Yet you seem to insist on its being finite. If it were infinite, wouldn't that, too, be a mere matter of fact?" My answer has two prongs, one general, one specific. First, generally, this world, while neither man-made nor just in man's mind, is yet one man can think; and for what he can think, I have come to believe, the difference between the finite and the infinite is momentous. As you will see, this idea dominates the assay of classes. Second, specifically, if the number of types were infinite, certain recursions could not get started; and if it were not for these recursions, the limits of thought would be narrower than they are. (Of this connection, I trust, you already have a sense.) Nor is the distinction without dialectical support. Presently we shall see that we cannot even (literally) think that the number of types is infinite. That alone makes their number being finite more than a mere matter of fact. But you may, if that helps, call it a contingent principle; for some such principles do determine what we can and cannot think. (For this, see Appendix A.) (c) If *PM*, supplemented by constants, could, as Russell thought, accommodate (statements of) facts, there would in its world be an infinite number of subsorts of atomic facts. In this world, what holds for the number of types holds, not surprisingly, also for the number of these subsorts as well as for the number of functions. If either were infinite, we couldn't (literally) think certain things which we can think and certain recursions would not be available.

We are ready for the question postponed. Is the new calculus a fragment of a higher calculus? In a higher calculus that deserves the name there is not only quantification over each type; there are also certain "connections," established by primitive sentences, which span more than just two successive types. In *PM*, for instance, there are, minimally, the primitive sentences of extensionality for any three successive types, and in addition, for certain purposes, the primitive sentences of choice. Without some such connections, a "higher" calculus is materially but a series of second-order calculi, obtained from the first member of the series by what Goedel called type-lifting (*Typenerhoehung*). Those who shared Russell's belief that arithmetic can not be grounded without a higher calculus which does deserve that name paid the price. I, no longer sharing the belief, need not pay it. Nor do I have any choice. If one accepts the arguments, just marshaled under the headings (A), (B), and (C), for the sharp contrast between classes and properties, he must for the latter abandon extensionality, which is the most indispensable I can think of among all those "connections." Thus, since there are in this world only a few higher types, the new calculus, or, as one says, the model that will be used in the new validity criterion, is materially but a short series of second-order calculi. Nor, as was mentioned earlier (p. 156), need we recoil from the price to be paid for that. Naturally, the new calculus will be neither decidable nor, in Goedel's sense, complete. That, though, is not a weakness of this world but, if anything, a strength, one more place where its blocks abut without gap. For the second-order calculus is complete in Henkin's sense, which (we shall see) is the one that does matter on ontological grounds.

What, finally, is the connection between the two new assays, of sameness and of the quantifiers? If there is one, should we not "add identity" to the calculus that corresponds to the latter? If one reads '=' as I do, such expressions as, say, '$f_1 = a_1$' and '$f_2 = f_1(a_1)$', although what they stand for is potential, are yet well formed. If one reads the two horizontal bars as in the calculi to which, as one says, identity has been added, these expressions are ill formed. Sameness just isn't identity in the axiomatic style; nor is it, as we shall soon convince ourselves once more, analytical equivalence in the style of Russell. The answer to the second question, about calculi, is thus obviously No. That does not, however, dispose of the first question. In the world, there are of course connections between sameness and quantification. The mathematical problems to which these connections give rise belong to combinatorial logic. Fortunately for us, Church and some others, who in the discussions about the so-called substitution rules of functional calculi more than a generation ago were the first fully to grasp these problems, also solved them. But the way I shall fit some bits of their elaborate researches into the new ontological schema is itself new and makes it imperative that, before starting on the new assay of the quantifiers, we get a glimpse of its connections with that of sameness.

Still speaking and writing conventionally, with variables, suppose that 'μ' stands for a first-level complex (i.e., briefly, as before, a complex-I) and that 'x' has no free occurrence in 'μ'; form the four expressions

$$(21\text{a})\ (x)[\,\mu \vee f_1(x)], \qquad (21\text{b})\ \mu \vee (x)\,f_1(x),$$
$$(21\text{c})\ (x)\,(\exists y)\ r_1(x, y) \qquad (21\text{d})\ (y)(\exists x)r_1(\,y, x);$$

let $\alpha_1, \beta_1, \gamma_1, \delta_1$ refer to the complexes they stand for; and consider four others:

(22a) $\alpha_1 \equiv \beta_1$,   (22b) $\delta_1 \equiv \gamma_1$,
(22c) $\alpha_1 = \beta_1$,   (22d) $\delta_1 = \gamma_1$.

(22a) and (22b) are quantificational I-complexes (briefly: q-complexes-I), and therefore among those to which conventional "quantification theory" addresses itself. Since γ_1 and δ_1 are q-complexes, so are (22c) and (22d); but, since they are of the second level (i.e., complexes-II), they are beyond the purview of the conventional "quantification theory." In this world, (22a) to (22d) are all available. (22a), (22b), and (22d) are accessibly actual. (22c), however, is accessibly potential; no longer surprisingly, I trust, in a world where even $(\alpha_1 \supset \alpha_2)$ $= (\sim \alpha_1 \vee \alpha_2)$ is potential, although, $(\alpha_1 \supset \alpha_2) \equiv (\sim\alpha_1 \vee \alpha_2)$ is of course actual. In a world without sameness, I repeat, (22c) and (22d) are not available. Some conventional calculi use (22a) as a primitive sentence. The condition that goes with it, x-not-having-a-free-occurrence-in-μ, is metalinguistic. So, by their very nature, are all derivation rules. Practically it is not difficult to decide whether these rules apply or those conditions are satisfied. Yet it has been anything but easy to state accurately rules and conditions which apply in all cases and to prove that it is recursively decidable whether or not they apply or are satisfied. This is part of what, proceeding metalinguistically, the combinatorial logicians did.

In this world, the two steps corresponding to the syntacticist's choice of primitive sentences and derivation rules read as follows. First we specify a small number of forms and claim (a) that a complex actually having one of these forms is either immediately available or recursively accessible to us; and (b) that as soon as we are presented with a complex actually being of this form, the actuality of the complex itself becomes transparent. Second, we specify a small number of tuples of complexes and claim for each tuple of any of these forms that the transition from all but the last of its terms to the last is Cartesian. So far, so good. I have merely "translated" from a calculus into the world. Nor of course is there any need, just as there wasn't in the p-case, for once more executing the two steps in detail rather than merely pointing out what matters ontologically. Two features, both already touched upon, matter so crucially that they ought to be pointed out immediately.

For one, the mode of any circumstance is at least recursively accessible to us. The circumstance itself, therefore, is either analytic or contradictory. To this very major feature of the taxonomic pattern we are, structurally at least, committed already. A sameness is the negation of a diversity. A diversity is a circumstance. Thus we shall have to show that not just (22c) and (22d) but every sameness whose terms are q-complexes-I is decidable. Nor will that be very difficult. Notice, though, that if one made the same claim for all equivalences between q-complexes-I, he would claim, absurdly, that the functional calculus is decidable. That illuminates once more the radical difference between sameness and analytical equivalence. For another, a q-complex-I having a formal feature is in this world itself a decidable complex-II. More precisely, depending on whether or not the latter is actual, so is the former. Thus we need not, or not yet, at this point throw away the ladder and take refuge in a metalanguage. What makes those complexes-II decidable, i.e., what additional immediately available transparencies (and what Cartesian transitions, if any) we must claim for the second level is a further question to which we shall attend in due course. Nor shall we run into a vitiating regress to higher levels.

This, then, is the long-range program. One must show, first, how in all cases to produce those complexes-II; and one must show, second, that the mode of the latter is recursively accessible. (For a first statement of the pattern in a special case, see p. 146.) To carry out this program is, I repeat, far beyond my mathematical skill. I shall merely show that, if a certain hypothesis, which I shall present and try to support in the last Section, does hold up, then the mathematicians can carry it out. For all I know, ignorant as I am in these matters, implicitly they may already have done it. The two kinds of specialized skill and involvement, mathematical and ontological, are by now so far apart that at the few places where mathematics and ontology are in fact inseparable the ontologist must have the courage to take his chances, just as in ontology some mathematicians take theirs. As long as no one pretends, no harm will be done and some good may come of it.

Now we can effectively renew an agreement that will greatly facilitate the exposition in the rest of this Section. I shall freely avail myself of some familiar notions usually called syntactical, such as, say, being molecular, being a q-complex, something having a free occurrence in something, something being a constituent of something, and so on; modifying them or introducing new ones only when the new ontology requires it. More precisely, I shall avail myself of those among these notions which, if taken metalinguistically (i.e., literally, arithmetically), are by one facet of Goedel's achievement beyond all doubt recursive. But I shall handle them as if they stood, or, if you please, with the reasoned hope that they can be made to stand, for decidable classes out there in the world; e.g., the class of all those and only those complexes-I which are (actually) molecular, or the class of all those and only those 2-tuples such that their first term is (actually) a constituent of the second, and so on.

Let 'f_1' stand for a universal [(0)]. Then (23') '$(x)f_1(x)$' and (24') '$(\exists x) f_1(x)$' stand for two of the "simplest" among the determinates we must assay. Let 'b' stand for a particular. Then (25') '$(x)f_1(x) \supset f_1(b)$' and (26') '$f_1(b) \supset (\exists x)f_1(x)$' stand for complexes whose actuality is immediately available. Adding another prime will distinguish the expressions from what they stand for. (23'), for instance, stands for (23'') $(x)f_1(x)$. The notation for the quantifiers, '$(x) \ldots x \ldots$' and '$(\exists x) \ldots x \ldots$', making use of bound variables, is in all four expressions still the conventional one. Yet I cannot bring myself to write instead of 'b' a free variable, say 'y', in (25') and (26'). That, you will gather, is a compromise. We cannot but start from the conventional notation. Yet, I repeat, since there are no variables, either bound or free, nor definite descriptions nor abbreviations in the world, there cannot be any of these devices in the ideal schema. Do not jump to the conclusion that I have suddenly changed my mind, making the construction of that schema the primary task. The task is and remains a new and, hopefully, adequate assay of the quantifiers. For this purpose, though, some improved notation is virtually indispensable. That makes the primary task virtually inseparable from the secondary one, of constructing a new fragment of the ideal schema. Yet, to repeat this, too, because all those linguistic devices are excluded from the ideal schema, the latter is all but unmanageable for a human mind. That leaves me no choice. Where it is needed, the new fragment will be put to work. At all other places I shall continue to use the conventional notation, or some conveniently relaxed modification of it, for the quantifiers and, occasionally, even free variables.

First. (25') and (26') are not rules of some sort but stand for determinates. Second, (23'') and (24'') are neither circumstances nor classes nor things but facts, and as such have modes. Third. (23'') is not a conjunction, either finite or infinite, nor even analytically equivalent to one. Similarly for (24'') and disjunction. Fourth. What connection there is, and there is of course a most important one, between (23'') and (24'') and particulars is grounded in the tautologies (25'') and (26''), respectively. Put differently, in words suggested by a medieval phrase, (25'') regulates the *descent* from (23'') for either b or any other particular, while (26'') regulates the *ascent*, again for either b or any other particular, to (24''). These four things I take for granted.

If (23'') and (24'') are facts, then the two quantifiers are functions. For a fact is the value of a function for some arguments, which are determinates; preferably for a single argument, otherwise what has already been gained by standardization would be lost. What, then, are the arguments of the quantifiers in (23″) and (24″)? The only obvious candidate in both cases is f_1. Yet it will not do. To see why it doesn't, ask yourself what the arguments of $(x)r_1(x, c)$ and $(x)[f_1(x) \lor f_2(x)]$ would be. The only consistent answer is $r_1 (\ldots , c)$ and $f_1(\ldots) \lor f_2$ $(\ldots)$, respectively. An argument, in order to be one, must first of all exist. That is why I just replaced 'x' by dots. But, again, whether with dots or with some adequate equivalent for 'x' (as in Appendix B), the two expressions with the dots will stand for existents if and only if there are derived characters. Since from this world those putative existents have been expunged, we haven't yet found the argument in the case. The only one I can think of, and which therefore I propose, is a 2-tuple such as, say, $\langle a, f_1(a) \rangle$. Writing $\bigvee$ and $\bigwedge$ for the all- and the some-quantifier, (23″) and (24″) then become in the new fragment (23) $\bigvee \langle a, f_1(a) \rangle$ and (24) $\bigwedge \langle a, f_1(a) \rangle$. A function, finally, in order to be one, must impose on its arguments a restriction beyond that of being a determinate. What, then, are the restrictions that go with $\bigvee$ and $\bigwedge$? The question must at least be raised at the very beginning. The answer will fit in better a bit later.

We must agree on some terms. A complex which is a value of $\bigvee$ or $\bigwedge$ will be called a $\bigvee$-*generality* or a $\bigwedge$-*generality*, respectively. A complex-I such that there is at least one quantification among the steps producing it will be called *q-complex*. A generality thus is a q-complex but not conversely. $f_1(a) \lor \bigvee \langle a, f_1(a) \rangle$, for instance is a q-complex but not a generality. a and $A(a)$ will be called the *target* and the *scope* of the quantifier in $\bigvee \langle a, A(a) \rangle$ and $\bigwedge \langle a, A(a) \rangle$.

32* Suppose that there is a quantification among the steps producing a class α_1. One still wouldn't want to call either α_1 or, say, $\alpha_1 \in \alpha_2$ a q-complex. Hence, since on the second level the classes appear, the temporary limitation to the first level in the definition of 'q-complex'. As you see, I adopt the usual relaxed notation, such as '$A(a)$' or 'B', for complexes in which a is or is not free. The four expressions, not current among syntacticists, which may be formed from the two pairs 'existential-universal' and 'instantiation-generalization', I find ontologically confusing; so I go out of my way to avoid them; hence 'ascent' and 'descent'. 'Scope', 'free', and 'bound' I use as everyone does. 'Free-for' and 'variant', which will presently appear, you will, I hope, find convenient. 'Free-for', as far as I know, has been introduced by Kleene.

Why just $\langle a, f_1(a) \rangle$ in (23) and (24)? Wouldn't $\langle b, f_1(b) \rangle$ or $\langle c, f_1(c) \rangle$, or any other 2-tuple in which still another particular has taken the place of a do as well? For the paradigm the answer is Yes. For most other facts it must be qualified. Thereby hang the familiar complications which the combinatorial logicians have finally settled. Of these in due course. First we must attend to some matters so fundamental that the paradigm will serve. Nor will any harm be done if for the most part we stay with $\langle a, f_1(a) \rangle$.

For any two particulars a and b, (27) $\bigvee \langle a, f_1(a) \rangle = \bigvee \langle b, f_1(b) \rangle$. This is the gist of the new assay. Or, if you please, this is the claim. Express it, without prejudice, by calling $\bigvee \langle a, f_1(a) \rangle$ and $\bigvee \langle b, f_1(b) \rangle$ *variants* of each other. As soon as it will be safe, the phrase 'of each other' will be dropped. At the moment it usefully calls attention to a corollary without which there would be no point to the claim. There is no further determinate, in addition to all the variants, "of" which the latter would all be variants. If that is the claim and this its corollary, two preliminary questions immediately arise. Phenomenologically, what grounds the claim? Ontologically, what sense does it make to say of one determinate that literally it is (not: has!) an indefinite number of variants?

Remember the third signpost at the beginning of this Section (p. 136). In the ordinary course of thought we are not presented with variants. Unless this assay of the quantifiers is first provided with a "phenomenological hookup," it does therefore not even make sense to ask what grounds the claim. This hookup, I promised, will be attempted in the next Section. Supposing it will succeed, we may until then make shift with the fiction that we are presented with variants.

Turn now to what I called the phenomenological claim concerning (27). To judge from what has transpired so far in this discourse, to make one claim of this sort often amounts to making two; namely, first, that one is presented with determinates of a certain sort, and, second, that one is also presented with their mode. The fiction allows us to claim that we are sometimes presented with (27). How, then, about its mode? We shall see in a moment. First we must answer the other preliminary question.

What ontological sense, if any, does it make to speak of variants? 'Variant' is the best word I could think of; yet it has some untoward associations; so we must detach them from it. A fact is the value of a function for an argument. If the latter two are there, the value—or, as we sometimes called it, the third—is eo ipso there. That does not mean that the fact is either the collection or the class of the first and the second. If it were the collection, it would in this world be nothing; since the second is not a determinate, there is no such class in this world. The third is, rather, the "whole" sui generis and without any further ground, whose nature is exhausted by the first fitting the re-

striction that goes with the second and by the second being inseparable from the first. Suppose now, abstractly speaking, three things.
(1) This function has for this argument this value. (2) That other
function has for that other argument that value. (3) This value and
that value are the same. I said abstractly speaking because in this world
if not only the arguments but also the functions are different, so are
the values; the case in hand being the only one where the arguments
may differ and the value yet be the same. This, though, is beside the
point. The point is, rather, that in all cases and in any world (1), (2),
and (3) clearly are all three ontological matters. Thus we are reassured. A variant is not one of a class of determinates, out there in the
world, such that each of its elements, presumably either accessible to
us or at least thinkable, "represents" something else, also out there,
which presumably is neither. Nor, again, is a variant anything in a
mind, or perhaps in language, such that alternative variants all "represent" the same thing not in the mind nor in language. That takes us
back to (27). First, though, we ought to take notice of something else.

Finally we have encountered what has been announced in the first
Section. *(23) and (24) are determinates with alternative foundations;* and as
for them, so of course for all q-complexes. Starting from $\bigvee \langle a, f_1(a) \rangle$
you will arrive at the four-member collection f_1, η, $\bigvee$, and a (twice) as
an ultimate foundation of (23). Starting from $\langle b, f_1(b) \rangle$, one arrives at
f_1, η, $\bigvee$, and b (twice). Clearly, the collection of f_1, η, $\bigvee$, and any particular (twice) will do. f_1 is a determinate all these alternative ultimate
foundations share. Presently such a determinate will be called a "constituent." But we are not yet quite ready for this notion.

How now about the mode of (27)? A while ago (p. 165) I reminded
you of what we are already committed to. Every sameness is decidable; i.e., its mode is either immediately available or recursively accessible. *The actuality of (27) is immediately available.* Granted the fiction,
the claim is both reasonable and indispensable. As the notion will be
articulated, (27) is also a tautology-II. That takes care of the paradigm. In the general case, $A(a)$ and $B(b)$ may be, and often are, so
"complicated" that the mode of (28) $\bigvee \langle a, A(a) \rangle = \bigvee \langle b, B(b) \rangle$ will not
be immediately available. Nor again, supposing, quite reasonably, that
the decision hinges on the (relevant) forms of $A(a)$ and $B(b)$, will the
latter be immediately available. In principle, therefore, three recursions must be at our disposition; the first two (I speak concisely) in
order to reach the forms, the third in order to reach the mode of (28).
Yet there is a crucial difference between the first two and the third.
A-determinate-being-of-a-certain-form, a-determinate-being-free-in-
another, and so on, are among the conventional "syntactical" notions

whose decidability, according to the plan by which we proceed, we may now take for granted. (28), however, involves the new sameness. Thus we must, without taking anything for granted, specify the third recursion. That will be most conveniently done at the end of the Section. But we see already that, since the new sameness is as alien to the conventional metalanguages as it is to their respective object calculi, the recursion for (28) must not be metalinguistic but in the new style, such as, say, the proof pattern, which we can learn, that leads for all molecular complexes to the decision as to whether they are p-tautologies or p-contradictions or neither.

A second phenomenological claim finds here its natural place. For any two complexes α and β, if $\alpha = \beta$ is actual, so is $\alpha \equiv \beta$, although not of course conversely. Equivalently and more formally, *the actuality of* (29) $(\alpha = \beta) \supset (\alpha \equiv \beta)$ *is immediately available.* Sweeping as it is, the claim is yet so obvious that it needs no support. But two comments should help.

First. Where the combinatorial complications suggest it, we shall of course check our phenomenological claims by making sure that the four "axioms of identity" hold. Not to do that would be less than convincing. Yet these so-called axioms will not be counted as complexes corresponding to the syntacticist's theorems, nor even as immediately transparent ones, or perhaps as schemata of such. For, if "two" things are one, what more is there to be said about, say, "substituting" the "one for the other"?

Second. Since the consequent of (29) may be a complex-I, (29) itself may be of mixed level. Its antecedent, however, is always a complex-II. That makes (29) an addition to our collection, started in Section III, of "new" tautologies of which we must claim that their mode is immediately available. That there must be such tautologies if the notion of analyticity is to be enlarged as intended, is obvious. Yet, remarkably, we shall not have to add any "new" Cartesian transitions. This, I submit, is part of the sound core of the claim, made by Quine and others, that only sentential logic and what they call quantification theory are "logic."

What restrictions do the quantifiers impose on their arguments? The question is so fundamental that attention was called to it at the very beginning of this assay. The best place to start answering it is here.

If the first and the second are there, so eo ipso is the third. This is the schema of canons (a) and (b). If the first is there, so eo ipso is the second. This is the schema of canon (c). In all three cases, though, it is of the very essence of a canon that what it specifies to be there is something else or new, something over and above, or in addition to, what already is and must be there, for it to be there. Otherwise, what would be the point of a canon? This is one of my basic gambits. To appreciate its import, just think of what, rather obviously, it will do for the assay of classes. No class is an element of itself. Right now it yields one of the restrictions we are looking for. *The target of a generality must be free in its scope.* And, of course, on the first level, the target and the scope must be a thing and a fact, respectively. Syntactically, when constructing a calculus, one may make (a) B well-formed even if a is not free in B, and so arrange matters that $B \equiv B$ becomes a schema, either primitive or derived. Notationally that may be a convenience. Ontologically it makes no sense.

A critic interrupts. May not, he asks, B be so "complicated" that one is under the impression of a being free in it when in fact it isn't, and thus also under the impression of thinking something when, if you are right, in fact he isn't? If so, how do we ever know whether we think anything? Hoping that a meek answer will turn away wrath, I reply that most of the time we don't. Less paradoxically, most of the time we think on credit; the creditor being the language habits we have acquired. In the ordinary course of thought, one stops to consider only when he is blocked. Some such blocks interest the philosopher. Just remember how the notion of the unthinkable was unpacked (p. 65). There is nothing new in what you say. Rather, you were at this point newly struck by what, although not emphasized, has been with us for a long time. Or may it not happen that (I speak concisely) one "thinks" a conjunction without being aware that one of its terms is "nonsense"? Nor, finally, is it surprising that you were struck at this point. Just consider the "complexity" of all generalities on the one hand, and, on the other, our incapacity, of which more in the next Section, to intend any of them without at the same time intending (images of) words.

Like the connectives, *the quantifiers are mediators of modes.* The patterns of mediation, naturally, differ for the two sorts of functions. That for the quantifiers is dominated by the *tautologies of descent and ascent,* (25″) $\bigvee \langle a, f_1(a) \rangle \supset f_1(b)$ and (26″) $f_1(b) \supset \bigwedge \langle a, f_1(a) \rangle$. And, to enter formally a claim already made incidentally, *the actuality of (25″) and of (26″) is immediately available to us.* Without this claim, there would be a gap in the phenomenology of logic. Fortunately, it can stand on its own feet without further support.

In both (25″) and (26″), $f_1(b)$ and the scope, $f_1(a)$, are substitution instances of each other. In (25″) $f_1(b)$ is the consequent; in (26″) the antecedent. In (25″), $f_1(b)$ descends from the generality; in (26″) it ascends to the latter. The scope and the substitution instances, being both facts, have modes; the substituends, being particulars, don't. The *range* of the target is (the collection of) all particulars. But all this is only too familiar. Why restate it in a new jargon? As long as one stays with (what corresponds to) the lower functional calculus, there is indeed no point in restating it. As soon as one tries to extend quantification to the second level, and, on the first, to the higher types, the notion of range needs rethinking and two more restrictions come to the fore. These novelties the new jargon fits better than any other I know.

In the general case the combinatorial complications come into play. For some $A(a)$, there are some b such that (25) $\bigvee \langle a, A(a) \rangle \supset A(b)$ and (26) $A(b) \supset \bigwedge \langle a, A(a) \rangle$ are not tautologies. Yet the following four requirements are fulfilled. *First.* There is for every $A(a)$ and for every b in the range of the target one and only one other complex, call it $A_b(a)$, such that (30) $\bigvee \langle a, A(a) \rangle = \bigvee \langle a, A_b(a) \rangle$ and (31) $\bigvee \langle a, A_b(a) \rangle \supset A_b(b)$, and hence also the descent (32) $\bigvee \langle a, A(a) \rangle \supset A_b(b)$ are all actual. *Second.* The modes of (30) and (31), and hence also of (32), are all recursively accessible. *Third.* Given $A(a)$, $A_b(a)$ can be reached recursively. *Fourth.* If and only if $A(a_i)$ is the scope of a variant of (25), i.e., if and only if $\bigvee \langle a, A(a) \rangle = \bigvee \langle a_i, A(a_i) \rangle$, then $A_b(b) = A_b^i(b)$. Succinctly, there is for each determinate in the range of the target of a $\bigvee$-generality one and only one complex, produced by substitution of the determinate for the target in either $A_b(a)$ or $A_b^i(a)$, call it in either case the *descent complex* for the determinate, such that this complex itself and the actuality of the descent from the generality to it are recursively accessible. Thus the essence of the mediation pattern, although it does not manifest itself as luminously as in the paradigm case, is yet safe. That is why I spoke of requirements. For, again succinctly, if they were not fulfilled, the function $\bigvee$ would not exist. To convince ourselves that they are fulfilled will take two more steps; one to be made presently, the other at the end of the Section. Right now just take note of them, so that you will be able to appreciate a completely general statement of the mediation pattern and of the two restrictions which it brings to the fore.

33* (a) *If* $\bigvee$ *were not in the world, there could not be any laws of nature.* That shows, by rewording it, the ontological clout of the aphorism that, if the four requirements were not fulfilled, there would be no quantifiers. Ever since Hume, philosophers have been so absorbed by the question of how, *if* there are such laws, we may come to *know* them, that they have become completely oblivious of this necessary, although to be sure not sufficient, ontological ground for there *being* any. (b) The description above of the conventional notation for substitution is metalinguistic, as of course is the notation itself for both

$A(a)$ and $A(b)$. I would rather say, nonlinguistically, that the complex-II (33) $(\exists c)subst\langle A(a),\ a,\ b,\ c\rangle$ is actual; *'subst'* being (the abbreviation for) the structural form corresponding to the familiar recursive quaternary notion. That there is at most one determinate *"c"* can, and of course must, be shown to be a tautology-II whose mode is recursively accessible. Notice, though, that I am again seeking the shelter of "linguistic devices," first an abbreviation, then a pair of double quotes. Talking without all such devices is arduous indeed. That is why, in writing (33) as I just did, I have already fallen back upon a more manageable *in-between notation for quantification,* which will be used whenever it does not affect the matter under consideration.

(1) *A determinate* (b) *is in the range of the target of the generality* $\bigvee\langle a,$ $A(a)\rangle$ *if and only if* $(\exists c)subst\langle A(a),\ a,\ b,\ c\rangle$ *is actual.* (2) *The scope must have a mode.* (3) *The mode of the descent complex for a determinate depends only on the identity but not on the mode, if any, of the latter.* (4) *The mode of the generality is actual if and only if all "its" descent complexes are actual.*

This is the mediation pattern. As for $\bigvee$, descent, and the descent complexes; so mutatis mutandis for $\bigwedge$, ascent, and the *ascent complexes;* we need not tarry. (2) *and* (3) *are the restrictions.* Call them the second and the third. The only other, call it the first, we know already. The target must be free in the scope.

A skeptic listened but remains unconvinced. What, he asks, is the point of all this generality. Let us see, first for the second level, then for the first.

Let α_1 and α_2 be two complexes. Is α_1 quantifiable in, say $\alpha_1\ \&\ \alpha_2$? Or, syntactically, is '$(\alpha_1)(\alpha_1\ \&\ \alpha_2)$' well formed? A glance at the third restriction shows that it is not. The mode of a descent complex, e.g., $\alpha_3\ \&\ \alpha_2$, depends only on the mode of the determinate, α_3, and not at all on its identity. Thus all the mediating there is to be done can be done by the "truth tables." In ontology this is a perfect rationale for exclusion. Nor of course does the level of the conjunction terms matter. On the first level, however, a generalization is within easy reach: *On the first level only things are quantifiable.* I.e., with the new terms, in the scope of a complex-I, the target must be a thing. Hence the clause, 'if any', in the third proposition of the mediation pattern.

On the second level, the three sorts of circumstances—diversity, the element nexus, and the meaning nexus—make their appearance. Keep ignoring the third; replace the first by sameness, for convenience' sake and also in order to take cognizance of the order and standardization diads, which are pervasive. That leaves us with (34) α_1 $= \alpha_2$ and (34') $\alpha_1 \in \alpha_2$; α_1 and α_2 being any two determinates of either level. Every circumstance has a mode which depends on the identities of its terms but not on their modes. Structurally we are already committed to that. For sameness we know it. As to classes, remember that in this world all complexes are determinates and that every determinate is an element of classes; let 'α_1' stand for '$f_1(a)$'; and you will see that the mode of (34') could not possibly depend on anything but the identities of its terms. The restrictions are all fulfilled; and we easily proceed from the generalization just made to another: *If* they are quantifiable at all, *complexes are quantifiable only on the second level.* Notice the condition. The case for the quantifiability of complexes on the second level has not yet been made. But notice, too, that if it can be made, the two generalizations fit the taxonomic schematism exceedingly well. Another, related feature of the new assay is so important in the overall dialectic that it should be presented at this point. The agreements about the notation the presentation requires you will find in 34* (e).

34* (a) Even if α_2 is not a class, (34') is in this world a complex, although of course potential. Syntactically, '$\alpha_1 \in \alpha_2$' is well formed, as, (34') being a circumstance, consistently it must be. Yet, even if α_2 is either a fact or a circumstance and thus has a mode, what affects the mode of (34') is not its mode but only its identity, which of course comprehends its not being a class. (b) Classes having no modes, a class and one of its elements cannot be target and scope. In the example, even if (34') is actual, '$\bigvee\langle \alpha_1, \alpha_1 \in \alpha_2 \rangle$' is ill formed.† In (34), on the other hand, both terms are quantifiable. All this is as it ought to be. (c) As has already been pointed out more than once, the limits of the classes, and of the complexes in which these classes occur, which we can *think* (intend) and not merely, as I shall say, *reason about axiomatically,* are narrow, more or less in the intuitionists' style. Within these limits, though, we have by now some assurance that the connectives and the quantifiers will be available. In this respect, therefore, we may expect not to be worse off than the axiomatic set theorists. (d) We also have by now a fair notion of what the second level is like. Diversities and element nexus whose terms are determinates-I (i.e., either things or facts-I) are the "atoms" from which all the rest is produced by any of the available steps, *except the (a)-steps of exemplification.* (e) Consider the definition that writes

'*conj* (x)' for '$\bigwedge\langle f_1(a), \bigwedge\langle f_2(b), x = f_1(a) \,\&\, f_2(b)\rangle\rangle$'

The definiendum does not occur in the ideal schema; the definiens does and, depending on what is put for 'x', is either actual or potential.

---

† Bergmann apparently means here that '$\bigvee\langle \alpha_1, \alpha_2 \rangle$' is ill formed, since $\alpha_1 \in a_2$ *does* have a mode.—WH

'x', since it serves as the "definitional variable," clearly is not a "variable" of the sort that has been expunged from the ideal schema. The role of the *word* 'conjunction', which occurs in the definiens, will be examined in the next Section. (With this understood, we can relax our notation and write, more nearly conventionally and less cumbersomely, '$(\exists\ \alpha_1)(\exists\ \alpha_2)(x =. \alpha_1\ \&\ \alpha_2)$' for the definiens. But keep in mind that in this in-between notation 'α_1' and 'α_2' are constants. 'x', 'y', 'f', 'F', and so on, and the Greek letters without subscripts will henceforth serve as definitional variables. The first few letters of the Latin alphabet, even when without subscript, have for some time been used as constants.)

Let 'α_1' and 'α_2' stand for $f_1(a)$ and $f_2(b)$; and consider the "definiens" of disjunction: (35) $(\exists\alpha_1)(\exists\alpha_2)(x = \alpha_1 \vee \alpha_2)$. Since (36) $x =. \alpha_1 \vee \alpha_2$ is the sameness, there is for every x a complex (35) which is actual if and only if x is a disjunction of two complexes. Since the notation is in-between and still unfamiliar, I restate this so that no doubt will be left. All that is required for (36) to be actual is that, by the restriction for disjunction, x be a disjunction of two complexes. The latter, however, are not subject to any further restriction. And, of course, subject to the combinatorial perils as they work out in the case of quantified complexes, any two other targets will do as well as $f_1(a)$ and $f_2(b)$. On the other hand, if x is a conjunction, a class, a universal, or a determinate of any other sort, there is still the potential complex (35), which grounds its not being a disjunction. As for disjunction, so for every other form$_2$ (ordinarily here called: form), provided only we can produce its "definiens," but not for the forms$_1$ which are ultimate sorts. How important the availability of these complexes is for thought accurately drawing its own limits we already know. What makes them available is the modified notion of range, jointly with the terms of a circumstance being subject to no other but the minimal restriction. To see how this modification, or loosening, reflects itself in the different notations, consider that if in a many-sorted world one uses different kinds of letters for the variables ("real" and not just definitional!) associated with the different sorts, and then uses these letters in the expressions for the quantifiers, as in '$(x) \ldots x \ldots$', he has already committed himself to a sort-homogenous range. Our notation does not so commit us.

What does this loosening do to the first level of a world such as ours, with higher types and quantification for all of them? Take color (*Col*), a color (*gr*), and a particular (*a*). Start from $\eta(gr, a)$ and consider (37) $\bigvee\langle a, \eta(gr, a)\rangle$. Since $Col(gr)$ is a complex, the range of the target in (37) is the collection of all particulars and all universals[0]. That destroys the meaning of quantification where we must not tamper with it. Unless there is a way out, we are blocked. As it happens, the one there is, is not just a way out but leads to a nodal point at which several features dialectically support each other. Remember what was said about the synthetic a priori (p. 80). If there were several exemplifications, say, at a minimum, one, call it η_1, for all atomic facts in which one universal is tied to one or several particulars, and one other, call it η_2, for all other sorts of atomic facts, the synthetic a priori would be grounded as deeply as one can ground it without collapsing it with the analytic. That points the way out. For (37') $\bigvee \langle a,\ \eta_1(gr,\ a) \rangle$ and (37'') $\bigvee \langle Col,\ \eta_2(gr,\ Col) \rangle$ the ranges of their targets are the collections of all particulars and of all universals[(0)], respectively. *We now introduce several exemplifications.* How many will depend on the numbers of ultimate sorts and of sorts of atomic facts. The actual numbers, as long as they are all finite, are a matter of relative detail. But, then, why should any of them be finite? If it is, or if they all are, isn't that, too, a mere matter of fact, or, at most, since the availability of certain recursions is a stake (p. 163), a matter of contingent principle? When the question first arose for the ultimate sorts, further dialectical support was promised. Now it can be provided. If there were an infinite number either of *functions* or of ultimate sorts, it stands to reason that we would be able to think, either that some of them have not yet been presented to us, or that some will be presented to us, or what have you. Ontologically, that amounts to quantification over either a function or an ultimate sort. Hence either the one or the other, or both, would have to be targets. A target, however, being a term of a diad, must be a determinate. As Russell might put it, with that infelicitous phrase I use only for demonstration purposes, we have "knowledge by description" of determinates but not of functions, and still less, of course, of ultimate sorts, which are merely entities. *This is a third sense in which all functions and all ultimate sorts are unique.* Notice, finally, that where 'function' is italicized above, it replaces 'quantifier' because we have also come upon an additional argument for there being only a finite number of connectives.

Let us stop long enough to count the number of threads in that dialectical knot. There is the notion of range which is characteristic of the new assay of the quantifiers; there is the new grounding of the synthetic a priori; there is the finite number of functions and of ultimate sorts; there is the uniqueness of both these ontological kinds; and there is the availability of certain recursions, of which more in the last two Sections. Five features dovetail at this point.

Notice, too, that the synthetic a priori is now grounded in canons, or, as some might still put it, in formation rules. No matter how one puts it, finding this feature grounded at such extraordinary depth not only makes one appreciate a major strand of the tradition; it also gibes with the phenomenological trichotomy of the imaginable, the dubitable, and the thinkable. The negation of what is synthetic a priori we cannot imagine. What we are directly aware of we cannot, while being so aware of it, doubt. What is presented to us with its mode we cannot, while it is so presented to us, think with the other mode.

Two comments will round out the ontologization of the quantifiers. Then we shall tackle the combinatorial complication.

First. How many quantifiers are there? The logicians again tell us that one will do. Starting from either $\vee$ or $\wedge$, they introduce the other by definition. We, having started with both, must add to their primitive schemata one of the four corresponding to the so-called duality formulae. That, though, is not the end of the matter. Since the considerations we applied to the connectives also apply to the quantifiers, we must inquire how many of the latter there can be, and, having coralled them, must ontologize them all. If you keep in mind that if there is to be any "quantifier-like" mediation at all, the antecedent must be actual in both ascent and descent, you will see that the only other quantifier is *None.* Ontologizing it together with *All* and *Some,* one must add one of the two schemata corresponding to 'if none then not any' and 'if for some then not for none'. But we need not bother. Having acknowledged those considerations and the need for consistency will suffice.

Second. The Russell of *Logical Atomism,* holding that "logical form" was nothing, yet also held that some expressions without either free variables or constants, such as, say, (38) '$(f)(x)(f(x) \vee \sim f(x))$', were truths, even "logical truths." Thus he expected them to have "constituents," and in the fifth chapter looked for them. Not having found any, he confessed his puzzlement; adding, very reasonably, that since the problem was rather new, there had not been much opportunity to consider it. Now, when these studies are no longer in their infancy, there ought to be an answer to his query. In this world there is one; very much to my relief, for I, too, have been puzzled ever since I first read that chapter. Call a complex of the sort the expressions he considers stand for a *limiting complex.* Among the members of any ultimate foundation of any determinate (not itself a thing) there must indeed be some things. The only difference, in this respect, between a limiting complex and any other determinate is that, as the former is stepwise produced, these things all become targets. In the case of (38), for instance, every five-member collection of *a* particular, *a* universal$^{(0)}$, $\vee$, $\bigvee$, and η_1, each the appropriate number of times, is *an* alternative ultimate foundation; the two things in due course become targets. A complex is a limiting complex if and only if it has alternative ultimate foundations which have nothing in common. Again, as we shall presently regulate the use of 'constituent' in ontology, a complex is a limiting complex if and only if it has no "constituents." That solves, or, perhaps better, resolves, Russell's problem.

35* If, as in this world, there are limiting complexes-I, then they are, by anyone's validity criterion, q-tautologies if actual, q-contradictions if potential. Also, a complex is a q-tautology if and only if it can be reached from an actual limiting complex by a (finite) succession of descents and ascents. But do not hastily conclude that the mode of every limiting complex is recursively accessible. If it were, the lower functional calculus would be decidable.

What precisely are the combinatorial complications? Replace in (39) $(a)r_1(a, b)$ the target and its free occurrence(s) in its scope once by b, once by c. The results are (39') $(b)r_1(b, b)$ and (39") $(c)r_1(c, b)$. Everyone agrees that (39) is the same as (39") but diverse from (39'). Or, if you insist, everyone who does not have the new notion of sameness will yet agree with us that while (39) and (39") are analytically equivalent, (39) and (39') are not. Take next

$$(40)\ (a)(\exists b)r_1(a, b)\ \text{and}\ (41)\ (a)[f(a) \supset (\exists b)r_1(a, b)];$$

try the descent from them, once for b, once for c. The results are

$$(40')\ (a)(\exists b)r_1(a, b) \supset (\exists b)r_1(b, b),$$
$$(41')\ (a)[\ f(a) \supset (\exists b)r_1(a, b)] \supset [f(b) \supset (\exists b)r_1(b, b)];$$

and

$$(40")\ (a)(\exists b)r_1(a, b) \supset (\exists b)r_1(c, b),$$
$$(41")\ (a)[f(a) \supset (\exists b)r_1(a, b)] \supset f(c) \supset (\exists b)r_1(c, b)],$$

respectively. Everyone agrees that while (40") and 41") are analytic, (40') and (41') are not. I keep repeating that everyone agrees. But how does anyone "know"? I claim that the actuality of (42") $(a)r_1(a, b)$ $= (c)r_1(c, b)$, that of (40"), and quite probably also that of (41") are immediately available. A critic, after remarking that he would indeed expect some such phenomenological claims at this point in this discourse, pounces upon the qualification (quite probably!) for (41") and asks me how I handle a scope so "complicated" that a claim of this sort, far from seeming plausible, is not even reasonable. And, he adds, how about the modes of $(42')$ $(a)r_1(a, b) = (b)r_1(b, b)$, of $(40')$, and of $(41')$. I promise to answer both questions; he is willing to wait.

What is the difference that makes the difference between a licit and an illicit transition; either as from (39), by replacing a target; or as from (40) and (41), by substitution? A transition from a generality to another is illicit if and only if there is in its scope an "occurrence" of a thing such that, while before the transition it was free, afterward it is either bound or has been substituted for by one that is bound. Conversely (and as I shall speak, more succinctly) *a transition is licit if and only if no bound is changed.* (The double quotes around 'occurrence' announce an objection I expect the critic to raise.)

Everyone agrees that this condition is both necessary and sufficient. But, again, how does anyone "know"? Let us stop and consider where we stand. We know the goal. The four requirements that were stated before the general mediation pattern was formulated (p. 174) must be fulfilled. The thing to do, therefore, is to determine the minimal phenomenological claims that secure their being fulfilled, and, having determined them, to support them as well as we may.

C1. *If* one can from one complex, $A_x(a)$, obtain another, $B_x(b)$, by substituting b for a and replacing one or several targets by others, although not necessarily providing for the same target the same replacement either in different generalities or in several occurrences of one, without thereby any bound being changed, then $\bigvee\langle a, A_x(a)\rangle = \bigvee\langle b, B_x(b)\rangle$ is actual and its mode is either immediately available or recursively accessible.

C2. (a) The actuality of $\bigvee\langle a, A_1(a) = \bigvee\langle a, A_2(a)\rangle \equiv A_1(a) = A_2(a)$ is immediately available. (b) For every molecular complex, (a) M $(a) = (b)$ M (b) is actual and its mode either immediately available or recursively accessible *if and only if* no bound is changed.

C3. $\bigvee\langle a, A_1(a)\rangle \supset A(b)$ is actual and its mode either immediately available or recursively accessible *if and only if* the following condition is fulfilled: $A_1(a)$ neither is, nor is there in it an occurrence of, a generality whose target is b and in whose scope a is free.

36* (i) notice that while the conditions in (C2b) and (C3) are necessary and sufficient, that in (C1) is there not claimed to be necessary. But it will not be difficult to prove, from (C2) in conjunction with the "sameness criteria" for the connectives, the stronger proposition, call it in anticipation (C1*), according to which it is also necessary. (ii) Given the strictness of our sameness notion, (C2a) does not come as a surprise. Yet it must be entered as a separate claim! The converse implication, on the other hand, which is but an instance of the univocality of all Meinong functions, is a special case of (C1). (iii) The condition in (C2b) is of course equivalent to $subst\langle M(a), a, b, M(b)\rangle$ & $subst\langle M(b), b, a, M(a)\rangle$. Just consider the examples (39), (39'), and (39'').

These three phenomenological claims I now make and shall next support by three comments. That will consummate the first of the two steps still to be taken. The second is the demonstration that these claims secure the four requirements of the mediation pattern being fulfilled. This demonstration belongs with the sameness criteria, which in turn fit best at the end of the Section. (If you wonder whether so piecemeal a method of exposition is the most economical, consider that (C1*) is in substance the sameness criterion for generalities, i.e., just to practice our terminology, the criterion for "two" generalities being variants of each other.)

First. The critic now raises the objection I foresaw. By (C1), he points out, (i) $f_1(a) \supset (\exists b)r_1(a, b)$ and (ii) $f_1(a) \supset (\exists c)r_1(a, c)$ are one complex (α_1). The condition in (C3), he adds, I must consistently hold to be fulfilled if and only if (the complex which is the "definiens" of) α_1-having-a-certain-form is actual. (ii) fulfills this condition; (i) does not. Thus, he concludes, I have settled myself with a most embarrassing complex which somehow manages to be both actual and potential. What happened, he surmises, is that inadvertently I used the syntacticists' 'occurrence' ontologically. They, though, he observes, replace the embarrassing complex with the ternary syntactical relationship of some-*expression*-being-free-in-another-for-a-third; distinguish the two expressions, β_1 and β_2, corresponding to (i) and (ii), respectively, and avoid embarrassment by holding, without any commitment as to what anything stands for, that $\beta_1 = \beta_2$ is analytic.

I reply as follows: You did spot a gap that needs filling. But I did use 'occurrence' deliberately, because I expect you to pick it up, thus providing me with the cue for doing what needs to be done where it fits best. The key idea we possess already: variant is an ontological notion. But we have not yet grounded it specifically. Consider, then, together with *an* ultimate foundation F_n^i, *of a complex*, α_1, the whole series, F_{n-1}^i, F_1^i; and form the class, call it γ^i, exists in this world. Call any such class a *cone* of α_1. A molecular complex-I has of course only one cone. Yet, clearly, no matter how many alternative cones a complex has, for a class to be one of its cones is a matter of ontology, rather than of a representation, either linguistic or otherwise. Hence, ontologically and speaking concisely, a variant "is" a cone. That fills the gap. As to words, adopting the syntacticists' term for an ontological use, we shall say that something-being-free-for-something-else-in-a-third-with-respect-to-a-fourth is a quaternary notion. Still about words, the notion of a cone also permits us either to get along without or to ontologize such prima facie syntactical expressions as 'being at a place', 'being a well-formed part of', and so on. Concerning 'constituent', see presently.

Second. How can one support the three claims if the complexes involved are "complicated"? This, you remember, was the critic's first question. I answer in three steps. (1) In "simple" cases, such as (40″), (42″), and "quite probably" (41″), the claims need no support. Consider (42″) $(a)r_1(a, b) = (c)r_1(c, b)$ together with (27) $(a) f_1(a) = (b) f_1(b)$. Granting the provisional fiction which will be got rid of in Section V, (27), whose immediate transparence has already been claimed (p. 00), surely needs no support. And if (27) doesn't, why should (42″)? Aren't they two sides of one coin, equally contributing to what is immediately transparent to us about $\bigvee$? (2) Each of the three claims specifies a condition which two complexes-I, α_1 and α_2, satisfy if and only if either (α_1, α_2), as in (C1) and (C2b), or $\langle \alpha_1, \alpha_2 \rangle$, as in (C3), is of a certain form, i.e., if and only if a certain complex-II, whose mode can be reached recursively, is actual. As α_1 and α_2 become more "complicated," reaching the mode of this complex-II takes an increasing number of Cartesian transitions, thus requiring some time and effort. But why, once its actuality is presented, is it not plausible, and more than just plausible, that the actuality of the complex-I about which the claim as originally stated is made can be reached as the consequent of a single Cartesian transition from that complex-II as antecedent? Seen in this light, (C1), (C2b), *and (C3) are claims that the actuality of certain mixed implications, whose antecedents and consequents are of the second and first level respectively, is immediately available.* (3) Remember what has been said about the variety of ways in which our thoughts *externally* depend on language (p. 150). The more "complicated" the thought, the greater the dependence. The thoughts about which the three claims are made are fairly "complicated." Thus our ability to think them depends in a variety of ways, including quite probably some images of some designs from artificial schemata, externally on language. That casts no doubt whatsoever on the three claims nor lends any implausibility to attempts of construing them as propositions about language.

Third. The critic also asked what I had to say about the mode of complexes obtained by illicit transitions. The answer depends on whether the complex obtained is supposed to be a sameness or merely an implication or equivalence. If the former, (C1*) and (C2) provide the answer. If the latter, one example will do. Take (43′) $f_1(b) \supset$

($\exists b$) $r_1(b, b)$, which is the consequent of (41′). All I can say is that, whatever the universals, its mode is not accessible to me. For all I "know," it may in our world be actual for some universals, potential for some others. Usually one is given what passes for counterexamples. For (43′), letting 'f_1' and 'r_1' stand for 'integer' and 'successor' does the trick. Two-is-an-integer is actual; there-is-an-integer-which-is-its-own-successor is potential; the mode of both, we shall see, is in this world presented to us. In this world, however, as we shall also see, integer and successor are not universals, i.e., to leave no possible doubt, they are not what some, including myself, used to call "descriptive" characters. What we are faced with is therefore not really a counterexample but, rather, an appeal to the validity criterion. But notice, too, that our schema for analyticity holds up. (43′) is neither a q-tautology nor analytic; the former by the criterion; the latter, because its mode is not accessible.

This concludes the ontologization of the quantifiers. The cause of the impression which you have gained that it limits targets to particulars is, no doubt, the way such letters as 'a', 'b', 'f_1', 'r_1' were in the course of it used in such conventionally suggestive expressions as '$f_1(a)$' and '$r_1(a, b)$'. At a few places a and b were even referred to as particulars. Being thus responsible for the impression, I must, before we turn to the next topic, correct it. As to words, notice that in the statements of the four requirements (p. 173), of the mediation pattern (p. 174), and of the three conditions (p. 180), the letters do not appear in any of those suggestive combinations but only neutrally, as in '$A(a)$'; and that the targets are not referred to as particulars but, neutrally, as determinates, which leaves the door open not only for universals but also, quite deliberately, for complexes. As for the words, so for the things. In a complex-I, we know, a target must not itself be a complex. Otherwise, though, as a brief reflection will show you, nothing that has been said depends either on the sort of the target determinate or, if it is a thing, on its position, either as subject or as predicate or both, in its scope.

36* For the phenomenological issues involved, (a) $f_1(a) = (b) f_1(b)$ may serve as an example. Anyone who claims that the actuality of this complex is immediately available to him will not hesitate to make the same claim for $(f_1) F_1(f_1) = (f_2) F_1(f_2)$; provided, of course, that there are in his world at least three types. As to the combinatorial complications, the descent for f_2 is by (C3) as illicit from $(f_1)(\exists f_2)$ $\sim(a)[f_1(a) \equiv f_2(a)]$, as it is, again by (C3), for b from (40).

*With quantification limited to particulars, (C1), (C2), and (C3) fit directly the formalization of the lower functional calculus, with vari-

ables but without substitution rules and with only optional propositional variables, in the third chapter of Church's admirable treatise.[5]
His formalization of the second-order functional calculus in the fifth
chapter, however, does use substitution rules, also for propositional
variables and expressions which, if no free variables occurred in them,
would stand for facts. Thus, since the second-order calculus is the one
we shall need, and since I am not familiar with any other formalization of it, this is one occasion on which I must take my chances. But,
then, I see no reason whatsoever to doubt that, just as Church's alternative formalization, with substitution rules also for propositional
variables and expressions which, if no free variables occurred in
them, would stand for facts, of the lower functional calculus in chapter 4 is equivalent to that in chapter 3, so there is an equivalent formalization of the second-order calculus that fits directly (C1), (C2),
and (C3), *with the limitation on the target removed*. (With respect to propositional variables as such, I have already committed myself earlier.)
In a first-level context they are, by the mediation pattern, merely notational conveniences.

When is a q-complex-I a q-tautology? Less clumsily, with one prefix and
the suffix suppressed, what is the (validity) criterion for a q-complex?
Our purpose, you remember, is so to modify the old, or classical, criterion that the resulting new one fits this world. Taking the old criterion to be familiar, I shall talk about it only selectively and very concisely, in a way that suits this purpose and, incidentally, another as
well. We ought to convince ourselves that, like the notion of a p-tautology, that of a q-tautology belongs to the excess. Since in this respect
there is no difference between the old and the new, we might as well
save time and space by using the old to get this job done.

Both criteria work with "models." The old model is a series of
classes, $\Sigma_1, \Sigma_2, \ldots, \Sigma_i, \ldots$ one for each cardinality, i is the cardinality of a class M_i^0, whose elements are for convenience' sake called
i-points. The elements of Σ_i are all i-points, all classes of them, all
classes of such classes, and so on; all classes of ordered pairs of i-
points, all classes and ordered pairs of such classes, and so on; all
classes of ordered triples of i-points, and so on; and so on.

37* (a) Σ_i is the sum (union) of a series of classes, $\mu_i^0, \mu_i^1, \ldots$
$\mu_i^n, \ldots$, for each finite n; all in the way described determined by μ_i^0,
and such that, if all elements μ_i^0 were particulars, those of μ_i^n would all
be of the (Russellian) type n. In this world, though, where classes are
not stratified, any determinate may be an element of μ_i^0. We have

5. *Introduction to Mathematical Logic*, Princeton University Press, 1956.

merely constructed a series of classes (Σ_i), each of which reflects the stratification of things. (b) Abstractly, the type of a relation need not be "homogenous," as, e.g., (0, (0)) and ((0), (00,)) are not; although by contingent principle there are no such relations in the world in which we all live. Abstractly, therefore, the models, both old and new, would have to be supplemented in order to accommodate such relations. But we need not bother. (c) Since it does not affect the matter in hand, let us, while treating it, indulge the ingrained and convenient habit of writing variables, both bound and free; using Latin and Greek letters, with or without subscripts, depending on whether they are constants or variables, in connection with q-complexes and the complexes of the model (briefly: c-complexes), respectively.

Take a q-complex, say, (43) $(x) f_1(x) \supset f_1(a)$; call it A_1. A c-complex "corresponds to A_1 for Σ_i," if and only if (the expression standing for) it can be obtained by substituting in the formula (43') $(\alpha) \gamma(\alpha) \supset \gamma(\beta)$ in which *the range of the bound variable is the class of all i-points,* for the free variables 'β' and 'γ' (the expressions for) *an i-point and a class of i-points,* respectively. This is of course merely an illustration. But we may take it for granted that there is this familiar "correspondence," that we can think it, and that it is a matter of decidable form. (As always outside of axiomatics, I avoid 'interpret' and its derivatives.) If one now calls a q-complex *i*-valid if and only if all the c-complexes corresponding to it for Σ_i are actual, the criterion can be stated very briefly: A q-complex is a tautology if and only if it is *i-valid for all i.* The three metalinguistic clauses that have been underlined can be got rid of, the first two by the device known as relativization of scope; the third because, except for their cardinalities, the Σ are arbitrary. The result is, for each δ_l, a (mixed) complex B(δ_l), such that the criterion, if it could be thought literally, would be expressed by (44) $(\delta)[\beta_{A_K}(\delta) \supset (\delta \text{ is actual})]$. The subscript of β marks its dependence on the q-complex for which it is the criterion. (44) shows that, as anticipated, the Unthinkability of the Iterated Mode relegates not only the notion of a p-tautology (p. 144) but also that of a q-tautology to the excess.

At this point (I imagine) a thoughtful reader interrupts. He observes, correctly, that I took two things for granted, namely, first, that there is quantification over complexes, as in (44), and, second, that there are these complexes $\beta_{A_K}(\delta_l)$ *and that, therefore, by the Principle of Presentation, we can think them. Then he asks why, if all this is taken for granted, the notion of a q-tautology cannot be retrieved from the excess by making (44') $(\delta)[\beta_{A_K}(\delta) \supset \delta]$* the criterion. I tell him that what might serve as a criterion surely is not the complex (44') but, if anything, (44')-being-actual. Thereupon he points out that no reason was given why (44′) should not sometimes be presented with its mode. To this I reply as follows: To be able to think a notion, i.e., more accurately, to think (literally) that a determinate satisfies a criterion, one must be able to think its satisfying that criterion irrespective of whether or not the intention of this thought is presented to him with its mode. But I readily admit that, since this refutation is the only use I shall ever make of the $\beta_{A_\kappa}(\delta_I)$, I was indeed a bit cavalier in taking some things about hem for granted.

Several other readers have during this exchange shown signs of wanting to speak up. Most classes of the old model and therefore also, as they correctly assume, of the new, being neither finite nor recursive, cannot in this world literally be thought (intended) and thus do not enjoy full, or primary, ontological status. The best one can do for such classes, besides reasoning about them axiomatically, which ontologically amounts to nothing, is to attach them, or as one says, interpret them into, what we can (literally) think, which, since it is spectacularly successful, confers upon them a sort of derivative, or secondary, ontological status. Of all this later. Yet I have already insisted on it more than once. That is why these readers expect now at least some justification of the use of such classes in the new model. Justification? No. Acknowledgment or account? Yes. The classes of the models, both old and new, are indeed of that very special sort. That accounts for what was said earlier. Both notions, of a p- and of a q-tautology, are beyond the limits of literal thought for the same reason: while the modes are sometimes presented to us we cannot (I express myself aphoristically) discursively reason about them. For the q-tautologies, though, there is the additional reason that the model employed lies beyond those limits.

Return to the main line of thought. Speaking concisely yet I trust clearly, since classes are by their very nature extensional, the old model is a series of higher calculi, one for each i. Since universals by their very nature are not extensional, it will not do. Yet testing it on the classical notion of the analytic will help. That requires one fiction and one unpacking. We must for the moment suppose that universals are by their very nature extensional, and we must articulate the classical notion of a *possible world*. First, though, for a word of caution. The phrase 'possible world' has an ontological flavor; in the tradition it has been used ontologically; and it is now being so used again. Let it be understood, then, once and for all, that while the analytic-synthetic dichotomy has ontological import, that pretty phrase, as here used, has none. It is merely a label for certain selections from the model which play a role in establishing that dichotomy.

Each thing, a, f_1, F_1, and so on, "determines," for at least one i, one element μ_i^0, μ_i^1, μ_i^2, respectively, so that, say, $F_1(f_1)$ is actual if and only if $\alpha_1^i \in \alpha_2^i$ is actual; different things determining different elements, and α_1 and α_2 being the two f_1 and F_1 determine. The converse, however, except for the i-points, does not hold. For an element of μ_i^1, for instance, there may be either no property or one (or, after we shall have dropped the fiction, several) which determines it, or conversely, which it "represents." (Notice that, as I speak in this context, "corresponding" on the one hand and, on the other, "determining," or, conversely, "representing," are two and not one. The former pertains to forms, the latter, to determinates.) *Classically, a possible world is, literally, a series of series,* $\mu_i^0, \nu_i^1, \nu_i^2, \ldots,$ *one for each i, such that ν_i^1 is an arbitrary subclass of μ_i^0, ν_i^2 an arbitray subclass of ν_i^1, and so on.* More cautiously, it may be argued that this is the notion which informed the early Russell's vision of what he called logical truth. The first who stated it accurately, although not for ontological purposes and only for the second-order calculus, was the logician Henkin. Next for a comment, then for the test.

Are the ν-selections really arbitrary? Not completely, if one considers certain contingent principles, such as that every particular exemplifies at least one property. Yet, surely, the limitations imposed by principles of this kind are too broad to affect these arguments. Besides, since they are all contingent, why consider them at all? How, then, an embattled anti-Platonist might wonder, about the exclusion of unexemplified universals? Is this, too, merely a contingent principle? I, for one, if I had to, would have no objection to calling it that. But there is in this world—and not, as we shall see, just contingently—no empty class; so I don't have to. An appeal to the Principle of Acquaintance (p. 65), on the other hand, would not, or at least should not, satisfy so anxious an anti-Platonist. For that principle is itself contingent, even anthropocentric.

(An1) Analytic is what is true by virtue of its form alone. (An2) Analytic is what is true in all possible worlds. Both formulas are familiar from the tradition. We know that since being analytic and being of a certain form are two and not one (p. 146), (An1) must be handled with caution. With this caution, though, and with 'analytic' and 'true' replaced by 'tautological' and 'actual', respectively, (An1) and (An2) are the gist of the classical notion of analyticity, stated in a way that permits us to test the classical criterion against them. The correspondence is such that the class of all c-complexes a q-complex, α, could determine depends only on the form of α. Hence, since by the criterion α is tautological if and only if all elements of that class are actual,

(An1) is satisfied. Moreover, if it is satisfied by a μ-series, it is also satisfied by all of "its" ν-series. For (An2), however, the latter do make a difference. Suppose that there is in our world for each property at least one other, not coextensive with it, such that (45) $(f)(\exists g)(x)[f(x) \supset g(x)]$ is actual. In some possible worlds all c-complexes of the form corresponding to that of (45) are actual. In some, but surely not in all! Thus the model excludes what the tradition, if fully articulated, must want to exclude. Even if in our world (45) were actual, it would yet not be analytic.

38* (a) Since the number of the particulars is a contingent feature, the model must take in all i. Hence, even if the particulars are denumerable, the "possible" universals are not. Once one moves within the interpreted axiomatic system, that raises no question that concerns the ontologist. But does it make ontological sense to say of any class of simples (things), or of that of all simples, that it is not denumerable? I shall venture a comment in Section VI. (b) A μ-series, you will have gathered, counts as one of "its" ν-series. Put differently *a* "full" world is a possible world. The italicized article accommodates the new model, in which more than one universal may determine the same class.

Dialectically the new model, or criterion, is virtually forced on us by the new notion of a possible world, which in turn is forced on us by the arguments, marshaled under (A), (B), (C), on p. 00ff., in support of the sharp contrast between classes and universals. What, then, is this new model? I proceed in three steps. *First.* Take three successive types, say, the first three. Since properties are by their very nature not extensional, the following may, and in most possible worlds will, happen. One class of particulars is the extension of several properties[(0)], say, f_1, f_2, f_3, of which a property[(0)], say, F_1, picks some but not all. E.g., $F_1(f_1)$ and $F_I(f_2)$ are actual; $F_I(f_3)$ is potential. Thus the ν-series will no longer do. We must replace them by λ-series, $\mu_i^0, \lambda_i^1, \lambda_i^2, \ldots$, being produced as follows. λ_i is a class produced by coordinating, abstractly as one says, to each of some subclasses of μ_i^0 either one or several determinates; λ_i^2 is in the same way obtained from λ_i^1; and so on. If you consider the boundless variety of possible worlds this procedure yields, reflection will show you that no q-complex that spans three or more types can be actual in all of them. Thus it cannot be a tautology unless, of course, it is a p-tautology, either directly or after reduction, in one way or another, to q-tautologies each of which spans only two successive steps. *Second.* It seems that what we anticipated (p. 163) has already been shown: *The calculus that goes with the new criterion is materially a short series of second-order calculi.* Yet we cannot be sure unless we make one more check. For some "subject" classes there may be, and in most of these presumable second-order calculi there will be, more than one "predicate." Does that make a difference? In view of the familiar feature reflected by the extensionality of the lower functional calculus, the answer, obviously, is No. The new model is what we anticipated it would be. *Third.* While none of these second-order calculi is complete in Goedel's sense, which doesn't disturb us, each of them is complete in Henkin's sense (p. 164). Thus a q-complex is analytic if and only if it satisfies the one criterion that in the light of (A), (B), and (C) makes ontological sense.

39* A careful reader points out what he thinks is a roughness. Unless the number of sorts of atomic facts were finite, certain crucial recursions could not get started. If, by contingent principle, it is finite, there is an integer N so that no relation is more than N-ary. In Henkin's theorem, on the other hand, there is no such limit. The roughness is easily smoothed out. Just distinguish between the world and the model. In our world there is such an integer. Yet, in a model suited for explicating the notion of tautology, there will be "possible worlds" for which this integer is higher than any one selected in advance.

Are complexes quantifiable? Or, as we speak, synonymously, can they be targets? Remember some of the conclusions at which we arrived (p. 174ff.). Syntactically, quantified propositional variables may be a convenience in any calculus. Ontologically, since the connectives according to their mediation pattern—i.e., as one says, according to the truth tables—can do all the mediating there is to be done among complexes on the first level, complexes, unlike things, can on this level not be quantified. The mediation pattern for the connectives is of course quite different from that for the quantifiers; the crucial difference being that, by the third clause of the latter, the mode of the descent (or ascent) complex $A(b)$ depends only on the identity but not on the mode, if any, of b. Thus it makes sense that by this pattern complexes *may* be quantifiable on the second level, i.e., that there may be determinates such as $\bigvee \langle \alpha_1, \alpha_2 \rangle$, where α_1 and α_2 are both complexes and α_2 is a complex-II. It would indeed be a flaw in the taxonomy of this world if there weren't such determinates; for there would be a slot one expects to be filled left empty. How, then, can we establish that there *are* in this world such complexes? Another appeal to the phenomenological rock bottom is in order.

Sometimes, when presented with a disjunction, say, $r_1(a, b) \lor F_1(f_1)$, one is, or at least I am, either simultaneously or in immediate succession presented with the actuality of $(r_1(a, b) \lor F_l(f_1))$-being-a-disjunction. This is the phenomenological claim. What, then, does one intend when being presented, either transparently or otherwise, with x-being-a-disjunction? Until the question has been answered, the claim is not fully articulated. In this world, to intend x-being-a-disjunction and to intend (46) $(\exists \alpha_1)(\exists \alpha_2)(x = \alpha_1 \vee \alpha_2)$ are one and not two. Or, with a twist, by the provisional fiction to be discarded in the next Section, there is in this world nothing for either disjunction (*disj*) or '*disj*(x)' to stand for; the latter being merely an abbreviation for (46). That is why, although officially—if that be the word for so relaxed a notation—'x' serves here as an abbreviation for (46') '$r_1(a, b) \vee F_1(f_1)$', I used, and on similar occasions shall continue to use, such letters as 'x', 'y', 'z' in order to keep you reminded that, if there were abbreviations in the ideal language, (46') would result from substitution for a definitional (!) variable in a *definiens*.

In all cases that "simple," the claim, thus articulated, is a straightforward phenomenological appeal so irresistible, at least to me, that it needs no further support. Dialectically, though, there is an objection that does not depend on how "simple" or "complicated" x, and therefore its form, happens to be. Also, this objection is so characteristic of a rather large strand in the tradition that one is tempted to call it classical. Thus, since, as we have just convinced ourselves once more, the claim it objects to is in this world as strategic as any, we had better listen to one who (I suppose) raises it.

40* (a) Written out properly for once, the claim for (46) is that the actuality of $\bigwedge \langle f_2(c), \bigwedge \langle f_3(d), r_1(a, b) \vee F_1(f_1) =. f_3(d) \vee f_2(c) \rangle \rangle$ is immediately available to us. Notice the choice, of which more in a moment, of the targets. Neither of them shares a "constituent" either with the other or with $r_1(a, b) \vee F_1(f_1)$. (b) Make a note of the corresponding negative claims, indispensable in connection with the sameness criteria, of which more presently, that the potentiality of $(\exists \alpha_1)$ $(\exists \alpha_2)(\beta_1 \bigcirc \beta_2 = \alpha_1 \vee \alpha_2)$ is immediately available to us. '$\bigcirc$' marks here, most irregularly, any step of the first two canons that is not disjunction. Equally indispensable are the further negative claims as to the immediately available potentiality of $(\exists \alpha_1)(\exists \alpha_2)(\beta_1 = \alpha_1 \vee \alpha_2)$, when β_1 is either a circumstance, or class, i.e., the product of the (c)-step from a selector, or a thing.

The objector now makes his point: suppose, if only for the sake of the argument, that there is the existent for which you make 'x' stand. Suppose, too, that there are the two acts you assay as intending x and $disj(x)$, respectively. But why insist that their intentions are two and not one? You appeal at this point to the testimony of the given. I, unswayed by such appeals in support of what seems to be a prior doctrinal commitment, find only one intention, namely, x, and locate the difference elsewhere. It may be the difference between two ways of intending; or perhaps that between "attending" once to one "aspect" of x, once to another; I need not commit myself on such relative detail. Concisely, then, and with the traditional words, what you locate in the "object," I locate, more plausibly and at any rate more simply, in the "subject." I reply as follows: Consider the analogous case of a colored object perceived. Upon the assay corresponding to your proposal, (what I call) the perceptual object is, all details apart, "subjective." What is "objectively" there is either (a) the color the object "really" has, or (b) no color at all but some feature of (what I call) the theoretical object which physicists and physiologists talk about when talking about "color." For what we are about, the difference between (a) and (b) makes no difference. Upon the assay I have long proposed, what is "objectively" there (and nonmental!) is the perceptual object, while the theoretical object is merely the denizen of an interpreted axiomatic calculus. Thus the prior commitment, if this is the way you want to put it, is to phenomenological realism; that is, as I would rather put it, to an adequacy criterion that avoids the two extremes, equally unacceptable, of representationalism and phenomenalism. With respect to 'aspect' in particular, two "aspects" of one theoretical object are in this world, even if potential, indeed two perceptual objects. This, as we both know, is the feature that caused some phenomenalists to speak, so misleadingly, of the theoretical object as a "construction." (See also Appendix C.)

Granted that the quantifiability of complexes is in this world of strategic importance ontologically, what are its peculiarities? What, if any, are the conveniences it offers and the inconveniences from which it suffers calculationally? Dr. Johnson once attended a circus performance where he saw dogs that had been taught to walk on their hind legs. When Boswell, who hadn't been there, asked him the next day how well it was done, he answered to the effect that when it came to this sort of thing, it didn't matter how well it was done; it was enough that it could be done at all. As for those dogs, so for quantification over complexes. What matters is that it can be done at all; or, rather, that on the second level the quantifiers produce complexes which would otherwise not be there. Calculationally, the conveniences are few, if any; the inconveniences, severe; so severe indeed that we had better first provide ourselves with the notion of a *constituent*, which will prove handy in taking stock of them.

Remember the notion of a cone (p. 181). Consider, *first,* molecular complexes-I, each of which has only one cone. A determinate is a constituent of such a complex if and only if it is an element of its cone. Consider, *second*, a q-complex-I, which has alternative cones. A determinate is a constituent of such a complex if and only if it is an element of all its cones. This is the idea. Formally, as here specified for all sorts of complexes, β-being-a-constituent-of-α is a (binary) recursive notion, which, as a moment's reflection will show you, is transitive. Thus it fulfills a promise made quite early in this discourse (p. 52).

Three examples will help. The constituents of $f_1(a) \vee r_1(b, c)$ are a, b, c, f_1, r_1, $f_1(a)$, $r_1(b, c)$ and all the required standardization and order diads I do not bother to write down. The constituents not either order or standardization diads of $f_1(a, b)$ & $(a) f_1(a, b)$ and a, b, $f_1(a, b)$, $(a) f_1(a, b)$. The constituents not either order or standardization diads of $f_2(c, d)$ & $(a) f_1(a, b)$ are b, c, d, f_1, f_2, $f_2(c, d)$, $(a) f_1(a, b)$.

Classes require special provisions. So take, *third*, complexes, either of the second level or mixed, produced without a (c)-step. If you consider that both α and β are elements of all cones of both (α, β) and $(\alpha M \beta)$, you will realize that no additional clause is needed in order to preserve transitivity. A determinate is a constituent of such a complex if and only if it is an element of all its cones. Turn, *fourth* and last, to classes. Both α and β are elements of all cones of $\alpha \in \beta$. *Classes are constituents.* But the structural suggestion so to specify the notion that *classes do not have constituents* is virtually irresistible. If one yields to it and wants to preserve transitivity, he must modify the specification of the notion in a way that brings its recursiveness out into the open. *A determinate β_1 is a constituent of another, α_1, if and only if it fulfills two conditions, viz., (i) β_1 is an element of all cones of α_1; and (ii) there is at least one determinate γ_1 satisfying (i) and such that, first, β_1 is an element of all cones of γ_1, and, second, γ_1 is not a class and has in α_1 at least one occurrence not in the cone of a class satisfying (i).*

40* What is the force of that structural suggestion? We shall fully appreciate it only later, in Section VI; but we are far enough along for three comments, in descending order of persuasiveness, to be helpful. (1) The only plausible candidates for being constituents of a class are its elements, the constituents of its elements, and so on. Yet, unlike constituency, the element nexus is notoriously not transitive. (2) Terminologically it may be convenient to call a determinate its own "improper" constituents. Ontologically it makes no sense. For it is, I submit, part of the very idea of a constituent that, if α_1 is a constituent of γ_1, there is, if I may so express myself, an existent "between α_1 and γ_1. If γ_1 is a circumstance (i.e., an existent (b)), either (α_1, β_1) or $\alpha_1 \in \beta_1$ or $\alpha_1 M \beta_1$, then β_1 is between α_1 and γ_1, α_1 between β_1 and γ_1. If γ_1 is a value (i.e., an existent (a)), then the function is between its argument and γ_1. But there is nothing between a class (i.e., an existent (c)) and any of its selectors. The latter have constituents, of course; but the "transmission line" has snapped. That fits very well with the arbitrariness of classes. (3) Classes and things, we know, share several features. E.g., since neither has a mode, neither can be a scope. If classes and things are both "simples" in the sense of having no constituents, then there is one more such feature.

* An acute reader balks at (2). For every determinate, say, α_1, there is, he points out, nothing between it and the (potential) diad (α_1, α_1). Thus he charges me with inconsistency. I admit an exception, rather than inconsistency; pleading that on the level of sameness and diversity, which are the most fundamental of all ontological notions, one such exception seems inevitable. Then I supplement this plea with three remarks. For one, $\alpha_1 \in \alpha_1$ and $\alpha_1 M \alpha_1$, although of course also potential, are yet, because of the order they involve, no exceptions. Thus there is indeed only one. For another, even in a world as different as Quine's, there is on this deepest level a "corresponding" exception. For his unit classes elementhood and sameness "coincide." And I remind you, third, of the asymmetrical and therefore, perhaps, not quite "consistent" way in which on this level I broke off a barren regress by assaying sameness as the negation of diversity.

Being a constituent and being quantifiable are not coextensive; yet the connection is perspicuous. On the first level, a constituent may be either a thing or a complex, but only the former are quantifiable. On the second level, not only things but also complexes are quantifiable, the latter subject to the third clause of the mediation pattern. I.e., if α_1 and α_2 are two complexes such that α_1 is a constituent of α_2, then α_1 will be quantifiable in α_2 if and only if the mode of α_2 depends only on the identity but not on the mode of α_1. In $(\alpha_1 \in \alpha_2) \vee \alpha_3$, for instance, α_1 and α_2 are quantifiable, $\alpha_1 \in \alpha_2$ and α_3 are not.

The unwieldiness of quantification over complexes has two sources; both, as one would expect, additional combinatorial complications. Suppose that α_1 is a constituent of α_2, and ask yourself whether (47) '$(\alpha_2)(\alpha_1)A$' stands for anything. Obviously, α_2 must not be held to have a free occurrence in $(\alpha_1)A$; which by one of our fundamental gambits makes (47') ill formed. For (47') $(\alpha_1)(\alpha_2)A$, *on the other hand, provided* α_2 is a constituent of A and α_1 has a free occurrence in it outside of α_2, there is no such difficulty. That spots one source. Consider descent from a generality, $(\alpha_1)A(\alpha_1)$, such that $A(\alpha_1)$ either is or has as a constituent $(\alpha_2)B(\alpha_1, \alpha_2)$. Then the descent to β_1 by substituting it for α_1 in $A(\alpha_1)$ will be illicit not only if β_1 is α_1 but also if α_1 is a constituent of β_1. That spots the other source.

When quantifying over complexes in the rest of this Section and later on in Sections VI and VII, we shall manage in spite of these additional complications. Yet, to design a calculus which masters them as completely as the combinatorial logicians mastered the lesser ones of the first level is quite a job, not only tedious as well as calculationally unrewarding but also, at least for me, formidable. But I see no reason why it couldn't be done. So I once more take my chances, leaving it to the mathematicians to teach this dog how to walk on its hind legs.

There are three more jobs to be done. We must, *first*, introduce the *irregular targets*, and, *second*, attend to the *sameness criteria*. Then we shall be ready to conclude by showing, *third*, that the three claims (C1), (C2), and (C3) guarantee the four *requirements* of the mediation pattern for the quantifiers.

First. Remember what has been claimed explicitly for one form, or more fully for once, for one structural form or feature. I claimed, first, that when presented with a disjunction, x, I am sometimes, either simultaneously or successively, presented with the actuality of its being a disjunction ('*disj(x)*'); and I claimed, second, that on these occasions I am transparently presented with (48) $(\exists \alpha_1)(\exists \alpha_2)(x =. \alpha_1 \vee \alpha_2)$; with the gap between '*disj(x)*' and (48) to be bridged in the next Section. Thus if the complexes α_1 and α_2 were not, as by the proposed mediation pattern they are, quantifiable in (48), the claim could not be sustained. (In the above notation for (48), 'α_1' and 'α_2' are of course abbreviations for complexes, say, $f_1(a)$ and (b, c); otherwise the expression would be ill formed. In other expressions they may be determinates from other ranges. In this respect our notation of convenience is as flexible as the new assay of the quantifiers.)

As for disjunction, so for all connectives, all the exemplifications, and the three (b)-steps, which produce the three sorts of circumstances. $(\exists \alpha_1)(\exists \alpha_2)(x = \eta_2(\alpha_1, \alpha_2))$; $(\exists \alpha_1)(\alpha_2)(x = \supset \langle \alpha_1, \alpha_2 \rangle)$; $(\exists \alpha_1)(\exists \alpha_2)(x = (\alpha_1, \alpha_2))$; $(\exists \alpha_1)(\exists \alpha_2)(x =. \alpha_1 \in \alpha_2)$ will do for one sort of atomic facts, for implication, diversity, and the class nexus, respectively. (In the first of these examples, f_1 and F_1 will do for α_1 and α_2; in the second, any two complexes, in the third and fourth, any two determinates.) We need not tarry to enter separate claims for each of these steps or, if you please, for the formation rules associated with them. Yet, checking the list, rather short and certainly finite, of such steps, we quickly discover that on three of them we are blocked; one is the (c)-step, from a selector to its class; the other, the $\vee$- and the $\wedge$-step, leading from the argument of a quantifier to its value. Classes, as already mentioned, have no structural form, although, as we shall see, they can be characterized transparently in context. Of this more later, in Section VI. That leaves the quantifiers. For them I now enter two separate claims, although, as before, nothing will be lost if we stay with $\bigvee$.

Sometimes, when presented with a $\bigvee$-generality x, say, $\bigvee \gamma_1$, I am, either simultaneously or successively, presented with the actuality of its being such a generality ('$\bigvee gen(x)$'). I.e., writing for once without the shortcuts of convenience, I am transparently presented with what '$\bigwedge \langle\langle a, f_1(a)\rangle, x = \bigvee \langle a, f_1(a)\rangle\rangle$ presumably stands for. Or, with the one shortcut here most helpful, I am so presented with what (49) $(\exists \gamma_1)(x = \bigvee \gamma_1)$ presumably stands for. In (49) the irregularity pierces the eye. Upon the notion of free, or, if you please, with the formation rule we have adopted, γ_1 is not free either in $\bigvee \gamma_1$, or in $x = \bigvee \gamma_1$, or, for that matter, in any presumable scope in which it occurs only as a constituent of the constituent $\bigvee \gamma_1$. Hence, (49), being ill formed, cannot stand for what I claim to be sometimes transparently presented with. Under such double pressure—phenomenological and, admittedly, systematic—the thing to do, I submit, is to so modify the notion, or, if you please, the formation rule, that expressions such as (49) do stand for a complex. Thus I stipulate that in scopes of the sort just mentioned *the argument of a quantifier is quantifiable;* or, concisely, that it is an *irregular target in irregular scopes.* Let us see whether we can gain some assurance that nothing untoward will happen and that this extension of quantifiability is not, in a pejorative sense, arbitrary. Five remarks should do the job.

(1) The mode of $\bigvee \gamma_1$ depends only on the identity but not on the mode of the irregular target. Thus the extension does not clash with the crucial third clause of the mediation pattern. (2) A calculus which accommodates the extension would list '$\sim(\gamma_1) \bigwedge \gamma_1$,' '$\sim(\gamma_1) \bigvee \gamma_1$,' '$(\exists \gamma_1) \bigwedge \gamma_1$,' '$(\exists \gamma_1) \bigvee \gamma_1$' among its theorems. The actuality of each of the four complexes these expressions stand for is indeed, if not immediately available, easily reached. (3) If quantifiability is extended to the irregular targets, is it not arbitrary to withhold it from the order and standardization tuples such as, say $\langle \alpha_1, \alpha_2 \rangle$ in $\langle\langle \alpha_1, \alpha_2 \rangle, \ldots \supset \langle \alpha_1, \alpha_2 \rangle \ldots \rangle$? Looking more closely, one sees first that, provided α_1 and α_2 do not fall under bound in the dotted context, the value of this quantification is analytically equivalent to that produced by successive quantification, in proper order, over α_1 and α_2; and, second, that, as was pointed out earlier, these latter quantifications would merely reproduce the truth-table pattern. Thus the exclusion is not really arbitrary. Notice, incidentally, that, since α_1 is a constituent of α_2, $(\gamma_1)(\ldots \bigvee \gamma_1 \ldots)$ is analytically equivalent to $(\alpha_1)(\alpha_2)(\ldots \bigvee \langle \alpha_1, \alpha_2 \rangle \ldots)$; unless, of course, a bound be changed, in which case we so change what

the complexes 'α_1' and 'α_2' stand for that this contingency is avoided. (4) Since the formation rules, or, as I would rather say, the canons have been mentioned, a remark about them, both as a reminder and for later reference, is in order. Such complexes-II as (48) and the one (49) stands for do not ground formation rules but, rather, a certain complex, x, being or not being of the same form as a certain other, in this case $\alpha_1 \vee \alpha_2$, which latter wouldn't be there if it were not for a certain formation rule. These rules themselves, however, lie irretrievably in the excess. (5) Take a class which in this world has primary ontological status, say, the pair whose elements are a and b; i.e., as we shall eventually write, the class $\lambda\langle c, (c = a) \vee (c = b)\rangle$. The notation is essentially that of Church, except that 'c' is, target-like, not a variable but stands for a thing. Why, then, if γ_1 is quantifiable in $\vee \gamma_1$, is it not quantifiable in $\lambda \gamma_1$? The answer is illuminating. 'λ', being a diacritical mark, stands for nothing! That is why, as has been argued a while ago, there being nothing "between" a selector and its class, the former would not, even if it were uniquely determined by the latter, be a constituent of it. And while, complexes being constituents of complexes-I, not every constituent is quantifiable, or, as one says, free, in every presumable scope, surely nothing is quantifiable in what it is not a constituent of. Thus the pattern continues to make sense and remains perspicuous. We may feel reassured. As to words, if you use 'free', as I do, synonymously with 'quantifiable', just don't also use it as a synonym for 'constituent'. (In the ideal schema that will be proposed in the last Section, there are all together four diacritical marks. The other three are '$\in$', 'M', and, with a modification to get rid of the linear order, '(. . .)'.)

Second. For each argument α_1 of the function ϕ_1 there is one and only one value, $\phi_1\alpha_1$, which the function makes out of it. As for these (a)-steps, so for the three (b)-steps and the (c)-step. Given two determinates and, for the element and meaning nexus, their order, there is one and only one circumstance of each of the three sorts of which they are the terms. Again, for each selector there is, reached from it by the (c)-step, one and only one class. Thus, what was just called the univocality of all Meinong functions, i.e., of the (a)-steps, holds for all steps. Given suitable material, there is one and only one determinate which a step produces from it, or, synonymously, builds out of it. This is one of our fundamental gambits. Without it I wouldn't know how to do ontology. Yet we also remember, from the opening of Section II, that there is nothing about a step, or canon, that determines whether (i) its product from this material is the same as, or diverse from, its product from that material, or, more generally, whether (ii) its product from this material is the same as, or diverse from, the product of another step from other material. That is how in that Section the need for "criteria," themselves ontologically grounded, for regulating such sameness or diversity was brought home to us. The reason, or at least one reason, why this need has not been felt is that these criteira are, with one major exception, so simple, or obvious, that they are easily either overlooked or taken for granted. We, though, have been alerted to them by that feature of the new assay for which the transparent actuality of $\bigvee\langle a, f(a)\rangle = \bigvee\langle b, f(b)\rangle$ is the paradigm. For $\langle a, f(a)\rangle$ and $\langle b, f(b)\rangle$ are "of course" two and not one. This is in our world the one major exception; it falls under (i); there is none that would fall under (ii). The one minor exception, safely and conveniently ignored until Section VI, is the classes.

The quotes I just put around 'of course' are there to tease. *a and b being diverse*, the criterion grounding this particular diversity is (50a) $(\alpha_1)(\alpha_2)(\beta_1)(\beta_2)[(\alpha_1, \alpha_2) = (\beta_1, \beta_2) \equiv. ((\alpha_1 = \beta_1) \,\&\, (\alpha_2 = \beta_2)) \lor ((\alpha_1 = \beta_2) \,\&\, (\alpha_2 = \beta_1))]$ which is one of those so simple or obvious that they are easily either overlooked or taken for granted. But, then, how about *a and b* being diverse? If, as in this case, α_1 and α_2 are simples (things), there is no further determinate that grounds by its mode the actuality or potentiality, as the case may be, of (α_1, α_2), i.e., in this case, (a, b). If you want to rehearse the arguments for there being no such "criterion complex" for simples reread parts of Section II. The reasons why there seems to be one you will find in Section V. As for (a, b), so for (a, α_2), i.e., for a thing and a complex. That leaves us with those cases where neither term of the diad is simple. What, if anything, grounds their being two and not one? The answer has two parts.

Let us first collect all the criteria so simple that, if they are presented at all, so is their actuality. They fall into two groups. One consists of all those which, for any two steps, exclude the abstract possibility (ii) above. (51a) $(\alpha_1)(\alpha_2)(\alpha_3)\sim(\alpha_1 \lor \alpha_2 =. \sim\alpha_3)$, (51b) $(\alpha_1)(\alpha_2)(\alpha_3)(\alpha_4)\sim(\alpha_1 \lor \alpha_2 =. \alpha_3 \supset \alpha_4)$, (51c) $(\alpha_1)(\alpha_2)(\alpha_3)\sim(\alpha_1 \,\&\, \alpha_2 =. \bigvee\alpha_3)$ are three of them. Since the number of different steps is finite (and rather small), so is that of these immediate transparencies. We need of course not list them all. The second group, also finite, limits the exceptions (i) to the quantifiers. (50a) belongs to this group. So does (50b) $(\alpha_1)(\alpha_2)(\alpha_3)(\alpha_4)[(\alpha_1 \supset \alpha_2) =. (\alpha_3 \supset \alpha_4) \equiv. (\alpha_1 = \alpha_3) \,\&\, (\alpha_2 = \alpha_4)]$. Again, we need not enumerate them all. The only ones not immediately transparent, unless γ_1 and γ_2 are very "simple," are of course $\bigvee\gamma_1 = \bigvee\gamma_2$ and $\bigwedge\gamma_1 = \bigwedge\gamma_2$.

(1) Since in the two groups of obvious criteria the targets are all ei-

ther terms of diversities or constituents of such, they are indeed quantifiable; the criteria themselves, as one would expect, are generalities-II. But since (speaking linguistically for the sake of conciseness) these quantifiers are all gathered in a prefix, one must not overestimate the importance of such closure. We might as well have proceeded as we were forced to proceed in the case of the p-tautologies, where the third clause of the mediation pattern is not satisfied, in the way that corresponds to the logicians' schemata, by claiming that the actuality of every "instance," obtained by the appropriate number of descents from one of these "criteria complexes," is immediately available. (2) From the four premises $x = x_1 \vee x_2$, $x_1 = y_1$ & y_2, $(\exists \alpha_1)(\exists \alpha_2)$ $(x =. \alpha_1 \vee \alpha_2)$, $(\exists \beta_1)(\exists \beta_2)(y_1 = \beta_1$ & $\beta_2)$, in conjunction with the appropriate sameness criteria from the two groups above, $(\exists \beta_1)(\exists \beta_2)$ $(\exists \alpha_1)(\exists \alpha_2)[(\alpha_1 =. \beta_1$ & $\beta_2)$ & $(x = \alpha_1 \vee \alpha_2)]$ can be reached by some of the "sentential" and "quantificational" Cartesian transitions already available to us. As in this case, so in all others; with the precautions required whenever complexes are targets. Notice, for instance, the order in the prefix of the conclusion.

Now for the generalities. How shall we decide whether, say, (52a) $\vee\langle a, A(a)\rangle = \vee\langle b, B(b)\rangle$ is actual or potential? Remember the sufficient condition in (C1) and pick a thing, z_1, of the appropriate type such that it is diverse from all things (of the same type) which are either constituents of, or targets in, either $A(a)$ or $B(b)$. Then, by (C1), $\vee\langle a, A(a)\rangle = \vee\langle z_1, A(z_1)\rangle$ as well as $\vee\langle b, B(b)\rangle = \vee\langle z_1, B(z_1)\rangle$, and, therefore, (53) $\vee\langle z_1, A(z_1)\rangle = \vee\langle z_1, B(z_1)\rangle$. Hence, by (C2a), if (52a) is to be actual, so is (53') $A(z_1) = B(z_1)$. If the two sides of (53') are either both $\vee$-generalities or both $\wedge$-generalities, we repeat the procedure, picking a z_2 diverse not only from everything z_1 must be diverse from but also from z_1 itself. If one side of (53') is a generality of one kind, while the other is either a generality of the other kind or molecular or a q-complex-I, i.e., a molecular compound of generalities-I, (52a) is potential. If both sides of (53') are q-complexes, we apply the obvious criteria until either by means of them we arrive at a decision or have to decide whether one or several generalities such as (52b) $\vee\langle a_1, A_1(a_1)\rangle = \vee\langle b_1, B_1(b_1)\rangle$ are actual or potential. The recursion, except for the obvious ones, is of course on the maximum number of quantifiers in the scope of another. In the last step, (C2b) comes into play. If you now reflect on this procedure, you will soon see that we have obtained not just one but three results. (i) We have established the decision procedure for the sameness or diversity of generalities. (ii) We have proved (C1*), i.e., that the condition in (C1) is both sufficient and necessary. (iii) We have, in the second step, established the decision procedure for q-complexes-I. Yet there remains a question. Can one be sure that there is always a sufficient number of "z's" available? Of that at the very end.

At long last we are ready to make sure that the requirements of the mediation pattern (p. 173) are fulfilled. Suppose that a_1 is not free for b in the scope of $\bigvee\langle a_1, A^1(a_1)\rangle$. Then in the innermost occurrence or occurrences $(b)\, B\,(b)$ or $(\exists b)\, B\,(b)$ of the target b in $A^1(a_1)$ we replace the latter by another thing, z_1, of the same type, such that z_1 is diverse from all things which are either constituents of, or targets in, $A^1(a_1)$; an occurrence being innermost if and only if there is in it no further occurrence of b as a target. In the complex which is the result of this first step z_1 either is or is not free for b. If it is not, we repeat the procedure, taking care that z_2 be also diverse from z_1; and so on. That establishes the recursion by which to arrive at a complex $A_b^1(a_1)$, such that, first, a_1 is free for b in $A_b^1(a_1)$, and, second, $\bigvee\langle a_1, A^1(a_1)\rangle \equiv \bigvee\langle a_1, A_b^1(a_1)\rangle$ is a special case of (C1). Hence, by the nature of $A_b^1(a_1)$ the actuality of (53a) $\bigvee\langle a_1, A^1(a_1)\rangle = \bigvee\langle b, A_b^1(b)\rangle$ is another special case of (C1). Furthermore, since the actuality of $\bigvee\langle b, A_1^b(b)\rangle \supset A_1^b(b)$ is immediately available as a special case (C3), so is, recursively, that of (54a) $\bigvee\langle a_1, A^1(a_1)\rangle \supset a_b^1(b)$. This is one half of what has to be shown. As for a_1, b, $A^1(a_1)$, so for a_2, b, $A^2(a_2)$. The actuality of (53b) $\bigvee\langle a_2, A^2(a_2)\rangle = \bigvee\langle b, A_b^2(b_2)\rangle$, as well as that of (54b) $\bigvee\langle a_2, A^2(a_2)\rangle \supset A_b^2(b)$, is recursively accessible. Suppose now that $\bigvee\langle a_1, A^1(a_1)\rangle = \bigvee\langle a_2, A^2(a_2)\rangle$ is actual. Hence, by (53a) and (53b), $\bigvee\langle b, A_b^1(b)\rangle = \bigvee\langle b, A_b^2(b)\rangle$ is actual. So, therefore, by (C2a), is $A_b^1(b) = A_b^2(b)$. In words, the result of the descent for b from a generality is uniquely determined by this generality and b. This is the other half of what has to be shown. Nor would it be difficult to show that if the results of descent of any b from "two" generalities are the same, the latter are one and not two. As for descent, so mutatis mutandis for ascent. I.e., concisely and with a twist which brings out that the mediation pattern is the very heart of quantification, the descent (or ascent) classes of two generalities do not overlap.

Can one be sure that the required number of *things* of the same type, z_1, z_2, $\ldots$, will always be available? The combinatorial logicians, and not they alone, build some of their proofs under the assumption that an ω-type series of *variables*, say, x_1, x_2, $\ldots$, is available. We, of course, must not resort to variables. That, though, is, if anything, an advantage. For it forces us to face the issue of some sort of "infinity axiom" independent of the issue of infinite classes, for which (we shall see) it is in this world not needed. How, then, about an inexhaustible supply of, say, particulars. The way acts are assayed in this world, each has a particular as a constituent and these particulars are all diverse from each other. As long as I shall be conscious, I shall thus not run out of "new" particulars. As for particulars, so plausibly for the universals[0] which in this world are called thoughts, and also, quite probably, as space is assayed, for those called shapes. For relations and higher-type universals, however, such inexhaustibility is neither plausible nor even remotely probable. Moreover, even if it were, it would be contingent in a way that should keep anyone, and certainly keeps me, from building his explication of analyticity on it. (Because of this contingency, I for once used 'axiom'.) What, then, can we do? What shall we say?

Consider in a "possible world" of three particulars and two binary relations the complex $(\alpha_1)[(\alpha_2)r_1(\alpha_1, \alpha_2) \vee (\exists\alpha_3)r_2(\alpha_1, \alpha_3)]$. As it stands, there is no descent complex for either α_2 or α_3. No can it be so recast—i.e., as the syntacticists would say, the "variables" in the expression for it cannot be so "rewritten"—that there are descent complexes for more than two of the three particulars. On the other hand, if there is reason to believe that the supply of things on hand exhausts all there are, we yet can, even if they do not suffice for the recursion procedures outlined, examine all the combinatorial possibilities which would be there if that belief were true. But we must, I submit, be prepared to say that if, having run into a boundary of this sort, we ignored it, we would be talking merely about calculi, or, at most, about the set-theoretical model in the criterion.

41* Anyone even slightly familiar with the work of the combinatorial logicians, and my own acquaintance is very slight indeed, will realize that I have barely skimmed one part of its surface. But, then, our purposes are very different. Theirs was to ground axiomatically and as deeply as possible not only these matters but also others. Mine is to make a contribution to the phenomenology and ontology of logic. Yet I have benefited from brooding over some of their work. So I want to acknowledge that.

V

Thought and Language

I now perceive a horse. More accurately in this world, I now perceive this-being-a-horse. There is yet no thing (property) for which the word 'horse' stands, as, ignoring shades, 'green' stands for a color. Or so at least it was claimed. But there is also the claim, or, more strongly, there is the fundamental gambit that whatever explicitly or implicitly one intends exists. Hence, negatively, unless a contradiction lurks at the very core of this world, a "perceiving" of this-being-a-horse cannot involve an "intending" of this-being-a-horse. How, then, positively, shall we assay what is there, on the side of the mind and the side of the horse, when one is perceiving a horse? Clearly, this is *an item of unfinished business* to which we must attend.

What a man "knows" is, while he knows it, either a complex explicitly intended by, and transparent to, an act of believing of his; or it is a-thing-being-of-its-ultimate-sort, which he explicitly intends in an act of grasping. On the side of the mind, we saw, such believings are evident; and so are all graspings. In this world that is the strongest sense in which one can "know" anything. Consider, then, (a') 'green-not-being-a-property', (a") 'green-being-a-relation', (b') 'exemplification-being-diverse-from-conjunction', (b") 'particularity-being-diverse-from-universality'. None of these four expressions stands for anything; (a') and (a") because the negated and the different ultimate sort are both unthinkable (p. 93); (b') and (b") by the canon requiring that both terms of a diad be determinates. Thus one cannot intend what the expressions purport to stand for. For one cannot in this world intend, let alone "know," what is not there. Or, if you would rather put it that way, if at this advanced stage of this discourse I had to admit that, literally, one can, and sometimes does, "know" the sort of thing the four expressions purport to stand for, my enterprise would have failed. Phenomenologically, though, it "seems" that we "know" things of this sort as well as anything. Such "seeming," on the one hand, and evidence, on the other, make in this world strange bedfellows. Nor does it improve matters if transparence is added as a third. Phenomenologically, thus, we "seem" to "know" what, ontologically, is not there. How shall we extricate ourselves from this predicament? Clearly, this is *another item* of unfinished business.

Sometimes we are transparently presented with the mode, either actual or potential, depending on what x is, of x-being-a-disjunction. Or so at least it was claimed. But it has also been claimed that there is nothing 'disjunction' stands for, even though, if we speak as literally as in phenomenological description one must, 'x is a disjunction' expresses most faithfully what on these occasions one is presented with. As for disjunction, so for all forms. How does one in these cases reconcile the apparently irreconcilable? Clearly, this is a *third item* of unfinished business.

There is still another such item. Having had your attention called to it rather emphatically in the opening passages of the last Section, you know very well what it is. But let us pretend that we don't. (1″) All-f_1's-being-f_2's is the schema of what on many occasions we "think." The schema, offered in the last Section, for the assays of what such "thoughts" are "about" is not, conventionally, (1′) $(x)[f_2(x) \supset f_2(x)]$ but, rather, alternatively and indifferently, $(1)\bigvee\langle a, f_1(a) \supset f_2(a)\rangle$ or any of its variants; indifferently because all those variants are one and not many. Yet the discrepancy, or phenomenological distance, between (1) and (1″) is greater than that between (1′) and (1″). The increment in such distance of the new assay, over and above the conventional one, from what we "think," although admittedly a matter of degree, is yet so large that it must be accounted for. Otherwise, as it was put in the last Section, the new assay would lose all phenomenological credibility. That spots the *fourth item* of unfinished business. We must provide this account.

Ontologically, the schema of what a "thought" of this kind is "about," or, if you please, of what the mind is about on these occasions, is indeed (1). This, I take it, has been established in the last Section. But we have, while establishing it, studiously avoided another question. What is the assay of the "thoughts," or, if you please, of what is there on the side of the mind, on these occasions? The account we are looking for must be built on some feature or features of this assay. How, then, shall we assay those "thoughts"? The question is but one among several, all so entangled with each other that in order to answer any of them one must also answer some others and at least probe the rest. Sometimes, when there is such a skein, there is at its core a single major issue or central question. In these cases one cannot satisfactorily answer any of the questions at the periphery without first answering the one at the center. The four items of unfinished business just listed do share such a core. What, then, is in their case the central question? One cannot even articulate it while the listener stands on one foot. To do that, i.e., articulate it and then at least start answering it, is the task of this Section. But the issue was acknowledged each of the several times we have come across it. So again you know very well what it is. But let us again pretend that we don't and try once more to identify it.

It will save words if we call the four paradigms the cases of (1) the horse, (2) the negated ultimate sort, (3) disjunction, and (4) the quantifiers, respectively. The first three share one feature. Something one would expect to be there isn't. 'Horse', (2*) 'green is not a property', and 'disjunction', respectively, purport to stand for this missing something. 'Horse' and 'disjunction' are nouns; (2*) is a sentence. With this grammatical difference goes one among things. In cases (1) and (3), each of the two sentences (1*) 'This is a horse' and (3*) 'x is a disjunction' *abbreviates* an expression which stands for a complex. On the side of the "referent"—the word will presently be introduced as a technical term—the task is, of course, to specify these complexes. In the case of disjunction we have done that already. The case of the horse will take some doing. Yet we shall manage. In both (1) and (3) there is such a complex. In this important respect they are alike and radically different from both (2) and (4). But (2) and (4) are also radically different from each other. They are, as it were, the extremes; (1) and (3) lie between them. Let us next see what that means. But do not in the meantime forget that the main task before us is to specify what in all four cases is there on the side of the mind.

(2*) stands in this world for nothing, either directly or (I speak concisely) as an abbreviation. Nor is there anything else that could more or less naturally stand in as a referent for what in this case we "seem to know." So we shall have to grub for a surrogate. If that makes (2) one extreme then we shall at the other expect to find an obvious thought about an obvious referent. More precisely, there ought to be in case (4) a referent such that, obviously in this world, there is a single thought about it; not in the broad sense in which I have until now quite deliberately used 'thinking', 'thought', and 'about' between double quotes, in order to get started; but in the technical sense of this discourse (p. 61), in which a thought is one of the two properties which together with one particular are the three constituents of an act, and in which such a thought is about what it intends. If, for example, you write '*bel*' for the species of believing and employ in this relaxed notation the usual corners to form from the expression for a complex a definite description for the thought intending it, (5) $bel(c)$ & $\ulcorner \bigvee \langle a, f_1(a) \rangle \urcorner$ (c) will be an act and (5″) $\ulcorner \bigvee \langle a, f_1(a) \rangle \urcorner$ M $\bigvee \langle a,$

$f_1(a)\rangle$ will be the circumstance that the thought in it intends the generality $\bigvee\langle a, f_1(a)\rangle$. Reflect now for a moment on this example and you will see that it is not only the simplest paradigm for (4) but also that other extreme we expect to find. For, obviously in this world, this thought is about this intention. (Nor need I this time use 'referent'!) The one thing unusual about it is what I called the increment in phenomenological distance. But, then, what is this distance between?

One cannot, or at least, by the incontrovertible witness of the given, I cannot "think" any generality such as, say, all-men-are-mortal without at the same time also "thinking" the words "*all-men-are-mortal.*" One need not, and I cannot, directly defend this appeal to the phenomenological rock bottom. But one can, and in this discourse must, restate it without the blurred use of 'thinking' which was used as an opening ploy. *One cannot believe, or doubt, or remember, and so on, a generality without at the same time also perceiving the appropriate words.* The words "appropriate" and "perceived" are those of the sentence, or, briefly, they are the sentence that stands for the "referent." In the simplest cases, the referent is the intention of a single act of believing, or doubting, and so on. In most cases that is more complicated. Of this presently. But notice right now that in all cases *the appropriate words are those of the (natural) language in which, as one says, we think.* This discourse, however sparingly and (I hope) judiciously, employs artificial (or improved) languages; it concludes with a proposal for the ideal schema. That makes at this point this distinction, between those "languages" or, rather, schemata, on the one hand, and the natural language in which we think on the other, the most urgent of all. Another distinction, not quite as urgent yet crucial for everything that follows, was made much earlier (p. 62). If you remembered it, you may have wondered whether the "perceiving" in the above formula was a perceiving or a perceiving$_1$. The answer will not be long in coming forth. But let us first attend to the two questions already before us. What is that extra distance in the case of the quantifiers between? What is the issue at the core of all four cases, of the horse, of disjunction, and so on? After having answered the first, we shall have gathered all the cues needed for answering the second.

Return to the paradigm (1″). The distance that strikes us is between what in this world is there, viz., (1) $\bigvee\langle a, f_1(a) \supset f_2(a)\rangle$, and what the words perceived, viz., (1t) "*All f_1's are f_2's,*" lead one to expect is there. Thus I was stretching the use of a word when calling this distance "phenomenological." Yet, since it is, as we shall see, a distance between two intentions, and since we cannot intend the former, (1), without intending the latter, (1t), I did not, I think, stretch it too far. But let us first spot what strikes us by the contrast with three other pairs: (6) $f_1(a)$, (6t) "*this is f_1*"; (7) $\sim f_1(a)$, (7t) "*this is not f_1*"; (8) $f_1(a) \supset f_2(a)$, (8t) "*If this is f_1 then it is f_2.*" The standardizations are mild; and there is virtually no phenomenological distance between the members of any of these pairs. How shall we account for this difference between (1) on the one hand and (6), (7), (8) on the other? Is it perhaps the greater complexity of what must be there on the side of the mind if we are to be conscious, or aware, of (1)? The answer, although negative, points the way; so I anticipate it. The conscious state, or awareness, whose referent is (6) is indeed less complicated than any of the three whose referents are (1), (7), (8), respectively. The latter three, however, are equally complicated; the reason for this being that, unlike the former, these three necessarily involve perceivings of the words (1t), (7t), (8t), respectively. What distinguishes (1), which is of course the case of the quantifiers, from (7) and (8) is one thing only. We are startled, or even shocked, by the distance I called phenomenological between (1) and (1t). The shock is wholesome; for it virtually forces us to explore, not just in this case but in all cases, the place which perceivings of words have in most, although not as we shall see in all, of our states of consciousness. Nor is that the first nudge we have received in this direction.

In the two cases of the horse and of disjunction, we were virtually forced to mention abbreviations, i.e., as one usually says, defined predicates and the left sides of definitions; 'horse' and 'this is a horse' in one case, 'disjunction' and 'x is a disjunction' in the other. Do, then, the perceivings of "*this is a horse*" and of "*x is a disjunction*" have a place in the assays of the corresponding awarenesses? The suggestion that they do is structurally irresistible. The quantifiers, the horse, and disjunction; that makes three out of four. In the last case, of the negated ultimate sort, the suggestion is not quite so compelling; nor in the nature of things could it be; just remember that this is the case in which we shall have to search for surrogate referents. Yet there, too, we shall see, the suggestion points to the assay that does the job; which will make four out of four. The central question at the core of the four items of unfinished business is identified beyond reasonable doubt. *What is the connection between thought and language?* In the more formal style of ontological discourse: *What is the place of perceivings of words in the assay of our awarenesses?* We are almost ready to tackle this major issue. First, though, for a few comments, then for some agreements about words and notations.

42* (a) The cases of the horse and of disjunction are alike in that both "*this is a horse*" and "*x is a disjunction*" are (I speak concisely) abbreviations standing for complexes. In two other respects they differ. The horse complexes, if I may provisionally so express myself, are never transparent; the mode of a form complex is always at least recursively accessible. This we know already. The former cannot be reached by "introspection"; the latter can be so reached. This we shall see. (b) Where we speak of canons the syntacticists speak of formation rules. Speaking as they do, an alert reader wonders why, since the formation rules presumably do not stand for anything, they are not *a fifth item*, of the same kind as the other four, of unfinished business. I start my reply by reminding him that there are three kinds of canons, (a), (b), (c), as we called them, for facts, circumstances, and classes, respectively. For the last two kinds, there is indeed nothing a "formation rule" could conceivably stand for. A canon (a), however, if read as a "rule," codifies the restriction, beyond the minimal one, a function imposes on its argument. Thus there is at least the function which, as it was put (p. 126), "represents" the canon. But I hurry to add that, as was also pointed out, the discrepancy between the representative and the represented is so great that the question makes excellent sense for all canons. Nor have they been excluded fom the list because their case is radically different but, rather, because it is more radical. For it lies at the very limits of thought, where the ladder must eventually be thrown away, which we shall not retrace until the very end of this discourse. Notice, though, that in this respect the case of the negated ultimate sort is more radical than those of the horse and of disjunction, which are in turn both more radical than that of the quantifiers. (Someone else may want to ask why the two "extensions," still to be introduced, of the theoretical objects and of those classes we cannot literally think, will not make *a sixth item* of the same sort. I reply that these two cases, although sufficiently different for each to be sui generis, are yet in other respects alike and so different from the other "five" that the "entities" they involve are "added" to this world as enjoying a secondary, or derivative, ontological status. But nothing would be gained by previewing these similarities and differences.)

Now for the agreements about words and notations we must make. *First.* Improved notations, including fragments of the ideal schema that will be proposed at the end, are used throughout this discourse *about* the world. But there is also some talk, particularly in this Section, about natural-language expressions which are the intentions of acts that occur *in* this world. Our notation ought to leave no doubt that these are two very different things. In order to make sure that it doesn't, I use both italics and double quotes; thus distinguishing a determinate, which may or may not be the intention of an act, say, $\sim f_1(a)$, from "*this is not f_1*", which is the intention of the second, auxiliary act, simultaneous and in the same mind, which in this world must be there if the first is there. The reason for sewing with the double thread of both italics and double quotes is, of course, that in this book all artificial expressions are italicized. For, if we write this way, the expressions for $\sim f_1(a)$ and "$\sim f_1(a)$" remain clearly distinct even if we use artificial expressions for the intention of the second act, either for the sake of convenience when it makes no difference, or when some act happens to intend an artificial expression. *Second.* Suppose that (5) on p. 203 is the intention of an act whose species is direct awareness (*draw*). Written out, even with the convenience of definite descriptions, the expression for this act is (9) $draw(d)$ & $\ulcorner bel(c)$ & $\ulcorner \bigvee \langle a, f_1(a) \rangle \urcorner (c) \urcorner (d)$. In what follows we shall repeatedly have to speak about several such acts at the same time. Thus we have no choice. If we do not want to drown in ink or choke on words, we must design some abbreviations. Fortunately that is not difficult. Every thought has exactly one intention. A determinate, if intended at all, as of course the overwhelming majority of them is not, is intended by exactly one thought. That makes "an act with this species (α) and this intention (β)" a description in which nothing but the name of the particular in the act is lost. This, though, causes no inconvenience; for no particular is a constituent of more than one act. Thus I propose to write '$(\alpha \| \beta)$' as an (artifical) abbreviation for the (nonitalicized!) phrase between double quotes above. If you agree, then we can instead of (5) and (9) write (5') '$(bel \| \bigvee \langle a, f_1(a) \rangle)$' and (9') '$(draw \| (bel \| \bigvee \langle a, f_1(a) \rangle))$'; two expressions which, although neither very short nor very handy, are yet shorter and more perspicuous than what they abbreviate. For another example, if we anticipate that the "perceivings" in the auxiliary acts are all perceivings$_1$, the auxiliary act associated with (5) will be (10) $(perc_1 \| "\bigvee \langle a, f_1(a) \rangle")$. But keep in mind, please, that the thought in (10) is $\ulcorner "\bigvee \langle a, f_1(a) \rangle" \urcorner$ and not either "$\bigvee \langle a, f_1(a) \rangle$" or $\bigvee \langle a, f_1(a) \rangle$. There will be other abbreviations as we go on. These, though, should suffice for you to get the hang of all of them. *Third.* Your or my perceiving this-being-a-horse is a conscious state, or awareness, either yours or mine. Should this state turn out to be a single act, its species would be a perceiving$_1$; and what either you or I am aware of, or conscious of, viz., this-being-a-horse, would be its intention. But suppose now that this particular awareness is a collection of several acts. Then there may among the latter not be any that intends "what the awareness is aware of." Should this turn out to be the case, we would be well advised to pick a single word to do the job of the phrase between double quotas. I propose that we pick 'referent'. The *referent of an* *awareness* is what the latter is aware of. Suppose next that (*perc*‖ "*this is a horse*") is one of the acts in the collection. Should that turn out to be the case then, clearly, this is the auxiliary act which, as has already been claimed, must be there if the awareness is there; and it should pay to introduce one more technical term. I propose that we call the intention of this auxiliary act the *text of the awareness*. Such an awareness, then, would have both a referent and a text.

43 * (a) The 't' after the numerals in the numberings of some expressions is of course the initial of 'text'. If, e.g., (7) is the referent of an awareness, (7t) is its text. (b) 'Referent', having been taken, improperly, from a present rather than a past participle, is barbarous. 'Object' and Meinong's 'objective', on the other hand, are too closely associated with what is here called a thing. Thus, since I couldn't think of another word, I reluctantly adopted the solecism already well established. (c) Clumsy as it is, idiomatically, to speak of an awareness, rather than its owner, being aware of something, intellectually the locution does not embarrass me; for it fits the assay I have long proposed for the Self. But I have nothing new to add to the latter; so it may as well be kept out of this discourse. 'Referent' helps with that, too.

With some important qualifications and additions, the tripartite thesis about to be proposed asserts of all conscious states what has just been supposed of one. Thus it will hardly come as a surprise. But, then, what is a *thesis*? There has been talk of fundamental gambits and appeals to the given, of adequacy criteria and contingent principles, of standardizations, extrapolations, and even extensions. If a thesis is one of these, why the new word? If not, what does the latter stand for? The question must and will be answered. But since it is of the second order, or, as one says, metaphilosophical, it will be best if we delay answering it until we have provided ourselves with an example.

(Th1) *Each awareness, 𝔄, is a collection of at least two acts, all simultaneous, such that at least one of them is a direct awareness, 𝔇, either of one other, or of a conjunction of others, among them.* (Th2) *Each act, 𝔞, of an awareness, 𝔄, which is not one of the 𝔇 of 𝔄, is either the intention, or a conjunction term of the intention, of at least one such 𝔇.* (Th3a) *In every awareness, 𝔄, which is not either a perceiving or an imagining, there is an auxiliary act, 𝔞𝔲, which is a perceiving₁ of the text of 𝔄.* (Th3b) *In some awarenesses that are either perceivings or imaginings there may be, but there need not be, the auxiliary act 𝔞𝔲 just specified.*

Five comments will take care of the obvious and the preliminary. (1) The Gothic letters to which, having run out of others, I reluctantly resort are not marks of an artificial language, either ideal or merely improved, but expedient additions to the vocabulary of the natural language in which this discourse is written. Put differently, if this discourse were syntactical, which of course it is not, they would be used as the Gothic letters are used in a natural, or, as one says, informal, metalanguage. (2) It will save words and do no harm if, instead of saying that an act a_u is a member of a collection $\mathfrak{A}$, we shall say—as I already did, except when stating (Th1)—either that a is *in* $\mathfrak{A}$ or that it is an act *of* $\mathfrak{A}$. (3) If you examine the wording you will see that it allows for awarenesses with more than one $\mathfrak{D}$ as well as for one a being intended by more than one $\mathfrak{D}$, either singly and therefore explicitly, or, as a conjunction term, implicitly. E.g., the collection $a_1, a_2, a_3, \mathfrak{D}_1, \mathfrak{D}_2$, such that $\mathfrak{D}_1$ intends a_1 & a_2 & a_3 while $\mathfrak{D}_2$ intends a_3, is, schematically, a possible $\mathfrak{A}_1$. The relevant meaning nexus in the example are, of course, f_1 M $\ulcorner a_1$ & a_2 & $a_3 \urcorner$ and f_3 M $\ulcorner a_3 \urcorner$, with 'f_1' and 'f_2' standing for the thoughts which are constituents of $\mathfrak{D}_1$ and $\mathfrak{D}_2$ respectively. These circumstances may be, either singly or conjointly, the referents, or part of the referents, of other awarenesses; but they are not the referent, or part of the referent, of $\mathfrak{A}_1$; just as not being acts, they are not in $\mathfrak{A}_1$. (4) Literally, in this world a collection is nothing. If that bothers you, think of an awareness as a class. Which, then, is it? On reflection you will see that the question is moot. As in the example just given, an awareness is "unified" by the meaning nexus between the thought in each of its $\mathfrak{D}$, on the one hand, and the conjunction that is the intention of this thought, on the other. (Remember that even a single act is a conjunction of atomic facts.) If, finally, an awareness is a collection of, say, two awarenesses, each thus "unified," as will be the case when, e.g., I think about something while having a pain, you may, if you wish, count it as two simultaneous awarenesses. For, again, the difference will make no difference. (5) By making all acts of an awareness simultaneous, I do not mean to ignore, but merely to bracket, the difficult problems of time. For some comments on the latter, see Appendix C.

A thesis, whatever else it may be, is the sort of thing its proponents must be prepared to defend; and, of course, the more detailed and complex the thesis, the more articulate and in depth its defense ought to be. As things stand in ontology, the tripartite thesis is both, detailed and complex. How, then, should one go about defending it? The thesis has two halves. One, call it the first, is (Th1) and (Th2); the second is (Th3a) and (Th3b). The first specifies some features every conscious state is supposed to possess. That makes it a thesis about the nature of consciousness in general. The second half, which, obviously, is an elaboration of, and inseparable from, the first, is an assertion about those conscious states in which—as one says, with a phrase we have unpacked—thought is inseparable from language. Hence, since perceivings and imaginings are the only conscious states which, by the second half, do not necessarily involve language, the defense of the whole will gain in depth and dialectical strength if it can be shown that, upon an adequate assay, these two sorts of awareness possess the features specified by the first half. That determines the strategy of exposition. I turn next to perception.

What I perceive when perceiving this-being-a-horse is a perceptual object, out there in the pasture, the kind of thing about which on some occasions I entertain all kinds of belief, such as that it is a "continuant" with a past and a future, that I now "see" only part of its surface, and so on. The tune is only too familiar; even so, 'continuant' and 'see' have been quarantined in order to leave no doubt that I used them as one ordinarily does, in a way from which philosophical puzzles may be elicited, without meaning to imply that, as some philosophers have used them in their study, there are continuants or that, phenomenologically, seeing a cluster is either the whole or a part of perceiving a horse. A cluster, in the terminology of this discourse, is a conjunction of atomic facts, all of the lowest type, some of which may be relational. Remember, too, that as perceiving has been contrasted with perceiving$_1$, while we perceive horses, meadows, trees, and so on, what is perceived$_1$ is always a cluster such that the particulars in it are all simultaneous with the particular in this particular act of perceiving$_1$.

Taking 'M' from 'molecular', let 'M_i' be a cluster, and write 'μ_i' for ($perc\|M_i$), i.e., for an act of perceiving$_1$ that intends M_i. Taking 'L' from 'law', let L_i be a generality such that, first, the particulars which are constituents of M_i are all those and only those which are also constituents of L_i; and that, second, L_i epitomizes, however schematically and selectively, the lawful connections among the past, present, and future particulars in a nonsubstantialist assay of a perceptual object; either a horse, or a meadow, and so on. Write 'λ_i' for ($bel\|L_i$), i.e., for an act of believing L_i. Suppose next two things; namely, first, that M_1 is the cluster which, as some would have it, is either all or a part of what I am aware of when now perceiving this horse; and, second, that L_1 goes with M_1 as just indicated; then consider the following proposition. (P1) *The referent of my now perceiving this horse, i.e., the complex which, if actual, makes, as one says, this perceiving veridical, is the conjunction* M_1 & L_1. I have long held, and still hold that, however schematic and selective, (P1) is yet (the paradigm of) an adequate assay of what there is on the side of the referent in perception. This, though, is only part of the story. Prima facie (P1) conflicts with the awareness. So we must next identify and then try to resolve the conflict. But let me first interrupt once more for some comments.

First. The only things called *perceptual objects* in this Section are those usually called physical objects, stones, trees, horses, tables, and so on. Elsewhere in this discourse the phrase is sometimes used more broadly, to mark the contrast to the "theoretical objects," which will be introduced in Appendix C. No harm will come to us from this ambiguity. *Second.* The proposed assay of perceptual objects is, of course, *nonsubstantialist,* or, as I used to call it, Berkeleyan. Historically and dialectically, I still believe, the latter appellation is fully justified.[6] Yet I have come to dislike its phenomenalistic associations; so I now abandon it. *Third.* If M_1 & L_1 can serve as assay of a perceptual object, so can any one of a countless number of different selections of varying complexity M_2 & L_2, M_3 & L_3, and so on. Literally, therefore, what has been proposed is merely an *alternative assay both selective and schematic.* That this is the best the ontologist can do should by now be abundantly clear; if only from the failure of more than two centuries of valiant efforts, particularly in the classical British tradition, to do better. Is, then, the best we can do good enough? For our purposes, I have long been convinced, it is; for in some respects, of which this is one, ontology is by its very nature merely schematic. The proof of the pudding is in the eating. Thus I merely add that what some may miss in those alternative partial assays they will in this world find either in nonphilosophical phenomenology or in science. As to words, since "the" not merely selective and schematic assay of a perceptual object is a myth, let us save as much ink and breath as possible by agreeing that in the appropriate contexts '*an assay*', and sometimes even '*the assay*', will henceforth stand for 'an alternative assay both selective and schematic'. *Fourth.* Suppose that the particulars in M_1 & L_1 are three, say a_1, a_2, a_3; introduce '*horse*(x_1, x_2, x_3)' as an abbreviation for '$M_1(x_1, x_2, x_3)$ & $L_1(x_1, x_2, x_3)$' and add to the ideal language the term thus defined. (In the ideal language itself there are of course no abbreviations.) Could the term added pass as a (schematic and selective) definition? No one who has any sense will in any "language" accept a relational definition of 'horse'. Thus it may be worthwhile to point out

6. For arguments to this effect, see "Realistic Postscript" in *Logic and Reality:* for the assay of space mentioned in the fourth of these comments, see "Synthetic A Priori," ibid., and the fourth chapter of *Realism.* The ontologization of such "derived characters" as, presumably, horse was first perpetrated in "The Revolt against Logical Atomism," written in 1956, which is reprinted in *Meaning and Existence* (University of Wisconsin Press, 1960).

that the difficulty can be overcome. As space is assayed in this ontology, a_1, a_2, and a_3 are all parts of a fourth particular, a; with part (P) being a simple relation. Thus one can, by conjoining $P(a_1, a)$ & $P(a_2, a)$ & $P(a_3, a)$ to the cluster, obtain '$horse(x)$' as an abbreviation for '$M_1(a_1, a_2, a_3, x)$ & $L_1(a_1, a_2, a_3, x)$'. *Fifth.* Presently I shall argue that one cannot by "introspection" reach the assay of this-being-a-horse. In this respect, as already mentioned (p. 206), the case of the horse differs from that of disjunction. These arguments, though, and the distinctions that go with them, had better wait.

(P2) *When perceiving this-being-a-horse, I am aware of just that, viz., this-being-a-horse, and of nothing else.* In particular, therefore, I am not aware of either M_1 or L_1 or their conjunction. Nor is this single awareness of mine really two, viz., μ_1 and λ_1, i.e., simultaneously, a perceiving$_1$ of M_1 and a believing of L_1. Broadly speaking, the apparent conflict is of course between (P1) and (P2). More accurately, there is no conflict. Nor is the issue whether M_1 & L_1 is acceptable as an assay of the referent. On this question I have already tipped my hand. The issue is, rather, how to bridge the gap between the referent, as assayed, on the one hand, and what we are aware of, on the other.

Ontology is one thing; phenomenology is another. Yet ontology starts with phenomenology and it ends with phenomenology. Ontology starts with it because we cannot do without that rock bottom, or jumping-off place, which we called the phenomenological basis. It ends with phenomenology because, even if adequate assays of all referents had been offered, the job would still not be done unless one can also—if only schematically and, as we shall see, by means of a "thesis"—bridge that gap.

How, then, in the paradigm, shall we bridge the gap between M_1 & L_1 and this-being-a-horse? It is now more than fifteen years that, convinced as I already was that ontology must start from and end with the given, I could no longer live with this question staring me in the face. So I tried to answer it; but the answer was disastrously wrong. Introducing '$horse(a)$' as a definitional abbreviation for '$M_1(a)$ & $L_1(a)$', I ontologized the word 'horse' into a "derived character," which thus at least was there to be perceived. Now, having got rid of those unfortunate supernumeraries some time ago, I am ready for a last try.

44* As mentioned earlier, the derived characters were meant to satisfy more than one need. On one side, there was the perceived horse to be accounted for. On the other side, I had come to believe that Russell's "analysis" of classes, which I uncritically accepted, cannot be grounded ontologically without these entities. This belief I still hold. But I now also believe that classes can and must be grounded differently. Under this double pressure I pursued so long and so stubbornly that *Holzweg;* which goes to show that sometimes a little knowledge is a dangerous thing. Yet, is it not better to err at whatever expense of time, effort, and anguish, than not to come to grips with the issues?

Direct awareness (*draw*) is a species among species; perceiving$_1$ (*perc$_1$*), believing (*bel*), remembering, and so on, are others. A direct awareness thus is an act; a believing is another, a doubting a third, and so on. Let $\mathfrak{A}_1$ be an awareness of the simplest possible structure. By (Th1) it is a collection of two acts, say $\mathfrak{a}_1$ and $\mathfrak{D}_1$. By (Th2) $\mathfrak{D}$ is (*draw*$\|$ $\mathfrak{a}_1$). Let α_1 be the intention of $\mathfrak{a}_1$. *Then the referent of $\mathfrak{A}_1$ will be α_1.* Call this proposition (A). One cannot consistently hold it without also holding that *by itself, or as such, no act is ever aware of anything.* E.g., for the $\mathfrak{D}_1$ of $\mathfrak{A}_1$ to be aware of its intention, there would have to be a further direct awareness (*draw*$\|\mathfrak{D}_1$). Otherwise, what would become of the obvious distinction between being aware of something, on the one hand, and being aware of this awareness on the other?

The new try, as always in ontology, is a proposal. What is being proposed is, in outline, a new ontology of mind; i.e., more literally, a scheme for the assay of all awarenesses (conscious states). The tripartite thesis is the foundation on which the proposal rests. (A) is one of the three propositions which are its cornerstones. As you see, it deals with "the nature of consciousness in general." So, we shall see in a moment, does (B). Language, as planned, will come in only with (C). To discover (B), let us examine an awareness, $\mathfrak{A}_1$, which is a perceiving of this-being-a-horse.

The referent of $\mathfrak{A}_1$ assays as M_1 & L_1. To this we are committed. Thus there are two possible $\mathfrak{a}$'s, viz., μ_1 and λ_1; and three possible $\mathfrak{D}$'s, call them δ_1, δ_2, δ_3, i.e., more fully, (*draw*$\|\mu_1$), (*draw*$\|\lambda_1$), (*draw*$\|\mu_1$ & λ_1), respectively. As I now propose to assay it, $\mathfrak{A}_1$ is the collection $\mu_1, \lambda_1, \delta_3$. Generally, an $\mathfrak{A}_i$, which is a perceiving not involving words, whose referent is M_i & L_i, is (the three-member collection of) μ_i, i.e., a perceiving$_1$ of M_i; λ_i, i.e., a believing of L_i; and a direct awareness whose intention is the conjunction μ_i & λ_i. The second cornerstone is the following proposition: (B) *When the crucial $\mathfrak{D}$ in an awareness $\mathfrak{A}$ intends a conjunction of several acts, then what $\mathfrak{A}$ is aware of is not the conjunction of the several intentions of these acts but, rather, what in matter of (phenomenological) fact it is presented$_2$ with.* If it can be justified, then, clearly, (B) bridges the gap that concerns us. Thus it should be worth our while if once more I interrupt for some comments.

First. Notice that (B) is not limited to perceivings and imaginings not involving words. For, we shall see, the only difference between these two kinds of awareness and one which involves words is that there is among the terms of the conjunction intended by the crucial $\mathfrak{D}$ of the latter a perceiving$_1$ of its text. *Second.* The only difference between imaginings and perceivings is the species of the act that intends the cluster. In the case of the former, it is imagining$_1$; in that of the latter, perceiving$_1$. Thus no more need be said about imagining. *Third.* The subscript in 'presented$_2$' has been used on some earlier occasions. Its only purpose, then as now, is to remind us that there is no species being-presented-with. Or, if one wants to expand that, what an awareness is presented with is not its referent, as assayed by the ontology, but, rather, what its referent would be if its text (if any) were mistaken for (an image of) a literal statement (in the ideal schema) of the assay (in the ontology) of its referent. Upon reflection you will see that this expansion merely restates (B). *Fourth.* How can one justify these assays and, in particular, that "fusion"—I use deliberately a word used and, alas, misused by the classical psychologists preoccupied with introspection—which, by bridging the gap, "saves the appearances"? I hope you will be patient a bit longer. It will pay if we first acquaint ourselves with the whole pattern and only then attend to that little knot of questions which (I quite agree) we must not ignore: What is a "thesis"? Under what conditions is an assay "acceptable"? What is "introspection" and where, if at all, does it come in?

In the normal course of our mental life we are only very occasionally aware of clusters, or, for that matter, of atomic facts, each of which, if of the lowest type, is a "minimal cluster." Yet, however rare and fleeting they may be, there are, by the incontrovertible witness of the given, such awarenesses. If we so choose, or, as the psychologist would say, with the appropriate set, one can even deliberately produce them. (Claude Monet and his fellow impressionists, one would think, were unusually skilled at producing them.) Let then $\mathfrak{A}_3$ be an awareness of this kind. I assay it, as consistently I must, as a collection of two acts, a_3 and $\mathfrak{D}_3$; the former being a perceiving$_1$ of a cluster; the latter, a direct awareness of the former.

A cluster, you remember, is either a single atomic fact (of the lowest type) or a conjunction of simultaneous ones. Hence neither $\sim f_1(a)$ nor $f_1(a) \lor f_2(a)$ is a cluster. Yet I am sometimes aware of such complexes. How, then, shall we assay these awarenesses? Let $\mathfrak{A}_4$ be one whose referent is $\sim f_1(a)$. Positively, as I assay it, $\mathfrak{A}_4$ is a collection of four acts, $\mathfrak{A}_4, au_4, \mathfrak{D}_4, \mathfrak{D}_4^*$; such that a_4 is a perceiving$_1$ of $\sim f_1(a)$ and au_4 is a perceiving$_1$ of "$\sim f_1(a)$", i.e., of the text of the referent a_4; while $\mathfrak{D}_4$ and $\mathfrak{D}_4^*$ are direct awarenesses, the former of the conjunction a & au_4, the latter of au_4 alone. Negatively, there is in this world no awareness such that its only members would be a_4 and a direct awareness of it. In other words, one cannot in this world be aware of $\sim f_1(a)$ without at the same time also being aware of its text. As for $\sim f_1(a)$, so for $f_1(a) \vee f_2(a)$ and for virtually all awarenesses more "complicated" than $\mathfrak{a}_4$. For, by (Th3a) and (Th3b), every awareness, except *some* perceivings and *some* imaginings, is of the kind in which, broadly speaking, the thought is "inseparable" from its text. (About this use of 'inseparable' more presently.)

If you now try to state the matter literally rather than broadly and let yourself be guided by what has so far been said about our paradigm, $\mathfrak{A}_4$, you will see that the following generalization suggests itself. (C) *Except for some perceivings and some imaginings, there are in every awareness, $\mathfrak{A}$, at least four acts. One, call it $\mathfrak{au}$, is a perceiving $_1$ of the text of $\mathfrak{A}$; another, call it $\mathfrak{D}^*$, is a (draw$\|\mathfrak{au}$), i.e., a direct awareness of $\mathfrak{au}$. A third, call it $\mathfrak{D}$, is a (draw$\|\mathfrak{c}$ & $\mathfrak{au}$), i.e., a direct awareness whose intention is a conjunction, $\mathfrak{c}$ & $\mathfrak{au}$, one of whose terms is $\mathfrak{au}$. The other factor, $\mathfrak{c}$, is either a single act, $\mathfrak{a}$, or a conjunction of acts. In the former case, $\mathfrak{a}$ is the fourth act and there are altogether four in $\mathfrak{A}$; in the latter case there are more than four. The referent of $\mathfrak{A}$, finally, is in the former case the intention of $\mathfrak{a}$ and in the latter case the conjunction of the intentions of the factors of $\mathfrak{c}$.*

(C) is one of the three pivots on which the new ontology of mind turns. The other two are (A) and (B). Thus they are all equally indispensable. Yet, in an obvious sense, (C) depends on, and completes, the other two. Also (C) unpacks (Th3a). Our paradigm, $\mathfrak{A}_4$, has the virtue of being an awareness as "simple" as any of the kind mentioned in (Th3a). Thus, since with the exceptions stipulated by (Th3b), all awarenesses are of this kind, there should be more we can learn, either directly or by way of suggestion, from a still closer examination of $\mathfrak{A}_4$. Seven comments will do the job.

First. Although in fact our strength falters very soon, in principle there always could be, and in fact there sometimes is, for each awareness, $\mathfrak{A}$, another one, call it $\mathfrak{A}'$, which is a direct awareness of $\mathfrak{A}$. What, then, we must ask, is (a) the referent, and what precisely is (b) the structure, of $\mathfrak{A}'$? Trying to answer (a), you will soon discover that you are faced with a "choice." If one's conscious state is $\mathfrak{A}_4$, is he presented with (a1) the conjunction, $\mathfrak{a}_4$ & $\mathfrak{D}_4$, of two perceivings $_1$, of $\sim f_1(a)$ and of its text "$\sim f_1(a)$," respectively; or is he presented with (a2) a perceiving $_1$ of $\mathfrak{a}_4$ and a perceiving $_1$ of its text, i.e., of "*this is a perceiving $_1$ of $\sim f_1(a)$*"? Phenomenologically, being presented with (a2), I have no choice. Just as importantly, though, the argument is by now far enough advanced to provide dialectical support for what, if choice there were, would be mine. Turn once more to $\mathfrak{A}_2$, which is a perceiving (not: a perceiving $_1$) of a horse without a text. The $\mathfrak{D}$ in $\mathfrak{A}_2$, without which the latter would not be an awareness, intends the conjunction μ_1 & λ_1. Yet, by (B), the referent of $\mathfrak{A}_2{}'$ is not a direct awareness of μ_1 & λ_1 but, rather, that-is-a-perceiving$_1$-of-this-being-a-horse. Unpacked and generalized, that amounts to two claims. For one, such "fusion" occurs whenever the relevant direct awareness intends a conjunction of acts. For another, whenever it does occur, it bridges the phenomenological gap between the referent as in fact presented, on the one hand, and its assay on the other. Reflect now and you will see that the only choice consistent with these two claims is (a2). Reflect some more and you will arrive at the only consistent answer to (B). The members of $\mathfrak{A}_4{}'$, in addition to those of $\mathfrak{A}_4$, are three. One, call it $\mathfrak{au}_5$, is a perceiving$_1$ of "*this is a perceiving$_1$ of* $\sim f_1(a)$." The other two are direct awarenesses, call them $\mathfrak{D}_5$ and $\mathfrak{D}_5{}^*$, such that, while the intention of the former is $\mathfrak{au}_4$ & $\mathfrak{au}_5$, that of the latter is $\mathfrak{au}$ alone.

A friendly critic speaks up; says that he has several questions on his mind; but readily accepts my suggestion to ask them one at a time.

Second. What you call a fusion (he begins) is a kind of "integration," a move from the microscopic to the macroscopic, as it were. In $\mathfrak{A}_2$ for instance, the move is from M_1 & L_1, which is an (alternative partial) assay of the referent, to the referent itself. In $\mathfrak{A}_2{}'$, the move is from the direct awareness of a conjunction of acts, one a perceiving$_1$ of M_1, the other a believing of L_1, to a direct awareness of a perceiving of the referent of $\mathfrak{A}_2$; even though by itself, or as such, "perceiving" is not a species nor even, literally, an existent. In $\mathfrak{A}_4$ and $\mathfrak{A}_4{}'$, on the other hand, the respective referents, $\sim f_1(a)$ and this-being-a-perceiving$_1$-of-$\sim f_1(a)$, are also their respective assays. Hence, I speak concisely, in these two cases at least, their texts are the texts of their assays. But, whether or not they are, what does it mean to integrate an existent with a text? And, whatever it may mean, what purpose does it serve? I reply as follows: In all cases but one, 'integration' is a tag as suitable as 'fusion' for some of the several jobs which in this ontology are assigned to direct awarenesses of conjunctions of acts. Take two perceivings, $\mathfrak{A}_2$ and $\mathfrak{A}_2$, based (I, too, speak concisely) on two alternative assays, say M_1 & L_1 and $\overline{M}_1$ & $\overline{L}_2$, respectively. One of those jobs is to make both $\bar{\mathfrak{a}}_1$ and $\bar{\mathfrak{a}}_2$ perceivings of this-being-a-horse, and for this particular job 'integration' is indeed a tag more suitable than 'fusion'. The exception, where 'fusion' serves better, is all the cases where, as in $\mathfrak{a}_4$, the intention of the relevant $\mathfrak{D}$ is a conjunction of two perceivings$_1$; one of a molecular complex that is not a cluster; the other of the text of this complex, which is also the text of its assay. In these cases the job is not to "integrate" some things into something else but, rather, to "fuse" the text into the nontext, or, if that helps, to "absorb" the former into the latter; and the reason why this job needs to be done, or as you put it, the purpose served, is that, if the nontext is not a cluster, there is in this world no awareness that is a perceiving$_1$ of it unless there is also a (simultaneous) perceiving$_1$ of its text in the awareness. Just compare a_4 with a_3, which are perceivings$_1$ of $\sim f_1(a)$ and $f_1(a)$, respectively, and you will see what makes the difference. The referent of the latter is a (minimal) cluster; that of the former, although molecular, is not. Thus while I may of course be wrong, I am once more at least consistent. All this, though, is not to deny that in most cases, such as, most perspicuously, a perceiving, call it $\mathfrak{A}_6$, of this-*not*-being-a-horse, the text, or, more accurately, the auxiliary act intending it, also does other jobs.

Third. My friend prefers that, before turning to $\mathfrak{A}_6$, I consider another question. First he grants, if only for the sake of the argument, that each awareness of certain referents is, as I put it, inseparable from a (simultaneous) awareness of the appropriate text. He even grants that this is so in all cases of which I claim it. But then he wonders whether I have not unnecessarily complicated matters by introducing into the act both $\mathfrak{D}$, which is a $(draw\|\mathfrak{c}\ \&\ \mathfrak{au})$, and $\mathfrak{D}^*$, which is a $(draw\|\mathfrak{au})$. Why couldn't the same purpose be achieved more simply by introducing, together with $\mathfrak{D}^*$, a $(draw\|\mathfrak{c})$? I reply as follows: Let $\mathfrak{A}_m$ and $\mathfrak{A}_n$ be simultaneous awarenesses, each inseparable from its text and such that neither is a direct awareness of the text of the other. Then there are, upon your "simpler" proposal as well as upon mine, at least four direct awarenesses in the total awareness. According to you, there are, schematically, $(draw\|\mathfrak{c}_m)$, $(draw\|\mathfrak{au}_m)$, $(draw\|\mathfrak{c}_n)$, $(draw\&\|\mathfrak{au}_n)$ while I hold that they are $(draw\|\mathfrak{c}_m\mathfrak{au}_m)$, $(draw\|\mathfrak{au}_m)$, $(draw\|\mathfrak{c}_n\ \&\ \mathfrak{au}_n)$, $(draw\|\mathfrak{au}_n)$. Compare the two quartets and you will see that the "complication" serves a purpose. The assay I propose associates each of the two nontexts with "its" text. In the one you propose there is no cue as to which text goes with which nontext. Yet the total awareness (or, as one would rather say, its owner) is, in an obvious sense, aware of what goes with what. Thus, clearly, your assay is incomplete in a way that makes it inadequate.

My friend, without necessarily accepting the overall pattern, yet acknowledges, within it, the dialectical force of this particular argument. Then he remembers that I was about to comment on $\mathfrak{A}_6$ and invites me to turn to it next. I tell him that I shall be glad to do that provided he permits me to dispose first of a closely related matter.

Fourth. By (Th3b) awarenesses that are either perceivings or imaginings are of two kinds. In some there may be, but there need not be, a direct awareness of their text; in some others there must be such an auxiliary act. Call for the moment the former "primary"; the latter, "secondary." Or, as I shall also say in order to save words when there is no danger of confusion, some awarenesses which are perceivings may be, but need not be, accompanied by their text; others are inseparable from it. As for perceivings so for perceivings$_1$. Some awarenesses that are perceivings$_1$ are primary; others are secondary. Or so at least one is led to generalize from $\mathfrak{A}_3$ and $\mathfrak{A}_4$. Again, as for perceiving, so for imagining. Thus one may, as I do, wish to strengthen (Th3b): *An awareness that is either a Perceiving or an Imagining is either primary or secondary.* As you gather, I have once more saved words by calling for the moment an awareness a Perceiving (an Imagining) if it is either a perceiving or a perceiving$_1$ (an imagining or an imagining$_1$). And, again, there will be no need always to mention both, Imagining and Perceiving.

Which awarenesses are primary, which secondary? $\mathfrak{A}_6$, you remember, is an awareness which is a perceiving of this-not-being-a-horse. $\mathfrak{A}_4$, you also remember, is an awareness which is a perceiving$_1$ of $\sim f_1(a)$. In my world, and therefore in this ontology, $\mathfrak{A}_6$ and $\mathfrak{A}_4$ are both secondary; i.e., they are inseparable from their respective texts, "*this is not a horse*" and "$\sim f(a)$". $\mathfrak{A}_2$, on the other hand, which is a perceiving of this-being-a-horse, is primary; and so is $\mathfrak{A}_3$, which is a perceiving$_1$ of $f_1(a)$. Hence it cannot be the difference between perceiving and perceiving$_1$ that makes the difference. What, then, does? Very probably you can anticipate the answer I am about to propose. But let us proceed slowly and first consider an awareness, call it $\mathfrak{A}_2'$, which is a perceiving, accompanied by its text, of this-being-a-horse. Its text is of course "*this is a horse.*" To its assay, reflection will show you, we are already committed. $\mathfrak{A}_2'$ has five members. Two, call them $\bar{\mu}_1$ and $\bar{\lambda}_1$, are "duplicates" of, or, as I shall also say, "identical with," the μ_1 and the λ_1 in $\mathfrak{A}_2$ (p. 216); i.e., they differ from the latter only in the particulars they involve. The other three are an auxiliary act, $\mathfrak{au}$, which is a $(draw \| "this\ is\ a\ horse")$, and two other direct awarenesses, which are a $(draw \| \bar{\mu}_1\ \&\ \bar{\lambda}_1\ \&\ \mathfrak{au})$ and a $(draw \| \mathfrak{au})$, respectively. As for $\mathfrak{A}_2$ so for $\mathfrak{A}_3$. The text of $\mathfrak{A}_3'$ is of course "$f_1(a)$"; its assay I leave to you. Thus we are ready for the question. What are the critical differences between the two pairs $\mathfrak{A}_4$, $\mathfrak{A}_6$, on the one hand, and $\mathfrak{A}_2$, $\mathfrak{A}_3$, on the other? I am struck by two. The texts of the two secondary ones do, while those of the two primary ones, *if* they are accompanied by a text, do not, contain 'not'. This difference not only stands out; it also suggests another. Every Perceiving involves a perceiving$_1$, whose intention, although always a molecular compound (M) of (simultaneous) atomic facts, is not always a cluster. In $\mathfrak{A}_2$ and $\mathfrak{A}_3$, the two paradigms for primary Perceivings, M is a cluster. In $\mathfrak{A}_4$, the "simpler" of the two paradigms for secondary Perceivings, it is not. How then about the other, $\mathfrak{A}_6$? Since its text contains 'not', it stands to reason that the M it involves is not a cluster. If you are prepared, as I am, to generalize from this pattern, also with respect to the "connectives" in the "sentence" of our language of which the text is an image, you will arrive at the following proposition: *A Perceiving or an Imagining is primary if and only if the M it involves is a cluster. If it is secondary then the "sentence" of its text will contain at least one "connective" other than "conjunction."*

45 * (a) The double quotes in the above proposition are to warn you that the words they surround are not, as almost always in this discourse, used ontologically, but, rather, I speak concisely, linguistically. (b) How about "quantifiers" in the "sentence" of the text? Reflection will show you that while we may believe a generality, or without believing it entertain it, and so on, we cannot either Perceive or Imagine it. But since by (Th3a) every awareness not either a Perceiving or an Imagining is inseparable from its text, one may, if one wishes, so extend the primary-secondary dichotomy that every awareness, of whatever kind, is either primary or secondary. If you do so extend it, you will have to amend the above proposition so that it mentions not only "connectives" and "quantifiers" but also some words we use when speaking about either classes or circumstances. (c) You may wonder why I broke off when, instead of specifying a suitable alternative M for $\mathfrak{A}_6$, I merely said that its not being a cluster stands to reason and let it go at that. The "geometry" of the mind is neither less difficult nor less compendious than that of space. Nor is it the main topic, nor even one of the main topics, of this discourse. I merely undertook to add to the "old" sketch, offered on earlier occasions, that measure of detail and correction which would suffice to make it fit with the major innovations and corrections now proposed. And this limited goal had (I believe) been reached when I broke off.

$\mathfrak{A}_6$ also is a paradigm, as clear-cut and yet simple as any, of still another job, often done by the auxiliary act, which is neither an integrating nor a fusing but, rather, a selecting and steering. Let $\mathfrak{A}_7$ be a secondary awareness which is a perceiving accompanied by *"this is not a cow."* Except for the auxiliary act, $\mathfrak{A}_6$ and $\mathfrak{A}_7$ may well be duplicates of each other. Or, to say the same thing differently, one M_1 & L_1 (and, therefore, one μ & λ) may serve as the "basis" for any number of alternative awarenesses with such texts as *"this is not a horse,"* *"this is not a cow,"* *"this is not a deer,"* and so on. Which, then, if any, will it be? That depends on the circumstances; just as, depending on which in fact it is, the subsequent awarenesses may, and more often than not will, be different. For the course of our mental lives depends, not exclusively, to be sure, yet to a very considerable extent, on the "associations" among the parts of that "inner speech" which accompanies most of it and without which all of it except our primary Perceivings and Imaginings would not be there. What, then, are those circumstances? What are those associations and how do they become established? Must we, in order to complete the assay, answer these questions? Being questions of cause and effect, they are, like all such questions, not ontological but, rather, scientific, in this case psychological. (Notice that, as just used, 'association' and 'inner speech' are psychological terms.) The ontologist must of course try to assay the connection—or, if that helps, the nature of the connection—between what both common sense and science call cause and effect. But he does not inquire into the specific causes and effects of anything. His business is to assay what is there, not to discover either why it is there or of what, if there, it is a (contributory) cause.

As for $\mathfrak{A}_6$, so for countless awarenesses which are primary perceivings accompanied by their texts, such as, e.g., $\mathfrak{A}_2^t$, $\mathfrak{A}_8^t$, $\mathfrak{A}_9^t$, with the texts (1) *"this is a horse,"* (2) *"this is a stallion,"* (3) *"this is a brown horse,"* respectively. There is no reason why the "bases" of $\mathfrak{A}_8^t$ and $\mathfrak{A}_9^t$ shouldn't be duplicates of that of $\mathfrak{A}_2$. Presently this example will come in handy. If (3) worries you, replace it, in the mildest of standardizations, by *"this is a horse and this is brown."*

At this point another critic, who has long been bothered by my calling Perceivings awarenesses of something *not* being something else, or even awarenesses of something being this *or* that, wants to intervene. But the first critic says that he has two more urgent questions which are closely connected. Thereupon I suggest, and they both agree, that before we listen to the second critic, the first will ask, and I shall try to answer, his last two questions.

Fifth. (a) The auxiliary acts (my friend begins) which are now so prominent in your ontology of mind are all perceivings₁. Hence, unless the texts, as you call them, which are their intentions, are not just molecular complexes but are all clusters, that would have to be a second auxiliary act, with a second text, if there is to be the awareness you insist must be there, which is a perceiving₁ of the first text; and so on. Thus you would be trapped in a vicious regress. I take it, therefore, that in your world *each text is a cluster,* i.e., a conjunction of atomic facts (of the lowest type). My first question is how, if challenged, you would defend this assay. (b) The connection between $\mathfrak{A}_2$ and $\mathfrak{A}_2'$ (p. 215) is, I suppose, paradigmatic of what you take to be the connection between any two awarenesses, $\mathfrak{A}$ and $\mathfrak{A}'$, such that the former is the referent of the latter. Now 𝔄, if I understand you, is an awareness, first, by virtue of a 𝔇 which is a $(draw\|c)$, such that (I speak again concisely) c determines the referent of 𝔄; and, second, *if required,* by virtue of a further direct awareness, 𝔇*, whose intention is the auxiliary act au for the text of 𝔄, in which latter case, i.e., if both 𝔇 and 𝔇* are required, the intention of 𝔇 is not just c but c & au. The awareness 𝔄', however, although of a direct awareness, *always requires,* or, as you say, is inseparable from, its text. Thus 𝔄' contains, in addition to the members of 𝔄, three further acts. One is a perceiving$_1$ whose intention is the text (not *in,* but) *of* 𝔄; e.g., in the paradigm, *"this is a perceiving of* $\sim f_1(a)$." The other two are of course the required direct awarenesses, call them 𝔇' and 𝔇'*. In your world, however, not only every act and every conjunction of acts but also, as I just argued you must consistently claim, every text is a cluster. So therefore is the intention of 𝔇'. Hence, or so at least you must again consistently claim, *perceivings$_1$ of clusters are, yet direct awarenesses of clusters are not, separable from their texts.* Considering the natures of these two species, perceiving$_1$ and direct awareness, that strikes me as odd, not to say counterstructural. My second question is how, if challenged, you would defend this oddity.

I reply as follows: (a) Being images, either visual or auditory, of sentences, either written or spoken, texts are indeed clusters. Yet there is a difficulty that must at least be acknowledged. Since one need not be literate in order to have secondary awarenesses, we had better stick with auditory texts. Speech sounds, being events of short duration, are readily schematized as atomic facts $g_1(b_1)$, $g_2(b_2)$, $g_3(b_3)$, and so on. A sentence, though, and even a word, is a succession of such sounds; and while the relevant relationships, b_1 preceding b_2, b_2 preceding b_3, and so on, are again atomic, the particulars in the pertinent conjunction are not, as in a cluster they must be, simultaneous; unless one considers as "simultaneous" all the particulars in a brief interval, of the sort philosophers call an (extended) *moment* or a specious present, as distinct from an (extensionless) *instant.* This is the difficulty. Since it pertains to the assay of time, which is sticky indeed, I here merely acknowledge it. You will find the resolution of it which I now propose in the reflections on time in Appendix G. (b) What strikes you as odd really isn't. The difference which matters is not that between the two species, perceiving$_1$ and direct awareness, but that between an awareness 𝔄 (or, synonymously, conscious state), on the one hand, and an awareness of an awareness, on the other. *All* of the latter are *reflective; some* of the former, viz., all primary Perceivings and Imaginings, are *nonreflective.* E.g., an awareness, 𝔄$_2$, which is a perceiving of this-being-a-horse is nonreflective; an awareness, $\mathfrak{A}_2{}'$, of this awareness is reflective; as is, in a different way, every Perceiving or Imagining not "based" on a cluster, such as, e.g., the awareness which is a perceiving of this-not-being-a-horse. Phenomenologically, the nonreflective-reflective dichotomy is clear and obvious. Ontologically, I ground it in the distinction between the awarenesses which are, and those which are not, separable from their texts.

46* (a) Distinguish this use of 'reflective' from the way 'reflexive' is sometimes used in philosophy. According to some (including I believe Kant) thought is reflexive in that every awareness is eo ipso aware of itself. As Brentano put it, most clearly, yet to my mind with a self-defeating clarity, every act has two intentions, one *empirisch,* the other *noetisch,* the latter being the act itself. In my worlds acts never were reflexive. In the new one of this discourse, an act isn't even an awareness unless it is supported by another act which intends it and whose species is direct awareness. (b) An awareness, I repeat, and, as I speak, a conscious state are one and the same. Direct awareness is a species of acts. Thus it is, like believing, perceiving$_1$, and so on, a nonrelational universal of the lowest type. I realize that my terms are not as sharply differentiated as one might wish. But 'conscious state' is very clumsy. Nor could I think of a suitable substitute for 'direct awareness' and 'being directly aware of'. 'Apprehension' and 'apprehending' are, I think, too compromised. (c) The higher mammals, one may plausibly suppose, have primary Perceivings and even Imaginings. Why would dogs otherwise bark in their sleep? But we have no reason whatsoever to believe that they are capable of reflective thought.

Now it is the turn of the second critic. I have long been bewildered (he says) by your insisting that we perceive facts, e.g., this-being-a-horse, rather than, as the tradition has it, things, e.g., a horse. But I discounted this as an idiosyncratic expression of your antisubstantialism, exacerbated as it is by the strange doctrine of bare particulars. Now, though, when making a point of our perceiving, rather than judging, this-not-being-of-that-kind, this-being-of-either-that-or-that-other-kind, and so on, you challenge the distinction between perceiving and judging. If that is a deliberate challenge to what is so deeply rooted in the tradition, I wish you would address yourself to the several issues it involves.

I reply in three steps. (a) Ignore for the time being the "bareness" of particulars and of things in general, of which more in Appendix A. That still leaves several issues. Yet it will suffice if I identify the one which dialectically controls and, if I may so express myself, defuses the rest of them. This controlling issue, I submit, is not which referents we perceive, which others we judge, and soon, but, rather, what is there, for the most part not in any mind, to be either perceived, or judged, or what have you. The point, then, is that in this world there are not only the actual atomic facts but also the potential ones as well as all nonatomic ones (and the circumstances); with their modes, unless they are analytic, being in principle inaccessible to us. On the side of the referents that defuses the issue. Nor need I here do more than identify it. For the defense of an ontology that "rich" is the burden of this discourse as a whole. (b) On the side of the mind, there remains the lesser issue of which kinds of awareness and which species go with which referents and intentions. I offer three observations. (1) Every Perceiving (or Imagining) is "based" on a perceiving$_1$ (or imagining$_1$) of a molecular complex such that—by a contingent principle of which again more in Appendix A—the particulars in it and that in the perceiving are "simultaneous." (2) We can believe but neither Perceive nor Imagine generalities. (3) The new assay of the analytic, in conjunction with what has been secured in Section II, allows for all the distinctions one may care to make among believing, judging, knowing, and "knowing." (c) You are quite right when you say that at this point I seem to set myself against the tradition. Most philosophers would agree that one sometimes perceives a spot, or, perhaps, even its being green, but would shy away from saying that one perceives, rather than judges, its being not green. Behind a reluctance so widely spread there is more often than not a phenomenological difference clearly felt, which must be grounded ontologically. In the case at hand I have no difficulty admitting that there is such a difference. For we have already grounded it in what distinguishes reflective from non-reflective thought. Thus my unorthodoxy is merely terminological.

47*Suppose an ontologist proposes a world so "poor" that all its existents are either actual atomic facts or clusters of such. How, you may wonder, can there be clusters in a world without conjunction? From where I stand, there can't be any. But if you consider how many still overlook, even after Meinong has insisted on it again and again, the obvious distinction between two simultaneous awarenesses, one of this, the other of that, on the one hand, and a single awareness of this-and-that, on the other, you will come to understand that among all connectives the one the need for whose ontologization is most easily overlooked is conjunction. Suppose next that in such a world a particular that is green ($f_1(a)$) is "judged" to be not red ($\sim f_2(a)$). All the material to make the judgment (and/or its referent?) out of is $f_1(a)$. What then is the bridge, or, if you please, who builds the bridge, from the material to the product? Classically, the mind does; in building it,

the mind—whether or not, as in the contemporary version, substituted for by language in use—is "active"; and this activity, or contribution, of the mind is the idealistic camel's nose under the tent of
realism. For, not just in this case but in all cases, the "poorer" the ontological material available outside of minds, the greater the contribution of the latter must be. The end of this particular road is absolute
idealism. Structurally, I believe, this is the very root of the advantage
"idealism" has had over the impoverished ontologies of "materialism."
But there are also two other roads with equally unattractive destina-
tions. If, as in the Humean tradition, the act is discarded, what could
in such a world an awareness be but itself a cluster whose particulars
are, presumably, "sense data"? Once this step has been taken, the two
roads become visible. If the "perceived" and the "perceiving" cluster
are "similar," as upon this gambit they would have to be, why not collapse them into one? The end of this road is the neutral monism
whose fiery sensa, however absurdly, either burn or do not burn depending on their "contexts." One more sophisticated will ask himself
how similar complexes manage to represent different things, once
what is presently either perceived or imagined, once what is remembered, once what is expected. The third way is to give up the notion of
"representation" altogether and rely for the required distinctions on
what, either in or outside of the mind, either causes or is caused by the
cluster which the mind presently "is." Yet this, too, is absurd; for a
present perceiving, or remembering, and so on, not only is, but also
presents itself as, just that, namely a perceiving, or a remembering,
and so on, irrespective of whatever it may cause or be caused by. This
(I believe) is the "contextualist" cross that lies so heavily on the shoul-
ders of the second Wittgenstein. Contrast these three alternatives with
the ontology of this discourse. In this world, everything that can become a referent is already there, ready to be presented, as it were, although in matter of anthropological fact it cannot be presented unless
in the minds to which it is presented there are also texts. That certainly gives "language" its due; yet it does not give it too much. Nor,
finally, not having speciously either to "make" or to "contribute" anything, are these minds "active" in a specious sense. Thus this world as
a whole is, or at least consistently may be, at the proper level and in
the proper sense, as "mechanistic" and "deterministic" as any.

The critics reserve judgment but invite me to go on. So I turn now
to the sixth and last in this series of general comments on how to assay
conscious states. Then we shall be ready for the second major question, already mentioned but postponed, as to how one can justify all
these assays. Once this general question will have been answered, we

shall not find it difficult, and it will therefore not take us very long, to apply the notions which we have acquired in the paradigm case of (1) the horse, to the three special cases of (2) the negated ultimate sort, (3) disjunction, and (4) the quantifiers (p. 202).

Sixth. The dependence of thought on language is either *external* or *internal.* The distinction was first made when the notion of a Cartesian progression was introduced (p. 149). A Cartesian progression, you remember, is a finite series of awarenesses, $\mathfrak{A}_1, \mathfrak{A}_2, \ldots, \mathfrak{A}_n$, each temporally preceding the next, in which transparence spreads from the first to the last. Such series, as was then pointed out, are very often interspersed with further, "instrumental" awarenesses, whose referents (not: texts!) are, typically though not exclusively, sentences of a language, either natural or artificial, such that, first, the instrumental awarenesses following $\mathfrak{A}_i$ and preceding $\mathfrak{A}_{i+1}$ are among the contributory causes of $\mathfrak{A}_{i+1}$, and, second, the referents of all of them (except often of the one immediately preceding $\mathfrak{A}_{i+1}$) are (I speak concisely) not the text of $\mathfrak{A}_{i+1}$. Thus we can formulate schematically: An awareness, $\mathfrak{A}$, is instrumental for another, $\mathfrak{B}$, if and only if (1) $\mathfrak{A}$ is among the contributory causes of $\mathfrak{B}$, and (2) the referent of $\mathfrak{A}$, although "linguistic," is not the text of $\mathfrak{B}$. With this formula at hand, one can usefully recast the earlier notion: An awareness is said to depend externally on language if and only if another is instrumental to it. Close as it is, this dependence of thought on language, i.e., more precisely, of one awareness on another, whose referent is linguistic, is yet merely causal. The dependence of thought on language I called internal is, as we now see, that of a single secondary awareness, $\mathfrak{A}$, on the auxiliary act, aa, and the (*draw*‖aa) which are in it. So we can now usefully restate the difference between the two kinds of dependence. Since aa and the direct awareness of it are in $\mathfrak{A}$ and therefore simultaneous with all the other members of it, and since, if they were not there, there would be no awareness at all, the dependence of $\mathfrak{A}$ on these two acts is not merely causal but internal, or, if I may so express myself, "constitutive."

There is one point left. Starting from a word, it is yet not just verbal. As I am here speaking, for an awareness to be internally dependent on language and to be "inseparable" from its text is one and the same. This is a new, and merely local, use of 'inseparable', radically different from the several ontological ones to which the word is being put throughout this discourse. For, clearly, this sort of inseparability, of certain awarenesses from their texts, is a matter of anthropological fact. Yet it lies very deep. Is it then a contingent principle? I see no objection to so classifying it, provided it is understood that among such principles it is as anthropological as any. To grasp firmly what that means, consider the other extreme. Our world is extensional (p. 160). This is a second contingent principle. There are in our world no inhomogeneous relations (p. 185). This is a third. But, unlike the one we just so labeled, neither of these two would lose that status if there were in our world no human minds. (I say human minds, rather than human bodies, because the parallelistic connection between conscious states and bodily states is itself a contingent anthropological principle, or, rather, more accurately, a huge class of such principles.)

When perceiving a horse, I repeat, what one perceives is just that, a-being-a-horse; not, for some i, $M_i(a)$ & $L_i(a)$. Again, when being aware of this awareness, what one is aware of is a perceiving-of-a-being-a-horse; not, for some i, μ_i & λ_i (p. 212). How, then, can one justify these assays, $M_1(a)$ & $L_i(a)$ and μ_i & λ_i, respectively, and all the others I have proposed, or consistently would have to propose, for the referents of our awarenesses, be they mental, like a perceiving of a horse, or outside of minds, like the horse itself? This is the major question to which we must now address ourselves. What makes those assays problematic is that, except for the referents of perceivings$_1$ and imaginings$_1$, one cannot, as it was put, "reach them introspectively." But what does that mean? What block, either real or apparent, does it produce? How can this block be removed? I shall of course start with the first question (A), then answer both the second and the third by framing an adequacy criterion for all assays (B).

A. When we say that someone is given to introspection, or of an introspective bent, what we mean, I take it, is that the stream of his mental life is significantly richer in awarenesses of awarenesses than those of most men. This notion of introspection is not at all problematic. Nor does it here concern us. The one that does has also been called analytical introspection. But no harm will come to us if we suppress the qualifying adjective. So understood, introspection is supposedly a method for what the elder Mill called the "analysis of the phenomena of the human mind"; a method first advocated by the British empiricists, particularly from Hume and Hartley to the Mills, and later on, roughly during the second half of the last century, "experimentally" practiced by such psychologists as Wilhelm Wundt in Germany, Alexander Bain in Britain, and E. B. Titchener in America. Let us again save words by calling all these philosopher-psychologists the introspectionists. Their notion of introspection is full of flaws and anything but unproblematic. Most of the results allegedly obtained by introspection are specious. Yet a small, sound core can and must be recovered. I shall first call attention to two flaws, then attempt the recovery.

Learning how to introspect, which according to the classical doctrine almost everyone can, is to learn how to induce in one's self a certain set. Having learned it, one can, always according to the doctrine, "decompose" any awareness of his into the "elements" of which it "consists." Now we can stop a film and, at our leisure, describe in any detail desired the frozen still on the screen. But one can not so freeze, inspect, and describe an awareness. For all awarenesses are momentary, and, even if they were not, would be interfered with by the attempt to "introspect" them. The best one can do is to produce, under that certain set, either one or several memories of $\mathfrak{A}$ or some other awarenesses which, by the witness of memory, stand in certain relations to $\mathfrak{A}$. This obvious flaw can be corrected, however, by specifying that the awarenesses produced under the introspective set are not literally elements but merely, in the sense explained (p. 218), duplicates of, or identical with, elements of $\mathfrak{A}$. The introspectionist's notion of element, being more or less that of the phenomenologically simple, is as such not problematic. But what does it mean for an awareness to be decomposable into others of which it consists? If one examines the classical answers, one discovers a second flaw, not as easily corrected as the first, which has both a phenomenological and a dialectical aspect.

There are several schools of introspectionism. The main division, though, is between those who do, and those who do not, hold acts to be introspectively indecomposable and, therefore, elements. In the history of psychology they are known as act psychologists and content psychologists, respectively. In the world of this discourse acts are of course not simples. For the purpose at hand, though, huge as it is, the difference makes no difference. Again, there are many kinds of awareness. For the purpose at hand, however, it will suffice to inquire how the two groups differ in analyzing our paradigm, the awareness $\mathfrak{A}_2$, which is a perceiving of a-being-a-horse. Ignoring all relative details—including the relations issue and the pervasive nominalism which assimilates sense data to perfect rather than to bare particulars, neither of which is really a matter of detail—the less thoughtful content psychologists decompose $\mathfrak{A}_2$ into a cluster, say, M_1^s, that differs from M_1 only in that its particulars, unlike those of M_1, are so-called sense data. Or, equivalently, they hold that $\mathfrak{A}_2$ consists of a cluster of sense data, each of which, as consistently they also must, and do, hold, is itself an awareness. According to the act psychologists, $\mathfrak{A}_2$ consists of two other awarenesses, one a perceiving$_1$ of some M_i, the other a believing of some L_i that goes with this M_i. (Naturally, these are but two schemata which ignore many variants, including the substantialist one open to the act psychologists.)

The phenomenalistic implications, or at least temptations, of the first gambit do not concern us. But what shall we think of either gambit as an "analysis" of the awareness $\mathfrak{A}_2$? Phenomenologically, one knows what an awareness $\mathfrak{A}$ is (and is not) by virtue of a simultaneous direct awareness, $\mathfrak{A}'$, whose referent $\mathfrak{A}$ is. In the case of $\mathfrak{A}_2$, we know by virtue of $\mathfrak{A}_2'$ that it is neither a cluster $M_i^?$ nor the conjunction of a perceiving$_1$ and a believing but, rather, a perceiving-of-a-being-a-horse. Generally and more radically, except for one being the referent of another, I do not even know what it could mean for an awareness to "consist" of others. Thus understood, the traditional formula goes to the heart of the matter. *Every awareness is indivisible.* That is why I have insisted that, even if simultaneous, two or more awarenesses are just that, namely a collection, which in this world is literally nothing, of two or more awarenesses. Phenomenologically, the claims of both content and act psychologists to have introspectively analyzed $\mathfrak{A}_2$ are thus specious. Dialectically, there is more to be said. Suppose, then, that some reader, although not himself a classical introspectionist, is yet willing to speak for them.

Rather significantly (the advocate begins) you have omitted an argument which you might have made. You might have argued that, if $\mathfrak{A}_2$ were M_1^s, its referent couldn't plausibly be anything but M_1, which all thoughtful introspectionists agree it isn't, even though they may not agree with your analysis, upon which the horse, or, as you quaintly insist, a-being-a-horse, is $M_1(a)$ & $L_1(a)$. The reason you suppressed (or should I say repressed?) this argument is, I suggest, that, had you made it, you would also have had to argue, in the act psychologists' case, that $\mathfrak{A}_2$ is not what in essence you say it is, namely, the conjunction of two awarenesses, one a perceiving$_1$, one a believing. (I say in essence because I ignore the various direct awarenesses with which you so questionably embroider your analysis, because you claim that without them there is no consciousness.) These, though, are but two instances of the blatant contradiction between what you now say and virtually everything you have so far said in this Section. For, having presented us with elaborate analyses of several kinds of awareness, you now tell us that every awareness is indivisible and, therefore, I take it, unanalyzable.

I reply as follows: An introspective analysis, to whatever extent there is such a thing, on the one hand, and an ontological analysis, or, as I would rather call it, an ontological assay, are two things and not one. Thus there is no contradiction but merely your ambiguous use of a badly overworked word. Nor do I "assay" a-being-a-horse as $M_1(a)$ & $L_1(a)$ or say that it "is" this complex. For there isn't in this world anything 'horse' literally stands for; even 'a is a horse' is merely an abbreviation of the expression for the complex which, speaking concisely, is in this world the only thing that is there. (I ignore for the moment that $M_1(a)$ & $L_1(a)$ is merely one of many alternative assays, each both selective and schematic.) As for 'horse', so mutatis mutandis for 'perceive'. Or haven't I stressed again and again that in this world there isn't anything 'perceive', as it is used in this discourse, stands for? Yet you have done us a service by getting us back to the main line of thought at a point where we can make use of what we have just learned.

There is a gap that must be bridged, between much of what is phenomenologically presented to us, on the one hand, and what is there in this world, on the other. Nor is there in this respect any difference between the horse and a perceiving of it. The elaborate assays of awarenesses which I now propose, embroidered, as you say, not only with various direct awarenesses but also with texts, are supposed to bridge, from the side of the mind, as it were, that gap. All this we have known. Introspection, except perhaps in some cases, cannot, by "reaching" them, justify all our assays. This we have now learned. The thing to do therefore is to secure our assays by means of an adequacy criterion which they all satisfy. Presently I shall propose and try to defend such a criterion. But it will come in handy later if we first recover that small, sound core where the notion of introspection makes sense and introspection does in fact reach the assays of a special yet important sort of determinates.

Imagine the following thought experiment. A psychologist first teaches his subjects to react to a certain cue, say, the sound of a certain bell, by shifting from the language they ordinarily speak to another, call it the residual language, which he has obtained from the first by removing a part of its vocabulary. After having thus trained his subjects, he asks them on many kinds of prearranged occasions the same question: What are you at this moment aware of? Then he rings the bell and asks once more: What were you aware of a moment ago? (The wording of the question may vary with the occasion. The subject may be asked what he sees, what he is thinking about, and so on.) The experimenter's hope is to discover a minimal residual language such that, after having put a sufficient number of subjects on a sufficient number of occasions through this routine, he will be able to infer inductively from his records a set of generalities that will allow him to deduce from the second response of any subject on any occasion the first response of that subject on that occasion. Even if an experiment as bulky as this one would have to be could be carried out, it surely would fail; for our fictitious experimenter's program is but the "behavioristic" version, or model, of the program of the experimental introspectionists, which, as by now everyone knows, has failed. That, though, is beside the point. The point is, rather, that the model provides us with the cue we need in order to locate that small, sound core of introspectionism which we shall need in order to resolve one of the four paradigm cases.

48* (a) If you wonder whether the thought experiment really is the model I claim it is, consider two points. For one, the idea of the minimal residual language (taking for granted that there is only one) realizes, however roughly, the introspectionists' notion, itself anything but polished, of the "decomposition" of a conscious state into its "elements." For another, the laws my experimenter hopes to discover are such that, while the second response uniquely determines the first, the converse does not hold; for the same thought may be "carried" in different ways. (The striking phrase is Titchener's.) You will find more elsewhere,[7] including some uses, both critical and in structural history, to which the model can be put.

Almost everyone, without necessarily knowing what 'defining' means, knows how to use some words or phrases for which he can, in reply to an appropriately worded question, provide some sort of more or less adequate definition. The better educated one is, the greater the number of such words in his vocabulary will be. Most terms usually called technical no one can learn how to use except by definition. Suppose now, first, that someone is in a conscious state, $\mathfrak{A}$, not necessarily a perceiving yet such that its text is of the form 'this is . . .'. Suppose, next, that this man knows a definition of the word or phrase in the place of the dots, and that this word or phrase is missing in the residual language in which he has been trained by our experimenter. Suppose, finally, that the latter asks the man the first question of the routine at the moment at which he is in the conscious state $\mathfrak{A}$, and, after it has been answered, rings the bell. Under the circumstances I have no reason to doubt, either from my own experience or other-

7. See the essay "The Problem of Relations in Classical Psychology," reprinted in *The Metaphysics of Logical Positivism* (University of Wisconsin Press, second edition, 1967); also, passim, Chapters 9 and 10 of *Realism,* concerning some other pertinent problems in introspectionism, particularly in connection with the distinct-indistinct dichotomy and some confusingly close, yet different, uses of 'analysis'.)

wise, that the man will in his second response report the referent of a remembering, $\mathfrak{B}$, which is identical with that of $\mathfrak{A}$, but that in the text of $\mathfrak{B}$ (I speak concisely) the definiendum has been replaced by the definiens. This is the core we have been looking for. Four brief comments will help us to appreciate its significance.

First. 'Text' has in the last paragraph been used technically. 'Defining', though, and its cognates have been used most nontechnically, as we all use them when speaking as we ordinarily do, without any logical or ontological sophistication whatsoever. *Second.* When $\mathfrak{A}$ in the above example is a perceiving, the remembering will often be accompanied by a so-called memory image which is identical with the referent of $\mathfrak{A}$. Notice, too, that I have avoided committing myself to a detailed assay of rememberings. But you will find elsewhere[8] one which (I believe) can be fitted into the improved, or at least more detailed, ontology of mind proposed in this Section.

Third. The alleged result of an introspective analysis is in an obvious sense "richer" than what it purports to analyze. This "excess" is still another flaw. As Angell[9] has it, in one of the most effective among the attacks that caused the downfall of experimental introspectionism in psychology, the alleged result is like a pâté de foie gras. One wonders how the illusion ever took hold. Yet I can think of two reasons which, although bad reasons, may seduce the unwary. The definiens "displays" what is "in" the definiendum. Thus, naturally, the text of the former is longer than that of the latter. This is one obvious bad reason. To state the other with as few words as possible, let me once more trot out the horse. Then I shall put it to pasture for good. (Incidentally, I borrowed it from Brentano, whose dictum that the horse he was thinking about was not in his mind but out in the pasture, made an indelible impression on me.) Suppose, then, that our experimenter puts his first question ("What do you see?") to someone whose conscious state at this very moment is a perceiving, without text, of a horse. If the first response is "a horse" the second may yet plausibly be "a white stallion with a long mane." One merely has to assume that the original awareness, the one without text, was based on a cluster sufficiently detailed to account for the second response. This is the other reason. It is a bad reason because the "excess" is merely one of the second response (not: awareness!) over the first.

Fourth. Ever since Socrates philosophers have used "linguistic analysis," by definition, either explicit or, as so misleadingly one says, im-

8. "Some Reflections on Time," reprinted in *Meaning and Existence.*
9. "The Province of Functional Psychology," *Psychological Review,* 14, 1907, pp. 61–91.

plicit, as one of their tools. The British empiricists wielded "introspective analysis" as a weapon against substantialism and what, often so carelessly, has been branded as rationalism. And there is of course also "ontological analysis," the sort of thing I would rather call the search for assays. I have here argued, and hope to have shown, that these three kinds of "analysis," ontological, linguistic, and to whatever extent there is such a thing, introspective, while radically different from each other, are yet in *some* respects sufficiently similar to be confused with each other, or, perhaps even worse, to be fused into one. Thus one comes to understand the mixture, almost always noticeable and at some places virtually inextricable, which (I believe) mars this strand of the tradition, whose strengths I have long admired.

How can one "justify" the assays of either awarenesses or perceptual objects, trees, stones, animals, and so on, that have been proposed in this Section? More radically, putting first things first, what is there about these recent assays that we haven't encountered when "justifying," without ado and without using the word, the earlier assays proposed in Sections II and III, either by grounding them directly in the intentions of our acts; or by introducing them either as extrapolations, as in the case of the modes of complexes whose modes in principle inaccessible are to us, or as standardizations, as in the case of assaying as $r_1\langle a, \langle a, b \rangle\rangle$ what is conventionally expressed by '$r(a, b)$'? There is, to be sure, the distinction between what is presented$_1$ to us in the intentions of our acts, on the one hand, and the referents of many of our awarenesses which are presented$_2$ to us, without being the intention of any of the acts in the awareness. This distinction, though, is not itself the new feature requiring justification, but merely a cue to it. I am virtually certain that you already know which feature I have in mind. But we are at a point where I would rather be tedious than misunderstood. So let us first recall the words I used when I pointed out, more than once, that there was such a feature and promised eventually to attend to it. There was talk of a "thesis," in particular the tripartite thesis (Th) on p. 208. No one would call a proposition a thesis unless it raises some questions and needs defense. There was also talk, in the case of the quantifiers, of an "extra phenomenological distance" between what is presented$_2$ to us and what it is assayed as; or, equivalently in this world, because accounted for by the "fusing" job assigned to the texts, there was talk about the "gap" between what the text of an awareness may lead one to expect, on the one hand, and the assay in fact proposed for its referent, on the other.

Let C be a complex; A, the assay of C; $\mathfrak{A}$, an awareness whose referent is C. There are in this world many C such that (1) their A is not (phenomenologically) presented to any $\mathfrak{A}$, and (2) their A cannot be reached (introspectively) from any $\mathfrak{A}$. The feature we are looking for is the conjunction of (1) and (2). The assays in need of a new kind of justification are those which have this feature. I shall try to justify them by making the case for the following adequacy criterion. *An assay A of a complex C which is neither presented₂ nor accessible to introspection is yet adequate if, first, it is otherwise adequate; if, second, it is the sort of complex, or conjunction of such, which can be intended by acts of ours of which we are directly aware; and if, third, the universals which are constituents of A are, by the Principle of Acquaintance, all available to us.* E.g., we do on some occasions spontaneously perceive₁ clusters; and we can induce in ourselves either of two sets, which cause us either to perceive₁ clusters or to believe any of the generalities whose conjunction is the intention of λ_i. Hence, if they are otherwise adequate, M_i & L_i and μ_i & λ_i are, by the criterion proposed, adequate assays of the referents of $\mathfrak{A}_2$ and $\mathfrak{A}_2'$, respectively.

49* Since introspection is always of an awareness, how can an introspectionist, unless he is a phenomenalist, ever arrive at either M_i or M_i & L_i as the assay of a perceptual object? If momentarily you are puzzled, you probably forgot what was said but not emphasized a while ago (p. 228). If the assay of an awareness is M_i^s, that of its referent cannot plausibly be anything but M_1. As to the other alternative, some of the more thoughtful introspectionists added to M_i^s another supposed cluster, L_i^s, whose conjunction terms they called "expectations." Thus they came in their style as close as they could to M_i & L_i. The trouble with this "assay" is that an expectation, being intentional, is an act in disguise and not, even if there were such things, a sense datum.

How shall we justify the criterion? I offer seven observations. Taken together, they amount to the best argument I can make, and, I believe, also as good as needs to be made.

(1) An assay, to be adequate, must not only be properly grounded; it must also fulfill several other requirements; i.e., as has been explained once more in Section I, it must also be dialectically adequate. The criterion under examination merely stipulates a new, and more liberal, way of grounding some assays. Hence the first clause: *if otherwise adequate.* (2) Speculation reaches for the unthinkable. Speculation I have, with two apparent exceptions, renounced at the very beginning (p. 62). The second and the third clause of the criterion guarantee that the assays it admits are *not speculative.* (3) The apparent exceptions are the two extensions, already mentioned more than once but as yet never more than just mentioned, i.e., certain classes and the theoretical objects of physics, neither of which we can literally think.

The two reasons the exception is merely apparent are, first, the extraordinary success of interpreting the two axiomatic systems, by which these "existents" are suggested, into what we do think, and, second, the merely derivative ontological status which, because of this mediation, is assigned to these "existents." What our criterion admits, on the other hand, does *not belong to an extension.* For we do sometimes perceive clusters; and so on. (4) A standardization, if I may so express myself, merely refashions what is presented, even transparently presented, yet could not, without it, be ontologized. $r_1\langle a, \langle a, b\rangle\rangle$, for instance, which has been proposed as the standardization of what is conventionally expressed by '$r_1(a, b)$,' merely refashions, without "adding" anything to it, an order transparently presented to us. Our criterion, however, admits assays which are *not just standardizations* of what is presented. (5) When attributing modes to all complexes, we extrapolated from the complexes whose mode is (transparently) presented to those whose mode is in principle not accessible to us. But to be inaccessible by contingent anthropological principle and not to be accessible to introspection on certain occasions are two and not one. Hence the criterion is, in an obvious sense, *less radical than extrapolation.* (6) Being neither speculative nor as radical as either an extension or an extrapolation, yet more radical than a standardization, the assays the criterion admits are of a kind all its own. That is why I thought it expedient to mark this kind by a word, calling a *thesis* every claim, whether a specific assay or more general, that one cannot justify without appealing to the criterion. (7) Our ontology of mind goes rather well with three beliefs now held by many, including myself, whether or not they are philosophers, and, if they are, irrespective of their philosophical beliefs. In this world we are conscious of an act only if it is accompanied by a direct awareness intending it. Thus, after a fashion, acts are "unconscious thoughts." That fits with what the psychoanalysts tell us. If one believes that their doctrine contains an important kernel of truth, the agreement is reassuring. In this world, all awarenesses, except primary Perceivings and Imaginings (and undoubtedly also some "Feelings"), are inseparable from their texts. That, to repeat, not only gives language its due without giving it too much; it also reassuringly recovers the sound core in a large body of recent and contemporary thought, both scientific and philosophical, from Watson to Wittgenstein. The Perceivings and Imaginings we called primary may, but need not, be accompanied by texts. In either case they are conscious states. (And again, as for them, so undoubtedly for some "Feelings.") Thus we may plausibly ascribe consciousness, although not of course reflective consciousness, to our humble friends among the higher mammals. That, too, I find reassuring.

After these long preparations, the resolution of the three paradigm cases, of the quantifiers, of the negated ultimate sort, and of disjunction, which is the last business of this Section, will prove so easy and take so little time that it will almost come as an anticlimax.

Let us start with the quantifiers. Our paradigm is a single complex, call it C, such that, if C is the referent of an awareness, call it $\mathfrak{A}_{10}$, its text is "$all\ f_1$'s are f_2's". C is what called a q-complex, i.e., a complex such that at least one of the steps by which it is built is either a $\bigvee$-step or a $\bigwedge$-step. What makes the paradigm as "simple" as it can be is that its single quantifier step is also the last step and that the arguments from which the quantifier builds c are themselves about as "simple" as they can be. Peculiar is one thing and one thing only. A quantifier, unlike a connective, builds one complex not just from one argument but, indifferently, from an indefinite number of alternative arguments. In the paradigm, $\bigvee$ builds C from $\langle a, f_1(a) \supset f_2(a)\rangle$, from $\langle b, f_1(b) \supset f_2(b)\rangle$, and $\langle c, f_2(c) \supset f_2(c)\rangle$, and so on. In the text of $\mathfrak{A}_{10}$, however, which determines, by fusion, what is presented to it, there is no cue to this multiplicity. Specifically, while the "all", the "f_1", the "f_2", and the connective structure of the actual text correspond to $\bigvee, f_1, f_2$, and the connective structure of C, there is no trace left of any of the alternative targets, a, b, c, and so on. Ontologically that causes no trouble. Just as there is only one actual text, so the quantifiers produce from each of the alternative arguments the same C. Phenomenologically, though, there is the contrast, or, as it was put, the extra distance between the actual text "$all\ f_1$'s are f_2's", on the one hand, and, speaking concisely, the alternative "texts" of the ideal language, '$\bigvee \langle a, f_1(a) \supset f_2(a)\rangle$', '$\bigvee\langle b, f_1(b) \supset f_2(b)\rangle$', and so on, all of which stand for the same c, on the other. This contrast, or distance, appears to be a difficulty. But if one is able, as we now are, to put the matter as we just did, then one sees that the appearance deceives. There is no difficulty. Such is the fusing power of texts.

One question remains but is easily answered. Can one induce in himself a set that causes him to intend what, in the language we speak, would be literally expressed by "generalized for this: if this is green then this is square"? No matter how artificial the set may be, the answer, of course, is Yes. Thus the criterion is satisfied. An analogy and a reminder should help to allay whatever scruples you may have. For one, Russell was right when he insisted that equinumerosity is "logically prior" to number. I, of course, would say "ontologically prior."

But I hasten to add that, even if he had been wrong, his gambit was of the kind an ontologist reasonably may, and occasionally must, make. For another, remember a point made in the last Section (p. 169). If by chance that most artificial way were our natural way of "thinking," we would sometimes be presented with the actuality of such complexes as $\bigvee \langle a, f_1(a) \rangle = \bigvee \langle b, f_1(b) \rangle$ provided, of course, that a and b are simultaneous.

Turn next to the case of the negated ultimate sort. Our paradigm is connected with the ordinary-language sentence (S) 'green is not a property'. Unless one is a philosopher, he will not ordinarily either assert or deny (S); more likely than not, he will not even utter it. Philosophers, however, not only have occasion to utter it; most of us, although perhaps not all, will claim to "know" what (S) purports to stand for as well as they "know" anything. Phenomenologically, that is reasonable. Ontologically, though, in this world, there is trouble. For, in this world, to make this claim is tantamount to claiming that (S) stands for a potential determinate sometimes transparently presented to an awareness whose text is (T) "*green is not a property*". Yet there is in this world nothing (S) stands for. That spots the trouble. The way out is to find a determinate such that, first, it may be, and sometimes is, transparently presented to an awareness, and, second, an awareness of this kind is by linguistic habit deeply ingrained (in philosophers) so closely associated with (T) that, on the appropriate occasions, (T) serves as its "text." Nor do we have to look very far for a "substitute referent." Remember that all graspings are evident and suppose that on a certain occasion a philosopher grasps that green is a property. Depending on his set, which in turn depends on the occasion, the "text" of the awareness based on this grasping may be either "*green is a property*" or "*green is not a property*," with either the former or the latter being taken to stand for what is grasped. As in this "simplest" case, so in all cases where there is no ideal-language sentence such that either it or its negation corresponds to a "text" as the ordinary-language sentence (S) corresponds to (T). Consider for instance an awareness based on three acts, two graspings, one of green being a property, the other of higher-than being a relation, and a believing to which green-being-diverse-from-higher-than, which in this world is an actual complex, is transparently presented. The text of this awareness will under the appropriate circumstances be "*universality*[(0)] *is diverse from universality*[(0,0)]." Notice, incidentally, that in this example any two universals would have served as well. That, too, helps to bring out the pattern by which in all these cases the block may be removed.

50* The block, I take it, has been removed; the question that looms behind it remains. What are the limits of thought? More traditionally and more poignantly as well, how, whatever they are, can thought itself determine them? You know that I have left this question to the very end. Yet surely you sense already that the answer some recent philosophers have proposed will not do. These "formalists," as they are called, construe such sentences as 'green is a property', 'green is not a property', 'green is a relation', 'universality is diverse from particularity', and so on, as referring to the features of a syntactically constructed calculus. If this were the whole answer, ontology would be a branch of geometry. Yet, we shall see, in the complete answer such calculi will have to be mentioned.

Consider finally the case I have left to the end because after what has been said its resolution is almost obvious. Our paradigm was disjunction. Sometimes, when a complex α_1 is presented to us, we are, either simultaneously or shortly thereafter, transparently presented with its being, or not being, a disjunction. In this world, we are on these occasions presented with a second complex, $disj(\alpha_1)$, and its mode. This second complex we have assayed as $\wedge\langle\beta_1, \wedge\langle\gamma_1, \alpha_1 = \beta_1 \vee \gamma_1\rangle$. That makes '$disj$' a defined term which does not stand for anything and does not occur in the ideal language. With the conventional notation, the actual definition, with a definitional variable, reads: '$disj(x)$' for '$(\exists\beta)(\exists\gamma)(x = \beta \vee \gamma)$'. How, then, shall we account for an awareness whose text is "x is a disjunction"?

No one but a philosopher uses 'disjunction' as it is used in this discourse, ontologically. Thus we deal here, as in the case of the negated ultimate sort, with very special sets and very specialized linguistic habits. Even an ontologist, though, cannot learn how to use 'disjunction' ontologically except "by definition." This is the key. We have come upon a case from the sound core of the notion of introspection. Now you see why, although small, this core is yet important. In terms of our thought experiment, the first and the second response in the paradigm case are "α_1 is a disjunction" and "there are two determinates such that . . . ," respectively. But notice that, in spite of the dots, there is nothing partial or alternative about the assay. The reason that there isn't, is, of course, that here we deal with what corresponds literally to a definition, and not, as in the case of perceptual objects, merely with a schema, although, to repeat, for the ontologist's very special purposes the schema will do. (More sweepingly, in case that pleases, we have come upon another manifestation of the contrast between the luminosity of Form and the opacity of Matter. Just remember that, unlike the mode of this-being-a-horse, that of this-being-a-disjunction is accessible.)

As for 'disjunction', so for all terms so misleadingly called syntactical. They can all be grounded in this manner. Or, at least, that is the idea. But there is still a wide gap between the idea and the execution. Just consider 'molecular fact' or 'molecular fact-I'. We know very well what (as one says) they mean. Yet, since the notions they stand for are recursive, one cannot ground them unless one first grounds the fundamental notion of being-either-this-or-the-next-and-so-on. To fill this gap is one of the tasks of the next Section.

VI
Classes

To be a class, (1) is to be a member (not: an element) of a certain ontological sort. So is being a particular, (2), being a disjunction, (3), being a generality, (4) being a diversity, (5), and, of course, also being a connective, (6), being a quantifier, (7), or being a function, (8), i.e., being either the one, (6), or the other, (7). The first five, being various sorts of determinates, are very different from the last three. But even among the former there are very major ontological differences. The members of (2), for instance, being all simples, are "hylomorphically compounded" Two-in-Ones, while those of (3), (4), and (5) are Two-in-Ones "pervaded" by modes and as such, as we speak, complexes having constituents. This surely is one major difference. Another divides the three sorts of circumstances, of which (5) is one, from all other complexes, such as those of (3) and (4). To recall this difference, consider two determinates, δ_1 and δ_2, of any sort. Since they are there, so eo ipso is the diversity (δ_1, δ_2), whose terms they are. If they are complexes, of whatever sort, they are also (ignoring standardization) the two immediate constituents of $\bigvee (\delta_1, \delta_2)$; the latter being a member of (3). Which reminds us that in order for a complex which is not a circumstance to be there, there must be, in addition to its immediate constituents, also an appropriate function; which latter, although not of course a determinate, is yet an existent.

All this we have long known. Why then rehearse it now? Because we are about to turn to classes, which are a sort of determinates all its own, radically different in at least one respect from every other one, and thus wholly sui generis, as one says. So far, however, that has in this discourse been merely an assertion, supported only by occasional asides and anticipated by some suggestive terminological distinctions. Classes, for instance, have been said to have elements but not, like complexes, constituents. Now the time has come to ground all these distinctions among words in the nature of things, phenomenologically as well as, by close reasoning, dialectically.

A suitable paradigm will get us started. For one cannot claim that there is an ontological sort without claiming, first, that he is on some occasions either explicitly or implicitly presented with some of its members, and, secondly, that either on these or some other occasions he is also (unless they are unique) transparently presented with their actually being of this sort. Nor, as we know, is providing such "phenomenological rock bottom" all that needs to be done for a proper grounding; that is merely the indispensable first step toward fitting the alleged sort into the schematism.

Take for example the particular a_1, the universal$^{(0)}$ f_1, and the atomic fact $\eta_1(a_1, f_1)$; write in our relaxed notation, with an abbreviation and without ontological commitment, 'At_0' for the smallest sort to which the fact belongs. Whenever presented with the latter, we are implicitly presented with both a_1 and f_1. But I have also duly claimed and argued that for each of these two things there is an act with the species of grasping (p. 94), to which the thing is explicitly presented and such that the latter's being of its ultimate sort is transparent. Again, I have claimed and argued that $\eta_1(a_1, f_1)$ may be explicitly presented. The mode of this fact, however, remains inaccessible. This is one of this world's fundamental gambits. It has also been claimed, but not yet argued, that '$At_0(\eta_1(a_1, f_1))$' stands for a complex whose actuality is accessible. More precisely, what has been argued so far, at the end of the last Section, is merely that, if At_0, or, for that matter, any other "syntactical predicate," is, in the sense there explained, a defined term, then every full sentence of it, such as '$At_0(\eta_1(a_1, f_1))$', will be the text of what is accessibly transparent if and only if it is the abbreviation of an expression standing for what is thus transparent. That, though, is clearly but an auxiliary point, in the sense in which the last section as a whole is but auxiliary. In the example, for instance, the heart of the matter is the claim, already recorded, that '$\bigwedge\langle a_2, \bigwedge\langle f_2, \eta_1(a_1, f_1) = \eta_1(a_2, f_2)\rangle\rangle$', which '$At_0(\eta_1(a_1, f_1))$' abbreviates, stands for what is immediately transparent. But there is of course much, much more that will have to be said about these "syntactical kinds." For one, as first mentioned in the concluding paragraph of the last Section, many of them cannot be grounded at all unless one first secures the ontological status of certain (infinite) classes. For another, there is, we shall see, a hierarchical qualification, in the style of Zermelo, which was mentioned at the very end of the last Section; and so on. As to words, finally, such phrases as 'syntactical predicates' and 'syntactical kinds', misleading as they are to the unwary, yet add a suggestive historical perspective without inconvenience to the forewarned. So I shall henceforth occasionally use them without either quotation marks or apologies.

Are there classes? Arithmetic cannot be grounded without them.

To the vast majority of those concerned with grounding arithmetic who take this for granted, that makes the pressure to answer in the affirmative virtually irresistible. Of this vast majority, as you already know, I am one. Yet no one can confidently claim that there are classes unless two kinds of difficulties are first overcome; one at the upper end, if I may avail myself of a spatial metaphor, one at the lower. At the upper end, there are the familiar difficulties which arise in the case of infinite classes. About these, both from inclination and necessity, I shall in the traditional mathematicians' way say as little as possible, although in my own way I shall say quite a bit. For the ontologist cannot ignore the troubles that beset the very notion of the infinite. Since the whole of classical mathematics is used and useful in talking about the world, he must face the notorious troubles of the non-denumerable, which caused the intuitionists to reject it out of hand. Nor can he ignore the lesser troubles of the denumerably infinite, which, unless it is decidable or, what amounts to the same, recursive, the intuitionists also reject. At the lower end, there is the task of phenomenological grounding on a meticulously specified rock bottom, to be followed (as we just reminded ourselves) by the dialectical systematization of what is thus provisionally anchored in the taxonomic pattern.

50* I interrupt for two comments; the first to adjust the focus, the second to point the way. *First.* The concern with the ontology of classes spread as it became clear that Russell's attempt of grounding arithmetic in a world without classes had failed. You will find the key to this deliberately provocative formulation in Appendix B. But I do not mean to imply that the vast majority of all concerned ever distinguished as emphatically as I insist one must between universals and classes on the one hand and between the axiomatization of an area, which essentially is always a cluster of universals, and the ontological grounding of a category, on the other. *Second.* Having come to share the sensibilities of the intuitionists, I shall, with one exception, limit the classes which have "full" ontological status in this world to the finite and the recursive ones; and I shall argue that this limitation is forced upon us by some of the most fundamental gambits of this ontology. Yet I also believe, and in this I disagree with the intuitionists, that somehow the whole of classical mathematics must be ontologically secured. Eventually, therefore, the "classes" which are excluded from full status because, as I shall argue, we cannot literally think them will be introduced through a back door, being granted an ontological status that is "derived." When in due course we shall see how that is done, it will also transpire that what in this world can be done

for "classes" we cannot literally think is, with a characteristic and illuminating difference, about as much as can be done for "physical objects," be they colorless apples à la Descartes, or electrons, or what have
you, in contradistinction to the "perceptual objects" of our *Lebenswelt*.
As much, I said. Of those who will read on, some would then perhaps
rather say: as little. This disagreement, I shall be prepared to argue, is
not on a point of ontology but, rather, as one now says, existential.

Are there classes? To the best of my knowledge, no one so far has
even made an attempt, as careful and as articulate as the importance
of the matter requires, to ground classes phenomenologically. Yet, for
an ontologist this job at the lower end is the most urgent of all. We
know how to start it. I shall select an "existent," let us refer to it by 'α_1',
to serve as a paradigm; and I shall claim, first, that α_1 and its likes are
sometimes presented to us, and, second, that on some of these occasions the actuality of $Cl(\alpha_1)$ is immediately transparent. '$Cl(\alpha_1)$,' with
'Cl' from 'class', like '$At_0(\alpha_1)$', is merely an abbreviation. What it abbreviates will of course be immediately transparent. The first task within
this general prescription is to pick the paradigm so conservatively that
these claims are indeed phenomenological rock bottom. So I shall
next select our *first paradigm*, then point out three respects in which it
is as conservative as possible.

Consider two atomic facts, $f_1(a_1)$ and $f_2(a_2)$, say, two particulars
being red (f_1) and green (f_2), respectively, as well as the class whose
only members are a_1 and a_2. Use 'α_1' and '$Cl(\alpha_1)$' to refer to this as yet
problematic existent and to its being a member of this as yet problem-
atic category. *When presented with $f_1(a_1)$ and $f_2(a_2)$, I may be, and sometimes am, also presented with either one or the other of the two existents 'α_1' and
'$Cl(\alpha_1)$' supposedly stand for; and, if I am explicitly presented with the latter,
its actuality is immediately transparent to me.* These are for α_1 the two
rock-bottom claims; or, saving words by combining them, this is *the
first claim for the first paradigm*. Eventually there will be a second and
third such claim for a second and a third paradigm. For there are, as
we shall see, fundamentally three kinds of full-status classes in this
world. Now for the three reasons why the first paradigm is as conservative as one can make it.

First. With the conventional relaxed notation, I chose to make the
claim for $\{a_1, a_2\}$, rather than either $\{f_1, f_2\}$ or one of four nonhomogeneous classes, $\{a_1, f_1\}, \{a_1, f_2\}$, and so on. From where I stand,
the difference between this choice and the others makes no difference. Yet it sidesteps two controversial points. For one, many ontologies, past and present, are single-sorted. Thus their classes, if any,
are necessarily homogeneous; and the "individuals" of such worlds
are more nearly particulars than universals. In a Russellian world, for

another, if, as he held, there were classes in it, they would be homogeneous; i.e., the elements of one would all be of the same sort (Russellian type). Much later in this section we shall come to a point where the convincing paradigm is a class of universals. Until then, though, our paradigm will do. Nor shall we ever have to return to these matters. The essential nonhomogeneity of this world's classes will soon be obvious.

Second. α_1 is finite. All but a few of the classes of the second and the third kind are infinite. These few, we shall see, such as, for instance, the class of all universals[(0)], for all we know, may be either finite or infinite. But the infinite, no matter how narrowly confined, and I have already indicated that I shall confine it very narrowly indeed, has problems all its own. The thing to do, therefore, is to divide and hope to conquer, which is done here by gathering all full-status finite classes into the first of the three kinds.

Third. α_2 has only two elements. I might as well have selected a class with three, or four, or perhaps five. But how about one of a thousand elements, or a million? A critical reader may doubt that we are ever presented with classes that large. Since it is my purpose so to extend the first claim that *all finite classes, however large, exist*, with full and not only derived ontological status; since upon my most fundamental gambit what exists can be thought and conversely; and since to say of something that it can be thought and that it can in principle be presented (intended) is one and the same, I must take this reader's doubt very seriously. So I first remind him of what Descartes said about the chiliagon. We cannot imagine it, yet we have an idea of it. Then I add that in this world, too, one cannot imagine all one can think; although causally the occurrence of a thought may, as explained in the last Section, depend on imaginings of words as well as of other things. Wondering whether this distinction makes room for the transparency of $Cl(\beta_1)$, in case β_1, is a very large yet finite class, the critic reminds me that what in the Cartesian analogy would be transparent is not just an idea but an idea both clear and distinct. That leaves no doubt in my mind that he worries about the right thing. By deliberately choosing α_1 I have indeed avoided certain issues. To focus on them, suppose that the critic agrees with my claim for very small classes. He may yet consistently wonder whether the actuality of $Cl(\beta_1)$ is even presented to us, either immediately or at least recursively. Since he thus raises a much broader issue, already acknowledged on an earlier occasion, and since this issue may with equal justification be raised again and again in the rest of this discourse, it will be best if, interrupting now, I face it once more.

51* How can "infallible" illumination be reconciled with our all too obvious fallibility whenever our intentions are as "complicated" as either (i) a tautology becoming transparent only after we have reached it by a long chain of Cartesian steps, or (ii) a disjunction such that the printed expression of each disjunct fills half a page, or, finally, (iii) β_1 being a class? This is the broader issue. In case (i) we must rely on fallibly remembered evidence (p. 89). In case (ii), when claiming to "know" that we are presented with a disjunction (and its text) without even "knowing" that (the texts of) the supposed disjuncts are well formed, we "borrow from language" (p. 172). In case (iii) and all others of large or infinite classes, we manage by a combination of what happens in cases (i) and (ii). The more "conservative" the example, the narrower this gap will be. That is why I picked α_1. Keep in mind, though, that this is not just a matter of classes but goes for all but the least "complicated" intentions. Is this then a defect of my method, casting doubt on all its results? No more, I believe, than the occurrence of computing errors casts doubt on the analyticity of a "complicated" arithmetical fact. If you disagree, the phenomenology you are committed to is the introspectionist poet's rather than the ontologist's. The latter (I believe), even when in search of phenomenological foundations, cannot and need not go very far beyond schemata for anything but the rock-bottom simple.

What, if anything, is one presented with when supposedly presented with $\{a_1, a_2\}$? The structural need for classes is so urgent that it may well father illusions. So I had better be very, very careful, saying too much rather than too little. Yet, if expected to answer while the listener can stand on one foot, I can only say that I am presented with *a* togetherness of a_1 and a_2, which is a togetherness all its own, manifestly different from all others, such as, e.g., those of a_1 and f_1, again different from each other, in $\eta_1(a_1, f_1)$ and (a_1, f_1), respectively. But I shall, as usual and as one must in all such situations, try to marshal all possible *indirect* support. This will turn out to be a rather longish business. So we might as well first stop for still another comment.

An existent is presented either explicitly or implicitly. The simples we ordinarily call things, for instance, are almost always implicitly presented; the only exception being those special acts we called graspings to which, although single and therefore explicitly, a thing presents itself with immediate transparence as of its ultimate sort. Thus the phenomenological truism that what is transparent to an act must be the whole of its intention is not violated. A complex, on the other hand, may to any ordinary act be presented either explicitly or implicitly. How, then, about the presentation of classes? If for the time being you take on trust what has as yet not been closely argued, viz., that not only, say, '$At_0(\delta_1)$' and '$Disj(\delta_1)$' but also '$Cl(\delta_1)$' abbreviates what stands for complexes with recursively accessible modes, you will see which answer best fits the schematism. The determinate in question may be either a fact or a circumstance or a class, as long as it is not a thing, there is, as it were, no need for a special act, such as grasping in the case of things, to which its actually being of its sort is transparent. In this respect, things have a position all their own; and quite properly so, since each thing and nothing but a thing is hylomorphically compounded of two entities (not: existents), one an ultimate sort, the other one of the items which are "the world's stuff." Still in this respect, therefore, of not requiring special acts for their being of their respective sorts to become transparent, classes and complexes go together, even though, unlike complexes, neither classes nor things have modes. In another respect, however, classes go together with things; for classes, although, since they have elements, they are not simples, are yet like the simples we ordinarily call things in not having constituents. That, though, brings us once more up against the distinction between elements and constituents, which has been anticipated so often without the close support which, you may think, is overdue. If you read on, you will see that it will come forth very soon. Again, and this is the matter of immediate concern that caused me to stop for these comments, if a class is never presented explicitly, you may plausibly think that when one wants to find out what, if anything, one is presented with when supposedly presented with a class, it would be prudent first to review the way, or the ways, in which a class may enter into what can be explicitly intended. As it happens, though, postponing this job for a page or two will improve the exposition by enabling us to pursue simultaneously two or even three closely intertwined lines of thought.

52* Notice the two things I just took for granted. (a) Unlike a complex, a class does not have a mode. (b) Unlike a thing, a class is not a simple. To clinch (a), a brief comment, although strictly speaking merely heuristic, will suffice. An expression standing for a class, not being a sentence, is neither true nor false; what stands for a complex, being a sentence, is either the one or the other. (b) anticipates the claim, still to be made good, that every class is "built on" a complex, or indifferently on any one of several complexes, which are called selectors, by canons of the kind we called (c).

We are finally ready to cast about for indirect support of the claim that the "togetherness" of a_1 and a_2 in $\{a_1, a_2\}$ is manifestly different from all other togethernesses. What I am about to do in this main context, which is of course phenomenological and for a while will remain so, will produce two incidental results. We shall, first, see that the word 'togetherness', although the most natural to start from, in the case of classes soon becomes awkward; at the end we shall even see that and why it is outright misleading. And we shall, second, come upon all the cues needed to construct the fragment of the ideal language that is about classes.

Suppose one intends, either explicitly or implicitly, the fact $\eta_1(a_1, f_1)$. If Section V holds up, he can do so without at the same time intending words. But suppose that he does. The words he intends are not, of course, those of an ideal language but, say, either (1) "this is green," or, in some implicit contexts called oblique, (2) "this being green," or, perhaps, for some reasons of either style or emphasis, either (3) "the fact that this is green," or (4) "the fact of this being green." One may, but one need not, think (3) or (4). (1) or (2) will always do. Let me state the difference between the two pairs, (1), (2) versus (3), (4), which makes this difference worth noticing, in the manner in which a certain group of linguistic philosophers first stated it, more than a generation ago, but which has the advantage of being still widely current. The words in (1) and (2), including 'is' and 'being', all belong to a (nonideal) "object language." 'Fact', however, which occurs only in (3) and (4), would not, if the object language were an ideal one of the conventional kind, occur in it but, rather, in its "metalanguage." This is quite independent of whether one holds that 'is' here stands for an existent, as I do but the vast majority of all philosophers including that group does not; and it is equally independent of whether one holds, as the members of that group also do, that 'fact' is merely a "syntactical predicate," or as I do (in spite of occasionally using that phrase) that being a fact is an ontological sort grounded in the nature of things.

53* I just spoke of ideal languages of the conventional kind. I could instead have said, more strongly, that none of the so-called syntactical predicates, such as 'fact', 'disjunction', 'class' and so on, occurs in any of the ideal (object) languages that have so far been proposed. In my world, this is not so. After having added the required definitions to its ideal schema, one can say, *positively*, that not only '$Fact(\gamma_1)$', '$Disj(\gamma_1)$', '$Cl(\gamma_1)$', but, with certain qualifications still to be specified, all sentences of this sort become available, and, standing for such determinates as γ_1-being-a-fact, and so on, express what is on this side of the line that separates what is literally thinkable from what is not. *Negatively* and just as importantly, while '$Fact$', '$Disj$', 'Cl', and so on, since they occur only in abbreviations, do not in isolation stand for anything at all, they stand least of all, as the linguistic philosophers of that group propounded, for certain features of marks, or strings of such, on paper. These, I submit, are two contributions, one positive, one negative, toward determining the exact limits of literal thought, which is one of the major purposes of this discourse.

There is a respect in which thought about facts (and circumstances) differs from thought about classes. In the texts associated with the former 'fact' (and 'circumstance') is dispensable; in those associated with the latter 'class' is not. In order to argue this proposition, we must select as a paradigm an intention involving a class which is as "simple" as possible, just as $\eta_1(a_1, f_1)$ is as "simple" as possible for facts. Thus, if a class as such, or in isolation, is never the whole of an intention, we have already arrived at the point where we must review the ways a class can combine with other existents.

In this world, either actually or potentially, a class (α_1) is diverse from every determinate (β_1); is an element of it; and has it as an element. With these abbreviations and still the conventional notation for elementhood, (α_1, β_1), $\alpha_1 \in \beta_1$, $\beta_1 \in \alpha_1$. Nothing will be lost if we select as paradigm for the ways classes combine with other existents the third of these alternatives, $\beta_1 \in \alpha_1$. But why the initial clause: in this world? Is it really necessary? There is indeed no ontology I know of such that its classes combine with anything in any but these three ways. In most worlds, though, if not perhaps in all, which pay explicit attention to classes, every existent is either a class or, at most, either a class or an "individual," the latter being some sort of particular. In those worlds, therefore, there are only these three ways for anything to combine with anything. In this world, however, where there are also facts not involving classes and the several ultimate sorts of things, the three ways set classes apart rather strikingly.

The case for elementhoods being indeed circumstances will presently be made in considerable detail. If they are, then $\delta_1 \in \delta_2$ and $\delta_2 \in \delta_1$ are both well formed, for any two determinates, δ_1 and δ_2, of whatever sort or sorts. Nor is it difficult to balance this overflow in a world with modes. Broad subcategories, i.e., collections of elementhoods that can be characterized categorically, will be potential. Suppose, for instance, that α_1 is a class and β_1 a fact or thing or circumstance not one of its elements; then $\alpha_1 \in \beta_1$ and $\beta_1 \in \delta_1$ will both be potential.

Stop now for a moment and look at the map. I have undertaken to show that the togetherness of the elements of a class is sui generis. By way of preparing the ground, I claimed that thought about classes differs in a certain respect from thought about either facts or circumstances (provided the latter are "simple" enough not to have classes as constituents). So I shall next support this auxiliary claim; then we shall be ready to start on the main argument.

Section V has, I take it, established that the only conscious states which need not, although they may, involve (acts of either perceiving$_1$ or imagining$_1$) texts, are themselves either perceivings$_1$ or imaginings$_1$, or either perceivings or imaginings; and that therefore the relevant texts, if they were involved, would be conjunctions of sentences, atomic in a sense there specified, such as "this is green" or "this is a horse," but neither "this is green or square" nor "this is not green" nor "this is not a horse." *Classes we may think; but we surely neither perceive$_1$ nor perceive them, neither imagine$_1$ nor imagine them.* I may, for instance, in a single act of perceiving, intend $f_1(a_1)$ & $f_2(a_2)$, or, simultaneously, in two such acts, $f_1(a_1)$ and $f_2(a_2)$; but I do not either perceive$_1$ (or perceive) or imagine$_1$ (or imagine) $\{a_1, a_2\}$. This is a further bit of phenomenological rock bottom, which, I submit, one may, and which therefore I shall, take for granted. It follows that, if the auxiliary claim is sound, we must, whenever thinking a class, also think a text in which "class" occurs. So we had better check how that works out in the "simplest" case we can think of.

Take once more α_1, which is $\{a_1, a_2\}$; let a_3 be a third particular diverse from both a_1 and a_2; and consider (1) $a_1 \in \alpha_1$ and (2) $a_3 \in \alpha_1$. That either (1) or (2) may be presented to us is but a corollary to the original claim I called the first, in conjunction with what has been said about the three ways. Presently I shall also argue that sometimes, when we explicitly intend either (1) or (2), the actuality of the former or the potentiality of the latter is immediately transparent. This, though, is not the business at hand.

Stay with (1) and ask yourself what sentence one must also think when thinking it. If, as I did, one uses (3′) '$\{a_1, a_2\}$', the answer is, of course, (1′) '$a_1 \in \{a_1, a_2\}$'. (3′), however, is merely a conventional abbreviation for the italicized clause in (1″) 'a_1 is an element of *the class whose only elements are a_1 and a_2*'. That bears out the auxiliary claim. But there is also something else that may strike one when looking at (1″). Why the double occurrence of 'element' before and after 'class'? Is that awkward? Not really, I believe, if one considers that in the language we speak it marks the connection, uniquely close as we shall see, between the two sorts of something-being-a-class and of something-being-an-element-of something. In the ideal fragment, by the way, the second '$\in$' will have dropped out. But we cannot find out what this fragment is like unless we get on with our reflections about things and thoughts rather than words.

The next cue comes from replacing (3′) with 'the class such that something is one of its elements if and only if *it is either (the same as) a_1 or (the same as) a_2*'. The clause italicized within the clause, or, equivalently, 'being (the same as) either a_1 or a_2', or, again, in the conventional notation with variables, (4') '$(x = a_1) \lor (x = a_2)$', is a condition$_2$. That suggests the following proposition: (C) *One cannot think α_1 without thinking it as the class of all those and only those things (determinates) which satisfy and appropriate condition$_2$*. A critic, who senses that this is a decisive move, interrupts. (C), he observes, has not the slightest tendency to prove that there are classes. All one can reasonably propose is that, *if there are any* (and if I have made no other mistakes), one can think *a* class only as *the* class of all those and only those things satisfying a condition$_2$.

Of course the critic is right. But he merely anticipates what has to be said next. For a while phenomenology, which is the main context of these reflections, has receded into the background. Now we are witnessing one of its epiphanies in this discourse. For the rock-bottom claim that α_1 is sometimes presented to us there is of course no direct support. I merely try to support it indirectly by supporting, again indirectly, the related, or partial, claim that the "togetherness" of a_1 and a_2 one is presented with when presented with α_1 is manifestly different from all others, presented in either a fact or a circumstance. And this argument has barely gotten started. So far we have only acquired some notion of "what goes on" when a class is intended. The next step is to compare this with, and make sure that it is manifestly different from, "what goes on" in other cases. But it will expedite matters if I first balance the phenomenological tilt with an ontological reminder. (The deliberate vagueness of the phrase which just appeared twice between double quotes reflects this tactical exigency.)

At the very beginning, in Section I, we distinguished among three types of determinates, marking them (a), (b), (c), respectively. A determinate that is not a simple is either a fact, (a), or a circumstance, (b), or a class, (c). With each of these types goes a schema for "its" canons, the reasons for distinguishing among the former being the differences among the latter. (C1) If the particular a_1 and the universal $^{(0)}f_1$ are there, then, since the function η_1 is also there, so is eo ipso the fact $\eta_1(a_1, f_1)$. (C2) If the two determinates δ_1 and δ_2 are there, so is eo ipso the diad (δ_1, δ_2). (C3) If a selector is there, so is eo ipso "its" class. The reason for the distinction marked by the new word 'selector' instead of 'condition$_2$', important as it is, can wait a while. An expression, however we call it, if it contains variables, does not literally stand for anything. Or, with a twist by now familiar, in the ideal language there are no variables. Yet what is usually called a condition$_2$ is in the usual relaxed notation represented by expressions with variables such as, e.g., '$(x = a_1) \lor (x = a_2)$'. Thus, as a matter of things and not just words, we shall have to cast about for determinates that can play the role of conditions. But we are not quite at the point where this bit fits best.

What, if any, are the differences among the "togethernesses," *as they are,* on the one hand, and *as they present themselves,* on the other? Our purpose being what it is, our main concern is with the second question. But we also know how to join the two. Suppose, for instance, that, with an inevitable metaphor, these several togethernesses, as they are, "reside" in different "places" or in different "ways" in their respective intentions. In this case the claim that, as they present themselves to the respective acts, they are manifestly different, will have the strongest possible indirect support; just as whatever differences there are will stand out more starkly against a shared background. So let us next look at what these three different kinds of acts, with their three different kinds of intention, have in common.

An existent that is there by virtue of a canon is not literally either a class or a group or a collection; nor is it any other kind of "complex" or "combination" or "compound" of its material(s). If it were, the ontologist would, as so many have, drown in the whirls of an infinite regress. This is the negative import of the tag *eo ipso*. On the other hand, though, we cannot either explicitly or implicitly intend (i.e., think under whatever species) any such existent without implicitly intending all of its material. In the case of our (a)-paradigm, (C1), we so intend a_1, f_1, η_1; in the subschema (C2), δ_1, and δ_2; in the schema (C3), the condition$_2$. In case (a) correspondingly, the "togetherness" resides in the function. That is why calling functions ties is sometimes so helpful. In case (b), the "way" the togetherness is presented at two "places," or, more literally, by (the identities of) the two terms, is such that one may, with a word which for reasons explained I rather avoid, call the three kinds of circumstances, of which elementhood is supposed to be one, internal relations. *In case (c), finally, the togetherness can only reside in the condition$_2$.* About (a) no more needs to be said. To (b), already familiar from the diads, we shall soon return, when attending more closely to elementhood. To provide the italicized formula for (c) with the expansion it needs, I next pick up a thread that was left pending because we have only now come to the point where tying it up will do the most good.

For classes, I said, the very word togetherness is awkward, even outright misleading. Now you see why. In our phenomenological context, it is much too "strong." In facts the togetherness resides strikingly in the existents called functions, in circumstances, in the identities of both terms. In the case of a class, however, say, α_1, what holds a_1 and a_2 together is merely a condition$_2$, or, as we called it, a selector. A "togetherness" between two (or more) determinates, thus "mediated" by their being those and only those which satisfy a "condition" external to both (or all) of them, is radically different from the togethernesses produced by the first two canons as well as, surely, the "weakest" of them all, so weak indeed that it hardly deserves to be called a togetherness. As it presents itself and, therefore, for the best of all possible reasons on this rock-bottom level, as it is, the togetherness of a_1 and a_2 in $\{a_1, a_2\}$ is thus sui generis. The indirect support we thought has come forth. We are at the end of one of the several lines of thought I am trying to pursue simultaneously. But the ontological import of taking even the first step toward grounding even in a single glass, since obviously one thereby does as much for the category, is so momentous, that I would rather seem rambling than hasty. So I interrupt in order to entertain two objections.

The first objector wonders whether the feature on which my case is built, the "mere" mediation by a condition, is really as "external" and therefore presumably as radically different and weak as I made it appear. For he anticipates, quite correctly, that whatever determinates are made to serve as the selectors of finite classes, one cannot be presented with such a class without being in its selector implicitly presented with every determinate it selects. I offer in reply two observations; for the rest beg him to be patient. For one, a selector and its class are two and not one. If that isn't beyond all doubt already, it soon will be. For another, the classes of the second kind are all infinite; yet no one, and I least of all, would claim that, whatever the selector(s) of such a class will turn out to be, one could, when presented with one, be implicitly presented with every thing it selects. Just think that if this were otherwise, there would have to be "infinite texts."

The second objector takes a different tack. What, he asks, is so unique about a condition being involved in (c). Isn't it in the subschema (C1) also a condition that the two things involved be a particular and a universal$^{(0)}$; not to mention that the use of 'condition' is easily so stretched that it covers the need for the appropriate function, in this case η_1, also to be there? Again, for all subschemata (b), is it not also a condition, albeit a very broad one, that for a circumstance to be there each of its terms must be a determinate rather than a function? When a while ago I quietly started adding a subscript to 'condition', I anticipated just this objection. The materials specified by a canon, whether (a), (b), or (c), must indeed satisfy a condition$_1$, e.g., they must be of a certain form (or forms). What sets (c) apart is, rather, that in this canon (part of) the condition$_1$ is that the selector be a condition$_2$. For, surely, even ignoring functions, not every existent can be made to serve as a condition$_2$. Nor does this dichotomy exhaust the ambiguity of the term in the context; hence the 'part of' just added in parenthesis. Just think of the notorious condition$_2$, first singled out by the great Cantor and so effectively exploited by Russell. In the conventional notation '$\sim x \in x$' stands for this condition$_2$; yet, not selecting a class, it is not a selector. Thus we are warned. The determinates which in this world will take the place of conditions are not all selectors; i.e., not every such determinate is material "on which a class is built." Or, to continue the subscript game, a condition$_2$, in order to be a selector, must satisfy further conditions$_3$. That takes care of the objection. Five comments will round it out. Then we shall be ready to widen the dialectic by closing in on the circumstance of elementhood.

54* *First.* In axiomatic set theory the idea of starting from conditions$_2$ is anything but new. I simply take it from the Zermelo-Fraenkel-von Neumann-Goedel line of the tradition. (The mathematicians, for reasons that do not compel me, use 'set' rather than 'class', reserving the latter for a use which, no matter how suggestive it may have been to von Neumann and Goedel, I find ontologically confusing.) *Second.* Mathematically the notion of a conditions$_3$ is problematic. The problems are those of the so-called comprehension formula; and one would not get anywhere, either in axiomatics or in ontology, if one tried to tackle them directly. The thing to do is to proceed constructively, as one says, i.e., by postulating that, given certain classes, there are also certain others connected with them in certain ways. But notice the difference between such an axiom (of the object language) and a canon (of the metalanguage) specifying how the determinates of a "new" ontological sort are produced from others not of this sort. Notice, too, that the ontologist must choose his axioms so that they are immediate transparencies, or, as I shall sometimes write, that they are "axioms." Of this more presently. *Third.* Having acknowledged these obvious debts, let me avoid a later interruption by acknowledging here a borrowed notation. Except for the elimination of variables and the diacritical 'λ', the ideal notation for classes that will presently be proposed is taken from Church. *Fourth.* Except where they are of use, the subscripts of 'condition' will henceforth be suppressed. The variable in the Cantor condition runs in this world over all determinates. This, though, we shall see, makes no difference. *Fifth.* In the case of tertiary classes the conditions$_3$ a condition$_2$ must fulfill to be a selector are not what anyone would call the form, or a form, of the latter. Nor is this just a detail. At the moment, however, we may safely ignore it.

The dialectic of elementhood is best introduced by introducing concurrently the ideal notation. In terms of the paradigm, then, and still writing conventionally, the two jobs are, first, to assay what, say, (2) '$a_3 \in \{a_1, a_2\}$' stands for, and, second, to design a notation that perspicuously represents this connection and therefore, of necessity, also the class in the case, which is of course what the abbreviations 'α_1' and '$\{a_1, a_2\}$' both stand for. In assaying (2), I expect to establish that elementhood is indeed a circumstance by showing that it has all the features which, as often anticipated but except in the case of diads not yet closely argued, the circumstances of this world are supposed to have. The assay of α_1 we in substance just completed. So let us start at this end, where the work is already done and all that needs to be provided is a notation that makes it as diaphanous as amber makes the insect it enshrines. In order to do that, we must first of all get rid of the variables in such "conditions" as, in the paradigm, '$x = a_1 \lor x = a_2$'; replacing them by suitable determinates which can serve as conditions$_2$ and are therefore the only ones that may be, although to repeat, they need not be, and unless they fulfill certain conditions$_3$ in fact are not, selectors.

This time the cue comes, not surprisingly, from the way we managed without variables in the case of the quantifiers when replacing, say (i) '$(x)A(x)$' by (ii) '$\lor\langle c, A(c)\rangle$', if and only if (c1) '$x$' has at least one free occurrence in '$A(x)$', '$A(c)$' being the result of substituting, 'c' for 'x' in '$A(x)$'; (c2) c is any determinate such that '$A(c)$' is well formed, and (c3) irrespective of whether or not 'c' and '$A(x)$' themselves are already partially rewritten in this style, no scope is altered by the substitution; and (c4) at least one free occurrence of 'c' in '$A(c)$' is not truth-functional. The clause (c3) takes care of certain cumbersome technicalities familiar from Section IV to which I shall pay no further attention. (c1) secures what I take to be part and parcel of the very idea of ontology. No canon may in any instance specify the existence of anything that would exist, provided all its materials as specified by this canon exist, even if there were no such canon. More suggestively, at the price of explicitness, *what a canon specifies the existence of is always something new.* If and only if (c1)–(c4) are satisfied, with (c1) stipulated also for the conventional notation, $\langle c, A(c)\rangle$ will be an argument for either $\lor$ or $\land$, whose values are what in the latter notation '$(x)A(x)$' and '$(\exists x)Ax$', respectively, stand for.

Guided by this cue, I now submit that *every 2-tuple, say (iii)* $\langle b, B(b)\rangle$, *such that its first term is a constituent of the second, can serve as a condition$_2$.* Thus I must answer two questions. First, how does one "transcribe" the conventional expression of a condition with variables into one without? Or, with a cleaner distinction between words and things, how does one get from such an expression as, say, '$A(x)$', which literally doesn't stand for anything, to a 2-tuple that can presumably serve as "this" condition$_2$? Second, what does it mean for the latter to be satisfied? As to the "transcription," (c1) and (c2) take care of themselves. Conditions not being anything that is quantified, (c4) is irrelevant. The technicalities necessitating (c3) control mutatis mutandis not only the "transcription" but also the answer to the second question. *A determinate, d, satisfies a condition of form (iii) if and only if* (c5) $\bigvee\langle d, B^d(d)\rangle$ *is a variant of* $\bigvee\langle b, B(b)\rangle$ *and* (c6) $B^d(d)$ *is actual.* (For the notion of a variant see Section IV. The choice of $\bigvee$ instead of $\bigwedge$ is of course irrelevant.)

Right now that will do. But don't think for a moment that this is all that needs to be said about conditions qua selectors. Just for an example, I shall argue that a condition$_2$ of form (iii) is a selector if and only if (c6) is decidable. This is indeed part of a major feature characteristic of this world, of which more in due course. But you see already that (c6) involves an "instruction." Thus one may wonder, isn't a condition of form (iii), if fully articulated, not just (iii) but, rather, (iii) in conjunction with an "instruction"; and must we therefore not make sure that the latter is not a (subjective) screen hiding something (objective) the ontologist must not ignore? This is indeed a good question. But it will pay if we postpone answering it until we have come to the second and the third paradigm, where the conditions as well as the instructions associated with them are so elaborate that the suspicion of something having been left out if the former alone are made to serve as "conditions" impresses itself more forcefully. Nor is this the only respect in which secondary and tertiary classes offer new problems. The selectors of recursive classes, for instance, whether of the second or of the third kind, although of course conditions$_2$, are yet not of the form (iii).

The primary classes, as we already know, are all finite, and conversely. For them, everything is simple and familiar. So I shall merely state the heart of the matter, then add a string of five short comments.

Every condition (iv) $\langle c, ((c = a_1) \vee (c = a_2) \vee \ldots) \vee (c = a_n)\rangle$, such that c is diverse from every a_i, is a selector of the finite class $\{a_1, a_2, \ldots, a_n\}$; and every finite class has such selectors. E.g., if c is diverse from both a_1 and a_2, $\langle c, (c = a_1) \vee (c = a_2)\rangle$ selects α_1.

First. Every 2-tuple such as (iv), but nothing else, will be called an *enumerator.* This use of the term is narrower than the set-theorists', but that is in the nature of this "finitistic" approach. *Second.* To see the need for the only explicit condition$_3$, viz., c being diverse from all the a_i, consider that, say, $\langle a_1, (a_1 = a_1) \vee (a_1 = a_2)\rangle$, being satisfied by every determinate, would not select the paradigm but what notoriously is not a class. *Third.* Two enumerators agreeing in everything except the order of the disjunction terms are in this world two and not one. Yet they select the same class. Obvious as that is in view of the familiar feature of extensionality, it is yet worth mentioning. For, otherwise, how could there be classes, among whose elements there is no order, in a world in which order has so explicitly so large a place? *Fourth.* More generally, if $\langle c, D(c)\rangle$ is an enumerator of a class and $\bigvee\langle c, A(c) \equiv D(c)\rangle$ is decidably actual, $\langle c, A(c)\rangle$ can also serve as a selector of it. Considering these nonstandard selectors jointly with the arbitrariness of the "dummy variable" c as well as that of the order of disjuncts, one realizes why, at least for primary classes, one must always speak of *a* selector. *Fifth.* Can one add to the ideal calculus a defined term, '*En*', such that '*En*(γ_1)' may serve as text for the literal thought "γ_1 is an enumerator"? The number of disjuncts having no upper limit, the answer involves recursion and will have to wait. As for this syntactical predicate, so for most that will appear in the sequel. An occasional comment will prepare the ground. But the complete answer will not come forth until we shall have examined a certain subkind of tertiary classes and introduced a certain hierarchy.

We are ready to develop the ideal notations, first for classes, then for elementhood. But the import of what follows will not be limited to primary classes, although, since we do as yet not know the selectors for the other two kinds, they are as yet the only examples available to us.

One can implicitly or even explicitly think a selector without thinking the class built on it, but one cannot (I hope I established) think the latter without implicitly thinking the former. In this respect the three schemata (a), (b), (c) are alike. E.g., one cannot think either $\eta_1(a_1, f_1)$ or (δ_1, δ_2) without implicitly thinking their respective material(s). Yet, to repeat, in all three cases, one must not, on pain of drowning in an infinite regress, think of the determinate, which by the relevant canon is there, as being the collection, or the sum, or what have you, of its material(s). *A selector, in particular, and the class built on it, are two and not one.* Thus, having found the expressions for (at least one kind of) selectors, we must search for others, to represent in the ideal language the classes built on them. In the case of α_1, for example, the expression standing for it must be different from $\langle c, (c = a_1) \vee (c = a_2)\rangle$, although the latter may, and plausibly will, be a part of it. What, then, we must ask, is the other part. Naturally, we shall expect our cues to come from the (a)- and (b)-canons.

In the (a)-paradigm, there is in addition to a_1 and f_1, or, more accurately, taking into account the standardization, there is, in addition to their diad, (a_1, f_1), the function η_1. That makes the "juxtaposition" of the two expressions '(a_1, f_1)' and 'η_1' the single expression for the fact, which is not only completely perspicuous but also unproblematic in the sense that each of the two expressions juxtaposed stands for something. Not so for the diad of our (b)-paradigm. There is no function, to "make," as it was put earlier, (δ_1, δ_2) out of δ_1 and δ_2. It suffices for the latter two to be there, then the former is eo ipso there, and its mode depends only on the identities (not: the modes) of the latter—in the familiar manner that causes some to speak of internal relations. *Hence the parenthesis,* '$(\ldots , \ldots)$', *in* '(δ_1, δ_2)' *does not stand for anything;* it merely *indicates* that the expression of which it is a part stands for a determinate *of a certain sort* which, δ_1 and δ_2 being there, is eo ipso there. Such mere indication of a certain sort is the very idea of a *diacritical mark.* More precisely, the opening and the closing arcs and the comma together are a single such mark. But let me add two observations and a query. (a) In the ideal schema of this world there are only a very small number of diacritical marks, all together four. Nor can I think of an alternative schema with even fewer; which is one of the reasons why I believe that the one proposed in this discourse is indeed the ideal one. (b) If you will allow me to anticipate that the 'M' in '$M\langle\delta_1, \delta_2\rangle$' which in the ideal schema stands for the meaning nexus, i.e., δ_1-intending-δ_2, is also diacritical, you will appreciate the italicized phrase 'of a certain sort'. (c) The juxtaposition of two marks is not, of course, itself a mark. Yet shouldn't it, too, be mentioned, if only for the sake of some indispensable distinctions, when there is talk about diacritical marks? There will be such mention in the last section, when we shall take a more systematic look at the idea schema as a whole.

Let α_i be a class, σ_i one of its selectors. If σ_i is there, so eo ipso is α_i. There is not, as in the case of determinates (a), a function that must also be there. Nor is there, as in the case of determinates (b), another determinate, in addition to σ_i, that must also be there. Yet, as we just convinced ourselves, α_i and σ_i are two and not one. That forces our hand. To obtain a notation ontologically perspicuous, one must choose a design, say, 'λ', set it apart as a diacritical mark, and replace the abbreviation 'α_i' for the class in the case by '$\lambda\sigma_i$'; e.g., for our paradigm, without any (relevant) abbreviation, by '$\lambda\langle c, (c=a_1) \vee (c = a_2)\rangle$'. In general, then, and, to repeat for the sake of emphasis, not just for primary classes, 'λ' *is a diacritical mark not standing for anything*, such that '$\lambda\sigma_i$' is well formed if and only if 'σ_i' stands for a selector, in which case '$\lambda\sigma_i$' *is the ideal notation for the class built on* σ_i; and the only job of 'λ' is to "indicate" that the expression for which it stands is a determinate "of a certain sort." We have found the notation for classes. For the time being that will do. But make a note of what has as yet not been closely reasoned. Unlike the three diacritical marks associated with the three sorts of circumstances, the fourth, 'λ', is the only one which requires that, if '$\lambda\gamma_i$' is to be well formed, γ_i be more than just any determinate or, for that matter, as we shall see in the case of tertiary classes, of a certain form. Nor of course is that chance. For the main problem, or difficulty, in the ontology as well as in the mathematics of classes, is to answer the question: what is and what is not a selector?

To insist on 'λ' being diacritical brings us most naturally back to the distinction, long familiar but not yet closely argued, between the *constituents of complexes*, on the one hand, and the *elements of classes*, on the other. Upon this notion of a constituent, whenever one determinate is a constituent of another, there is at least one existent "between" the former and the latter (p. 192). A selector of a class, however, since 'λ' is merely a diacritical mark, is not a constituent of its class in this sense. A critical reader might agree while yet insisting that, in some other sense, the elements of a class are (among) its constituents. If he is determined to use his words in this way he may of course do so. But I would try to dissuade him as follows.

An element of a class may be, as in the case of primary classes they in fact all are, a constituent of a selector of it. If that bothers you, consider, first, that not only in this world but (I believe) in any viable one there is need for a transitive notion of constituency (by whatever name); and consider, second, that, if a selector is not a constituent of the class built on it, there is no difficulty in something being a constituent of the former but not of the latter. Elementhood, on the other hand, is notoriously intransitive. Moreover, to mention a second feature, classes, although built on selectors and therefore not (simple) things, are yet like the latter, which of course have neither elements nor constituents, in that they have no mode; thus they occupy among all determinates a position all their own, between things and complexes, as it were. Add thirdly that this very special position of classes, apart from all Two-in-Ones of either of the two kinds, is, as we just saw, further accentuated by their being the only determinates that cannot combine with any other except in a circumstance. If you consider these three features, you will (I hope) agree that the proposed terminological distinction between elements and constituents has the merit of spotting a cluster of similarities and differences among determinates that is a nodal point in the overall dialectic.

It will not hurt, even though it may not be necessary, to support the proposed ideal notation for classes with two concluding remarks. (a) It is the very ideal of the ideal schema that every part or fragment of it reflects perspicuously what it stands for. Not so in the case of natural languages. Whatever reflection there is (and must be) in them is more often than not anything but perspicuous. Nor, given the anthropological facts of human nature and language, is this surprising. That makes it worth mentioning that, given two propositions which I believe to have established, the proposed notation, $\lambda\sigma_i$, is not only ontologically perspicuous but also remarkably close to natural language, i.e., to be explicit for once, to the texts without which we cannot think most of our thoughts. By the first, more general, of these propositions, classes are among the existents we cannot think without words. The second specifies that one cannot think a class without thinking the clause "the class such that . . . ."; with the dots marking the place of what, speaking as we ordinarily do, we would all call a condition. The diacritical 'λ' and the 'σ_i' in '$\lambda\sigma_i$' thus correspond respectively to the first four words and the condition in these texts. Could anything be more perspicuous? (b) This remark is a word of caution. In spite of the seductive texts that go with it, '$\lambda\sigma_i$' is not some sort of definite description, of which by the way in our ideal language there are none. Nor, for that matter, would it make any difference if there were. For, to mistake '$\lambda\sigma_i$' for a definite description amounts to "deriving" what is presumably in the "object language" from a canon, which belongs irretrievably to the "metalanguage," in the sense in which 'the present king of France' may be said to be "derived" from 'being a present king of France.'

Return to *elementhood*. How shall we assay the connection conventionally written (5) '$\delta_1 \in \delta_2$'; and what, if anything, does in this notation '$\in$' stand for? There is no point in pretending that I haven't long ago committed myself. Elementhood is supposedly one of three kinds of circumstances of this world, which in turn means at least three things. It means, *first,* that (5) is a text corresponding to what in the ideal schema is well formed and therefore expresses what is thinkable for any two determinates δ_1 and δ_2. It means, *second,* that '$\in$' literally stands for nothing. It means, *third,* that the mode of (5) depends only on the two identities, or, as it has also been put, on the nature and being, of the two determinates, and on nothing else; and, in particular, not on their modes, as structurally one would expect if '$\in$' stood for a function; just as, if it did, it would be counterstructural for the restriction imposed on δ_1 and δ_2 not to be narrower than the one we called minimal, of their both being determinates.

There is, I said, no point in pretending. I would indeed be disappointed if you were not by now accustomed to associate the notion of a circumstance with these three features. But there is every point in insisting that conditioning, however persuasive, to an overall pattern cannot take the place of the strongest possible support, both phenomenologically and by close reasoning, for every major feature of it. And such support of the three features has so far only been offered in the case of the diads. For the meaning nexus the argument is left to the last appendix. The time and place to make it for elementhood is here and now.

55* (a) There is still a *fourth* feature equally fundamental. The mode of a circumstance is either immediately or recursively accessible. For the moment I would rather keep this feature in the wings; but it will not be long before it comes to occupy the very center of the stage. (b) There is in this world *no empty class*. If there were such an existent, there wouldn't be complexes for '$Cl(\gamma_1)$' to abbreviate. Since there isn't, being-a-class and having-an-element are in this world equivalent. I shall even argue that the connection between these two categories—and therefore, on the side of the words, between 'γ' and '$\in$'—is uniquely close. All this will soon be out in the open. Keeping it in mind until then should help smooth out a roughness which you may feel at a place or two before we get there.

What is the proper assay of elementhood? Let us start answering by touching once more the phenomenological base. Two examples will serve.

Look at (1) and (2) on p. 248; rewrite them now as follows (6) $a_1 \in \lambda\langle c, (c = a_1) \vee (c = a_2)\rangle$, (6') $a_3 \in \lambda\langle c, (c = a_1) \vee (c = a_2)\rangle$. No one who has been persuaded that the class in (6) and (6'), which is of course our paradigm, is sometimes implicitly presented to us will object to my now registering, without further support, still another claim. *Not only are (6) and (6') sometimes explicitly presented to us, but so are immediately, on many of these occasions, their modes; actuality in the case of (6), potentiality in that of (6').*

Take as a second example two determinates, δ_1 and δ_2, such that the latter is not a class. Suppose they are a fact and a particular, respectively. *If* elementhood has the first feature, which stipulates only that δ_1 and δ_2 must satisfy the minimum requirement, then '$\delta_1 \in \delta_2$' stands for a determinate. *If* there is such a determinate, then it is of course potential, and its mode, whenever we explicitly intend it, transparent.

That much is obvious. The only question, therefore, is whether there are these "odd" things? As a skeptic might put it, is it proper thus to multiply existence for the sole purpose of preserving the first feature. On the phenomenological side, is it even "credible" that we can think what in such cases '$\delta_1 \in \delta_2$', presumably well formed, would stand for. I answer by repeating two points that have been made earlier. One cause, if not perhaps the cause, of the alleged oddness and incredibility of there being such determinates as a-certain-fact-being-an-element-of-a-certain-particular and of our sometimes intending them, is that in all other ontologies there are so few categories that the issue doesn't arise. In this world, on the other hand, with an adequate number of categories, where the issue most naturally arises, there are also the two modes. And in such a world, the structurally proper way of controlling the resulting plenitude of existents is to make large subcategories of them transparently potential. I point out, finally, that the "decision" is purely local; i.e., there is no place in the total dialectic that is nontrivially affected by either admitting or excluding all these potential elementhoods. Thus, rather than put up a show of phenomenological support, I "decide" to preserve the first feature of elementhood by admitting them. How, then, about the second and the third features?

As I proposed we speak, every selector is a condition$_2$, though not conversely. But only the selectors of primary classes and (as we shall see) of one of the two kinds of tertiary ones are 2-tuples, say again, $\langle c, B(c) \rangle$. The selectors of all secondary classes and of the other kind of tertiary ones, which both encode the recursion pattern, are more complex. Hence, naturally, what in the two recursive cases corresponds to (c6) is also more complex. Only in the nonrecursive case, for which the completion formula holds, is there a single determinate, $B(c)$, such that, as specified by (c6), $d \in \lambda \langle c, B(c) \rangle$ and $B^d(d)$ are either both actual or both potential for every d. Important as this difference between recursive and nonrecursive classes is in many contexts, for the task at hand, of securely establishing elementhood as a circumstance, it makes no difference. Nor will anything be lost if we stay, as we must, with the one case so far familiar to us, of finite classes and their enumerators, where we need not bother with variants. We may even safely limit ourselves to arguing for α_1; the only difference that makes is that what for α_1 is immediately transparent is for larger classes only recursively accessible.

The third feature requires that the mode of (7) $d_1 \in \lambda \langle c, (c = a_1) \vee (c = a_2) \rangle$ depends only on the identities of d_1 and of α_1. Now, by (c6) the mode of (7) is that of $(d_1 = a_1) \vee (d_1 = a_2)$, which in turn depends only on the modes of $d_1 = a_1$ and of $d_1 = a_2$, and therefore, since the latter are two negated diads, only on the identities of d_1, a_1, and a_2. Hence, since in view of the extensionality of classes, of which more in due course, the identities of a_1 and a_2 determine that of α_1, and conversely, the mode of (7) depends only on the identities of d_1 and of α_1, and on nothing else. Thus the third feature is secured.

Two comments find here their natural place. Then we shall turn to the second feature and, what amounts virtually to the same, the ideal notation for elementhood.

First. Since the standard selectors of primary classes are enumerators, since '$c = a_1$' merely abbreviates '$\sim(c, a_1)$', and since the terms of diads are subject only to the minimal restriction, the following four propositions hold for all primary classes. (i) No function is an element of a class. (ii) Every determinate is an element of classes. (iii) Classes need not be homogenous, i.e., the several elements of a class may be of several sorts, either things of one or several ultimate sorts, or classes, or facts, or circumstances. In other words, as I proposed we speak, these classes are arbitrary. (iv) Given any determinate and any class, the former being an element of the latter is decidable. As for a world with only primary classes, so, as we shall arrange matters, also for ours. With respect to (iv), two points are worth noticing. Notice, first, that '$B^d(d)$' being well formed for every d in the case of all enumerators (and, as we shall see in due course, for all selectors) is one good reason for calling a "decision" made a while ago (p. 260) merely "local." Notice, second, that (iv) involves the fourth and last major feature, so far kept in the wings, of being decidable, which in this world is associated with all circumstances. As to (i), (ii), and (iii), disappointed as I would be once more if you didn't by now expect them to hold in this world, there is yet no harm in recording that only at this point do they follow strictly from what up to this point has been argued closely in this discourse.

Second. The diversity, and therefore, the sameness, of any two determinates is decidable; i.e., to repeat for once, the mode of (δ_1, δ_2) is either immediately or at least recursively accessible, or, still differently, it is thus transparent. This, too, is a proposition to which I am already structurally committed. In a world like this, but without classes, call it the core of ours, the proposition follows from the finite and not very large number of complexes which in Section IV were called the immediate transparencies of sameness and diversity (p. 197). Thus, for instance, any conjunction is diverse from any determinate of any other form; "two" conjunctions are one and the same if and only if their conjuncts are pairwise the same; and so on. After having provided ourselves with what the text "$Cl(\gamma_1)$" abbreviates, we shall be able to add to these transparencies another smallish number, such as, e.g., $(\gamma_1)(\gamma_2)(\gamma_3)[Cl(\gamma_1 \neq. \gamma_2 \vee \gamma_3]$; thus grounding the diversity of every class from every determinate which, not being a class, has a form. Hence, since our notion of a full-status class will be so limited that '$\gamma\sigma_i$' is well formed if and only if $Cl(\gamma\sigma_i)$ is decidable, the sameness and diversity of any class and any other determinate, of whatever form, will also be decidable. But what about two classes, none of which has a form? As long as only primary (i.e., finite) classes are added to the core, the diad of any two of them is obviously decidable. In our world, though, with its secondary and tertiary classes, a question arises. There is, to be sure, the rock-bottom transparence, or as I said I would occasionally call it, there is the "axiom," in the phenomenological sense of the word, of extensionality. Two classes are the same if and only if every element of the one is also an element of the other, and conversely. This, though, is not enough. It does not follow that we can for any two classes decide the right side of the transparent equivalence. Thus the question remains. We shall have to check whether this structural requirement, to which I have long been committed, of any two determinates being decidably either the same or diverse, is still satisfied after all its full-status classes have been added to the core of this world. As we shall see, it remains satisfied; with one exception, which, however, is anything but counterstructural. Rather, it will strengthen the overall schematism by adding support to the claim that we cannot literally think the nonrecursively infinite. But it is, I fear, rather late in this discourse for so many anticipations. So let us get on.

Let d_1 be any determinate. What, if anything, does '$\in$' in (7") '$d_1 \in \alpha_1$' stand for? Consider a function, say, a connective, ϕ_1, and two complexes, δ_1 and δ_2. From either the diad of the latter or from their 2-tuples, as the case may be, ϕ_1 produces a value, say, $\phi_1\langle\delta_1, \delta_2\rangle$. Given the modes and the identities of δ_1 and δ_2, the mode of the value will still depend on (the identity of) ϕ_1. That alone makes this function indispensable ontologically, even if it were not, phenomenologically, a characteristic "togetherness" conspicuously presented to us. The mode of (7"), on the other hand, depends only on the identities of δ_1 and δ_2. From this angle, therefore, '$\in$' would not need to stand for anything. It doesn't follow that it doesn't. Just consider $\eta_1(a_1, f_1)$, which is like (7") in that its mode depends only on the identities of a_1 and f_1. Yet the existent η_1 is indispensable, not necessarily because phenomenologically it is unique and conspicuously presented, but because without it there would be no ground ontologically for what in a molecular intention such as, say, $\eta_1(a_1, f_1) \vee \eta_1(a_2, f_2)$, goes with what. Why, then, can't '$\in$' stand for a function?

What exactly is one presented with when presented with (7″)? Speaking for myself, as on these occasions one must, I am presented with the actuality or the potentiality, as the case may be, of d_1 being the same as either a_1 or a_2. More generally, in the case of larger primary classes, I am presented with $B(d_1)$ and its mode; analogously, though not as simply, for secondary and tertiary classes. But d_1 satisfying σ_1 is not anything one could think of (or "see") as a "togetherness" of d_1 and σ_1, particularly since, even though one cannot think the latter without thinking σ_1, they are yet two and not one. Not counting the relevant text, there is thus nothing to be presented except the satisfied condition, which surely is not anything a function, either by itself or jointly with d_1 and $\lambda\sigma_1$, could plausibly stand for. I conclude, with the tag we are accustomed to, that *if δ_1 and δ_2 are there, so eo ipso is $\delta_1 \in \delta_2$*, and *that, therefore, '$\in$' is a diacritical mark.* That establishes the second feature.

The job of a diacritical mark, we know, is not to stand for anything, but, rather, to indicate the sort of the determinates represented by the expressions of which it is a part. For '$\in$', since in elementhood order is of the essence, the other part of the expressions cannot but be '$\langle\delta_1, \delta_2\rangle$'. Thus once more we have no choice, which again is reassuring. The ideal notation for δ_1-*being-an-element-of*-δ_2 is '$\in\langle\delta_1, \delta_2\rangle$', i.e., without abbreviations except for the determinates, '$\in(\delta_1, (\delta_1, \delta_2))$', where '$\in$' is a diacritical mark. But we shall, as usual, unless dealing with the ideal schema itself, continue to write '$\delta_1 \in \delta_2$'; thus taking advantage of one of the situations where the order of things in the world can conveniently be made to appear *in ipsissima persona* as an order among marks on paper.

Let us take stock. I have (I take it) established the following things. We are sometimes presented with (primary) classes and with elementhoods. Thus assured that there are these determinates, we proceeded to assay them and, concurrently with deciding on the ideal notation for them, concluded that elementhood has three of the four features which are in this world associated with the notion of a circumstance. How, then, about the fourth? To this issue we shall turn next. First, though, for a digression that should put in perspective what has been established for the first three.

56* The sharp distinction in this world, between universals, including nonmonadic ones, on the one hand, and classes, including classes of tuples, on the other, and the equally sharp distinction between the several 'η', standing for the several exemplification functions, and the diacritical '$\in$', which stands for nothing, are but the two sides of the same dialectical coin. Keeping that in mind, one is tempted to characterize the contemporary situation in ontology as follows. If properties were classes, exemplification would be the same as being-an-element-of and therefore not an existent but nothing at all. Yet, rather ironically, a world such as Quine's is nowadays often called "realistic" for the sole reason that there are classes in it, although it is a world of classes only and of course without functions. Equally strikingly, '$\in$' and '$=$', which in this world are diacritical, are in the calculi which go with those others styled as the only two undefined predicates; with the result that they are neither defined expressions nor diacritical, except in the odd sense that, like all predicates of those "nominalistic" calculi, they are not supposed to stand for anything. As to 'λ', finally, whether diacritical or otherwise, there is neither need nor room for it in worlds where every existent is a class. This is still another stark contrast with this world of mine, where it doesn't even make sense to speak of classes except as something built upon a world core of things, facts, and circumstances. Put differently, with a suggestive metaphor, those worlds begin and end with classes. The metaphor reminds me of how in those same calculi order is grounded in classes, which come only at the very end, even though it first appears, very near to where the world begins, in (relational) atomic facts.

For any two determinates the modes of the three kinds of circumstances they grounded are supposed to be decidable. This is the fourth feature of all circumstances to which I have long been committed. But, to repeat, commitment to a schematism, and perhaps even growing confidence in it, are not the same as the strongest possible support, phenomenologically and dialectically, for one of its features. How, then, about elementhood? Is $\delta_1 \in \delta_2$ decidable for any two determinates? Or, equivalently, by another quick agreement about words, *are all classes decidable?* The first who, in his way, so limited the very notion of a class was Brouwer. None of his arguments ever struck me or now strikes me as cogent. Yet his is the great merit of having first forced attention upon a cluster of issues, not just in mathematics but also in ontology.

Some of the classes critically needed to ground the whole of classical mathematics are not decidable. Yet, like Brouwer's, the classes of this world all are; in our sense of the word, i.e., the mode of every $\delta_1 \in \delta_2$ is either immediately or recursively accessible; which obviously, in our way, corresponds to his limitation. So I shall try to establish it in three steps. First I shall show that the limitation is *prostructural*. The reflections of the second step are, if I may so express myself, *economic;* designed to show that we can still "get all we need," so that the ontologist's pruning knife has not turned, as of course it must not turn, into a meat axe. These two steps, though, are merely auxiliary. Only the third will show, as for a limitation so radical so high up in the structure one must, that it is forced by the gambits which shape its very base.

First. Let us look at what I just called the *core,* i.e., a world otherwise like ours but without classes, and, in it, at the other two kinds of circumstances, diads and the meaning nexus. (a1) The diads of the core are all decidable. That follows from its transparencies of sameness and diversity, finite in number, in conjunction with each of its complexes being producible by a finite number of steps, either (a) or (b), from a finite ultimate foundation (with no more than a finite number of repetitions for each member, if and as required). (a2) On the meaning nexus I have in the one respect which here matters not changed my mind. While acknowledging the pervasive need of temporarily borrowing from language for all but rather "simple" intentions, I have always held and still hold that the actuality of a-thought-meaning (intending)-what-it-intends is immediately accessible to us. I.e., as I wrote and unless concerned with the ideal schema for its own sake shall continue to write, the actuality of $\ulcorner P_i \urcorner MP_i$ is immediately transparent; where P_i is a complex either within or without the core, and $\ulcorner P_i \urcorner$ is the universal (0), *if any,* which is *the* thought intending P_i; and $\ulcorner P_i \urcorner$, therefore, is an abbreviation for a definite description that fails if and only if there is no such thought, as of course there isn't for the vast majority of all complexes either actual or potential. What I did change my mind about is 'M'. When first introduced, long ago, it stood for a function; now it has become diacritical, which means that I have got rid of an existent, and of course, that the meaning nexus is now a circumstance ($M\langle \delta_1, \delta_2 \rangle$). The minor adjustments this change requires and the bit of dialectic that goes with it you will, as told before, find in the last appendix. But we retain now that the other two kinds of circumstances do have the fourth feature, the diads as long as only finite classes are added to the core, the meaning nexus without any qualification. (b) One of the most characteristic features of this world is the opacity of exemplification. The mode of all atomic facts is in principle inaccessible. If, in contradistinction, the mode of every elementhood is recursively accessible, the contrast, already noticed, between 'η' and '$\in$' is powerfully reinforced. Nor is all the benefit that local. Should it turn out, after the secondary and tertiary classes have also been added to the core, that not only the class "axioms" but also all instances of elementhood are transparent, the former immediately, the latter at least recursively, then we are well on the way toward that sought-for notion of analyticity which makes arithmetic analytic;

within, of course, the boundaries Goedel has drawn to this feature once and for all. That is part of the dialectic still to be worked out; the stage for it has been set in Section IV. But we surely need not wait until it has been worked out, any more than we need to wait until all the details about the new assay of the meaning nexus have come forth, in order to see that in this world the decidability of all (full-status) classes is *prostructural*.

Second. Even if one insists on the decidability of all classes, he can, I said, get all he needs. What does one need and how is that achieved? (a) As you may have gathered from the meat-axe image, I shall not settle for a smidgen less than the whole of classical set theory. The distinction making that possible runs between two kinds of ontological status. *Full* status has only what we can literally think (intend). This is the most fundamental and therefore also the opening gambit of this discourse. The lesser status, I called it *derived,* is acquired by all the "entities" of an axiomatic system usefully interpreted into the world, i.e., for this world, into what we can literally think (intend). I shall so interpret the set-theoreticians' axiomatic system(s). The interpretation, as you probably anticipate, is of the sort called partial, i.e., not all "entities" of the system are interpreted into what we can intend. But again, one does not need to wait for the details to anticipate how that will be done. The "decidable classes" of the axiomatic system will, and the "nondecidable" ones will not, be interpreted into the full-status classes of this world, which are all decidable (without double quotes). Notice that the double quotes around 'entity', and so on, do not mark derived status but, rather, the complete lack of ontological status of all the "entities" of an axiomatic system until and as long as it is usefully interpreted. (They merely mean that I have run out of decent words and shrink away from such quaint ones as 'denizen'.) The so-called "interpretation" of one such system into another is by any name— model making or what have you—a purely mathematical affair. (b) The secondary classes will enable us to ground elementary arithmetic and to show that within Goedelian limits it is analytic. (c) The tertiary classes will enable us to claim that, with a suitable hierarchical qualification in the style of Zermelo, the syntactical predicates are all not only thinkable but decidable. To unpack that again, each full sentence of such a predicate abbreviates what stands for a complex we can intend and whose mode is either immediately or recursively accessible. In these three respects the proposed limitation is also *economic*.

Third. "What we can think is an existent; what we can't think isn't. Thinking something here means intending it, either explicitly or implicitly, under whatever species. Whenever so presented with something, we are *uno actu* presented with its identity, i.e., perhaps more suggestively, with its nature and being, which do not, however, include its mode." These are the gambits, among those shaping the very basis of this world, which force the equivalent of Brouwer's limitation on its full-status classes. Or, rather, this is the claim I must now support.

Negatively, a determinate's identity is not another determinate; that would be the most gratuitous duplication of existents. That it isn't a function is obvious. Nor are a determinate and its identity a Two-in-One. I.e., a determinate's identity neither pervades it, as its mode pervades each complex; nor is there anything such that, compounded with it, its identity would become the determinate, as an ultimate sort compounded with an item becomes a thing. Thus, not even being an entity, a determinate's identity has no ontological status whatsoever. It neither is nor has a mode. Nor, unlike the modes of most complexes, is it hidden from us. Quite to the contrary, when presented with a determinate, with or without its mode, we are also presented with its identity. That is the import of the tag *uno actu,* which I take from the Roman law; with allowance being made, as always, for the inevitable provisional borrowing from language.

Positively, what is a determinate's identity? Let us first look at the atomic fact (8) $\eta_1(a_1, f)$, then at α_1. Sometimes, though by no means every time and therefore surely not *uno actu,* when (8) is presented, so is, transparently, what the abbreviation (9) '$At_0(\eta_1(a_1, f_1))$' stands for. 'At_0' itself, which seems to stand for what, following the tradition, I called a "form," occurs merely in the abbreviation and thus stands for nothing. Nor, if there is a (tertiary) class coextensive with a form, is that class literally the same as the form. For the phenomenology of the latter, you may, if you feel the need, return to the last pages of Section V, about "definitions." Right now I want you to consider the connections between the form and the identity of (8). Being both literally nothing, aren't they perhaps the "same"? There are three reasons why they are not. First, the form of (8) is that of all values of η_1 whose arguments are diads of a particular and a universal[0]. Hence, if it were the identity of one of these values, it would be that of all. Thus it cannot be that of any. Second, what I am presented with when presented with (8) is, with an old phrase that comes in handy, *this* particular, a_1, and *this* universal[0], f_1, being tied by η_1; while what (9) abbreviates is not (8) but, rather, there being *a* particular and *a* universal such that (8) is the value of η_1 for their diad. Of this distinction much more in due course. Third and again obviously, when presented with the identity of (8), we are also presented with what we can grasp although not literally say, viz., a_1 and f_1 being two Two-in-Ones compounded of this and that item with particularity and universality[0], respectively. (About the special position of grasping, at the exact boundary between what we can and cannot literally think, there has been talk already and there will be more in the last Section.)

This, I submit, is all that can and all that need be said by way of unpacking what is meant by the identity of (8). In case of any other complex such that no (c)-step is required to produce it from its ultimate foundation, I would do the same thing, or, more accurately, I would do more of the same thing, step by step. Since I merely unpack a phrase without adding anything to our basic inventory, this will do. But there are the (c)-steps and the classes they produce. So I turn to α_1.

Recall that one can be presented with a selector without its class but not conversely. That adds credibility to the claim that, when presented with α_1, I am, *uno actu*, either immediately or very nearly so, presented with its selector(s) selecting a_1 and a_2, while rejecting all other determinates. Does this mean that the selection of each element of a class and the rejection of all other determinates by its selector(s) exhausts the identity of a class? The answer is both Yes and No. To the extent it is Yes it is merely another way of asserting the arbitrariness of classes. Or, if you like paradoxical formulations, to this extent a class has no identity. Less paradoxically, *as such* the identities of its elements do not fully and directly enter into that of a class, as those of the constituents of a complex enter into that of the latter. Yet they do enter, indirectly, as does that of every other determinate, in that their being either selected or rejected depends, as we know, only on their respective identities, jointly with that of the selector. This is the exact extent to which the answer is No. On the delicate balance between this Yes and this No, jointly with the fundamental principle that one cannot be presented with a determinate without *uno actu* being presented with its identity, I rest my case. *One cannot think "a" class unless one can for every determinate decide whether it is either selected or rejected by the selector(s) of the class.* The obvious necessity to drop the requirement of immediate decision is merely the by now familiar relaxation, as in the case of the chiliagon. Thus the fourth feature, too, is established for all elementhoods. Or, if you prefer, it is grounded as deeply as any of this world.

The indefinite article in the italicized sentence above is surrounded by double quotes in order to distinguish between two intentions such as, say, $a_1 \in \alpha_1$ and $Cl(\alpha_1)$, i.e., in terms of texts, between "a_1 is an element of *the* class such that . . ." and ". . . is *a* class." The distinction brings to mind what we ought to do next. So far, we have not yet established that there is for every determinate γ_1 a complex $Cl(\gamma_1)$. Yet it is the second half of the first claim, if I may so put it, that '$Cl(\gamma_1)$'

stands for what is sometimes immediately transparent. Nor could we, if there were not all these complexes, literally think the immediate transparence known as the extentionality axiom, viz., $(\alpha_1)(\alpha_2)\{Cl(\alpha_1)$ & $Cl(\alpha_2) \supset [(\alpha_1 = \alpha_2) \equiv (\delta)(\delta \in \alpha_1) \equiv \delta \in \alpha_2)]\}$; for in this world, where not all determinates are classes, the antecedent is indispensable. That leaves no doubt how best to proceed. I shall next argue that like, say, '$At_0(\gamma_1)$', '$Disj(\gamma_1)$', '$Fact(\gamma_1)$', although with a characteristic difference, '$Cl(\gamma_1)$', too, is definable; and I shall then avail myself of this result in order to list and discuss the class "axioms." First, though, I interrupt for two comments on the way I shall henceforth often speak and already have spoken in the last paragraphs.

57* (a) Given a nonrecursive class, $\lambda\langle b, B(b)\rangle$, a determinate, d, is "either actually or potentially" an element of it if and only if $B^d(d)$ is "either actual or potential." As for these classes, so mutatis mutandis for the recursive ones. It will, for all of them, lighten the burden of talking properly about a world with modes, where everything is "either actually or potentially" an element of everything, if we can make an agreement that reduces the number of times the phrases between the double quotes must be repeated. So I propose, whenever the meaning is clear, to express myself as follows: A selector of a class *selects* all its elements and *rejects* all other determinates. (b) You are by now no doubt thoroughly familiar with the idea that '$Cl(\gamma_1)$', '$Disj(\gamma_1)$', and so on are in this discourse merely the definienda of definitions whose definientia only stand for certain complexes. Yet, because this idea is so familiar, it will be safe, except in a few crucial contexts where I shall avoid all shortcuts, to speak as if both definienda and definientia stood for those complexes; particularly since I am about to start on an accurate assay of the latter. Similarly for the use of 'define' in such phrases as 'defining the notion of a class'. Nor should it be necessary either to keep reminding you that those definienda may of course serve as texts, or to refer again to what has been said about the phenomenology (if I may so put it) of "definitions" in Section V.

Let us start with a look at, and some comments on, the definientia of '$At_0(\gamma_1)$,' '$Disj(\gamma_1)$', and '$Fact(\gamma_1)$' which are, respectively,

(10) $(\exists x_1)(\exists f_1)(\gamma_1 = f_1(x_1))$,

(11) $(\exists \alpha_1)(\exists \alpha_2)(\gamma_1 = \alpha_1 \vee \alpha_2)$,

(12) $At(\gamma_1) \vee (Neg(\gamma_1) \vee Disj(\gamma_1) \ldots) \vee$
$(\exists \beta_1)(\exists \beta_2)(\gamma_1 = \vee\langle\beta_1, \beta_2\rangle \vee \gamma_1 = \langle\beta_1, \beta_2\rangle)$;

where x_1, f_1, α_1, and α_2 are a particular, a universal[(0)], and two complexes; β_1 and β_2 are a target and a scope such that $\langle\beta_1, \beta_2\rangle$ is an argument for the quantifiers; At is the disjunction of a relatively small number of complexes, one for each of the several subsorts of atomic facts, of which At_0 is one; and the complexes $Neg(\gamma_1)$, $Disj(\gamma_1)$, and so on correspond each to one of the small number of connectives. With respect to the quantifiers in (10), (11), (12), you see once more that one can enjoy the advantages of the new assay of them without always submitting to the rigors of the ideal notation. Now for the comments. All should help with the task at hand; some will also serve as signposts.

First. Some but not all syntactical predicates are coextensive with classes. (10), we shall see, is; (11) and (12) are not. Equivalently, with the new shortcut, $\langle \gamma_1 At_0(\gamma_1) \rangle$ is a selector; $\langle \gamma_1, Fact, \gamma_1 \rangle$ and $\langle \gamma_1, Disj(\gamma_1) \rangle$ are not. Why that is so we shall understand soon, when examining what I shall call the broad Cantor axiom. *Second.* If '$\lambda \langle \gamma_1, Fact(\gamma_1) \rangle$' stood for a class, the order of the disjuncts in (12) wouldn't matter. But since it doesn't, how about *'Fact'*, or as some might want to say, how about its meaning? Ontologically, since the word stands for nothing, the question is specious; or, rather, there is no question. But perhaps it bothers you that, phenomenologically, the word occurs in texts. If so, I suggest, your uneasiness is merely a liminal case of the one I tried to allay in the case of the word 'horse'. *Third.* Compare the notion of *Fact*, as in (12), with that of a molecular fact (*Mol*) in a world otherwise like ours but shorn not only of its classes but also, except for the usual order and standardization tuples, of all circumstances. As a result of this further restriction on its "core," no determinate of the remaining "nucleus" of this world has either a class or a circumstance which is not either an order or a standardization tuple as a constituent. In our complete world, on the other hand, the negation of any diad (δ_1, δ_2), i.e., conventionally written, $(\delta_1 = \delta_2)$, is a fact, and so is, for instance, the disjunction $(\delta_1 = \delta_2) \vee (\delta_1 \in \delta_2)$; with δ_1 and δ_2, irrespective of whether or not they are either classes or circumstances, among their constituents. That shows that *Fact* is much more comprehensive than *Mol*. Yet the complex (12), for the former, is easily devised by disjoining (I speak concisely) the several (a)-steps, including of course all the exemplifications in $At(\gamma_1)$. As for Fact, or *'Fact'*, so for *'Circumstance'*, by disjoining the three (b)-steps; and hence also, by disjoining *'Fact'* and *'Circumstance'*, for *'Complex'*. *'Mol¹'*, on the other hand, which is so much less comprehensive, we shall not be able to define until we have mastered the ontology (!) of recursion. After that, though, we shall also see that while $\langle \gamma_1, Fact(\gamma_1) \rangle$ is not, $\langle \gamma_1, Mol^1(\gamma_1) \rangle$ is a selector.

Fourth. Hans Hahn, when once, in the discussion group that has since become known as the Vienna Circle, searching for words to express both suggestively and succinctly a familiar view, called the whole of mathematics "trivial" yet not "banal." As he meant these words, our definientia are "trivial" in two ways; but there are also two reasons why they are not "banal." (a1) The determinate γ_1 is actually a disjunction if and only if the last of the steps producing it is the (a)-step that goes with the function $\vee$. Accordingly, a disjunction $(\alpha_1 \vee \alpha_2)$ occurs in $Disj(\gamma_1)$. Doesn't this "circularity" (in a bad sense) trivialize (11)? If such "circularity" occurred in a complex which is claimed to ground a formation rule, it would indeed not just trivialize the claim but vitiate it. As to (11), however, and similarly for (10), how could γ_1 being either actually or potentially of a certain form be specified without the use of an instance? Otherwise the "form," which is literally nothing, would be an existent; or, equivalently in the case at hand, '$Disj$' would stand for something. In this sense, (10) and (11) are "trivial." (a2) Consider (10') $(\exists x_1)(\exists f_1)\ (f_2(x_2) = f_1(x_1))$ and (11') $(\exists\alpha_1)(\exists\alpha_2)(\beta_1 \,\&\, \beta_2 = \alpha_1 \vee \alpha_2)$, which are $At_0(f_2(x_2))$ and $Disj(\beta_1 \,\&\, \beta_2)$, respectively. (10') is actual; (11'), potential. Neither is either an immediate transparency corresponding to a primitive sentence of classical logic or one of its theorems. Yet to many, including myself, they are no doubt immediately transparent. Those who don't find them so will easily reach them by a very small number of Cartesian steps if they start from the appropriate transparencies of sameness and diversity which have already been added to those of classical logic. This is a second sense in which (10') and (11') are "trivial." Why, then, are they not "banal"? (b1) Heavily charged as 'complex' and 'intending' are in philosophical discourse, there is yet a sense in which, in spite of profound differences among them, many philosophers would agree that $f_2(x_2)$ stands for a complex which we can intend. Yet the vast majority of them would insist that there is no complex, for us to intend, which (10') could stand for. Thus it can't be "banal" that in this world there is one. (b2) As for (10) and (11), so for every (a)- and (b)-step. Being not yet in possession of the definiens for $Cl(\gamma_2)$, which I am about to provide, we must for the last time ignore the (c)-steps. But surely it is not "banal" that *(speaking very succinctly and ignoring the qualifications that will be specified in the last section) every form involving only (a)- and (b)-steps is available and its mode recursively accessible.*

We now have the background against which to build (the definiens of) $Cl(\gamma_1)$. But we also need something new, an important proposition as yet not argued. Nor would I know how to argue at any length for what, I believe, the ontologist ought to acknowledge is rock bottom; although, alas, I feel bound to add, among living ones, as far as I know Nelson Goodman is the only one who agrees.

There is in the world no empty class, or null class. If there were such a class, its selector would select nothing, and nothing is not an existent. To claim this as phenomenologial rock bottom is fully compatible with acknowledging the practical advantages as well as the anthropological (causal) indispensability of the two *flatus vocis*, or marks; '0', which the Arabs transmitted to us from its Indian inventors; and, say, '0' in the set-theoretical systems. Their practical advantages are obvious. By calling them causally indispensable, I mean, as you may guess, for this is after all the burden of Section V, that one could not without the texts in which they occur think many of the thoughts which some of us sometimes think. Nor should there be any doubt left that, except for rather simple intentions, the ideal notations could not serve as texts. The marks are thus "indispensable"; yet there is nothing for them to stand for. Ontology is not the anthropology of thought. Two comments will add some perspective. Then we shall look for the definiens of $Cl(\gamma_1)$.

First. If one rejects this specious existent he cuts out a little job for himself. It will be shown, in Appendix C, that the decidable "center" of set theory can be interpreted into the full-status classes of this world even though there is no "ontological Null" among them. *Second.* It is rather ironical that this Null which isn't there is in some modern axiomatizations the one and only class whose existence is "postulated." I hope you will remember this and therefore not think that I splurge when, unlike Quine, I shall very soon insist, as by the strongest possible structural compulsion I must, that a determinate and the class of which it is the only element are always two and not one.

If there is no empty class then every class has at least one element. Nor, as we know, is there any determinate not a class that (actually) has any. One is tempted to try out a formula: Being-a-class and having-elements are one and the same. If one may say that, we have already in (13) $(\exists \alpha_1)(\alpha_1 \in \gamma_1)$ found a definiens as simple and as perspicuous as one can hope for, also because it indifferently comprehends all three kinds of classes. May one say, then, that these "two," being-a-class and having-an-element, are literally "one"? Certainly not literally; for the very good reason that neither the "one" nor the "other" is literally anything. Yet, if you take it cautiously, as an aphorism, the formula will help you by pulling into the dialectic two points to which attention has already been called. The definiens for $Cl(\gamma_1)$, while in the four respects, (a1), (a2), (b1), (b2), like those of (10) and (11), is also, and this is the first point, in one respect characteristically different. If one accepts (13) this respect pierces the eye. Disjunction and implication are defined in terms of $\vee$ and $\supset$; the two sorts of operator facts in terms of $\vee$ and $\wedge$, respectively; being-a-diad in terms of a diad $((\exists\alpha_1)(\exists\alpha_2)(\gamma_1 = (\alpha_1, \alpha_2))$; and so on. Being-a-class, however, would, without such "surface circularity," be defined in terms of having-an-element. The connection between being-a-class and being-an-element, or, on the side of the words, between the diacritical marks 'λ' and '∈', was said to be uniquely close. Now we see what this closeness consists in. The former is definable in terms of the latter. The second point merely brings out the import of the first.

On these four similarities, (a1)–(b2); on this characteristic difference, the (c)-step being the only one such that the category of its products can without "surface circularity" be defined in terms of another one, which is a circumstance; on the resulting unique closeness between these two categories; as well as, last not least, on the very special position, exhibited in detail a while ago, which classes occupy among all determinates, I rest my case for the solution the above formula suggests. Explicitly, then, except for ignoring that 'γ_1' is itself but an abbreviation playing the part of the free dummy variable needed in all definitions, '$Cl(\gamma_1)$' *abbreviates* '$\wedge\langle\alpha_1, \alpha_1 \in \gamma_1\rangle$', *which in the ideal notation stands for the complex* γ_1-*being-a-class*. We have come to the end of a line of thought. Three comments will round it out.

First. The new contextualism, it was said much earlier, has two sound cores. One we encountered long ago (p. 151). Now we have finally come upon the other. Speaking for once deliberately in a certain way, for the sake of spotting this point, one could say that while '$Neg(\gamma_1)$', '$Disj(\gamma_1)$', and so on are with "apparent circularity" defined in terms of '∼', '∨', and so on, '$Cl(\alpha_1)$' is the one category of nonsimples defined in terms of something else, viz., '∈', and that in this sense the definition is contextual. That is but another way of calling attention to the unique closeness.

Second. You must have been uneasy about the blur with which I have lately used 'form'. So was I. Yet, since it is both slight and harmless, I let it go until we would come to the point, at which we are now, where clearing it up would do most good. Upon the *standard* use of 'form' in recent analytical philosophy, a form of this world is the category of a determinate produced by (a)- and (b)-steps only. That makes its definiens, on the side of the words, an expression with a prefix of existential quantifiers, one for each step, followed by a conjunction of samenesses; or, of course, it may be a disjunction of such expressions. In this standard sense, things, being Two-in-Ones not produced by any steps, do not have forms. Their ultimate sorts are merely entities and thus, although something, completely "undetachable" from their items; while standard forms, although literally nothing, are yet "detachable" in the sense that there are the complexes which we call, with a shortcut agreed upon, their *definientia*. Class, we know by now, is just as "detachable"; for there is the complex $Cl(\gamma_1)$. Yet, once again, things and classes stand apart and together, in that the latter complex, unlike the former ones, is not standard. The reason it isn't is that we could not (on the side of the words) begin the unpacking by '$(\exists\sigma_1)$ ($\gamma_1 = \lambda\sigma_1$)', which, since '$\lambda$' is diacritical, is ill formed; even if being a selector were, as it is not, a matter of standard form. In the standard sense, therefore, *a class has no form*. Nor would terminological expediency ever tempt me to say that it does. For there is a strand in the tradition that reverberates in this formula and that also fits very well the assay here proposed, upon which a class is "merely a collection" (which as such is nothing) that owes its ontological status to the "weak togetherness" due to all its elements being selected by the same selector. In this world, though, with its sufficiency of categories, there is a complication. Let δ_1 and δ_2 be two classes and consider the fact $\delta_1 = \delta_2$. Its most explicit form, if we shall decide to call it that, goes with the complex $(\exists\alpha_1)(\exists\alpha_2)(\exists\beta_1)(\exists\beta_2)[Cl(\alpha_1)$ & $Cl(\alpha_2)$ & $(\beta_1 = (\alpha_1, \alpha_2))$ & $(\beta_2 = \sim\beta_1)$ & $(\beta_2 = \gamma_1)]$; γ_1 serving again as the free dummy. Because of the first two conjuncts this is not a standard form. Suppressing them, however, one obtains *a* form, viz., that of all negated diads, which is standard (p. 270). Under the circumstances, I would rather not press a new word into technical service but, instead, whenever there are such "class conjuncts" speak of a form in the *broad* sense. Nor, shall I, having once been so pedantic about these distinctions, which I think was necessary, henceforth fuss over them where it is not.

Third. A critic wonders: How can a definiens as simple as you propose help you to come to grips with the notorious difficulties of the notion? If it does not, what purpose does it serve? Yet you claim it is important. I answer as follows: Do not forget that 'γ_1' is merely an abbreviation serving as a free-variable dummy. I cannot think that γ_1 is a class but only that this or that or that other is a class, where the pronouns stand for '$\lambda\sigma_1$', '$\lambda\sigma_2$', '$\lambda\sigma_3$', respectively. 'σ_1', 'σ_2', 'σ_3', however, are themselves merely abbreviations, supposedly for selectors. And we both know that the difficulties you have in mind come all out into the open as one proceeds to determine which conditions$_2$ are, and which are not, selectors. But do not conclude rashly that I plead guilty to superficiality. Separating the "superficial" definiens, which is relatively easy to find, from the notoriously very difficult, does serve at least one purpose. Just remember what was anticipated a few pages back (p. 269). If there were not the complexes located by that definiens, there would not be that other complex, for us to intend, which we intend when thinking the "axiom" of extensionality.

The critic subsides and invites me to start on the task of which both he and I are reminded by my answer. I shall next list, and start the discussion of, the "axioms" for all three kinds of classes. Then we shall be ready to tackle, with the help of a second paradigm, the second kind.

It will pay to start with a reminder and a few bits of overall information. (1) The ontologist, or at least this ontologist, does not call a complex an "axiom" unless he holds that its actuality is immediately transparent. The familiar mathematical use of the word knows no such restriction. While engaged in the tasks at hand, I shall therefore always mark the ontologist's use of the word by putting 'axiom' between double quotes. (2) An "axiom" on which the ontologist must insist if he is to ground phenomenologically what needs to be grounded may thus be the counterpart of a theorem deduced from axioms which, for reasons of his own, the mathematician prefers, although the ontologist in turn would not accept all of them as "axioms." For an example of this difference between the two approaches, see 58* below. And it is but a facet of the same difference that, while economy is always commendable, the ontologist has no real stake in minimizing the number of his "axioms"; in mathematics, although perhaps not a burning issue, such minimization is always a legitimate one. (3) The number of "axioms" I shall need and list is very small; smaller, as far as I know, than that of the axioms of any system of set theory. Nor is that surprising; for, unlike those of these systems, the (full-status) classes of the former are all decidable. (4) The four "axioms" that will be listed will be marked, and referred to, by Roman numerals. I. is the counterpart of what (as far as I know) is in those systems always a theorem. II. yields, for finite sums, the counterpart of the so-called sum or union axiom. III. is the complex of extensionality. IV. will be called the strengthened Cantor "axiom," because the classical Cantor transparency, $(\alpha_1)[Cl(\alpha_1) \supset \sim(\alpha_1 \in \alpha_1)]$, follows from it, but not conversely. There is, however, no "axiom" of infinity, which is, I shall argue, ontologically a very significant feature of this world. And there is, of course, no power "axiom," no "axiom" of choice, and none from which, in conjunction with the others, a counterpart of Fraenkel's axiom of substitution could be deduced. For the connection between IV. and the regularity axiom, see again 58* below. (5) You will in these paragraphs find a new use of upper-case letters that will stay with us for quite a while. E.g., I shall write '$CONST(\delta_1, \delta_2)$' rather than '$const(\delta_1, \delta_2)$' for δ_1-being-a-constituent-of-δ_2. The reason for this innovation is that we cannot literally think what the words thus distinguished purport to stand for; or, equivalently, that there are no definienda for them in the "object language." Eventually, as already promised, all possible sheep will be separated from the irretrievable goats in the last Section. In the meantime, the innovation will keep us reminded that sometimes I am not just writing in a relaxed notation what can more circumstantially be expressed in the ideal one; while, on the other hand, we need not give up a manner of writing that not only saves ink but also helps many, including myself, to grasp what is being said more easily and more quickly.

$$\text{I. } (\alpha_1)(\exists\beta_1)(\delta_1)(\delta_1 \in \beta_1 \equiv. \delta_1 = \alpha_1)$$

In words: for every determinate there is the unit class whose only element it is. The conjunct $Cl(\beta_1)$, which one might have added, follows immediately from I. and (13). That in this world a determinate and its unit class are always two and not one follows by an elementary proof from IV. But it may be worth mentioning here that, irrespective of IV., if even a single determinate not itself a class and its unit class were the same, this world would immediately and irremediably collapse. For, if the "element" were a thing, it would either be exemplified or exemplify or both, while the "class" which presumably it also is, neither is or does either one or the other. Again, if it were a complex, it would be a disjunct or a conjunct, and so on, while the class, which presumably it also is, is neither; and so on. Yet to claim of "one" that what holds of it qua this does not hold of it qua that, and conversely, is no longer ontology. That shows how in a world with a sufficiency of categories one is forced to think ontologically, even if the trend as at present is to think mathematically.

$$\text{II. } (\alpha_1)(\alpha_2)(\exists\alpha_3)[Cl(\alpha_1) \text{ \& } Cl(\alpha_2) \supset. (\delta_1)(\delta_1 \in \alpha_3 \equiv. \delta_1 \in \alpha_1 \lor \delta_1 \in \alpha_2)]$$

In words: for any two classes there is a third such that a determinate is an element of the latter if and only if it is an element of at least one of the two. The third is called the sum or union of the first two. As for two classes, so of course by repeated application of II. for any finite number, $\alpha_1, \alpha_2, \ldots, \alpha_n$. Infinite unions, however, exist in this world only if they are grounded in recursion. Some of these are indeed indispensable for what I have undertaken. Yet we shall have to wait for them until the recursive classes among those of the third kind are grounded.

$$\text{III. } (\alpha_1)(\alpha_2)[Cl(\alpha_1) \text{ \& } Cl(\alpha_2) \supset. (\alpha_1 = \alpha_2) \equiv (\delta_1)(\delta_1 \in \alpha_1 \equiv \delta_1 \in \alpha_2)]$$

In words: "two" classes are one and the same if and only if every element of the one is also an element of the other, and conversely.

III. needs no comment; IV. requires some preparation. So I present next some comments on the first three "axioms." (a) I. and II. are the simplest examples of the "constructive" feature (p. 161) I can think of. (b) Since I had to remind my last critic that III. requires that (13) be available, it may be worth mentioning that so does II. (c) If c_1 and d_1 are two determinates, $\langle c_1, c_1 = d_1 \rangle$ is an enumerator of $\{d_1\}$. If $\langle a_1, A_1(a_1)\rangle$ and $\langle a_1, A_2(a_1)\rangle$ are enumerators of α_1 and α_2, respectively, $\langle a_1, A_1(a_1) \vee A_2(a_2)\rangle$ is a selector of their union, although not, unless they don't overlap, an enumerator of it. Why, then, someone may ask, do we need I. and II. He needs to be reminded of the all-important difference between an "axiom," or for that matter an axiom, which can be expressed in the ideal notation, on the one hand, and a formation rule, which is irretrievable, on the other.

(A) No determinate is its own constituent. Being a constituent is transitive. Hence no determinate is a constituent of one of its constituents. Nor is it a constituent of a constituent of one of its constituents; and so on, any finite number of times. (B) No class is one of its elements, nor either an element or a constituent of one of its elements; nor either an element or a constituent of one of the latter; and so on, any finite number of times. Our last "axiom" is the conjunction of (A) and (B). They both flow from the same fundamental principle. Every canon produces in each case something new. Such a principle, though, is not an "axiom."

A new notion will permit us to state IV. more conveniently. Let 'α_2 is *material* of α_1' be short for 'α_2 is either a constituent or an element of α_1'. In symbols, write '$\alpha_2 MAT\alpha_1$' for '$(\alpha_2 CONST\alpha_1)\vee(\alpha_2 \in \alpha_1)$'. Now we can write our "axiom" as follows.

IV.1. $(\alpha_1)\sim\alpha_1 MAT\alpha_1$

IV.2. $(\alpha_1)(\alpha_2)\sim[(\alpha_1 MAT\alpha_2) \,\&\, (\alpha_2 MAT\alpha_1)]$

IV.3. $(\alpha_1)(\alpha_2)(\alpha_3)[(\sim\alpha_1 MAT\alpha_3) \,\&\, (\alpha_3 MAT\alpha_2) \,\&\, (\alpha_2 MAT\alpha_1)]$

and so on, any finite number of times. As you see, IV., or, as I shall call it, the strengthened Cantor "axiom," is not really a single complex but a series of such which we can make as long as we want, or, more realistically, as on any one occasion we need.

For I., II., and III., the immediate transparency of an "axiom" needs, I submit, no support. In the case of IV., however, some close reasoning is in order. (1) By the immediate transparencies of sameness and diversity, classes have transparently no constituents. Hence, for any class β_1, $\beta_1 \in \beta_1$ is transparently equivalent to $\beta_1 MAT\beta_1$; similarly, if γ_1 is a determinate not a class, for $\gamma_1 CONST\gamma_1$ and $\gamma_1 MAT\gamma_1$. (2) $\sim (\beta_1 \in \beta_1)$ *is an immediate transparency that cannot be reached by any Cartesian chain from what is thus transparent.* This bit of phenomenological rock bottom is one of Cantor's crucial insights; or so at least I am inclined to believe; hence also the name I chose. For his crucial insight follows, as we just saw, immediately from IV. and thus from the "strengthened Cantor axiom," but of course not conversely. (3) Turn next to a "pure" $\in$-chain, $(\beta_1 \in \beta_2)$ & $(\beta_2 \in \beta_1)$, or, in general, $(\beta_1 \in \beta_n)$ & $(\beta_1 \in \beta_{n-1})$ & . . . & $(\beta_2 \in \beta_1)$. Is its potentiality, too, immediately transparent? If n is large enough, the intention will be too complicated for the immediate to be the instantaneous. Yet in due course one is again presented with a transparence that cannot by Cartesian steps be reached from any other, including Cantor's. If this were otherwise, the principle to which I appealed at the beginning of this argument would not be as fundamental as it is. (4) Let now α_1 and β_1 be two classes and consider a "mixed" chain, say, $(\alpha_1 CONST(\alpha_1 \in \beta_1)$ & $((\alpha_1 \in \beta_1) \in \alpha_1)$, which begins and ends with the same determinate. I claim again that the potentiality of such chains is transparent, immediately although not necessarily instantaneously, and that it is not by Cartesian steps accessible from other transparencies. In the example, the actuality of the first conjunct is of course so accessible; but the potentiality of the second, unless the classes are finite, is not. (5) The potentiality of a pure $CONST$-chain beginning and ending with the same determinate can be reached from the immediate transparencies of sameness and diversity. Thus IV. could be "weakened," though only at the price of less perspicuity now and less convenience in later handling. Besides, it is not our business but, rather, if anyone's, the mathematicians', to either weaken, or reduce the number of, our "axioms" as much as possible. This is all I can say, and, I believe, all that needs to be said to establish the immediate transparence of IV.

In the axiomatic systems of the set theorists, of classes only, there are of course only pure $\in$-chains. Write those here relevant as they are sometimes conveniently written: $\alpha_1 \in \alpha_1$, $\alpha_2 \in \alpha_1 \in \alpha_1$, . . . , $\alpha_1 \in \alpha_n \in \alpha_{n-1} \in$ . . . $\in \alpha_1$. The set theorists deduce the negation of all these chains by an elementary proof from a single axiom, the so-called regularity axiom; (R) "Every (nonempty) class β_1 has at least one element β_2 such that β_1 and β_2 have no element in common." Why then bother with the series in IV.? The answer throws light on the difference between the ontological and the mathematical approach. To me (R) is neither immediately nor accessibly transparent. If to you it is, I doubt that you and I mean the same by 'transparent'. In other words (R), however elegant as an axiom, is not an "axiom." A digression will further illuminate the difference.

58* *First.* (R') "For every determinate δ_1 there is at least one other δ_2, such that δ_2 is material of δ_1 and there is no determinate δ_3 which is material of both δ_1 and δ_2." Call (R') the strengthened regularity axiom. From (R') as a premise one can, by duplicating the elementary proof of the set theorists, deduce IV. But since (R') is not immediately transparent, this proof serves no particular purpose in ontology. *Second*. Jointly with other axioms not available in this world (R) also excludes the infinite descending series . . . $\alpha_n \in \alpha_{n-1} \in \ldots \in \alpha_2 \in \alpha_1$. This we can of course not match. Yet we need not worry. The number of constituents of any determinate is finite. And as far as elementhood is concerned, we shall see that if $\alpha_1 \in \alpha_2$ is actual, α_1 and α_2 lie on successive levels of a well-ordered hierarchy whose basis corresponds to Zermelo's *Urelemente*. Thus there are in this world no such series.

What are the uses for which Cantor's "axiom," i.e., roughly IV.1., needs to be strengthened? I shall give an example that will for the time being close a line of thought. The example, being familiar, should add to the sense of closure. $\langle \gamma_1,(\exists \alpha_1)(\exists \alpha_2)(\gamma_1 = \alpha_1 \vee \alpha_2) \rangle$ is of course a condition$_2$. Yet it is not a selector; or, equivalently, there is no class such that a determinate is actually an element of it if and only if it is a disjunction. To see why this is so, assume *e contrario* that there is this class, write '$\widetilde{disj}$' for it, and notice that $(\beta_1)[\beta_1 \in \widetilde{disj} \equiv Disj(\beta_1)]$ would be actual. Now let δ_1 be any determinate, δ_2 any complex, and consider (14) $(\widetilde{disj} = \delta_1) \vee \delta_2$. Whether or not this complex is actual, its being a disjunction transparently is, and so therefore is its being an element of $\widetilde{disj}$, i.e., $[(\widetilde{disj} = \delta_1) \vee \delta_2] \in \widetilde{disj}$. Thus, if there were this class, it would be a constituent of one of its elements, which contradicts IV.2. The source of the trouble is not hard to spot. There are in this world classes whose elements are facts (or circumstances) having classes as constituents, classes whose elements have elements that are facts (or circumstances) having classes as constituents, and so on. That is why, for instance, the collection of all disjunctions is not a class and therefore literally nothing. But could one not perhaps stratify such collections into a hierarchy of levels, or types, such that at least each of the latter is a class? You gather why I just said that we are "for the time being" at the end of a line of thought.

When assaying the primary classes, we first picked a paradigm as "simple" as possible and then branched out from it, as it were, in the order suggested by it and by the ideal notation for it. The strategy worked well; so I shall employ it again in the assay, to which I now turn, of secondary classes; for, naturally, the two jobs are similar. Yet they differ in two respects. A good deal of what has been said on the occasion of the primary classes also holds, as has been pointed out, for the secondary and tertiary ones; thus it will not have to be said again.

This difference makes the job now at hand less difficult, or at least less lengthy. The two jobs are also alike in that each requires a new idea so basic that it cannot be introduced into ontological discourse without a paradigm and some rock-bottom appeal. The other difference, which makes the second job more difficult, is between the two basic ideas. In the primary case, the new idea is that of a class, i.e., a fundamental category. This category, we know already only too well, is a very special one, with peculiarities all its own. Yet, since it is a fundamental category, its idea is, as ontology goes, as graspable as any. The new idea, from which the assay of the secondary classes must start, is not as graspable, or palpable, or specific. I leave the choice of metaphor to you. Without metaphor, as far as that is possible, it is not as manifestly and directly grounded. What, then, is it, and in what sense, if any, is it "basic"? Thus put on the spot, I beg leave to introduce the second paradigm.

Let a_1, b_1, f_1, g_1, be two particulars and two universals[(0)], respectively. Our second paradigm, call it π_1, is the "class" such that its elements are *"all those and only those"* determinates which are *"either $f_1(a_1)$ or, next, $f_1(a_1) \vee g_1(b_1)$,"* *"and so on."* In a familiar relaxed notation, π_1 is the class (14) $\{f_1(a_1), f_1(a_1) \vee g_1(b_1), (f_1(a_1) \vee g_1(b_1)) \vee g_1(b_1), \ldots\}$. In this notation, though, the dots are made to bear the whole burden of the idea of *iteration*, which, though not perhaps literally the whole of the new basic idea, surely is its very heart. So I shall use this notation only most sparingly. In $\{a_1, a_2, \ldots, a_n\}$, on the other hand, where the dots are followed by a comma followed by the mark for an element, they are, for finite n, an abbreviation as unproblematic as any. As to the iterations we are concerned with, they are all finite, not transfinite, i.e., while each of them moves along the whole sequence of the integers, none moves beyond them. Thus we may safely skip the qualifying 'finite'.

Attend next to the typographical devices in the second sentence of the proceeding paragraph. The double quotes around 'class' are to remind us, not only that the very use of the word is as yet problematic, but also that, should it be cleared, its place would in the ideal notation be taken by 'λ'; just as that of the part of the sentence following it would be taken by the selector. The longish phrase italicized in this part is the condition the selector to be proposed must ontologize. This condition, or, rather, any condition of this sort, is the new basic idea. That is why the longish phrase is italicized. The three shorter ones within double quotes are the key part phrases in the expression of the condition. I add three remarks, one about each of them, anticipating what will soon be so obvious that we shall not need to return to it. In the first phrase, "all those and only those," the last three words can be suppressed if the third is enlarged to "and so on, and nothing else." The second phrase could be replaced by "either, first, $f_1(a_1)$, or, second, $f_1(a_1) \vee g_1(b_1)$." But why use ordinals when the notion to be conveyed is merely that of the order in a 2-tuple, for which 'next' will do as well? The third phrase, "and so on," signals in the context of the other two the iteration.

Is there such a class as π_1? Or, equivalently in this world, since the selector on which it is presumably built does involve a new and basic idea, even though at this point the notion of a class as such does not, are we sometimes presented with π_1? Supposing we are, are we on some such occasions also presented, either immediately or at least recursively, with the actuality of what '$Cl(\pi_1)$' purports to stand for? Eventually I shall support the affirmative answers. Until then the phenomenological status of π_1 remains problematic. Even so, I want to do some other things first; that will help the exposition as a whole, which, although not as lengthy as the first time, in the case of the primary classes, is yet laborious. First of all, therefore, I shall try to make you willing to share in these labors by previewing, informally, selectively, and in a free-ranging manner, what will be achieved in case they succeed.

A. Write, with Peano, (15) $0,0',0'',0''',\ldots$; suppose that the familiar marks stand for a sequence of determinates satisfying his five axioms (hereafter: PI–PV); and you will surmise, correctly, that (14) is an *ontologist's* attempt to locate in the world of his discourse the pattern the great *axiomatist* was the first to propose. That is why, just as in tribute to Meinong I occasionally call the functions of this world Meinong-functions, its secondary classes will occasionally be called *Peano-classes*, or, briefly, P-classes. Nor need I remind you that Russell was the first to recognize that elementary arithmetic cannot be grounded without interpreting the pattern.

Always supposing that there is such a class, does π_1 satisfy PI–PV? I invite you to consider, informally and selectively, PIII. Written more or less conventionally, it reads '$(\alpha)(\beta)(\alpha' = \beta' \supset . \alpha = \beta)$'; with the stroke abbreviating a definite description based on a relation on which the five axioms jointly impose certain conditions. When it comes to interpretation, therefore, the first thing to do is to make sure that there is at least one such relation in the world. Now, if the latter were to be descriptive, either simple or (I speak concisely) defined, we have *in fact* no very good reason for either believing or not believing that there is one. Moreover, if *per absurdum* one had the best possible reasons for believing this sort of thing, they would still not provide him with grounds for all demonstrable arithmetical complexes being, in the sense of this discourse, analytic. In arithmetic and in successfully interpreted axiomatic set theory there are of course such "relations." Appealing to them, however, is in the context clearly question-begging. Ontologically significant interpretation of Peano's pattern is thus faced with a dilemma from which in the ontologies I am familiar with there is no escape. (The double quotes around 'relation' mark once more my reluctance, even when speaking succinctly, to use 'relation' thus broadly, for what is a class of tuples rather than either a non-monadic universal or at least, although of course without ontological status, defined in terms of such universals.)

In this world one proceeds as follows. In the case of π_1, let 'succeeding$_{\pi_1}(\gamma)$' abbreviate '$(\exists \alpha_1)(\gamma = \langle \alpha_1, \alpha_1 \vee g_1(b_1) \rangle)$', which is an expression for γ being of a certain form, viz., a 2-tuple such that if γ_1 is its first term, $\gamma_1 \vee g_1(b_1)$ is the second. Thus, given any 2-tuple $\langle \gamma_1, \gamma_2 \rangle$, its being or not being of this form is immediately transparent. Also, we are provided with the instructions how, given any determinate γ_1, to find *the* other such that they are, respectively, the first and the second term of a tuple of this form; as well as, given any determinate γ_2, with the instructions how to find *the* determinate, *if any*, such that they are, respectively, the second and the first term of such a tuple. Moreover, it follows from the appropriate tautologies of sameness and diversity that in every 2-tuple of this form each term uniquely determines the other (which justifies the use of the words I just italicized). Thus π_1 transparently satisfies PIII. All that remains is to connect with the usual notation by writing 'successor$_{\pi_1}(\alpha,)$', or even more fragmentarily when there is no danger of ambiguity, (α_1'), for the definite description usually based on 'succeeding$_{\pi_1}$'. As for π_1, so for all P-classes. We have escaped the dilemma. *In this world the successor "relation," being part of its form, is not only unproblematically there but also, by virtue of the formation rules and the tautologies of sameness and diversity, decidable;* which latter it would not be for a descriptive relation, even if there were one that satisfies the five axioms, since our very strict notion of decidability requires either immediate or recursively accessible transparence. *Again, π_1 transparently satisfies* PIII. If we can secure the transparence of the other four axioms, a *first crucial feature* of all secondary classes will be established. But I would rather postpone this job until we start proceeding systematically and instead continue the preview in two directions, (B) and (C), suggested by what has been said already in connection with PIII.

B. Among the features which by the general schematism of this world all its (full-status) classes are supposed to have, the one that stands out, if only because it is the most restrictive, is their decidability. I.e., if α_1 is such a class and β_1 any determinate whatsoever, the mode of $\beta_1 \in \alpha_1$ must be at least recursively accessible. How, then, about π_1? β_1 (actually) is an element of π_1 only if it is either $f_1(a_1)$ or a disjunction one of whose terms is $g_1(b_1)$, say, $\beta_2 \vee g_1(b_1)$. If β_1 is either the former or neither, the decision is immediate; if it is the latter, there is the obvious recursion on β_2. As for π_1, so for all P-classes. They are all decidable. This is a *second crucial feature,* which it didn't take us long to establish. The idea is the same as before. *In this world what matters is "thrown upon," or "located in," its transparent form.* But notice, too, that the "instructions" as to how to arrive at the decision, as well as the statement that the procedure they prescribe is recursive, belong irretrievably to the metalanguage.

C. When Russell tried to interpret Peano's axioms, he noticed that there was something amiss. What he missed was, to be sure, not a further axiom, to be added to Peano's uninterpreted ones, so that they may all six be interpreted into the world, but, rather, an "axiom," i.e., a proposition about the world, which, if it held, would allow him to interpret the original five. I refer, of course, to his axiom of infinity, according to which there is an infinite number of particulars in the world. Unfortunately, this proposition asserts, as above under (A), the sort of thing we have no very good reason either to believe or not to believe. Nor, again as above, even if there were such an infinity, would it have provided him with grounds for all (demonstrable) arithmetical complexes being analytic. This he himself recognized. The qualification, demonstrable, acknowledges the limitation Goedel subsequently discovered. For still other reasons why the interpretation Russell attempted lacks ontological significance, see Appendix B.

What Russell hoped to achieve by means of his axiom is here achieved without it, by means that do not prejudge the analyticity of demonstrable elementary arithmetic, on the much "deeper" level of the formation rules and the transparencies of sameness and diversity, neither of which involves the notion of infinity. Specifically, since any two members but the first of the sequence in (14) are diverse, although they are of course tautologically equivalent, the required infinity of determinates is in this world available among its facts. Thus there is no need for "postulating" an infinity of (simple) things (of the same ultimate sort). This is a *third crucial feature.* Again, the idea is clear, and broadly speaking, the same as in (A) and (B). Yet it would not be convincing if I left it at that without answering a question raised by a friendly mathematician. I do (he says) appreciate the ontological scruples to make you want to avoid the postulation of an infinity of simples, either of the same ultimate sort, or, for that matter, since you, too, reject Russell's requirement of homogeneity, of any sorts. But could you not achieve your purpose more simply if, adopting Zermelo's version of the set theorists' infinity axiom, you claimed, not either as an axiom or as an "axiom," but rather, as you would say, as phenomenological rock bottom, that, if γ_1 is a determinate of any sort, the Zermelo-class, as for the moment I shall call it, which is conventionally written (16) $\{\gamma_1, \{\gamma_1\}, \{\{\gamma_1\}\}, \ldots \}$, is sometimes presented to you, as is, on some of these occasions, its actually being a class? Starting my reply with two acknowledgments, I *acknowledge, first,* that by substituting γ_1 for the empty class, my friend has freed Zermelo's original pattern from what is here not at issue. I *acknowledge, second,* that, since the classes of this world, although they do not have constituents, are yet not simples; and since Zermelo's iteration step, from a determinate to the class of which it is the only element, is by our "axiom" I. available, and produces by IV. a sequence any two of whose members are diverse, it should be possible to find in this world a selector for (16) without the sort of postulation from which I recoil. But I *add, third,* that while there are indeed such selectors, we shall see that the classes built on them are among those which in this discourse are called tertiary; and that, as we shall also see, these classes require, in addition to "something else," the ontologization of a recursion pattern more complex than that in (14). Thus, if I followed my friend's suggestion, I would without gaining anything scramble what the ontologist ought to unscramble. I *conclude, fourth,* with an anticipation that will (I hope) serve as a signpost. Being a selector of either a primary or a secondary class is a matter of (transparent) form. Being a selector of a tertiary class, however, is not.† This limitation of the strategy that throws as much as possible on the world's form involves the "something else" just mentioned.

D. It will not be difficult to establish that π_1 satisfies PI – PV and that successor $_{\pi_1}$ well-orders its elements with the Peano-null, $f_1(a_1)$, as its first. Once this is done, elementary arithmetic is in principle grounded; all the rest can be safely left to the mathematicians. To them, unless I

---

†There is a penciled comment at the bottom margin of the rough copy of Section VI that begins: "That now seems dubious to me." This comment, dated 10/12/77, is marked by an asterisk at the end of the sentence *ending* with the phrase: ". . . is a matter of transparent form." But it is the sentence *following* the asterisk that is underlined (in pencil). It is thus not clear whether Bergmann came to doubt that being a selector of a primary or secondary class *is* a matter of form, or, on the other hand, that being a selector of a tertiary class is *not* a matter of form. All that's clear is that the note expressing the doubt was written (approximately) two years after the text itself was written. See Editor's Note.—WH

am greatly mistaken, that is obvious. Thus a *fourth crucial feature* will be established. But in case there is a reader who knows even less than I do of what the mathematicians have achieved during the last half century or so, let me point out to him that if one wants to ground (elementary) arithmetic, one need not, as Russell thought, pick out a sequence of existents and offer them as the assays of what '1', '2', '3', and so on supposedly stand for. All there needs to be, we have been taught, is a class of P-classes, together with those the mathematicians call enumeration functions, to count off any two of the former against each other and every finite class against an initial segment of any of them. The gap thus left between what is claimed to be there, on the one hand, and the texts with their ordinals and cardinals that enable us to think, on the other, can—and, as you already know, I insist, *must*—be bridged in the style of Section V. But again, my mathematical friend would not be happy if I stopped here without making one more comment. Mathematicians, I gather, can make "formal" pictures of elementary arithmetic without an infinity axiom. From where I stand, they pay for what is thus gained by their kind of ingenuity with a loss of ontological significance. For the basic idea, which in fact we have, of infinity and of counting is not, or so at least, I am profoundly convinced, about (the always finite number of) marks on paper but about an "actual" infinity of existents in the world. (This use of 'actual' is of course not mine but the one long customary in this very special context.)

This will do for the preview. What is now to be done systematically? Several things, of course; but it will be best if we start with Peano's axioms.

Let me restate the burden of (D). If arithmetic is to be grounded by grounding π_1 in a manner not prejudicial to its analyticity (within Goedelian limits), each Peano axiom must be transparently satisfied by π_1. That faces us with three alternatives. Either (1) the axiom can be recursively reached by Cartesian steps from immediately transparent tautologies already available to us, or (2) it holds by virtue of the formation rules for secondary classes; in these two cases I shall say that it is automatically satisfied. Or (3) we must claim that the actuality of the axiom is immediately transparent, add it to the four class "axioms" for which this claim has already been supported, and do for it the same. Let us look at the situation abstractly. Even if none of the five were automatically satisfied, we could, as it were, bully our way through by matching each of them with an "axiom." In terms of structural economy, however, if that were necessary the game would no longer be worth the candle. I, for one, would start looking for another way of grounding arithmetic and, if that failed, for a more adequate ontology. Concretely the situation lies between the extremes in a way that is structurally illuminating. PI–PIV are automatically satisfied. Of PIII we remember that from the preview. The induction axiom, PV, requires a new "axiom." I shall now write down PI–PV for the paradigm, comment on the way they present themselves in this world, show next that PI, PII, PIV are automatically satisfied, follow up with a consideration of our fifth "class axiom," PV, and conclude this first job with a digression.

(PI) $f_1(a_1) \in \pi_1$

(PII) $(\alpha_1)[\alpha_1 \in \pi_1 \supset . (\alpha_1 \vee g_1(b_1)) \in \pi_1]$

(PIII) $(\alpha_1)(\beta_1)[(\alpha_1 \vee g_1(b_1)). = .\beta_1 \vee g_1(b_1) \supset . \alpha_1 = \beta_1]$

(PIV) $\sim (\exists \alpha_1 (\alpha_1 \in \pi_1) \& (\alpha_1 \vee g_1(b_1)). = .f_1(a_1)]$

(PV) $Cond(f_1(a_1)) \& (\alpha_1)[(\alpha_1 \in \pi_1) \& Cond (\alpha_1) \supset .$
$Cond(\alpha_1 \vee g_1(b_1))] \supset :(\alpha_1)[(\alpha_1 \in \pi_1) \supset Cond(\alpha_1)]$

π_1 and '$Cond$' are abbreviations. The former stands for '$\lambda\sigma_1$', with 'σ_1' in turn standing for the selector. That is as far as at the moment we can go. Specifying the determinates that can serve as selectors for secondary classes will be our second job. '$Cond(\gamma_1)$' stands for γ_1 satisfying a certain condition, whatever the latter may be. More often than not, it will be that γ_1 is an element of a certain class, say α_1. If so, '$Cond(\gamma_1)$' abbreviates what becomes of '$\gamma_1 \in \alpha_1$' after 'γ_1' and 'α_1' have been replaced by what they abbreviate. What I wrote when avoiding abbreviations, as in the fragments '. . . $\vee g_1(b_1)$', narrowly fits the paradigm and nothing else. *Practically* that is the best one can do. Since in $\lambda\sigma_1$ neither σ_1 nor any of its constituents are quantifiable, the most one can do *in principle* for any *sort* of classes in the ideal notation is to write down the form, if any, shared by all the selectors of such a class. For primary and secondary classes, according to the signpost I just erected, that can be done; although only most laboriously; for we must not use such abbreviations as the stroke and the Peano-null or any other of the many notational conveniences available to the mathematician in his axiomatic treatment of classes. Nor are these just conveniences. Given the nature of our minds, when mathematical work is to be done, they are necessities. Thus the mathematician cannot but choose the axiomatic approach to classes. The ontologist, on the other hand, need not shrink away from an indefinitely large number of propositions, such as PI–PV, which could only by the most complicated set of instructions be connected with a finite number of manageable "schemata" in the metalanguage. For his purpose, unlike the mathematician's, is not to deduce much from little but, rather, to discover what is there by determining what can be said, no matter how laboriously and for our minds unperspicuously, in an ideal language in which admittedly no human could think. (More accurately, this is *a* way of stating the ontologist's purpose, the one that fits the need of the moment.)

Turn now to PI, PII, and PIV. The first two hold "by virtue of the formation rules for P-classes." The thing to do, if one wants to show that, is to unpack the phrase; then the rest will be obvious. The heart of the formation rule for a class is that of its selector(s). A selector, σ_1, we know, must provide an adequate basis for, and in this sense encode, although it does not literally express, the "instructions" how to decide, for every determinate γ_1, whether $\gamma_1 \in \lambda\sigma_1$; which in this world is the very touchstone of thinkability. How that works in the case of the primary classes we have seen. Nor need we wait for the details in the case of the secondary ones in order to anticipate that, by the instructions for π_1, $f_1(a_1)$ is an element of it, and that, if α_1 is one, so is $\alpha_1 \vee g_1(b_1)$; and that, therefore, PI and PII are automatically satisfied by virtue of the formation rule. But notice, too, that while PI and PII are in the object language, the formation rule and the instructions belong irretrievably to the metalanguage. That is why I said that PI and PII become transparent "by virtue" of the formation rules, rather than that they can be "deduced" from them, as PIII can be deduced from the tautologies of sameness and diversity. In the case of PIV, finally, we know by virtue of the instruction that the successor of each element of π_1 is a disjunction one of whose terms is $g_1(b_1)$, and we deduce from the appropriate tautology of sameness and diversity that every such determinate is diverse from $f_1(a_1)$.

The actuality of PV I claim, as I must, to be sometimes immediately transparent. Suppose it is, why is that structurally illuminating? Remember a less formal claim. π_1 was said to involve a new idea, represented, as we ordinarily speak, by the formula ". . . all those and only those . . . either *this*, or, next, . . . and so on." PV is similarly represented by "If *this* satisfies the condition, and if something does so does the next, then all do." Looking at the two formulae together, one is struck by the very close connection between what they respectively represent. Yet you will rightly insist that the nature of the connection be clarified. This I do as follows. "On some of the occasions on which either π_1 or $Cl(\pi_1)$ is presented to me, the latter with its mode, so is immediately the actuality of PV." The immediacy excludes, as before, the deducibility of PV from $Cl(\pi_1)$; and, again as before, the immediate need not be the instantaneous; if either the secondary class or the condition or both are "complicated," it won't be. This, and nothing else, is the nature of the "connection." Now you point out that I have merely supported one phenomenological claim with another. You are right, of course. The second, however, I submit, is rock bottom and thus not only needs no support but supports in turn the earlier one that PV may and must be admitted into this world as an immediate transparence, i.e., as I have taken to calling it, an "axiom," *provided* of course that either π_1 or the actuality of $Cl(\pi_1)$ is sometimes presented to us. So you want to know whether we do in fact sometimes intend these two. It will pay if once more I postpone answering this question.

We have closed in on the new idea. Broadly speaking, it is that of a narrowly limited sort of "actual" infinity. In the order in which this world is being built in this discourse, it is at this point certainly new. But in what sense is it also basic? One sense, or reason, is obvious. The new idea wouldn't cut any ice unless it were buttressed by an immediate transparency as closely tied to it as the immediately transparent p-tautologies are to the connectives. That is why the need to count PV as an "axiom" is structurally enlightening. But there are other reasons, both pro and con, for the idea being basic. If you will allow me one anticipation, amounting to no more than a simple assertion that will be made good presently, this is the best place for collecting all these reasons.

The idea of an ultimate sort is basic; so is that of an M-function, whether connective or quantifier. Their being basic shows itself in there being special existents, which are not determinates, "corresponding" to them, one to each of them, such as particularity, $\vee$, $\wedge$. The ideas of the three circumstances are basic; so is that of a class. Their being basic does not show itself in corresponding existents in the world but merely in four corresponding diacritical marks in the ideal notation. Our new idea surely is not of the first kind. Is there then perhaps a special diacritical mark corresponding to it? If there were one, the phrase in our formula it would most likely take is "and so on." Here the anticipation comes in. We shall see, first, that the ideal notation for the selector of a P-class does not require any new mark, either diacritical or otherwise; and we shall see, second, that in the metalanguage of the instructions the job of that phrase can be done without it. Does that leave the immediately transparent actuality of PV as the only reason for the new idea being basic? I submit that it does; and if having momentous consequences is part of what makes an idea basic, there is still another. Nor is the consequence I have in mind merely that, positively, one can with this idea find arithmetic, which surely is momentous enough, but just as much that, negatively, it is *the* root of the Goedelian limitation that will force us to make do with second best when completing the tautological-analytic schema from the beginning of Section IV for classes. Of this more in Section VII; now for the concluding digression.

59* (a) If one starts, in the style of the earlier axiomatists, from the three "nonlogical" constants, 'N,' corresponding to 'π_1'; '0'; and '′', PV is also needed to secure well-order and thereby categoricity of interpretation. For a counterexample, consider the class whose elements are zero, all even positive integers, and all odd integers, both positive and negative, with zero as the Peano-null and $x' = x + 2$ as the stroke-function. PI–PIV are satisfied; so is the antecedent of PV for the condition of being either zero or a positive integer; yet its consequent is not. In the context of this discourse a "numerical" counterexample is at this point of course improper. It is easy, though, as long as one requires of the stroke-function merely that it be decidable and one-one and that each element of N have a successor, to construct from 2-tuples of molecular compounds of $f_1(a_1)$ and $g_1(b_1)$ a counterexample that is isomorphic to the numerical one above. We need not tarry to construct it; yet I must report a twist that appears when one does. The selector of this proper counterexample makes it a tertiary class. If, however, again quite properly, one limits the iterative feature as I presently shall, then, as far as I can see, PV is not needed to secure well-order. In the style of the modern axiomatists all this is of course moot; they (I speak concisely) start from well-order and in due course prove Peano's five propositions. But consider now in the light of these comments the three phrases "all those *and only those*," ". . . next . . . ," "and so on"; and you will see that as long as the second is not appropriately specified, it needs the support of the last three words of the first; just as, after all, the third, even though it be the heart of the matter, needs the support of the second; all of which is as it ought to be; if it were otherwise, why speak of *one* idea both new and basic? (b) Let us retrace the steps toward the transparence of PIV in the case of the P-class, call it π_2, conventionally written

$$\{[g_1(b_1) \lor g_1(b_1)] \lor g_1(b_1), ([g_1(b_1)] \lor g_1(b_1)] \lor g_1(b_1)) \lor g_1(b_1) \ldots\}.$$

By its formation rule, by the tautologies of sameness and diversity, and by a few Cartesian steps we "know" that, first, successor π_2 is one-one; second, its Peano-null is the successor π_2 of $g_1(b_1) \lor g_1(b_1)$; third, every element of π_2 is of the form $(\alpha \lor g_1(b_1)) \lor g_1(b_1)$; fourth, every determinate of this form is diverse from $g_1(b_1) \lor g_1(b_1)$; and, fifth and finally, PIV for π_2. For the paradigm the progress was less "complicated." Its "complexity" will increase with that of (the selector for) the class. But if the idea of iteration, as expressed by the formation rules, is properly specified, there is no reason to believe that (the actuality of) PI–PIV cannot always be reached, if necessary by also appealing to the immediate transparence of PV. So we need not, for our non-mathematical purposes, pursue the matter nor later return to it.

What are the selectors on which the P-classes are built? Answering this question systematically is our second job. I shall start with two preliminary remarks, then get down to the nuts and bolts of it.

A. A selector of a class must be determinate; otherwise it could not *ontologize* the condition satisfied by all those and only those determinates which are elements of the class. But it must also contain all the material (I avoid the unnecessarily anthropomorphic 'information') required to carry out the instructions that lead for every determinate to the decision as to whether it (actually) is an element of the class. Otherwise the condition would not be *adequately* ontologized. If, on the other hand, a determinate does so ontologize the condition of a class, then, by extensionality, it determines the latter *uniquely*. Thus it can serve as the selector, or, in case there are several, as one of them. In the primary case, for instance, with $B^c(d)$ decidable for all d and instructions to the effect that d is an element of a certain class if and only if $B^c(d)$ is actual, $\langle c, B(c) \rangle$ can serve as a selector for this class. Yet, to repeat, a selector as such and the class built on it are two and not one. The connection between them, brought out so well by the ideal notation, '$\lambda\langle c, B(c)\rangle$' for the latter, is that the former, since it adequately ontologizes the latter's condition, can serve as a selector for it. Speaking about notations, the strategy that worked so well for the primary classes will work again. Finding the selectors for P-classes and finding the ideal notation for them are not really two tasks but two aspects of one. So I shall again pursue them together.

B. What exactly are the nature and role of *instructions?* In the strict sense that concerns us, the two notions of instructions and decidability are inseparable. An instruction, that is, to be one, must, if followed, guarantee success. The first time we encountered the notion was in the case of the decidable p-calculus; the second time, when in the case of the q-calculus, which, whether first-order or enlarged, is itself of course not decidable, we retraced the combinatorial logicians' instructions for deciding whether $\langle a, A(a) \rangle$ and $\langle b, B(b) \rangle$ are variants of each other; the third and last time so far, in the case of the selectors for primary classes. The first case, being the most familiar as well as, in a familiar sense, completely noncontroversial, will provide the most serviceable example for the purpose at hand. Take, then, a sentential complex, α_1, and suppose that, starting from three immediately transparent sentential actualities, one can after seven Cartesian steps arrive at being transparently presented with the actuality of α_1 in the seventh. The texts, of the three initial transparencies and of the seven steps, are in the object language. Written down sequentially, the ten sentences form a pattern called a proof. The statement that they are a proof, however, as well as the instructions which, if followed, will cause us to move through this Cartesian progression, is in the metalanguage. As in this case, so in all others. *All instructions are irretrievably in the metalanguage;* so are in substance all formation rules. In their context all logicians agree. That is the familiar sense in which this distribution, if I may so express myself, between object and metalanguage is completely noncontroversial. Yet it is anything but noncontroversial in its ontological context, particularly in the world of this discourse, where it is at the core of one of the fundamental gambits.

Each Cartesian step is, or, perhaps better, it culminates in, an awareness whose referent is transparent. Between any two such awarenesses, though, there may be and often are one or several others. Call these latter awarenesses for the moment the interstitial ones; the former, the illuminations. The occurrence of the interstitial awarenesses is indispensable for that of the illuminations. That is why in Section V they were called auxiliary.[†] This we remember. When carrying out an instruction, one exercises an acquired disposition in order to produce a series of illuminations interspersed with certain interstitial awarenesses. This we now clearly see. The context of both these comments, about what we remember and about what we now clearly see, is strictly causal. This, too, I trust, is clear. Where, then, is the ontological issue, where the controversy in which I undertook to uphold my side? We are finally ready for them.

Except for perceivings and imaginings one cannot in this world reach any referent, i.e., briefly, one cannot think without words (texts). In all these cases we think *by means of words.* In the interstitial awarenesses of a Cartesian progression, e.g., when carrying out instructions, we *think about words;* or, more precisely, we think either about

[†] In Section V Bergmann defines an 'instrumental awareness' as an awareness that (i) has a linguistic string as its referent, and that (ii) is causally necessary for the occurrence of some subsequent awareness; the former awareness is thus "instrumental" in bringing about the latter. It is not entirely clear here in Section VI that the concept of an 'interstitial awareness' is or is not identical with that of an instrumental awareness as define in Section V, although it seems so. In any case, *instrumental* awarenesses—and, if this is the same concept, *interstitial* awarenesses—are *not* auxiliary *acts*, as they are defined in Section V. Bergmann never, in fact, introduces a notion of 'auxiliary *awarenesses*'. See p. 208, and also p. 225, where he defines 'instrumental awareness'.—WH

texts or, jointly with texts, about some designs of a calculus, which is a sort of geometry, and some relations between those texts and these designs. The texts by means of which we think these thoughts about words (and designs) are those of the metalanguage. Keep this in mind and return to the Cartesian progression that ends in α_1. Brush aside what is unessential by supposing that of all the referents of its illuminations, which of course are all either facts or circumstances, none involves either words or the geometry of a calculus. If so, then none of the referents we think about in those interstitial awarenesses can literally be any feature, or aspect, or what have you, of the facts or circumstances that are the referents of the illuminations. Yet, clearly, the former are somehow, and not just causally, relevant to the latter. You recognize the dilemma; you are aware of the two extreme stands that have been taken. In my words rather than necessarily theirs, one side holds that the metalanguage is indeed about marks on paper and nothing else; the other side insists that there is no metalanguage, or at least none that makes any sense. I take my stand with neither extreme. All ontological discourse, including of course this one, is not merely about marks on paper but in its own peculiar way about the world; but its way is peculiar indeed; for, what it tries to say is strictly speaking unthinkable and therefore not literally sayable. The "reason" for this being so is that, while the discourse reaches out for what cannot but be somehow "rooted" in the world, it is yet not, upon the very terms of the discourse, "grounded" in the world and therefore, unlike everything we can literally think and say, does not, still upon those terms, "exist." The insight (not: 'illumination') which this "reason" provides is very major indeed; and the reason itself not only rich in detail but one of a web of others, jointly productive of other rewarding insights. Such discourse, I plead, deserves better than to be thrown away like a ladder, as if the literally unsayable were a besieged refuge rather than an enduring dialectical challenge. This plea I shall repeat once more, at the very end, when gathering several of the reasons that support it. My main purpose now has not been to plead for anything, but, rather, to argue that in this discourse, even though it may be found wanting in other respects, one can consistently speak of instructions that are literally unthinkable and therefore a fortiori literally unsayable without either adding to, or omitting anything from, what upon its terms exists.

60* Isn't a formation rule also an instruction? A verbal handle is there. E.g., when you have come upon a particular and a universal[(0)], *make* a diad out of the two; *make* next out of the latter and η_1 the complex; then, if you intend the latter's being an atomic fact, its (actually) being one will be transparent to you. Against the temptation in the "making" we are warned. If the two things are there, so eo ipso is their diad; whether or not, having first intended (grasped) them separately, we exercise the disposition to intend that diad; and so on. But, then, the referents of the Cartesian progression leading to α_1 are also there, whether or not anyone does intend them, and they are tautologies whether or not they are transparent to one who does. Thus, while a formation rule, not being about conscious states and how to produce them, is of course not an instruction, you may, if that clarifies your thought, think of it as "corresponding" to an instruction that is rather odd.

We are ready for the nuts and bolts. Which determinate or determinates can serve as selector(s) for our paradigm π_1? Equivalently, what must we be able to read off the ideal notation for it or them? The assurance that the two questions are equivalent we acquired in (A) and (B).

We must be able to read off, first, that $f_1(a_1)$ and $f_1(a_1) \vee g_1(b_1)$ are the Peano-null and its successor, respectively. We must be able to read off, second, what exactly the iteration step is that leads from the former to the latter and how "the same step" leads from any determinate (already established to be an element of π_1) to its successor. We must, third, specify the very notion of iteration, spell it out in the ideal notation, as it were, not just for π_1 but for any P-class, so that it realizes the new basic idea. Let me stop here and jot down five points we had better keep in mind while looking for such determinates.

(1) Notice that I saved ink by writing 'successor' instead of 'successor$_{\pi_1}$,' while on the other hand, since not every determinate needs to be an argument of every successor function, I added in the last paragraph the phrase in parentheses. (2) Notice, second, that the phrase "and so on" does not occur in the last paragraph, and that, therefore, it will not occur in the instructions how to decide whether a determinate is an element of π_1. (3) Since there are tuples in this world, there is also finite serial order. Thus we may not only in speaking about the (candidates for) selectors freely and without prejudice use 'first', 'second', 'third', and so on, but also use the corresponding subscripts when writing them down, not in the ideal notation, to be sure, where they may appear only as effective parts of marks, yet in the working approximations to that notation, with which for the usual psychological reasons we shall stay wherever they will do the job. (4) Since the succeeding in a P-class must be decidable, the iteration step must (I speak as before) be thrown upon the "form" shared by all 2-tuples whose first and second terms are an element and its successor, respec-

tively. (5) Remember two questions that arose at an earlier point (p. 275). Are there in the ideal language definientia corresponding to 'constituent' and to 'material'? If there are none, are there at least limited ones, for the first level and for each of the strata of the second level? Since at that point an artificial notation was expedient, I abbreviated 'constituent' and 'material' by '*CONST*' and '*MAT*' rather than '*const*' and '*mat*', in order to indicate that, since, whatever the answers, $CONST(\delta_1, \delta_2)$ and $MAT(\delta_1, \delta_2)$ are decidable, the two questions were, and then could be, left open. As then, so now. All we need for what follows is that δ-being-the-result-of-substituting-γ-for-β-in-α is decidable. This time we shall get along without artificial notation. Yet it should help the continuity to realize that, if it paid, I would be writing $SUBST\langle \alpha, \beta, \gamma, \delta \rangle$ rather than $subst(\alpha, \beta, \gamma, \delta)$, either with or without a stratification index. (Hence also the double quotes around 'form' in the last sentence of (4).)

Write τ_1 for the selector of π_1 we are looking for. Clearly, $f_1(a_1)$ must be a constituent of it. Does that also hold for $f_1(a_1) \vee g_1(b_1)$? Or, with a twist, if the latter were also a constituent of τ_1, would the two suffice? In other words, or very nearly so, could $\langle f_1(a_1), f_1(a_1) \vee g_1(b_1) \rangle$ serve as a selector of π_1? In this special case one may be able to guess successfully that, first, the third element is $(f_1(a_1) \vee g_1(b_1)) \vee g_1(b_1)$, and, second, each element but the first being a disjunction of $g_1(b_1)$ and another term, its successor is obtained by substituting it in itself for that other term. Guessing, however, will not do. Yet we have already come upon part of the answer. In the light of what has been said, the proper specification of iteration in this world is a decidable substitution. But, then, for substitution to produce an iteration, it must each time be the "same." Thus we must encode this feature in a way that also precludes all guessing. Then we shall have the rest of the answer.

Consider the 3-tuple $\langle \langle i_1, f_1(a_1) \rangle, \langle i_2, i_1 \vee g_1(b_1) \rangle, \langle i_1, i_2 \rangle \rangle$. If I ask you to try whether it can serve as τ_1, you will want to know what i_1 and i_2 abbreviate. As I use them in this working approximation to the ideal notation, i_1 and i_2 are two determinates which are, except for the ever-present need to avoid substitutional embarrassment, completely arbitrary. For π_1 two particulars, say, *c* and *d*, will do very well. Call these dummy variables the first and the second *iterator*. The notation picks them out without any need for guessing. i_1 is the first term in both the first and the third 2-tuple of the 3-tuple; i_2 is the first term in the second and the second term in the third. The instruction reads: the first element of the class is the determinate associated with i_1 in the first 2-tuple; every other element is obtained from the one preceding it by substituting the latter for i_1 in the determinate associated with i_2 in the second 2-tuple. We have our answer. This 3-tuple of 2-tuples will do. *Accordingly,* $\lambda\langle\langle i_1, f_1(a_1)\rangle, \langle i_2, i_1 \vee g_1(b_1)\rangle\langle i_1, i_2\rangle\rangle$ *is "an" ideal notation for* π_1. Since the identity of the selector varies with the choice of the iterators, there is of course a plurality of such; hence the indefinite article. But that causes no trouble.

An example will make us appreciate the indispensability of the iterators. Consider the two classes

$$\lambda\langle\langle i_1, f_1(a_1)\rangle, \langle i_1,(i_1 \vee f_1(a_1)) \vee f_1(a_1)\rangle, \langle i_1, i_2\rangle\rangle$$

and

$$\lambda\langle\langle i_1, f_1(a_1)\rangle, \langle i_2, (i_1 \vee i_1) \vee f_1(a_1)\rangle, \langle i_1, i_2\rangle\rangle.$$

To make sure that they are diverse, compute their third elements, which are, aside from the different bracketing, disjunctions of five and of seven terms, respectively. Yet either could, with equal plausibility, or implausibility, be "guessed" from $\langle f_1(a_1), (f_1(a_1) \vee f_1(a_1)) \vee f_1(a_1)\rangle$.

61* There are two iterative sequences of which 3, 9, is an initial segment. The usual mathematical notation, 3^n and $3^{2(n-1)}$ for the one and the other, eliminates all ambiguity. So in its more cumbersome way does our notation; we hardly need to check that. Yet the later Wittgenstein found here a reason for concern. His argument, if I am not mistaken, is that in order to understand the notation '3, 9, . . .' one must understand the instructions, but in order to understand the latter . . . . Presumably he sees a regress where I don't. The issue thus joined, if I may once more trot out the tired labels, is that between the views of meaning as reference, on the one hand, and as use, on the other. The author of the *Philosophical Investigations* embraces the latter; I follow the author of the *Tractatus* in embracing the former. Trying to support either the one or the other view explicitly in a brief digression, rather than, implicitly, by the whole of one's ontological discourse, would be merely silly. Yet it may be worth pointing out that *if,* taking the reference view, one holds that such "simple" words as 'green' and 'all' and the "simplest" sentences in which they occur do not involve us in a regress, he has *no* reason whatsoever to believe that we become so involved in the case of the notations and instructions here discussed, not just for P-classes and not just abstractly, yet with concrete support from the proposed ideal notation for our paradigm.

The third and last job of this assay of the secondary classes does not, like the first two, center on one issue. We merely have to organize as well as we can a group of more or less connected leftovers. Then we shall be ready for the tertiary classes.

Still with the abbreviation, is π_1 ever presented to us? If it weren't, we know, everything would collapse. Classes, we also know, unlike things, are never grasped. How, then, about a complex as "simple" as (17) $f_1(a_1) \in \pi_1$? I have no phenomenological scruple that would keep me from claiming, first, that (17) is sometimes presented to me, and, second, given the very special role of $f_1(a_1)$, which is so perspicuously reflected in the ideal notation, that on at least some of these occasions I am immediately presented with the actuality of (17). Nor would I know how to support the first class indirectly, except of course by everything that has been said so far about P-classes. Yet a comment that may at first strike you as carping should help. Some may be prepared to agree that we are sometimes presented with the class of all integers, and yet, in the case of π_1, strain at what they would probably call the strange and clumsy machinery of the $f_1(a_1)$ and $g_1(b_1)$, not to mention the claimed diversity of what is merely analytically equivalent, on which ultimately, or perhaps not so ultimately, everything here depends. To such a one I would say that with respect to the integers he borrows too trustingly from the language we are accustomed to, while with respect to π_1 his phenomenological sensitivity, however commendable as such, is of the wrong kind. His concern, that is, is more with the shades and the flavors which only the great writers know how to bring to our admiring attention, than with those on which it is the ontologist's business to concentrate, even, if necessary, at the expense of those others. But, then, which is the right and which is the wrong sensitivity? At this point, I agree, direct argument ends; hoping he in turn will agree that the proof of the pudding is in the eating, i.e., without metaphor, in one's ontological discourse as a whole.

Are we ever presented with the actuality of $Cl(\pi_1)$? You know that, as I must, I have also made this claim. Remember, then, that '$(\exists \alpha_1)$ $(\alpha_1 \in \pi_1)$' is the definiens for '$Cl(\pi_1)$'; remember also the second claim just made for (17), together with the relevant one among the existential tautologies first listed with those of sameness and diversity, and you will see that this claim, too, has already been made good.

Quickly and easily as the last result came, it involves a point that tests the kind of phenomenological sensitivity which (I believe) the ontologist must have. If the actuality of $Cl(\pi_1)$ were not immediately accessible, at will, if I may so put it, one would consistently have to say that when he takes himself to be presented with what, say, '$\alpha_1 \in \pi_1$' purports to stand for, he merely "borrows from language" (or from his memory), until he has moved through the Cartesian progression that ends in that transparency. The point plays a role in the very next paragraph; it will come to the fore as soon as we shall turn to the tertiary classes.

The four class "axioms" had already been singled out as immediately transparent actualities for all classes when the only ones we had studied in detail were the primary ones. The fourth was Cantor's axiom. Call the fifth, which had to be added for secondary classes, Peano's. As you see, I just dropped the double quotes around 'axiom'. If you agree that we do that whenever there is no danger of confusion with the axiomatists' use, we can say that the five class axioms are, or were claimed to be, immediately transparent for all classes. But we had better check how this claim stands up for the secondary ones. For the axiom of the unit class (I.), the finite-sum axiom (II.), and extensionality (III.), I said earlier and now repeat, the claim needs no support. That leaves the axioms of Cantor (IV.) and of Peano (V.), the latter of course only for secondary classes, i.e., in the case of the paradigm (p. 286), PV. But it has already been argued (p. 287) that *if* $Cl(\pi_1)$ is immediately transparent, which as we just saw it sometimes is, then so is PV; also immediately, since there is no deductive inference involved but, at most, an interstitial willing that causes one act of intending to be followed by a certain other. That leaves only IV. Are we ever transparently presented with π_1 being neither an element of itself nor material of any of its elements (and so on, as long as you wish)? If IV. is to hold up as axiom, then we ought to be. So I shall in three steps support the claim that sometimes we are. (1) No determinate of the first level is a class and no such determinate has as its material a class (and so on as long as you wish). Also, all elements of π_1 are of the first level. This is just a fragment of the hierarchy of which more in Section VII. (2) As one may read off the ideal notation, being even implicitly presented with π_1 is to be so presented with its first element and iteration step. This does not mean that on all such occasions one is even implicitly presented with all elements of π_1 being of the first level, and so on. If, however, on some such occasions, the intending having turned from implicit to explicit, $Cl(\pi_1)$ is transparently presented, then so is, either with or without an interstitial willing, π_1 being neither an element of itself nor material of one (and so on as long as you wish). (3) The sufficient indirect support for the claim in (2) comes from the fragment recited in (1).

62* As for π_1, so for any other P-class, π_2, that is homogeneous, not in Russell's sense, of course, but in the much broader one that all its elements belong either to the first level or to the same stratum of the second. The Peano null and the iteration step of π_2 may of course be very "complicated," just as it may take a Cartesian progression to identify the stratum; yet that makes no difference; what matters here is only the connection between the two transparencies, of (the specialization for π_2 of) IV. and of $Cl(\pi_2)$. But there are also nonhomogeneous secondary classes, such as, most simply, for any α_1, $\lambda\langle\langle i_1, \alpha_1\rangle$, $\langle i_2, i_1 = \alpha_1\rangle,\langle i_1, i_2\rangle\rangle$ and $\lambda\langle\langle i_1, \alpha_1\rangle,\langle i_2, i_1 \in \alpha_1\rangle,\langle i_1, i_2\rangle\rangle$. In all these cases, sufficient indirect support for the immediate transparency of IV. comes from another feature. When moving from an element of such a class to its successor, one also moves, as we shall see, from a lower to a higher stratum. But we need not tarry; making an exhaustive list of all subsorts of full-status classes is really a mathematician's job; ours is merely to make sure of those needed to "close" this ontology. Nor would anything be lost if for "complicated" secondary classes, we had for a while to borrow from language; which, as we shall soon see, is the rule of tertiary ones.

What, if any, is the "form" shared by all determinates τ_i selecting secondary classes, or, equivalently, such that '$\lambda\tau_i$' is a well-formed expression standing for a secondary class? The double quotes around 'form' remind us again that in the ideal language of this world there may be only the definientia for a plurality of such forms obtained by stratification. This, though, will not affect the little that needs to be said. Nor, of course, is it new to us that, whether form or forms, the formation rule, or canon, for the secondary classes is, like all canons, irretrievable. So let us inspect the candidates.

Starting from the 3-tuple $\langle\langle i_1, \alpha_1\rangle,\langle i_2, \alpha_2\rangle,\langle i_1, i_2\rangle\rangle$, what can one say about α_1 and α_2? For α_1 any determinate will do. α_2, however, must have i_1 as a constituent and we can conventionally write for it '$\alpha_2(i_1)$'. Thus all elements from the second on are complexes. From the third on they are obtained by substituting for i_1 in $\alpha_2(i_1)$ a complex. That leaves two alternatives. If α_1 is either a thing or a class, every primary occurrence of i_1 in α_2 must be as terms of a circumstance. If α_1 is itself a complex, such an occurrence may also be in (or, in the case of negation, as) the argument of a connective. This, I believe, is all, except that if you now reexamine the 3-tuple you will see that $\langle i_1, i_2\rangle$ is expendable. The two iterators are picked out without ambiguity as the first terms of the first and the second 2-tuple of the 3-tuple, respectively. Thus $\langle\langle i_1, \alpha_1\rangle,\langle i_2, \alpha_2(i_1)\rangle\rangle$ will do. The emphasis on the iterators, however welcome otherwise, that the addition of '$\langle i_1, i_2\rangle$' provides, is in an ideal notation out of place. The only advantage of writing thus redundantly, as I did, is, as we shall see, that it makes the notation continuous with that for tertiary classes.

There is one last matter to which we must attend. The sameness or diversity of any two classes of this world must be decidable. So we had better check for secondary classes. If one of the two classes is primary while the other is secondary, the decision is obvious. If they are both secondary, choose the same iterators, so that, most economically written, '$\lambda\langle\langle i_1, \alpha_1\rangle,\langle i_2, \alpha_2(i_1)\rangle\rangle$' and '$\lambda\langle\langle i_1, \beta_1\rangle,\langle i_2, \beta_2(i_1)\rangle\rangle$' stand for them. They will be the same if and only if α_1 and $\alpha_2(i_1)$ are the same as—not just analytically equivalent to—β_1 and $\beta_2(i_1)$, respectively. If these four determinates are all on the first level then, we know, this condition is decidable. If there are classes among their constituents then there will, as we shall proceed, a recursion be available. So we may safely turn to the tertiary classes.

The tertiary classes are of two kinds. One involves a new idea, not basic this time, yet sufficiently novel to account for a significant enlargement of what we are familiar with from the primary classes and to add to the old issues some new wrinkles, as is usual even with such limited novelty. The other kind combines this new idea with the basic one, already familiar from the secondary classes, of recursively controlled infinity. That virtually dictates both order of exposition and nomenclature. We shall first deal with the kind first mentioned, calling these classes the *nonrecursive tertiary* ones, or, briefly *n-classes*. And we shall deal next with the other kind, calling these classes the *recursive tertiary* ones, or, briefly, *r-classes*.

As 'enumerate' is used in this discourse, much more narrowly than in mathematics, the only classes whose elements one can enumerate are the finite ones. These classes, we called them primary, are *among* those of whom a mathematician would say that their conditions can be written down in closed form; i.e., in the language of this discourse, they are *among* those whose selectors are 2-tuples, $\langle b, B(b)\rangle$, such that $d \in \lambda\langle b, B(b)\rangle$ is actual if and only if $B^d(d)$ is. What makes them primary classes is that among their selectors are those we called enumerators; i.e., schematically they are the classes $\lambda\langle c, (c = a_1) \vee (c = a_2) \vee \ldots \vee (c = a_n)\rangle$. But, then, you notice it makes no sense to use 'among' the way it has just been used twice unless there are other such classes. So you ask which they are. In order to find them one merely has to remember the feature that most radically distinguishes the full-status classes of this world from those of all others, except the intuitionists'.

All full-status classes of this world are decidable. Thus, for $\langle b, B(b)\rangle$ to select a class, $B^d(d)$ must be decidable for every determinate d. It follows immediately that every primary occurrence of b in B must be a term of a circumstance.[†] This, though, is merely a necessary condi-

---

[†] Bergmann has penciled in here "How about $\lambda\langle b, f_1(b) \equiv f_1(b)\rangle$ or $\lambda\langle b, f_1(b) = f_1(b)\rangle$?"

tion. '$\lambda\langle b, B(b)\rangle$' will be well formed, or, equivalently, the collection determined by a decidable B will be a class if and only if the four general class axioms, I.–IV., are satisfied. The first three, as before, cause no difficulty. The touchstone, as from the history of axiomatic set theory one would expect, is IV. We have already come upon cases in which Cantor's axiom is, and upon others in which it is not, satisfied. So let us see what lead we can get from examining these again.

Take first (18) $\langle b, b \in b\rangle$ and (19) $\langle b, disj(b)\rangle$. In both cases the would-be class violates IV. Thus neither tuple selects an n-class. Yet there is a difference. If the argument made earlier for IV. being an "axiom" stands up, then in the case of (18) the violation is immediately transparent; (19), on the other hand, takes some doing. To speak less loosely although still with some shortcuts, what we did was the sort of thing mathematicians do when answering a question that is, in our strict sense, not necessarily decidable by following an instruction (p. 290). We "found" a counterexample and then made its being one transparent by substituting it for the definitional variable in the definiens of '$disj(x)$'. Similarly for complement formation. In the simplest case, for any determinate α_1, if '$\lambda\langle x,\sim(x = \alpha_1)\rangle$' were well formed, $\lambda\langle x,\sim(x = \alpha_1)\rangle \dotplus \{\alpha_1\}\rangle$ would by I. and II. be the class of all determinates and therefore, contrary to IV., an element of itself.

Take next (20) $\langle b, (\exists f_1)(\exists a_1)[b = \eta_1(f_1, a_1)]\rangle$.† The condition in (20) is the definiens of what we wrote as '$At_0(b)$', i.e., of the form all *members* of a certain subsort of atomic facts share with, say, $f_1(a_1)$. Remember now that there is only a finite number of such subsorts in this world, say, n; abbreviate accordingly '$At_1(x)$' '$At_2(x)$', . . . , '$At_{n-1}(x)$'; write with still another abbreviation '$At(x)$' for '$At_0(x) \vee At_1(x) \vee . . . \vee$ '$At_{n-1}(x)$'; consider (21) $\langle b, At(b)\rangle$, whose (unabbreviated) condition is (the definiens of) the form shared by all *members* of the collection of all atomic facts; and ask yourself whether (20) and (21) select n-classes. We "know" that they both do; for we "know" that the two conditions are decidable and that in both cases IV. is satisfied. The issue is how we come to "know" these things. Staying for the moment with the axiom, in the case of (20) its being satisfied may without any interstitial thought be immediately transparent to some. Those to whom it isn't can reach IV.1 easily, though not by instruction, by first intending (α_1) $(At_0(\alpha_1) \supset \sim Cl(\alpha_1))$, which is one of the immediately transparent tautologies of diversity. (For the other parts of IV., concerning the materials of atomic facts, see below, 64*. In the case of (21), finally, with its

---

†Bergmann's original formula was $\langle b, (\exists\alpha)(\exists\beta)[(b = \eta_1(\alpha, \beta)] \& \sim(\exists\gamma)(\delta)(\alpha = \langle\gamma, \delta\rangle \vee \beta = \langle\gamma, \delta\rangle)]\rangle$. Marginal notes indicate that it was to be altered as I have altered it.

longish disjunction, almost everyone will, at least at the beginning, need some interstitial Cartesian progression.

Suppose that '$B(x)$' is both well formed and decidable for every determinate. If so, is there a decidable feature such that $\langle x, B(x) \rangle$ selects an n-class of this world, or equivalently, such that '$\lambda\langle x, B(x) \rangle$' is well formed, if and only if the would-be selector actually has this feature? If one assumes that, concisely speaking, every '$B(x)$' of an n-class is (the definiens of) a form, then it is not hard to show that there is such a feature or criterion. Of this more in the next Section. But, then, *how about the assumption?* I do not know how to prove it. On the other hand, though, I cannot even imagine what any other '$B(x)$' would be like. Thus it seems safe to proceed, as in the next Section I shall, under this assumption; also because, while the result we shall reach with it is broader than the one that can be obtained without it, even the latter will suffice to secure what is here our main concern, namely, the stratification of all forms. That makes the search for, or, as I would rather expect, the exclusion of those other recondite n-classes another thing we can safely leave to the mathematicians.

63* The following comments on what has been said in the last paragraphs have been placed here because I did not want to interrupt the line of thought. (a) Since all definitions and therefore all definienda are outside of the ideal language, I do not hesitate to make the artificial notation for the dummy variable in them more suggestive by using 'x', the mark which is in our minds so strongly associated with the notion of a regular variable. But recall, for the phenomenological import of some definitions, what has been said in Section V. (b) Notice, in connection with '$At(x)$', how structurally important it is that this world, unlike Russell's, is one in which certain alternatives are finite. Here it is of course the number of types, including relational ones; in the next to the last of these comments it will be the number of connectives. (c) No doubt you realized why, where the word was italicized above, I used 'member'. Using 'element' would have prejudged the issue, viz., whether the candidate does or does not select an n-class, as e.g., $\langle b, At_0(b) \rangle$ and $\langle b, disj(b) \rangle$, respectively. You also understand that in either case one may be, and sometimes is, presented with the mode of, e.g., $At_0(\alpha_1)$ and $disj(\alpha_1)$ for any α_1. Why then (you may wonder again) keep worrying whether there are the corresponding classes? The crunch comes (I repeat) when the form considered can only be defined recursively, as, e.g., being-molecular-I ('Mol'). For in all these cases, unless the corresponding r-classes (and the n-classes on which we shall see they are built) were there, there would not be the required definientia in the world, and thus nothing for which, e.g.,

'$Mol(\alpha_1)$' could stand. (d) Notice that some very broad categories are easily defined without recursion. "$At(x) \lor (\exists\alpha_1)(x = \sim\alpha_1) \lor (\exists\alpha_1)(\exists\alpha_1) (x = (\alpha_1 \lor \alpha_2) \lor x = (\alpha_1 \& \alpha_2) \lor \ldots) \lor (\exists\alpha_1)(x = \wedge\alpha_1 \lor x = \lor \alpha_1)$, for instance, and, even more obviously, '$(\exists\alpha_1)(\exists\alpha_2)[(x = (\alpha_1,\alpha_2) \lor x = (\alpha_1 \in \alpha_2) \lor x = (\alpha_1 M\alpha_2)]$' will serve for '$Fact(x)$' and '$Circumstance(x)$' on either level and, if on the second, in any stratum. The finite disjunction marked by the dots runs of course over the binary connectives. (e) If, finally, you want to make sure that there are '$B(x)$' such that '$\lambda\langle x, B(x)\rangle$' is ill formed on the sole ground that the would-be class is not decidable, consider the otherwise suitable '$\lambda\langle x, (\exists y)[(y = x) \& gr(y)],$[†] where '$gr$' stands for the universal green.

Is there an n-class corresponding to particularity, i.e., a class such that a determinate is one of its elements if and only if it is a particular? Are there such classes for universality[(0)], universality[(0,0)], and so on, one for each of the ultimate sorts, whose number in this world, we know, is finite? Since we grasp things and since no thing is a class, it does not look as if we shall have to worry about either decidability or a threat from the Cantor axiom. The one thing needful is to produce for each ultimate sort an appropriate selector.

Suppose that there are in our world only four ultimate sorts, particularity and the universalities associated with the superscripts (0), (0,0), ((0)). Define (22) '$\overline{Part}(x)$', (23) '$\overline{Univ}^{(0)}(x)$', (24)'$\overline{Univ}^{(0,0)}(x)$', (25) '$\overline{Univ}^{((0))}(x)$' in this order by

(22a) $(\exists\alpha_1)(\exists\alpha_2)(\exists\alpha_3)\{(x = \alpha_1) \& [\eta_1(\alpha_3,\langle\alpha_2, \alpha_1\rangle) \lor \sim\eta_1(\alpha_3,\langle\alpha_2,\alpha_1\rangle)]\}$,

(23a) $(\exists\beta_1)(\exists\beta_2)\{(x = \beta_1) \& \overline{Part}(\beta_2) \& [\eta_1(\beta_1, \beta_2) \lor \sim\eta_1(\beta_1,\beta_2)]\}$,

(24a) $\underline{(\exists\gamma_1)(\exists\gamma_2)(\exists\gamma_3)\{(x = \gamma_1)}$
$\& \quad \overline{Part}(\gamma_2) \quad \& \quad \overline{Part}(\gamma_3) \quad \& \quad [\eta_1(\gamma_1,\langle\gamma_2,\gamma_3\rangle) \lor \sim\eta_1(\gamma_1, \quad \langle\gamma_2,\gamma_3\rangle)]\}$,

(25a) $(\exists\delta_1)(\exists\delta_2)\{(x = \delta_1) \& \overline{Univ}^{(0)}(\delta_2) \& [\eta_2(\delta_1,\delta_2) \lor \sim\eta_2 (\delta_1,\delta_2)]\}$.

The four selectors we must produce are $\underline{(22b)}$ $\langle b, \overline{Part}(b)\rangle$, (23b) $\langle b, \overline{Univ}^{(0)}(b)\rangle$, (24b) $\langle b, \overline{Univ}^{(0,0)}(b)\rangle$, (25b) $\langle b, \overline{Univ}^{((0))}(b)\rangle$; with, of course, the abbreviations (22)–(25) replaced by their definientia (22a)–(25a). The following four comments, more often suggestively concise than strictly literal, will show why this is so and what it involves.

(1) The reason for putting the appropriate tautological disjunctions into the brackets of (22a)–(25a) is, of course, that what matters is not which of the disjunction terms is actual but that they are both well formed. (2) The conjunction terms '$x = \alpha_1$', '$x = \beta_1$', and so on are indispensable because the '$B^d(d)$' of a closed selector must be well-

---

[†] Bergmann has penciled in "or why not more simply '$\lambda\langle x, gr(x)\rangle$'?"

formed for every 'd'. The extra baggage we are thus forced to carry is not heavy. (3) Under the supposition made, we managed in (22a)–(25a) with functions and variables only. What made that possible is the plurality of exemplifications. But the number and, within limits, the kinds of ultimate sorts are a contingent feature of a world. So you will ask whether we could thus manage in all worlds. I shall answer in the next digression. (4) Ultimate sorts being neither determinates nor even functions but merely entities, there is nowhere in this discourse an artificial mark, either ideal or of convenience, for any of them. *Absentia fulgent*. On the side of the intention, we know, the feature thus signaled is that each thing is a Two-in-One of its item and its ultimate sort, while, on the side of the act, we can transparently think (grasp) a thing as a Two-in-One yet not literally say what such texts as "this is a particular" purport to express. About the systematic import of this feature more toward the very end of this discourse. For the moment, the bar in the abbreviations (22)–(25) will safeguard the distinction between what we can and what we can't literally think.

At one later point these special classes will be needed. But they also have a feature of considerable intrinsic interest. How many universals[0] are there? We have no very good reason for either believing or not believing that their number is finite. Yet it is commonsensical and in this dialectical context respectable to assume that the number of those we have so far encountered is finite, say, n. Then there is the primary class $\lambda\langle c, (c = f_1) \vee (c = f_2) \vee \ldots \vee (c = f_n)\rangle$. Call it $C^{(0)}$ and ask yourself whether $C^{(0)} = \lambda\langle b, \overline{Univ}^{(0)}(b)\rangle$ is actual or potential. Obviously we can't decide. Or, to say the same thing differently, the number of elements of the special class remains forever indefinite. As for this ultimate sort, so for all others. Yet the sameness or diversity of any two determinates of this world is supposed to be decidable. Shall we then give up or shall we tolerate this single "exception from a principle"? I suggest that we tolerate it, if only because, if I may so express myself, it spotlights the extraordinary impact of even the indefinite, which, for all we know, may or may not be finite. As for the indefinite, so for the infinite. Its impact, even if recursively controlled, is even more drastic. Of this in the next Section.

64* (a) For an anticipatory reference to $C^{(0)}$ as perhaps the most plausible paradigm for the point just made see p. 243. (b) With these special classes, such complexes as $(\alpha_1)(\overline{Part}(\alpha_1) \supset \sim Cl(d_1))$ become literally thinkable and, if explicitly intended, immediately transparent, with or without some interstitial thoughts; which in turn opens the way to the mode of IV.1; we need not, I think, dwell on the details. Again, with respect to the other part of IV., it will suffice if I now answer a question deliberately left open. It is immediately transparent that a_1 and f_1 are the only materials of $f_1(a_1)$ and that they in turn have no materials. Thus the actuality of IV.2 for $\lambda\langle b, At_0(b)\rangle$ become transparent; and so on, and so on. (c) Can one in every world get along with only functions and variables in the selectors for its special classes? The answer, also postponed (p. 303), is No. The obvious counterexample is a world in which particularity and universality[0] are the only ultimate sorts. In this case one needs at least one thing that will enter as a constituent—and not just, upon our assay of quantification, as a target—into the definientia. With f_1 available, for instance, define '$\overline{Part}(x)$' by $(\exists\alpha_1)(\alpha_1 = x)$ & $[\eta_1(f_1, a_1) \vee \sim \eta_1(f_1, a_1)]$ and then '$\overline{Univ}^{(0)}(x)$' as in (23a). The contextualist may think that this grants the core of his thesis. I disagree. The core of anticontextualism, not at all affected by the situation, is that, when presented with a single thing, one can "know" its ultimate sort. In this discourse, such "knowing" is called a grasping. That, though, is a matter of words. (d) Since the number of ultimate sorts is finite, there is the disjunction needed for the selector of the *class of all things*. This is the special class we shall need later on.

Is there a class such that a determinate is an element of it if and only if it is either (1) an atomic fact, or (2) a disjunction of (two) atomic facts, or (3) a disjunction of an atomic fact and a disjunction of (two) atomic facts, *and so on*? That the collection of all atomic facts is an n-class, we have, I take it, established. The ideal notation for it is '$\lambda\langle b, At(b)\rangle$'; but it will save breath and ink if we abbreviate this by 'C_1', and, without prejudice, write 'C' for the class into whose existence we inquire. If there is such a class, then, plausibly, we shall arrive at a selector for it by starting from 'C_1', which is the class of all determinates mentioned above under (1), in a position analogous to that of the Peano-null in P-classes, proceeding from it by the analogue of a (secondary) P-step to C_2, i.e., the class of all determinates mentioned above under (2), then by the "same" step to C_3, and so on. In other words, if there is the class C purports to stand for, it is of the sort I called *r-classes*. Again, if there is that class, it is as "simple" as any of this sort is likely to be and therefore well suited to serve as our third paradigm. How, then, is one to argue that there is this class? Or, as we speak, how shall we ground it? In the general case, the thing to do first is (a) to make sure that the analogue of the Peano-null is an n-class. The next thing is (b) to identify the iteration step and make sure that it is decidable as well as, for every i, the same from C_i to C_{i+1}. Thirdly, we must (c) secure the recursive decidability of C by establishing the analogues of the Peano axioms. Fourth and finally, we must (d) convince ourselves that the candidate for class status does not violate Cantor's axiom. In the case of the paradigm, we know already that (a) is satisfied; to (b) and (c) I shall presently attend; about (d) something will be said in the first, and more general, of two general comments I should like to make first.

First. Unlike the primary and secondary classes, the tertiary ones of the r-sort are so "complicated" that for them borrowing from language becomes the rule rather than the exception. This does not mean that for them our limited task becomes proportionately more difficult and lengthy. It does mean that as a rule one cannot gain access to the transparencies of Cantor and Peano which one must reach in order to be really presented with the class in question, without first going through some interstitial chains, each starting from some tautologies of sameness and diversity and such that the intention of its last link is either itself one of the required transparencies or a partial cause of the latter becoming immediately transparent in a next thought. All this, though, is merely more of what we are already familiar with. Thus, since, as I have limited the task throughout this discourse, it is not to attend to every detail, either phenomenological or of the sort better left to mathematicians, I shall, while of course pointing out the new, discuss only selectively or even pass in silence what is merely more of the same. The next of these two comments calls attention to a new twist. But when then turning to the job of grounding the paradigm I shall attend to (b), select PIII and PV for discussion under (c), and pass in silence what has to be done under (d).

Second. Supposing that the paradigm can be grounded, distinguish the class C from the sequence, call it C^*, conventionally written C_1, C_2, C_3, ... C^* is a Peano sequence whose members are classes, i.e., there is a successor function such that, again conventionally written, $C_2 = C_1'$, $C_3 = C_2'$, and so on. C, on the other hand, is the class of all d such that $d \in C_1$, or $d \in C_2$, and so on. Conventionally written, C is thus $\cup \ C_i$, or $\Sigma \ C_i$, i.e., as one says, the (class-theoretical) sum of all the classes which are members of C^*. If you now turn back to II. on p. 276, you will see how it all hangs together. By virtue of II., there are in this world all finite class-theoretical sums; the only infinite ones, however, are our r-classes, i.e., those, such as C, where the infinity is recursively controlled, as in C^*. That is why, in order to secure the recursive feature, one must establish Peano's axioms for C^*. To see how this distinction between the sum and the sequence may affect matters, suppose that one deals, as often one must, with an r-class, D, such that by virtue of its iteration step D_i is a proper part of $D_{i+1}(D_1 \subset D_2 \subset D_3 \subset \ . \ . \ .)$. In such cases, having established that, say, $d \in D_n$, one cannot conclude that it takes n steps, but merely that it takes at most n steps to reach d from D_1. Thus, if one looks for the often needed one-one correspondence that "stratifies" the elements of D, one has to shift to the sequence E^* such that $E_n = D_n \cdot \overline{D_{n-1}}$. (The last observation also illustrates the sort of thing which as rule I shall pass in silence.)

Now for the selective grounding of C. Writing Roman capitals for classes, the iteration step becomes, in the conventional notation, (26a) $\gamma_1 \in X_1' \equiv (\exists\alpha_1)(\exists\beta_1)[(\alpha_1 \in C_1) \,\&\, (\beta_1 \in X_1) \,\&\, (\gamma_1 = . \,\alpha_1 \vee \beta_1)]$; with '$C_1$', as above, for the n-class of all atomic facts. Obviously nothing will be lost by so limiting this successor function that every element, rather than merely some, of each of its arguments is a complex. Equally obviously, if X_1 is decidable, so is X_1', and conversely. To establish PIII, add (26b) $\gamma_1 \in Y_1' \equiv (\exists\alpha_1)(\exists\beta_1)[(\alpha_1 \in C_1) \,\&\, (\beta_1 \in Y_1) \,\&\, (\gamma_1 = \alpha_1 \vee \beta_1)]$ and suppose $X_1' = Y_1'$. If there were an element δ_1 of X_1 but not of Y_1, $\delta_1 \vee \delta_2$ would be an element of X_1' but not of Y_1' for every atomic fact δ_2, and so on; all of this being matters of decidable form. Thus PIII is established. As for it, so, as before, for PI, PII, PIV. PV, finally, again as before, or, more accurately, its specialization for C, must be added to our stock of immediately transparent actualities or "axioms." This, though, is merely what structurally one would expect; so I have no difficulty in doing just that; nor, I hope, will you.

We are ready for the more general case. Write either 'A' or '$\lambda\sigma$' for the r-class considered; thus making 'σ' an abbreviation for a selector of A. Write either A^* or $A_1, A_2, A_3, \ldots$ for the sequence that goes with A. The best way to find σ is again to inquire into an ideal notation for it. Each of the A_i being an n-class, write for them '$\lambda\langle i_1, A_{1c}(i_1)\rangle$', '$\lambda\langle i_2, A_{2c}(i_2)\rangle$', '$\lambda\langle i_2, A_{3c}(i_2)\rangle$', and so on. The second subscript, 'c', as, e.g., in '$A_{3c}(i_2)$', marks the second term, i.e., the one corresponding to the *c*ondition of, e.g., A_3, in a selector of it. To judge by what we have learned about the selectors of P-classes, one would expect, *positively*, that 'σ' contains two expressions for, or closely related to, A_1 and A_2, respectively, such that jointly they encode without ambiguity the instructions for specifying (a) the Peano-null, which is of course A_1 itself, as well as (b) the iteration step; just as, *negatively*, with this step thus specified, one would not expect to find in 'σ' expressions for A_3 and the classes following it in A^*. The role of the second iterator, i_2, is I trust already obvious. If it isn't, consider in the next paragraph the comment about the first, i_1, which applies to both.

Ad (a). If it were only a matter of encoding (a), including as a constituent into 'σ' the expression abbreviated by (27) '$\langle i_1, A_{1c}(i_1)\rangle$' would do. The '$\lambda$' to be put in front of it is easily absorbed into the instruction. 'i_1', on the other hand, is indispensable. For how would we without it know which determinate among the constituents of A_{1c} is the one whose place is in the conventional notation for conditions marked by a variable? If it were only a matter of encoding (a), I said. When trying also to encode (b), one soon discovers that because of certain complications (27) will in fact not do. The complications are the familiar ones, connected with "substitution," which, after having "systematized" them in Section IV, I decided to ignore wherever one can. But we are at a point where one can't. So we must find out how they come in and what has to be done about them.

Ad (b). The iteration step is always the "same". Let us explore how this feature can be encoded by inquiring whether

(28) $\langle\langle i_1, At(i_1)\rangle, \langle i_2, (\exists\alpha_1)(\exists\beta_1)[S(\alpha_1) \,\&\, At(\beta_1) \,\&\, (i_2 = \alpha \vee \beta)]\rangle\rangle$

could serve as a selector for our paradigm C. Write for the second term of the second 2-tuple '$B(i_2)$'. The tuple itself, $\langle i_2, B(i_2)\rangle$, is of course not supposed to be a selector of C_2, but, rather, a matrix from which the selectors for C_2, C_3, and so on can be obtained by iteration. To see how that is made possible by the newcomer, "S", examine the following provisional instruction: $A_{2c}(i_2)$ is obtained by substituting "A_{1c}" (i.e., in the paradigm, "At") for S in $B(i_2)$; $A_{3c}(i_2)$ is obtained by substituting "A_{2c}" for "S" in $B(i_2)$, and so on. The formula is inadequate in two respects, (i) and (ii), below. Notice, though, that if these inadequacies can be amended, it will adequately reflect the sameness of the iteration step. Notice, too, the peculiarity which I have marked by double quotes; for it will turn out, not surprisingly, to be the major source of the inadequacies. '$At(i_1)$', '$At(\beta_1)$', '$A_{2c}(i_2)$', and so on all abbreviate ideal-language expressions, each of which does stand for a complex. When writing "At", "A_{2c}", however, I merely took advantage of a conventional parsing whose results, since they do not stand for anything in this world, cannot be either expressions of its ideal language or abbreviations of such. As for these two, so for '$S(\alpha_1)$' and "S". The former abbreviates what stands for something, the latter does not. The only difference is that we have so far left open what the former stands for. If we now tackle the inadequacies, we shall soon discover what it may usefully be made to stand for.

i. Suppose that '$S(\alpha_1)$' abbreviates $\alpha_1 = a$, where a is a particular so chosen that it avoids any obvious substitution embarrassment but otherwise arbitrary. Since the occurrence of 'α_1' in '$S(\alpha_1)$' of (28) is closed, the flawed formula may plausibly be taken to enjoin us, not to *substitute* anything for anything, but, rather, to *replace* '$\alpha_1 = a$', in the first step by '$A_{1c}(\alpha_1)$', in the second step by '$A_{2c}(\alpha_1)$', and so on. For, replacing, as we speak in this discourse, is literally something done to marks on paper only. But we also remember that, as we here speak, every statement in which 'replacing' occurs can be rephrased in terms of substitutions and variants, which are both (also) ontological notions. Why then now fret about this verbal flaw? I introduced it deliberately into the provisional formula because clearing it up confronts us with the familiar complications. *Every time one replaces* 'S(α_1)' *one must take care that no scope is affected.* This I take to be obvious. If, however, you cast about for a reason, consider that if one didn't, there would be no sense, or at least none I can think of, in which the iteration steps would all be the "same." In the paradigm, although not of course in general, nothing will happen in the first step; but from the second step on one must, even in the paradigm, amend the inadequate instruction to the effect that, in the Kth step, 'S(α_1)' is replaced, not by '$A_{KC}(\alpha_1)$' but, rather, by an appropriate variant of it, i.e., as we write, by an '$A_{KC}^{\alpha 1}(\alpha_1)$', such that $\bigwedge\langle i_2, A_{KC}^{\alpha 1}(i_2)\rangle = \bigwedge\langle \alpha_1, A_{KC}^{\alpha 1}(\alpha_1)\rangle$. This is the first amendment.

ii. Since "S" is ontologically opaque, we must design a bit of machinery that isn't, which can do its job of marking the place(s) of the "substitution(s)." The easy solution, already anticipated, is to choose a complex as simple as possible and, in particular, without quantification, of which α_1 is a constituent but otherwise arbitrary, such as $\alpha_1 = a$ above, with the instruction that in each iteration step, say, in the $(k+1)^{th}$, every occurrence in '$B_2(i_2)$' of either '$i_2 = a$' or '$\alpha_1 = a$' or '$\alpha_1 = a$', and so on, is to be replaced by appropriate variants, '$A_{KC}^{\alpha 2}(i_2)$', '$A_{KC}^{\alpha 1}(\alpha_1)$', '$A_{KC}^{\alpha 2}(\alpha_2)$', and so on. This in the more general case. The $B_2(i_2)$' of our paradigm, as written out in (28), where "S" occurs once in a context of the type '($\exists\alpha_1$) (. . . S(α_1) . . .)', is merely a special case. This is the second amendment. We need not, I think, bother with the amended formula. So let us see whether we can find a selector, or, what amounts to the same, the ideal notation for it.

The thing to try, it would seem, after having chosen a suitable auxiliary complex, is to fit it into a larger one, as suggested by (28), in a manner that marks it without ambiguity and enables it to the job. Try then,

$$(29) \ \langle\langle i_1, S(i_1), A_{1c}(i_1)\rangle,\langle i_2, B_2(i_2), \text{``S''}\rangle\rangle;$$

where, with the same choice of auxiliary complex as above, '$S_1(i_1)$' stands for '$i_1 = a$'; and the double quotes are now merely a harmless abbreviatory notation, herewith agreed upon, to signal at least one occurrence from among '$S(i_2)$', '$S(\alpha_1)$', '$S(\alpha_2)$', and so on, as detailed above under (b). (29) is of course still an abbreviation. Yet one can read off it that what it abbreviates can serve as 'σ'. $S(i_1)$ is the second term of the 3-tuple; that picks it out. Its constituent i_1 marks the place that must be mentioned in the instructions. Comparison with the alternative selectors proposed for P-classes will make all this even clearer. But again, as in their case, I find the mildly redundant

$$(30) \; \langle\langle S(i_1),\, A_{1c}(i_1)\rangle,\langle i_2,\, B_2(i_2,\, \text{``}S\text{''})\rangle,\langle i_1,\, i_2\rangle\rangle$$

more suggestive than (29), which probably is the most economical. Nor is such "choice" of selectors (and notations) an embarrassment of riches. To be sure, alternative selectors (and notations) correspond to instructions with alternative texts. Yet each pair, selector plus instruction, selects the same class. Thus the "choice" is vacuous and therefore, far from being perplexing, illuminates the characteristic nature of classes.

Since the decidability of the condition of a would-be n-class is not itself a matter of decidable form, there is of course no form shared by all those and only those 3-tuples (30) which are selectors of r-classes. All one can do, therefore, is to single out among the several necessary conditions, all more or less obvious, the two which perhaps deserve mention. (a) "S" must occur in B_2 as above specified; for, if it didn't, there wouldn't be an iteration step. (b) It must be decidable for every determinate whether or not it can by this step be reached from other determinates. I.e., more briefly, the iteration step must be decidable. In our paradigm, (b) requires that we be able to decide, as of course we are, whether or not a determinate is a disjunction. Nor can I think of any candidate for the status of a recursive form-class whose iteration step would not be decidable. Thus, given the limits of our concern, we shall never have to worry about (b) being satisfied. (A *form-class*, as I shall henceforth call it in order to save words, is a class such that its elements are all those and only those determinates which share a certain form, either broad (p. 274) or narrow, either recursive or nonrecursive, as the case may be. Form-classes, thus, just to practice the new term, by the self-imposed limits just mentioned, are the only r-classes we shall be concerned with in what follows.)

If you noticed that in the last few pages I spoke twice of the schema (30) as the "more general" case, you probably wondered what was the really or "completely general" one. I am now ready to put this card on the table, except that it will help if we first address ourselves, although again only for the "more general" case, to another issue, already familiar from the first two sorts of classes but requiring closer attention in the case of the tertiary ones. The sameness or diversity of any two classes must in this world be decidable. As long as the classes admitted to full ontological status are all either primary or secondary, this requirement, we know, is fulfilled. But we do not yet know what becomes of it if the tertiary classes are added. That is the issue.

Let A be an r-class; $A_1, A_2, A_3, \ldots$, the sequence associated with it. Suppose that A_1 is an n-class; this we have so far taken for granted; presently we shall see that it makes the difference between the merely "more" and the "completely" general. But we see already that if A_1 is an n-class as well as, by the limitation I shall no longer mention, a form-class, so are all members of A^*. The decidability of the (actual) diversity of each of these r-classes, such as, e.g., A, and of each of these n-classes, such as, e.g., A_1, on the one side, from each finite class and from each P-class, on the other side, we may safely take for granted. That leaves the three cases of (a) two-n-classes, (b) an n-class and an r-class, and (c) two r-classes. In order to handle them with a minimum of symbols, let B be another r-class such that all the members B_i of B^* are n-classes.

(a) How can we reach the mode of (31) $A_1 = B_1$? A_1 and B_1 being both nonrecursive form-classes, (31) will be actual if and only if the respective form(s) are one and not two. And we have long known how to decide whether or not they are by building according to obvious instructions a Cartesian chain that starts from the appropriate tautologies of sameness and diversity. (b) Consider next (32) $A_1 = B$. A_1 being nonrecursive, all its elements are of the same nonrecursive form. The elements of B, on the other hand, are distributed into an infinite number of nonrecursive form-classes, such that all the elements of each of them, but not all the elements of any two of them, are of the same nonrecursive form. Thus A_1 could only be the same as either a single B_K, or a single B_K' such that $B_K' \subset B_K$, or the finite class-theoretical sum of several such B_K and/or B_K'. As for A_1 and B, so for any n- and r-class, respectively. (32) is in all cases decidably potential.

(c) For (33) $A = B$ things are a bit more complicated. So I shall first introduce a few symbols, in the mathematical style and of course without any ontological import; then outline the overall strategy and merely indicate the main ideas. Write 'I' and 'J' for the iteration steps of A and B, respectively; and accordingly, '$I^K A$' for 'A_K', '$J^K B_1$' for 'B_K'. That $A_1 = B_1$ and $I = J$, both decidable, are jointly a sufficient condition for (33) being actual is obvious. If one hopes to show that this condition is also necessary, in which case (33) would be decidable, one must examine the alternatives (c1) $A_1 = B_1, I = J$; (c2) $A_1 \neq B_1, I \neq J$; (c3) $A_1 \neq B_1, I \neq J$, and show that for each of them (33) is potential. This is the overall strategy. The gist of the execution can be presented by examining (c1). Let us first get rid of what is unessential by supposing that both A and B are cumulative, i.e., that each member of each of the sequences A^* and B^* is a subclass of its successor in this sequence (e.g., $A_1 \subset A_2 \subset A_3 \subset \ldots$). Let next b_1 be an element of B_1 but not of A_1, i.e., in the usual notation, $b \in B_1 \cdot \overline{A}_1$. (If there is no such b_1, there is a corresponding a_1; otherwise $A_1 = B_1$. And, again, nothing essential will be lost if we suppose that (34) $B_1 = A_1 \dotplus B_1 \cdot \overline{A}_1$.) If (33) is to be actual, there must be a $K_1 \geq 2$ such that $b_1 \in I^{K_i} A_1$. As for b_1, so for every $b_i \in B_1 \cdot \overline{A}_1$. Moreover, all these b_i have an upper limit and hence also a lowest upper limit, say, $\overline{K}$; otherwise the n-class $B_1 \cdot \overline{A}_1$, which is also a form-class, would be an r-class, which has already been excluded under (b). That makes, in view of (34), $\overline{K}$ the smallest integer such that (35) $B_1 \subseteq I^{\overline{K}} A_1$. Call now, with still another ontologically noncommital notation, 'ϕ_1' and 'ϕ_2' the forms shared by all the elements of A_1 and of $B_1 \cdot \overline{A}_1$, respectively, and notice that, since the two classes have no element in common, there is no determinate that shares them both. Hence, as usual, by the tautologies of sameness and diversity, there is no determinate that could be reached by applying $\overline{K}$ times the same iteration step, starting either from determinates at least one of which is of the form ϕ_2, or, alternatively, from determinates which are all of the form ϕ_1. Yet, by (35), there is such a determinate. Upon (c1), therefore, (33) is potential. As for (c1), so mutatis mutandis for (c2) and (c3). Thus we arrive at the following instructions: In order to decide (33), decide $A_1 = B_1$ and $I = J$, both of which we already know to be decidable; (33) will be actual if and only if they are both actual.

65* The way elementary arithmetic has been used in (c1) is very familiar. But is it legitimate in this unfamiliar context? In case you want that argued, I offer three comments. (1) The proof in (c1) is, as one says, in the metalanguage; so, like all instructions, are the instructions for deciding (33) which it yields. (2) Yet it is worth remembering on this occasion that, once PI–PV are secured, as I take it they are, for the classes in (c1), one can in principle use elementary arithmetic in arguing about them in the object language. "In principle" here, as often elsewhere, merely means that we have left to the mathematicians the sweat and the tears of executing what is but a variant of the long familiar. (3) But notice, too, that if the "instructions," instead of being the ones actually arrived at, required the determination, in either the object or the metalanguage, of the integer $\overline{K}$, they would not, or at least not on the grounds here presented, yield a decision procedure for (33), and thus, as we here speak, not be instructions.

Let R_1' be an r-class of the "more general" sort just considered; suppose that there is an iteration step, decidable, as all such steps are, and leading from R_1' successively to R_2', R_3', R_4', and so on; and consider the would-be class, call it R_2, which is conventionally written $\cup R_i{}^1$, or, also, $R_1^1 + R_2^1 + R_3^1 + \ldots$. In axiomatic set theory, if R_1^1 is a class (set), so of course is R^2. We, however, must make up our mind. Shall we admit R^2 among the (full-status) classes of this world? Since both R_1^1 and the iteration step are decidable, I do not see how we could consistently refuse. We must admit R^2. Nor is there anything to keep us from continuing this game. Just as R_1^1 may be the Peano-null (R_1^1) of an R^2, so R^2 may be the Peano-null (R_1^2) of an R^3; and so on. The result is a "fractionation" of the r-classes. An r-class is an r_1-class if and only if its Peano-null is an n-class; it is an r_2-class if and only if its Peano-null is an r_1-class; and so on. *Roughly*, at least, this is the "completely general" case. Presently I shall try to deepen our understanding of it by offering as an example one particularly important r_2-class, which will be needed in the next Section. First, though, for three comments. (A) will also prepare us for the example. (B) will indicate how to close a line of thought that the fractionation reopens. In (C) I shall review and relate some technical terms that have already been introduced into this discourse in order to increase their usefulness in the rest of it.

A. I just said "roughly" because there is still another multiplicity due to there being n-classes such that r-classes are among the constituents of their selectors. In itself this is but another detail which, within the limits we have set ourselves, we can safely ignore. As it happens, though, we shall need two sorts of such form-classes, one in the example, the other in the next section. So I now introduce these two in order to show how such classes are arrived at. Let 'X_1' stand for an r-class such that among its elements there are at least two, say, α_1 and α_2, for which '$\vee \langle \alpha_1, \alpha_2 \rangle$' and '$\wedge \langle \alpha_1, \alpha_2 \rangle$' are well-formed. Then '$\lambda \langle i_1, (\exists \beta_1)$ $(\exists \beta_2)[(\beta_1 \in X_1)\ \&\ (\beta_2 \in X_1)(i_1 =. \vee \langle \beta_1, \beta_2 \rangle \vee \wedge \langle \beta_1, \beta_2 \rangle)]$' or, with a further abbreviation, 'QX_1' stands for an n-class of this sort. If, for instance, M^1 is the class of all things and of all atomic and molecular facts of the nucleus (p. 270), which not surprisingly, we shall see, is an r-class, then QM_*^1 is the n-class whose elements are all the q-facts produced by a single quantification whose scope is one of those atomic or molecular facts; hence the 'Q'. As for QX_1, so for the class, write for it '$CircX_1$', of all circumstances whose terms are both elements of X_1. The only difference is that in this case X_1 does not need to satisfy any condition for '$CircX_1$' to be well formed.

B. Is $R_1 = R_2$ decidable for any two recursive classes? If you go over the proof sketch we just went through, you will see, first, that its paradigm is an r_1-class, and, second, that among its premises is the accessible diversity, previously established, of any two form-classes one of which is an n-class, and, second, that among its premises is the accessible diversity, previously established, of any two form-classes one of which is an n-class while the other is an r-class. In the completely general case the question is thus still open. But it is not hard to supplement the proof so that it covers all cases. The Peano-null of an r_n-class is a r_{n-1}-class; and just as an r_1-class cannot be the same as an n-class, so an r_1-class cannot be the same as an r_{n-1}-class; and so on. That shows the way. The supplement that (metalinguistic) proof requires is just one more induction.

C. Let T and M be the classes of all things and of all molecular facts-I, respectively. Write 'A' for the class of all atomic facts, '$\bar{M}$' for the sum $M\dot{+}A$, 'M'¹ for the sum $\bar{M}\dot{+}T$. You will see in a moment that we could do without M; yet it was introduced earlier; so I include it now. More importantly, so far only the existence of A and T is secured; $\bar{M}$ and therefore M¹, are still problematic. But let us first look at the connections one can assert once they, too, are secured. A *determinate-I*, or, more fully for once, a determinate of level I is either a thing or produced from things by a series of (a)-steps including quantification. M¹, speaking concisely, excludes quantification. Hence every element of M¹ is a determinate-I but not conversely. Recall now how we used 'nucleus' when speaking of the *nucleus* of our world, and you will see that 'nucleus' and 'level I' are two expressions for the same collection. Is this collection a class? The example to which we are about to turn is important because it answers the question in the affirmative. The nucleus and the *core* of our world, however, are two and not one. One arrives from our world at its core by suppressing all its classes. That leaves us, in addition to the nucleus, with the circumstance of diversity (I continue to ignore the meaning nexus until the very end) and all the facts that can be made out of diversities. Yet each diversity is a *complex-II*, and each such fact is also a *fact-II*. For, to arrive from the world's core at its nucleus, one must suppress all circumstances. Thus every determinate, whether class or fact or circumstance, that is not either a thing or a fact-I, is a member of the residual level II, which is the one we shall stratify in the next section.

Our example is the r-class, call it N, that is coextensive with the nucleus. But one cannot argue that there is this class without first securing the existence of $\bar{M}$ and M¹. The former, $\bar{M}$ is the r_1-class.

$$(36) \quad \lambda\langle\langle S_1(i_1), At(i_1)\rangle, \langle i_2, B(i_2, \text{``}S_1\text{``})\rangle, \langle i_1, i_2\rangle\rangle,$$

where '$B(i_2, \text{``}S_1\text{``})$' stands for '$S_1(i_2) \vee (\exists\alpha_1) [S_1(\alpha_1) \& (i_2 = \sim\alpha_1)] \vee (\exists\beta_1)(\exists\beta_2) \{S_1(\beta_1) \& S_1(\beta_2) \& [i_2 = [(\beta_1 \vee \beta_2) \vee \beta_1 \& \beta_2) \dots .]]\}$', and the disjunction in the bracket runs over all the binary connectives. To convince yourself that we have indeed got hold of a selector for $\bar{M}$, notice three things. (1) The Peano-null of (36) is the class of all atomic facts. (2) The iteration step from, say, X_1 to X_1' specifies that a determinate is an element of X_1' if and only if it is either itself an element of X_1 or produced by a connective from either one (in the case of negation) or two elements of X_1. (3) The recursion is thus cumulative. To see why it must be, let α_1, α_2, α_3 be atomic and consider that otherwise the second step would "skip" or "lose" $\sim\sim\alpha_1$ as well as $\alpha_1 \vee (\alpha_2 \,\&\, \alpha_3)$. To produce a selector for M^1 requires only one change in that for $\bar{M}$. Replace in (36) the second term of the first 2-tuple by '$i_1 \in (T + \lambda\langle K, At(K)\rangle)$'. The shift to class membership merely replaces one selector by another which is of the form that will be needed in the example. The disjunctive addition of T, on the other hand, adds all things to the Peano-null without, in view of the relevant formation rules, in any way affecting the iteration step.

N is larger than M^1. The difference, or the excess of the former over the latter, is produced by quantification steps. To exhaust this excess recursively, form first $M^1 + QM^1$; then the class M^2 of all "molecular" facts whose "atoms" are the elements of $M^1 + QM^1$, and form $M^2 + QM^2$; and so on. N, reflection will show you, is the r_2-class whose Peano-null is M^1 and whose iteration step leads from $M^1 + QM^1$ to $M^{N+1} + QM^{n+1}$. In symbols, N is

$$(37) \quad \lambda\langle\langle S_2(j_1), j_1 \in M^1 + QM^1\rangle,\langle j_1, j_2 \in B_1 + QB_1\rangle, \langle j_1, j_2\rangle\rangle,$$

with 'B_1' standing for

$$(38) \quad \lambda\langle\langle S_1(i_1), S_2(i_1)\rangle, \langle i_2, B(i_2, \text{``}S_1\text{''})\rangle,\langle i_1, i_2\rangle\rangle$$

and the 'B' (but not of course the 'B_1') being the same as in (36). The notation, even though only partially expanded and therefore not yet the ideal one, forces upon our attention the two features of such classes I had in mind when remarking, a while ago, that the example will deepen our understanding of them. So I attend next to these features.

First. The positions of 'S_2' in (37) and (38) make it clear that the instructions to be read off the ideal notation for N prescribe the "substitution," or, more accurately, the "replacement" of a constituent of a selector of a class, which latter is in turn a constituent of a selector of N. But a class, we know, has no constituent to be either substituted for or replaced. At first sight the block seems formidable. Yet two steps remove it. (a) First expand the instructions so that they include the specification of a selector on which (38) is built. (b) Then prove—and the tedium of this proof, however great, is but the familiar one of the machinery of variants—that the result, i.e., in the example, not only N but also all the classes of the sequence N^*, will be the same, whatever the selector on which (38) is built. Thus we are reassured that what we have done is not just axiomatically, but ontologically, significant.

Second. As Goedel has taught us, there is in the arithmetical part of his syntactical metalanguage a recursive class of integers, N_1, such that $d_1 \in N_1$ if and only if d_1 is the Goedel number of an expression of his object language, 'd_1', standing for a determinate d_1; and the recursion for N_1 is of that simplext kind called *primitive.* In the recursion here presented with the purpose of grounding N, on the other hand, two others so interlocked that it is of the kind called *general.* This sea change, from primitive to general recursion, is, or so it would seem, the price to be paid for so enlarging the boundaries of the object language that $d_1 \in N$ becomes literally thinkable (and '$d_1 \in N$' literally sayable). The change is instructive; yet it is but a relatively minor and rather technical feature among those dialectically connected with accurately determining that boundary; thus I shall not mention it again.

Being a determinate-I is to be of a certain form. That makes N, which is the class of all determinates-I, a form-class. Having secured the existence of N, we may safely take for granted that of all classes corresponding to forms shared by some but not all determinates-I and nothing else. On the second level, however, i.e., for form-classes such that some or all of their elements are determinates-II, we know already (p. 279) that certain difficulties arise. These, though, as already mentioned more than once, can be overcome by stratifying the second level in a manner reminiscent of the cumulative stratification of all classes first proposed by Zermelo. While attending to this job, in the first part of the next Section, it will at a certain point be helpful to be able to refer to a sort of classes I first mentioned (p. 284) when considering alternative ways of securing the existence of secondary classes. Since Zermelo in his version of the set-theorists' infinity axiom "postulated" a class of this sort, I called them *Zermelo classes.* The point then made about them was that, since appearances to the contrary notwithstanding they are tertiary classes, they could not be used to secure the existence of the secondary ones. So I conclude this Section by securing the existence in this world of this special sort of tertiary classes.

Consider, then, the class conventionally written

(16) $\{\gamma_1, \{\gamma_1\}, \{\{\gamma_1\}\}, \ldots\}$

where γ_1 is any determinate, and together with it the class

(16a) $\lambda\langle\langle S_1(i_1), i_1 = \gamma_1\rangle, \langle i_2, (\alpha_1)(\alpha_1 \in i_2 \equiv .S_1(\alpha_1))\rangle, \langle i_1, i_2\rangle\rangle.$

Or, rather, replace '$S_1(i_1)$' and '$S_1(\alpha_1)$' by '$i_1 \in b_1$' and '$\alpha_1 \in b_1$', respectively, where b_1 is any particular diverse from γ_1. For, with 'S', which I wrote because it makes the structure stand out, (16a) is of course merely a schema; after the replacement it comes at least reasonably close to the ideal notation for a tertiary class. Call this class Z and determine the classes Z_1, Z_2, Z_3, and so on, all (except for Z_1) produced by successive application of the iteration step to be read off (16a), and such that

$$Z = Z_1 \dotplus Z_2 \dotplus Z_3 \dotplus \ldots.$$

Z_1 is of course the class whose only element is γ_1. Z_2 is the class of all i_2 such that $(\alpha_1)(\alpha_1 \in i_2 \equiv. \alpha_1 = \gamma_1)$; Z_3, with an appropriate variant, the class of all i_2 such that $(\beta_1)(\beta_1 \in i_2 \equiv. (\alpha_1)(\alpha_1 \in \beta_1) \equiv. \alpha_1 = \gamma_1))$, i.e., the class whose elements are all and only those classes whose only element is γ_1; and so on. In other words and more simply, Z, whose existence is secured by its being built on a well-formed tertiary selector, and the class conventionally written (16) are one and the same.

VII

The Linguistic Turn Contained

Properly speaking, one can think only what exists. From this, its fundamental gambit, the second Section of this discourse started. It continues with the clarifications, which we need not repeat, that make the proposition convertible. What one can, properly speaking, think exists, and conversely. Not much later a distinction was made among existents. Much of classical mathematics and many scientific theories explore what, since we cannot properly speaking think it, does not have full but only derived ontological status. These latter existents, however indispensable to those disciplines, we left to an Appendix, thus arriving at another refinement of the gambit. *One can, properly speaking, think only what has full ontological status, and conversely.* But it will save words and do no harm if we agree to use in this Section 'exist' so that what exists has full ontological status. Similarly, I shall suppress the qualification "properly speaking," except occasionally, for the sake of contrast with another.

To accept the fundamental gambit of this discourse is to be committed to its method. It starts from what I called the phenomenological basis and at all crucial points appeals to what I called the phenomenological rock bottom. In this sense, *the method of ontology is phenomenological.*

The ontologist attempts to make an inventory of what exists and to describe its structure. Or, with a phrase that comes easily, he tells us what is and what is not there. Easily as it comes, the phrase is yet incendiary. Ontologists, including myself, say such things as "green is not a relation," even though there is neither in my world nor, as far as I know, in that of any other ontologist, an existent green-not-being-a-relation. Thus, by the fundamental gambit, the ontologist cannot think, and therefore obviously not say, what supposedly at least some of his discourse is about. Or, more in line with some sensibilities now fashionable, there is *a* use of 'thinking' and another of 'saying', which are the ones here relevant, with which no one can say what he cannot think. Yet the ontologist does "say" such things, and, after a fashion at least, they do make sense. Obviously again, some distinctions are needed; otherwise I am in trouble. What got me into it so quickly was a simple twist to the fundamental gambit. As things have gone in philosophy in this century, another twist, just as simple, will bring us just as quickly face to face with a challenge, not just to this or that ontology, mine or another's, but, rather, with the classical phrase, to the very possibility of metaphysics, or, as I would rather say, of ontology.

The beginning of the century witnessed the rise of a movement sometimes referred to us as the linguistic turn in philosophy. By now, having reached maturity, it has jelled into two extremes. Both sides agree that, since, taken literally, all ontological discourse turns out to be about nothing, ontology is a futile enterprise. Or, to put the same thing differently, they agree that there is no such thing as ontology. This disagree on what they believe can be "saved" from it by "interpreting" it as they do. According to one side, the salvage operation results in a body of statements of the kind linguists and other scientists make about the language people speak. The other side replaces language and the scientist by the geometrical designs called calculi and the mathematical logician, respectively. I believe that there is a discipline called ontology, of which neither of these two "substitute subject matters" is a part, even though in his way and for his purposes the ontologist often speaks about logic and must at least once take cognizance of linguistics. That is why, as I also believe, it is high time that the linguistic turn be contained. Not that at this late point that is news. There are, scattered throughout the discourse, arguments and reflections in support of both beliefs. Yet they have so far not been supported by a connected line of reasoning both fully explicit and conclusive. So I shall in this last Section do three things at once. I shall do my best to make good all the promises made in the earlier Sections but not yet kept; I shall add whatever else must still be said in the main body of this discourse; and I shall so arrange the exposition that the Section as a whole will become a connected argument, as explicit and as conclusive as I can make it, for ontology in general and for the containment of the linguistic turn in particular.

The distinctions the need for which became apparent so quickly are two. To introduce them properly and apply them effectively is a major part of the business in hand. But it should provide direction if I now gather into a single paragraph some characteristic sentences mentioning them.

The statements of ontological discourse are of three kinds. Some speak *literally* about existents which, if one is a philosopher, he sometimes does think. An ontologist who says about a fact, rather than about an expression of either a language or a calculus, that it is a disjunction, or a generality, or of some other form, makes a statement of this first kind. Those of the second kind are about existents which the ontologist sometimes thinks but can only *nonliterally* talk about; as, e.g., when he tells us that green is a property or that this-being-either-green-or-not-green is actual. The third kind, to which the bulk of all ontological discourse belongs, is the most problematic, at least in my world with its fundamental gambit. For an example, take the one long familiar from which once more I started. If there is no existent green-not-being-relation, then one can neither think nor say that green is not a relation. Yet, ontologists are trying to talk about such things; as, incidentally, I am at this very moment. That a "statement" of this kind is at best nonliteral is clear. But does admitting that sufficiently protect it against the fate, which if the members of the movement had their way, would be shared by all ontological discourse? Using 'thinking' itself literally, I cannot of course consistently deny that, since one cannot think what such utterances are about, they are mere strings of words rather than statements. Yet I shall defend them on the ground that whenever I utter such a sequence in earnest, I do think, although of course *only after a fashion,* about what, while excluded from the inventory of all existents I have proposed, is yet a feature of what that inventory includes. That is the idea; the details must wait, of course.

The two distinctions, as you have long gathered, are *literal* vs. *nonliteral* and *properly speaking* vs. *only after a fashion;* the former applying to speaking and to language; the latter, to thinking and to thought. Notice, too, that now, in the crunch, if I may so express myself, I no longer save words, as occasionally I did on earlier occasions, by using 'literal-nonliteral' also in connection with thoughts. Still about words, you remember no doubt that 'feature', as used in this discourse, has no ontological import.

(i) *We can think all forms, and, within the familiar limits of a schema, express, or represent, our thoughts about them in the schema called the ideal language (IL).* One job still to be done is the completion of the argument in support of (i), which, as repeatedly anticipated, involves the stratification of the second level. In the *first subsection* below I shall try to do this job. Supposing that it can be done, it suggests a connection between what can be expressed in the IL, on the one hand, and what can be "said literally" in the language we speak, on the other. As I shall use the crucial phrase, the two notions are coextensive; or, rather, I propose to explicate the latter by means of the former. (ii) *What can be expressed in the IL can be said literally in the language we speak, and conversely.* Nor is this just an arbitrary agreement about a phrase. In the direction from the expressible to the literally sayable it is indeed merely part of the very idea of an IL. The second job, still to be done, which is the heart of the matter, is in the other direction. More precisely, we must first sufficiently articulate the notion of the ideal schema, which as yet we haven't, and then argue as closely as one can, which we haven't yet either, that, given that notion and certain features of the ontology we have established by the phenomenological method without any appeal to language either natural or artificial, (iii) *there are in this world existents which cannot be represented in the IL.* This is the job I shall try to do in the *second subsection.* Supposing that it, too, can be done, what will have been achieved with respect to the three kinds of ontological statements?

We shall be able to replace (i) by the proposition that we can think all forms and literally speak about them. It follows that all statements of ontological discourse which are about forms are of the first kind, provided only that such a statement does not purport to be also about something else which cannot be said literally, such as, e.g., that if a fact is of a certain form it is actual. Are all ontological statements of the first kind about forms? I cannot think of any others. Nor, if there were, would that, as far as I can see, make any difference for the major concerns of this discourse. (There is, to be sure, one exception. We can think, literally say, and even "know" whether or not a certain existent is a class. Yet, as we chose our terms, being-a-class is not a form. The exception is as harmless as the choice is well grounded in the feature of there not being a form a determinate has if and only if it is a selector.) (iii) will be established by means of two paradigms which spot two important subclasses of the second kind. One can think but not literally say that a thing is of its ultimate sort; and one can think some complexes with their mode but not literally say that they are pervaded by it. Do these two subkinds, together with the statements compounded either from them alone or from at least one of them and some statements of the first kind, exhaust the second kind? Again, I cannot think of any others; and again, if there were, it wouldn't make any difference. What does matter, both structurally and dialectically, is, as we already know and shall have occasion to emphasize once more, that there are the two subkinds.

In the third subsection I support as carefully as I can the claim that (iv) *the canons are unthinkable.* But neither the second nor the third subsection could reach its goal if, taken together, they did not contain everything that still has to be said about the IL. In the *fourth subsection*

I unpack as completely as I can the notion of *analyticity*.[†] But, again, this cannot be done without making good a last group of promises not yet fulfilled. The concluding *fifth subsection* offers some comments on the *overall dialectic* of this discourse.

'*Det*-I(α_1)' abbreviates '$\alpha_1 \in N$'; N being the form-class whose existence we secured at the end of the last Section. Let now α_1 be any second-level determinate; ϕ, any of the forms of any of them. As to the plural, forms, see p. 135. That '$\phi_1(\alpha_1)$' is but an abbreviation I take for granted and continue to cut verbal and notational corners wherever it is safe. Can we literally think and say $\phi_1(\alpha_1)$ and recursively reach its mode? We cannot even start answering unless we first look closely at the collection of all determinates-II, i.e., all those and only those which are not determinates-I. The latter, we know, are all those and only those which are, except for the indispensable standardization and order tuples, produced out of a (finite) number of things by a finite number of steps, we called them (a)-steps, each of which involves either a single exemplification or a single connective or a single quantifier. As one moves to the second level, exemplification drops out and the (b)- and (c)-steps come in. With the meaning nexus relegated to the last Appendix, that leaves us until then with two (b)-steps and class formation. Starting from the first level, one can by a single one of these steps reach all diads, (α_1, α_2), and all elementhoods, $(\alpha_1 \in \alpha_2)$, such that $(\alpha_1 \in N)$ & $(\alpha_2 \in N)$, as well as all classes, β_1, of this world such that $(\gamma_1)(\gamma_1 \in \beta_1 \supset . \gamma_1 \in N)$. But the only limitation on the number of successive steps of this kind is that it be finite. That makes the collection of all determinates-II not only vast but less than readily mastered. Part of the difficulty is the one that causes Russell and Zermelo to propose their theories of types, homogeneous and cumulative, respectively. In this world, where in addition to particulars (or *Urelemente*) and classes there are also facts of either level as well as circumstances, there is still another difficulty. To spot it, we only need to recall briefly what we know already.

66* Write '$\underset{0}{Diad}(\alpha_1)$', '$\underset{0}{El}(\alpha_1)$', '$\underset{0}{Cl}(\alpha_1)$' for $(\exists\beta_1)(\exists\beta_2)(\alpha_1 = \beta_1, \beta_2))$', '$(\exists\beta_1)(\exists\beta_2)(\alpha_2 = \beta_1 \in \beta_2)$', '$Cl(\alpha_1)$ & $(\gamma_1)(\gamma_1 \in \alpha_1 \supset . \gamma_1 \in N)$'. '*Diad*' and '$\underset{0}{El}$' are obviously forms in the broad sense (p. 274). So we shall see are $\underset{0}{Cl}$ and all stratified class notions, of which it is the first. Being a class ($\overline{Cl}$), on the other hand, as for good reasons we speak (ibid.), is not a form. Nor is any of the classes $\overline{Part}$, $\overline{Univ}^0$, and so on, of the

---

[†] Of all the premises Bergmann makes here, this is the only one he does not appear to even make an attempt to keep. There is no fourth subsection on analyticity here, although there were among Bergmann's papers some very rough notes on such a subsection.—WH

several ultimate sorts of things (p. 302). For more about these latter classes, see II and III, below. But notice right now that, since they occur in all selectors of N, determinate-I is a form only in the broad sense. Notice, finally, that all elements of $\underset{0}{El}$ are potential.

'$Disj(\alpha_1)$', abbreviating '$(\exists\gamma_1)(\exists\gamma_2)(\alpha_1 =. \gamma_1 \vee \gamma_2)$', is not only thinkable but also decidable, even immediately so. $Disj$ is thus unproblematically a form. Yet one must not take for granted that the collection of all disjunctions is a class. To convince ourselves that in fact it isn't, we considered (p. 279) that, if there were a class, $\widetilde{disj}$, coextensive with that collection, $[(\widetilde{disj} = \delta_1) \vee \delta_2] \in \widetilde{disj}$ would for any determinates δ_1 and δ_2 be an actual complex. Again, $disj$ would actually be a constituent of $(\widetilde{disj} = \delta_1) \vee \delta_2$. Hence, $\widetilde{disj}$ would be among its own materials, which violates the Cantor axiom. It follows that, while $Disj$ is a form, there is yet no class coextensive with it. Whenever, as in this case, the definiens of a form neither is nor involves a class, that makes no difference. But there are also forms whose definientia either are or involve classes and which, therefore, we couldn't think if there were not these classes. Just remember that if N and M (pp. 313, 314) were not two recursive classes, there wouldn't be, for us to intend, the two forms shared by all those and only those determinates which are of the first level, and by all molecular ones among them, respectively. In these two cases, as in all others where all the determinates sharing the form are of the first level, there is no danger of Cantor's axiom being violated. On the second level, however, one cannot secure the existence of the classes required without stratifying it, i.e., without distributing all determinates-II into strata, or, as I would rather call them, *layers*, L_1, L_2, L_3, and so on, which will themselves turn out to be classes involving recursions. Thus there will also be for each layer a form shared by all those and only those determinates belonging to it. These layers will be most conveniently so defined that they are cumulative ($L_1 \subset L_2 \subset L_3 \subset \dots$), which in turn makes it often convenient to call the first level L_0. Proceeding in this way, we shall for instance be able to specify classes, $\widetilde{disj}^{n+1}$, *and therefore also corresponding forms*, $Disj^{n+1}$, shared by all those and only those disjunctions whose disjuncts are elements of L_n. As for this form, so for all others. That brings out the idea. Let us next equip ourselves with the tools needed for realizing it. The two things I shall always look out for are, as you may expect, that the would-be classes we need are decidable and that they conform with the Cantor axiom. The other checks can once more be left to the mathematicians.

Remember the chains (3) $\alpha_1, \alpha_2, \dots, \alpha_{k-1}, \alpha_k$, introduced when we strengthened the Cantor axiom (p. 278), such that their links, $\alpha_k \, MAT$

α_{k-1}, α_{k-1} *MAT* α_{k-2}, . . . , α_2 *MAT* α_1, are all actual; where 'μ *MAT*ν' stands for (μ *CONST*ν) $\vee$ ($\mu \in \nu$) and the upper-case letters were to remind us that being-a-constituent-of (*CONST*) and hence also being-material-of (*MAT*) may not be forms. Now we know that unless stratified they can't be. For, constituency being obviously a recursive notion, there would have to be a coextensive class (of 2-tuples), call it $\widetilde{const}$, such that *CONST* $\langle \widetilde{const}, \widetilde{const} = d_1 \rangle$ and $\langle \widetilde{const}, \widetilde{const} = d_1 \rangle \in \widetilde{const}$ are both actual for every determinate d_2; thus $\widetilde{const}$ would be among its own materials. Call now (3) a chain *of* α_1, or one of *its* chains; k, the *length* of this chain. In this world without empty classes, every determinate not a thing has at least one chain of a least length 2. $\{a_1\}$, a_1 and $f_1(a_1)$, a_1, for instance, are chains of maximum length of $\{a_1\}$ and $f_1(a_1)$, respectively; are both of length 2; and are the only such chains. Most determinates, though, have several chains of varying length. The number of steps by which in this world a determinate is produced from (any of) its ultimate foundation(s) is always finite. It does not follow, however, that for each determinate the lengths of its several chains have a finite maximum. Just consider the two classes π_1 (p. 280) and Z (p. 316), writing them informally yet suggestively, as before, $\{f_1(a_1), f_1(a_1) \vee g_1(b_1), (f_1(a_1) \vee g_1(b_1)) \vee g_1(b_1), \ldots \}$, and $\{\gamma_1, \{\gamma_1\}, \{\{\gamma_1\}\}, \ldots \}$, respectively. $f_1(a_1) \in \pi_1$ is a chain of π_1; but so is $f_1(a_1)$ *CONST* $[f_1(a_1) \vee g_1(b_1)] \in \pi_1$ and so on. Again, $\gamma_1 \in Z$ is a chain of Z; but so are $\gamma_1 \in \{\gamma_1\} \in Z$, $\gamma_1 \in \{\gamma_1\} \in \{\{\gamma_1\}\} \in Z$, and so on. In either case there is no chain of maximum length. Yet there is also a difference. No matter how long a chain of π_1 may be, the number of $\in$-links in it is 1. For the chains of Z, on the other hand, there is no maximum for the number of $\in$-links in them. Let us in a first step limit ourselves to determinates for which there is a finite number, i, such that *the number of $\in$-links in any chain of the determinate is $\leq i$, and, in at least one of them, $= i$*. Call this index the *type* of the determinate and mark it by a right superscript. If, that is, α is of type i, we shall, whenever it serves our purpose, write 'α^i' instead of 'α', and, in general, speak of determinates^i, facts^i, classes^i, and so on. $\{a_1\}$, $\{\{a_1\}\}$, $(\{a_2, \{a_1\}\}, a_1)$, and $(\{a_1, \{a_1\}\}, a_1) \vee f_1(a_2)$, for instance, are all determinates^2, and a class^2, a circumstance^2, and a fact^2, respectively. This notion of type adapts, although so far of course only within the finite, Zermelo's to a world in which not all determinates are either simples (*Urelemente*) or classes. In conjunction with two lemmas, (A) and (B), to which I turn next, it will enable us to stratify the second level.

A. Let X be a class^{i+1}, i.e., a class with at least one element of type i and the types of all others $\leq i$. (4) $Cl(\alpha)$ & $(\beta)[\beta \in \alpha \supset \beta \in X]$ is actual for all those and only those determinates which are classes all whose elements are elements of X. Mark this connection by writing 'Cl-$[X]$' for '$Cl(\alpha)$ & $(\beta)[\beta \in \alpha \supset . \beta \in X]$'. By the lemma we shall need, *if every determinate[k] such that $k \leq i$ is an element of X, Cl-$[X]$ is a(broad) form coextensive with a class.* Thus, limiting our check as indicated, we must show (a) that (4) is decidable, and (b) that the collection it picks out conforms with Cantor's axiom. The latter condition, (b), is obviously satisfied. For, if the collection is a class, it is a class[i+2] all whose elements are classes with types $\leq i + 1$. Concerning (a), as long as we do not "know" that 'α' is well formed, we are merely "borrowing from language" and there is nothing to talk about. If we "know" that 'α' is well formed, we also "know" whether or not α is a class. If it isn't, we "know" by virtue of the first conjunct that (4) is potential. In case α is a class, one must, in order to decide (4), decide the second conjunct, $(\beta)[\beta \in \alpha \supset . \beta \in X]$. Now, α and X being classes and the (full-status) classes of this world all being decidable, we can decide $\beta \in \alpha$ and $\beta \in X$ for every β. It doesn't follow, alas, that we can decide $(\beta)[\beta \in \alpha \supset . \beta \in X]$. The way out of this apparent impass is provided by a certain assumption, mentioned earlier (p. 301), which we must now examine more closely.

A class is of one of three sorts. If it is primary (finite), there is, as usually, no problem. In secondary or Peano classes, the iteration step does not (I speak concisely) raise the type. In a secondary class, therefore, all elements are of the same type, call it j, and the class itself is of type $j + 1$. A tertiary class is either an r-class or an n-class. If it is an r-class, its iteration step may or may not, always decidably, "raise the type." If it does, the class is among those we have for the time being excluded from consideration. (The only such class we have so far come across is Zermelo's Z.) For every other recursive class, α, be it secondary or tertiary, there is an integer, j, which, given α, is recursively accessible to us, such that α is of type $j + 1$. It follows that, if we "know" X to be of the kind specified in the lemma and of type $i + 1$, (4) will be decidably actual or potential depending on where $j \leq i$. That leaves only the n-classes, which is where the assumption comes in.

If $\langle \alpha, \beta(\alpha) \rangle$ selects an n-class, $\beta(\alpha)$ is (the definiens of) a form. This is the assumption. We have long known that it is not convertible. Just think of *Disj*, which is a (nonrecursive) form but not (coextensive with) a class. Forms are by their very nature decidable. That takes care of the condition (a). Concerning (b) make a distinction. Either it does or it doesn't specify or at least limit ($\leq j$) the types of all the constituents of the determinates it collects. *At, M,* and *N* do; *Disj* doesn't. In the former case, i.e., when the relevant types are specified or at least limited, Cantor's requirement is secure and one can argue as before to the effect that (4) is decidably actual or potential depending on whether or not $j \leq i$. In the latter case, one always can, by a procedure analogous to the one followed for '$\widetilde{disj}$' and '$\widetilde{const}$', show that '$\lambda\langle\alpha, \beta(\alpha)\rangle$' is ill formed and that, therefore, there is no class for which to decide whether it is an element of $Cl\text{-}[X]$. Thus, granted the assumption, the lemma is established. If you wonder whether the indispensable order and standardization tuples interfere with the type machinery, check and you will see that they don't. For a further comment on the assumption, see below, at the very end of this subsection.

B. Let X be a class^{i+1}; try making it the Peano-null of what is, hopefully, an r-class, X^*, with the cumulative iteration step (5) $Y'(\alpha) \equiv Y(\alpha) \vee (\exists\beta)[(\alpha = \sim\beta) \ \& \ Y(\beta)] \vee \ldots \vee (\exists\beta_1)(\exists\beta_2)[(\alpha = \beta_1 \ \& \ \beta_2) \ \& \ Y(\beta_1) \ \& \ Y(\beta_2)]$. (As you notice, I use the Peano stroke.) The disjunction in (5), running over all (a)-steps including the two quantifications as well as the two (b)-steps that remain if we keep ignoring the meaning nexus, is, except for these four additional disjunctions, the same as in the iteration step for M^1 (p. 314). Nor do these further disjuncts keep (5) from being decidable; i.e., if Y is decidable, so is Y'; which, if the rest works out, guarantees that, of the two conditions for X^* being a class on which we check, (a) will be satisfied. How, then, about (b)? Since (5) contains no disjunct for class formation, it does not raise the type. Hence, if X is a class^{i+1}, the other members of the Peano sequence, X', X'', and so on, as well as X^*, will all be collections of determinates of type $\leq i$; which in turn guarantees their all being classes^{i+1}. Thus the second lemma is established. *If X is a class^{i+1}, so is X^*.* For an example, take the nucleus, N, or, as it is now more convenient to call it, L_0, and you will see that L_0 *is the class of all determinates, of either the first or the second level, which are of type o.*

67* a_1 and $f_1(a_1)$, being elements of L_0, are both of the first level; $(a_1, f_1(a_2))$, $(a_1 \in f_1(a_1))$, and $(a_1, a_1 \in f_1(a_1))$, however, are three elements of L_0^* that belong to the second level. Incidentally, every elementhood which is an element of L_0^* is potential; the exemplification steps produce no determinate which is not already an element of the Peano-null; and so on.

We are ready to stratify, under the assumption mentioned, all determinates. Consider the sequence (6) L_0, L_1, L_2, and so on, such that $L_1 = L_0^* \dotplus Cl\text{-}[L_0^*]$, $L_2 = L_1^* \dotplus Cl\text{-}[L_1^*]$, $L_3 = L_2^* \dotplus Cl\text{-}[L_2]$, . . . Since L_0^* and $Cl\text{-}[L_0^*]$ are classes, so by the second class axiom is their sum L_1. Also, L_1 is the class^2 of *all* nonclasses^0 and *all* classes^1. Again, since L_1 is a class, so is L_2, and it is the class^3 of *all* nonclasses of *at most* type 1 and *all* classes of *at most* type 2; and so on.

There are only three more things to be done. We must finally stratify all those forms, such as *Disj*, which do not either specify or at least limit the types of all the constituents of the determinates they collect. We must get rid of the limitation to a finite *i*. And we must show that what is essential to this discourse would be safe even if the assumption which I can neither prove nor imagine a counterexample of, were false.

First. Our paradigm will serve once more. Write '$_nDisj(\alpha)$' for '$(\exists\beta_1)(\exists\beta_2)[\alpha =. \beta_1 \vee \beta_2) \& (\beta_1 \in L_{n+1}) \& (\beta_2 \in L_{n+1})]$. L_{n+1} comprehends the class of *all* nonclasses of a type $\leq n$. $_nDisj$, therefore, being decidable, is the form shared by all those and only those disjunctions whose disjuncts, being both of at most type *n*, are themselves of this type. Nor is it difficult to specify one that is exactly of type *n*. That makes $_n\widetilde{disj}$, *if* there is this class, of type *n* + 1. Now, being a class rather than a disjunction, $_n\widetilde{disj}$ cannot be its own element; nor, therefore, can it be among its own materials, unless it is among those of at least one of its elements, which latter, however, are all of at most type *n*. Hence there is a class coextensive with this form. As for disjunction, so mutatis mutandis for all stratified forms.

Second. As one sees at a glance, (6) is the Peano sequence of a recursive class whose iteration step does raise the type (by a finite integer) and for which therefore there is no finite *j* such that the type of all its elements is $\leq j$. So let us call it L_a. The simplest class of this sort, and the only one we have so far encountered is *Z*. Yet it is easily shown that the collection of all such classes, provided only their respective Peanonulls are of finite type, is itself a class. Taking it from here, every graduate student in mathematics knows how to get rid, although in this world of course only within the denumerable, of the requirement that *j* be finite. Thus, just as, having grounded a single secondary class, we did not pursue the grounding of elementary arithmetic, there is at this point no need for us to pursue.

Third. If there were n-classes not coextensive with forms, we might not be able to decide of which type they are. If so, we could not stratify all determinates. Yet we could, by proceeding as we did, stratify the collection of all those which either are not themselves such classes or have at least one of them among their materials. Thus we could still stratify all forms.

II

(a) A thing being of its ultimate sort is an existent we sometimes think; so is, for some complexes, their being pervaded by their mode (for most complexes that is merely an extrapolation); yet, (b) in neither case can these existents be expressed in the IL. (a) follows from the fundamental gambit in conjunction with two appeals to the phenomenological rock bottom. The business of this subsection is to present the strongest possible argument for (b). The next two paragraphs collect two groups of premises, (A) and (B), from which by the strategy already outlined the argument must start. (A) gathers some ontological propositions we have established without any appeal to language, either natural or artificial; although, in the opposite direction, we have used them and others obtained by the same method, which is phenomenological rather than linguistic, to ascertain what certain fragments of a calculus must be like if as a whole it is to represent perspicuously everything that exists, which is the very idea of the IL. (B) gathers some features of the IL; or, perhaps better, it unpacks by articulating these features the part of that idea we shall need.

(A1) A thing is a composite, or *composed* of, an item and an ultimate sort, two existents so special that we set them apart as belonging to two of the three subsorts of a sort we called entities. (A2) Items and ultimate sorts are mutually inseparable; which makes things one of the two kinds called Two-in-Ones. The notion of mutual inseparability— or, as it was then called, total inseparability—was stated in non-metaphorical language long ago (p. 13). Less strictly speaking, an item, being a mere identifier, "cannot" exist unless "its" sort also exists; an ultimate sort, being a quasi-universal (p. 58), "cannot" exist unless at least one of "its" items also exists. (To get the import of the modal metaphor, consider that a connective "couldn't" exist unless at least one atomic fact or diad existed, while there "could" be a world of diads, things, and exemplifications but without any other functions.) (A3) Every complex, whether fact or circumstance, is *pervaded* by "its" mode; and the two are mutually inseparable. The only members of the third subkind of entities are the two modes; the second kind of Two-in-Ones are the complexes. (A4) A complex pervaded by its mode is not again pervaded by one. That follows from the fundamental gambit in conjunction with a third appeal to the phenomenological rock bottom, the one I dubbed the Unthinkability of the Iterated Mode. In Section III there is, as you remember, a whole list (pp. 87 ff.) of such "unthinkabilities," all available to us as premises in the several cases of which we shall examine only two. (A5) an existent is an argument of a connective if and only if it has (is pervaded by) a mode.

Turning to the second group of premises, let us leave to the next subsection what must still be said about juxtaposition, about the linear order in which the expressions of the IL are customarily written, and about the parentheses which occur in them. (B1) the IL consists of its primitive marks and certain finite linear strings, with repetition, of primitive marks, that are called well formed. Let us use 'expression' so broadly that not only well-formed strings but also primitive marks are expressions. (B2) A string is an expression if and only if it has certain geometrical properties. Whether or not it has them can, as one usually says, be decided recursively, or, as I shall say instead, can be *certified* without recourse to anything but the shapes and the order of the primitive marks in the string. (B3) the number of diacritical expressions, i.e., those not standing for existents, must be as small as possible. In the IL proposed in this discourse, there are only four such expressions and they are all primitive marks. (B4) Every other expression stands for one and only one existent. (B5) There is an expression for each connective.

The converse of (B4) does not hold. There is not for every existent an expression that stands for it, or, to list for once all the synonyms here used, expresses it, represents it, or corresponds to it. Just stop as long as it takes to draw one breath and you will see that this is the burden of the argument for which, after a digression, we are now ready.

67* (a) One reason I believe that the IL proposed in this discourse cannot be too far off is that I do not see how one could do with even fewer than the four diacritical expressions mentioned in (B3). Concerning these four, which are all primitive marks, nothing needs to be added to what has already been said about 'λ' and '$\in$', the two which appear in the expressions for classes and elementhoods. About the parenthes*is*, '(. . . , . . .)', there will be more in the next subsection. The fourth, 'M', appears in the expressions for the meaning nexus; the argument for its being diacritical will be made in the last Appendix. (b) Why was in (B2) 'certifiable' pressed into service to do the job, which, as the logicians speak, is done by 'recursively decidable'? As the latter is used in this discourse, a complex is recursively decidable if and only if there is a procedure one can learn, such that, if he follows it, the mode of the complex will become transparent to him. The cue for the procedure (if any) to follow is provided by the form of the complex; the limiting case is the immediately transparent. What one does when testing a string is similar in that he, too, follows a procedure one can learn, that leads to the desired result. An obvious difference is that, as the logicians speak, every (finite) string is "recursively decidable," while as I chose my terms, only complexes of certain sorts are. But there is also, behind this difference in the words, a crucial difference in the things, as well as, not surprisingly in view of the similarity, a connection between the two procedures. When certifying a string of a calculus, one infers deductively from certain geometrical configurations having certain geometrical features that these or certain other geometrical configurations have certain other geometrical features. To do this sort of thing is to do geometry. Now in this world, as I shall presently complete the explication of analyticity, while not every analytic complex is recursively decidable (nor even such that its mode is in principle accessible, which is a much weaker condition), certain sorts of analytical complexes are the only ones that are recursively decidable. Nor in this world is geometry analytical. Thus, when one certifies a string, his thought moves along a Cartesian chain of steps whose kind and order can be learned, from the never transparent to the never transparent, while when a complex becomes transparent there is such a chain, for some sorts also learnable, at the end of which the complex becomes transparent. This is the crucial difference; now for the connection. The logician may, although in the case of this elementary task he surely need not, proceed as follows. He lays down certain rules for "coordinating" to every finite string, well formed or otherwise, exactly one integer, such that the string will be of a certain geometrical kind, e.g., well formed, if and only if the integer coordinated to it is of a certain arithmetical kind, e.g., to simplify starkly, if and only if it is the product of either five or seven odd powers of prime numbers. To see that this connection does not obliterate the crucial difference, consider that, unlike a string's being of a certain geometrical kind, which is never analytic, an integer's being of a certain arithmetical kind is not only always analytic but in certain cases also recursively decidable. Notice, too, that when the logician proceeds in this way, by "Geodelization," the situation is in the crucial respect the same as in analytic geometry. E.g., while two linear equations in two variables having at most one solution is analytic, two straight lines in a plane intersecting in at most one point is not. *The mathematical logician, we shall see, is always either a geometrician, analytic or otherwise, or a student of "pure" arithmetic.* About the use here made of 'coordinate' more later. (c) Turn now to the key phrase in (B2): without recourse to anything but the shapes and the order of the primitive marks in the string. When the logician-geometrician attends only to shapes and order he is, as one often says, a *syntacticist* attending to "form" only. This use of 'form' differs from the ontologist's, as in this discourse. But there is again not only a difference but also a connection, both of which we must grasp firmly. Since this time there is only one word, I resort for the moment to subscripts. The syntacticist studies $form_1$, which is a matter of geometry. The ontologist says that a complex—which may be, but in most cases of course is not, geometrical—is of a certain form$_2$ if and only if a certain other complex, of which the first is a constituent, is actual.[†] About the details of form$_2$ we have already heard more than enough. The connection is that a complex is of a certain form$_2$ if and only if the expression standing for it (in the IL) is of a certain form$_1$. This does not, however, affect the crucial difference that, while form$_2$ is always recursively decidable, form$_1$, being a geometrical feature, is not even analytic. At this point a careful reader asks to be heard. In Section V, he begins, you claimed that as a matter of anthropological fact our minds, more often than not, could not move along a Cartesian chain, from illumination to illumination, without "interstitial" awareness (p. 225)[‡] between at least some of its successive links; which latter awarenesses are either imaginings, either auditory or visual, or visual perceivings, in case one works with pencil and paper, either of sentences of the language we speak or of expressions of some artificial language, not to mention all sorts of diagrams, i.e., in all cases, of materials that are never transparent. Is it not, he then asks, odd or even incongruous that the unilluminable thus becomes, more often than not, an indispensable stepping-stone to our illuminations? Not at all, I assure him, provided only one thinks through completely the overall dialectic of this discourse, thus clarifying completely, among other things, the way phenomenology, ontology, and anthropology are interlocked in it. To put it negatively and into a formula, once illumination is reached it does not matter how it has been reached. To this formula I shall return at the very end. But let me add right now that, since such thinking-through is part of making the case for ontology and against the excesses of the linguistic turn, which is the major purpose of this concluding Section, much of the material in it, including virtually everything in this digression, is not wholly new but brought together from earlier Sections, for the sake of articulating it as fully and examining it connectedly and as closely as this purpose requires.

Using once more the old standbys, start from the four sentences (1) 'green is a universal$^{(0)}$', (2) 'this-being-either-green-or-not-green is actual', (1′) 'green is not a universal$^{(0)}$', (2′) 'this-being-either-green-

[†] Note that the distinction between form$_1$ and form$_2$ here is *not* the same as that drawn by means of the same terms in earlier chapters. Here "form$_1$" designates the geometrical shape of a linguistic string (its "syntactical" structure); in Section III "form$_1$" is any "nondeterminate with the one-many-feature," that is, a mode, an ultimate sort, or a function. "Form$_2$" here means the logical form of a complex that is represented by a linguistic string. This is roughly the same meaning this locution was given in Section IV.—WH

[‡] Bergmann in fact, in Section V, calls these "instrumental awarenesses." See note on p. 291.—WH

or-not-green is not actual'. By (A2) and (A4), in conjunction with the opening sentence (a) of this subsection, (1) and (2) stand for existents. (1') and (2'), by the appropriate unthinkabilities, stand for nothing. What after a fashion a philosopher thinks and, of course nonliterally, says when uttering in earnest either (1') or (2') will be explored in the next subsection. That leaves (1) and (2). We must show that there is in the IL no expression that could stand for either of the two existents to which they call attention; and that therefore, as we choose our terms, those sentences speak only nonliterally about these existents, even though by Section V we could not, in matter of anthropological fact, be aware of the latter if the former were not available to us, to serve as the texts of the awarenesses.

(1) and (2) go with the propositions (A2) and (A4). If you reread the latter, a difference in wording will remind you of a distinction first made in Section III. Each thing is "composed" of two entities; each complex is "pervaded" by one. There were of course in that early Section some comments about the difference thus marked between the two sorts of Two-in-Ones. But we are only now ready to articulate it fully. Because of it, I shall first argue the case of the thing. First of all, though, let us agree to save words by writing throughout these reflections 'expression' for 'expression of the IL'.

Suppose that there is an expression standing for the existent to which (1) calls attention. If there were one, there would have to be two others, standing for the item and the ultimate sort of green. Would these two have to be primitive marks, say 'i_1' and 's_1'? We may safely assume that they are; for, as you will see if you will check at the end of this brief argument, it makes no difference. Nor does it matter whether or not there is also a primitive mark, say 'f_1', that stands for the color. If there is 'i_1', 's_1', and 'f_1' will all three occur in the expression that stands for the existent; if there isn't, only 'i_1' and 's_1' will. Nor need we further specify this expression. So let either (3) '$[i_1, s_1]$' or (4) '$[i_1, s_1, f_1]$' abbreviate it. Let next each 'i_k' stand for an item; each s_l for one of the much smaller number of ultimate sorts. Substituting into (3) for 'i_1' and 's_1', respectively, two marks 'i_{k_1}' that do not stand for two entities that compose a thing, one obtains a string which by the appropriate unthinkability is ill formed. For, since the item is the identifier, if, for instance, 's_2' stood for the ultimate sort of particularity, '$[i_1, s_2]$' could only stand for green-being-a-particular. Similarly for (4). If, in order to avoid the predicament, one modifies the effective notation, dividing the 'i_k' into different subkinds, 'i_1^1', 'i_1^2', . . . , 'i_2^1', 'i_2^2', . . . , and so on, to go with 's_1', 's_2', and so on, one is starting on an infinite regress (p. 103). The predicament is that, by (B2), a string must be certifiable without recourse to anything but the

shapes and the order of the primitive marks in the string. We conclude, first, that there are *no expressions for either items or ultimate sorts*,
and, second, that *neither (3) nor (4) abbreviates an expression*. Concerning the different marks for the different sorts of things (not: items),
see what will be said in the next subsection about something "showing
itself" in the IL. But let us check right now how it all fits with what is
usually called epistemology.

(i) Every thought (not: awareness) intends explicitly one and only
one existent, its intention (not: referent), and for each existent there
is, if any, only one thought that explicitly intends it. (ii) An awareness
to which green-being-a-universal[(0)] is transparently presented consists, in addition to the two direct awarenesses required, of an evident,
explicit grasping of the thing itself and a perceiving of the text "*green
is a universal.*"[(0)] (iii) whenever one intends a thing implicitly, he is presented with that thing but not with its being of its ultimate sort. (iv) A
thing is never explicitly intended except by an act of grasping, which
latter are all evident and intend only things. Hold the first of these
four propositions together with the other three and you will see that it
all fits smoothly. Not so in the case, to which I now turn, of (2) and the
existent to which it calls attention.

Although modes and ultimate sorts are both quasi-universals
(p. 327), there are yet, in the case of the complex, all together only two
existents, viz., the Two-in-One and the mode that pervades it, rather
than, as in the case of the thing, three, viz., the Two-in-One and the
two entities that compose it. This claim we must now argue more
closely than when it was first made. The argument divides into three
parts; the first, (C), examines the expression or expressions involved;
the second, (D), assays the complex; the third, (E), concerned with the
thought or thoughts involved, spots and tackles an "epistemological"
difficulty. But let us once more agree to save words by calling, without
prejudice, "sheer complex" that third, whose existence is at issue,
which, if it existed, would correspond to the item in a thing.

(C) Let 'α_1' and 'α_2' be two abbreviations; 'α_1' for the expression
which, if we spoke the IL, would take the place of 'this is either green
or not green'; 'α_2' for the expression, if any, that stands for the
existent to which (2) calls attention. As to 'α_2', there surely must be the
expression it abbreviates, and it must, by (A4), (A5), (B5) be the one
that combines with others of the same sort into the expressions for the
familiar complexes, negation, conjunction, and so on. Otherwise, irrespective of whether or not there is the sheer complex, the calculus
surely couldn't be the IL. Also, if there is an expression 'α_2' abbreviates, 'α_1' must, together with an expression for the mode of the complex, occur in it. Again, we need not further specify 'α_2'; again, there-

fore, we would make use of brackets as in (3) and (4); but since there are only two modes, we may conveniently instead of 'α_2' write either 'α_1^+' or 'α_1^-', depending on whether the mode of the complex is actuality or potentiality. Yet by (B4), only one of the two "existents" 'α_1^+' and 'α_1^-' purport to stand for really is one. Hence, only one of the two strings is well formed and we find ourselves once more in the predicament of not being able to pick out the one which is in the manner required by (B2). If that causes you a moment's puzzlement, recall from the opening of Section IV that to identify as actual all complexes represented by expressions sharing the relevant form with 'α_1' requires resources excluded by (B2). Thus we may conclude that, *whether or not there are sheer complexes, there are no expressions for the modes; nor, if there are sheer complexes, expressions for the moded ones.*

(D) Are there sheer complexes? If there were these existents, they would not only be the ones we always can and sometimes do explicitly intend when intending a complex, but also, unless the latter is analytic (and its mode is at least in principle accessible) the only ones ever presented to us on these occasions. (The qualification in the parenthesis is needed because of Goedel's most famous contribution, of which more in the fourth subsection.) This, though, is awkward. For one, a sheer complex and its mode would be mutually inseparable; and one cannot explicitly intend what is mutually inseparable, nor even what, like the functions, is one-sidedly inseparable. For this, see also what has been said on p. 114 about degrees of independence. For another, since complexes are of many different forms, a sheer complex could not, as the analogy with items suggests, be a mere identifier. Moreover, the very notion of something "structured" that is merely an entity is repugnant. These are two weighty reasons for assaying complexes as single determinates pervaded by a mode. Strong as the structural suggestion is, we must not yield to it before stating without any metaphor a third reason, which, since when it first came up we were not yet ready for that, I hid behind one. "The connectives operate on the sheer complex." These are not the words, but this is the impact of that treacherous metaphor (p. 143). It is treacherous because, if there are no sheer complexes, what is there for the connectives to operate on? The following two propositions, since established, say nonmetaphorically what needs to be said. (a) A value of a function is neither a "sum" nor a "class" nor any other kind of "compound" of its argument(s) and the function itself, but an existent whose whole nature (identity) and being exhausts itself in being the one that is eo ipso there provided the argument(s) and the function are there. (b) If a complex is not atomic, i.e., very concisely speaking, if it has subcomplexes, then, while it is pervaded by its own mode, it is not also pervaded by the modes of its subcomplexes; if, for instance, $f_1(a_1)$ and $g_1(b_1)$ are actual and potential, respectively, $f_1(a_1)$ & $g_1(b_1)$ is pervaded by its own potentiality but not also by the actuality of $f_1(a_1)$ and the potentiality of $g_1(b_1)$. If you remember that the mode of a circumstance depends only on the identities but not on the modes, if any, of its terms, you will see why I just spoke of the value of a function rather than, more generally, of the product of a canon. Notice, too, that I did not add to (b) the clause "either wholly or in part," which in the light of (a) would be misleading.

Notice, finally, that one cannot reverse the order of (C) and (D). For one cannot, or at least not out of hand, reject the possibility of there being two expressions (not: thoughts) for one existent. Just think of the plurality of expressions, due to the plurality of dummy variables, for a single generality or a single class.

(E) Without the third which we called the sheer complex, the pervaded one is the only existent the thought (not: expression) in these situations can explicitly intend, irrespective of whether one is aware of the complex either (a) without or (b) with its mode. (2) being nonliteral, the only expression available fits (a). That causes no difficulties. About the thought, or thoughts, in (a) and (b), however, there is a serious question. Are they two or are they one? When first faced with it, I merely claimed, again because we were not yet in a position to do better, that they were one and the same. Even so, I pointed out, there was no difficulty in distinguishing between the two acts; qualitatively, as one says, i.e., not merely by the diversity of the particulars in them; since in (b) but not in (a) the particular in the act exemplifies evidence. Then, speaking of transparence and illumination, I added for good measure two words from the tradition. If, for instance, an awareness (a) is followed by an awareness (b) of the same complex, the intention remains the same but becomes transparent, or illuminated. In the meantime we have also learned that, since no analytic complex is a cluster and, therefore, texts are indispensable in both (a) and (b), the two awarenesses also have different texts. All this helped and still helps. Yet, much more incisively, by the "epistemological" proposition (i) on p. 332, if there is only one intention, there can be only one thought. How, then, shall we account—not causally, of course, which is the job of science, but ontologically—for the difference between what is presented to us in (a) and (b), respectively? The question is serious because in this world (i) lies deep; how deep will come out impressively in the last Appendix. I answer by appealing to the distinction, already made in Section V and thus not ad hoc, between the (nonexisting) *referent* of an awareness, on the one hand, and the *intention*, or intentions, of the nonauxiliary act, or acts, of it, on the other.

The intention in (a) is the same as in (b); what differs are merely the referents.
Thus (i) is preserved. There remains the fact that this new appeal
to the old distinction must be made for awarenesses much simpler
than the ones which first suggested and required it; so simple indeed
that the single nonauxiliary act in them may intend something as
simple as this-being-either-green-or-not-green. This may well be a
sign that we have reached not just the limits of logical atomism but,
rather, to use still another phrase of Butchvarov's, those of ontological
analysis.

We have come to the end of this longish argument. Let me add two
comments that will place it; the first about a supplement it requires,
the second about the importance of what it secures.

The three parts of the argument for (2) correspond to the threefold
distinction between thing (D), thought (E), and language (C). "Language," though, will not quite do; for there is the familiar gap between the ideal calculus which is not a language and the language we
speak which is not a calculus. One may refuse to fuss once more about
the familiar, as I did quite early in the game, and yet admit, as I also
do, that there are two reasons why I must check whether this gap
affects the significance of the proposed notion of the literally sayable,
upon which something is literally sayable if and only if an expression
(of the IL) stands for it. One reason is that in the IL all thoughts are
simple characters; the other, that the matter involves the assay of the
meaning nexus. Since this assay has been left to the last Appendix, it
will avoid repetition if the required check, or supplement, will be presented together with it.

Remember the three kinds of ontological discourse. In the order
they were listed (p. 318), the first is literally, the second nonliterally,
about what we can think; the third, nonliterally of course, about what
we can think only after a fashion. If it were not for the first kind, we
could not literally say, as we saw one can, that a certain complex is of a
certain form. That there is the second kind I have just done my best to
establish. In the next subsection I shall reason as closely as I can that
talk about the canons belongs to the third kind of philosophical
discourse.

III

The canons, together with the world's things and functions, determine everything there is in it. These canons, we remember, are of
three types, (a) for facts, (b) for circumstances, (c) for classes. Three
examples, one from each type, stated as we eventually stated them,
will call attention to one respect in which they are all alike, as well as to

another in which the variation is very narrow. (a1) If there is a diad such that its terms are a particular and a universal[(0)], then, since the appropriate function is also there, so is eo ipso the fact they jointly "produce." (b1) If there are two determinates, so is eo ipso the diad whose terms they are. (c1) If a determinate is an enumerator, there is eo ipso the class it "selects." To the respect, marked by the Latin tag, in which all canons are alike, attention was called quite recently. The "product" of a canon is neither the sum nor the class nor any other sort of compound of its "material." This, incidentally, also lays the ghosts of the metaphors that linger on in such words as 'produce', 'select', and their derivatives. In canons (b) the material is a collection of two existents, subject only to the restriction, we called it minimal, that they are both determinates. In canons (c) the material is a single determinate; with the condition, alas, not being in all cases a matter of form. The material of a canon is thus either *two determinates;* or *one determinate and one function;* or a *single determinate.* In this respect the variation among the canons is very narrow.

What is the import of the "eo ipso" for the IL? Continue to use 'expression' for 'expression of IL'; start with the canons (a) and (b), whose materials are two existents; take any one of them and let 'α_1' and 'α_2' abbreviate the expressions for any two existents that are material for this canon; then ask yourself what the expression for the product will have to be like. Clearly, this expression must do one and only one thing. It must single out the product and call attention to its being just that, viz., the one determinate which is eo ipso there, provided only α_1 and α_2 are there. As long as one writes linearly, the obvious way of doing that is by *juxtaposition;* or, rather, less haphazardly and in order to avoid the familiar ambiguity which '$\alpha_1(\alpha_2, \alpha_3)$' and '$(\alpha_2, \alpha_2)\alpha_3$' exemplify, by writing the two expressions to the left and to the right of the comma in a parenthes*is*. As you see, we have already arrived at the answer; and it turns out to be so fundamental that we shall be well advised to add it as a sixth to the five earlier propositions about the ideal language. (B6) *The juxtaposition of two expressions is diacritical.*

For an example, use 'a_1' and 'f_1' once more as so often before, and consider (1) '(a_1, f_1)' and (2) '$(\eta_1(a_1, f_1))$'. Since their diad is the *only* circumstance which *any* two determinates jointly ground, (1) cannot but stand for the diad whose terms are a_1 and f_1, just as (2) cannot but stand for the familiar atomic fact. Thus we have at long last conclusively established that the parenthesis in (1) and the inner and the outer parenthesis (2) do all three the same job. The only liberty I have taken and shall continue to take is the familiar one of omitting the outermost parenthesis. Notice, too, that since '(,)' is a single diacritical mark, I deliberately use the singular, parenthes*is*.

Turn now to the remaining canons, for classes and the other two sorts of circumstances. The expressions for classes, we have long known and can easily confirm by a glance at (c1), require a second mark, the one for which I use 'λ', such that, writing pedantically for once, '(λ, α_1)', which is well formed if and only if α_1 is a selector, may stand for the class that is eo ipso there if and only if α_1 satisfies the condition. That leaves elementhood and the meaning nexus. Both are circumstances; both, unlike diads, involve order but not only order. Take, then, any two determinates, α_1 and α_2, and consider one of them, say, α_1, together with their diad, (α_1, α_2). The latter two are jointly the material for three different determinates, viz., the order, the elementhood, and the meaning nexus, conventionally represented by (3) '$\langle \alpha_1, \alpha_2 \rangle$', (4) '$\alpha_1 \in \alpha_2$', and (5) '$\alpha_1 M \alpha_2$'. How must we, or how may we, expand these three in the IL? One could, of course, introduce three more diacritical marks, '$\in$' and 'M' as before, and, in addition, 'O' for order; which would yield (3') '$((\alpha_1, (\alpha_1, \alpha_2), O)$', (4') '$((\alpha_1, (\alpha_1, \alpha_2) \in)$', (5') '$((\alpha_1, (\alpha_1, \alpha_2), M)$'. Yet there is a difference between 'O', on the one hand, and '$\in$' and 'M', on the other. (3') stands for what is always actual and never involves anything but order. (4') and (5'), however, provide different notations for two determinates which, although they both involve order, are yet two and not one. It follows that, while '$\in$' and 'M' are indispensable, 'O' is not. Thus one may omit it; which reduces the number of diacritical marks to the minimum of four mentioned in (B3). Nothing will be lost; perspicuity will be gained; once more the practice we have long followed is at last conclusively established.

Notationally, juxtaposition and serial order are, as it were, at opposite poles. In the IL of my world, juxtaposition stands for nothing. In the conventional notations, however, some of which some ontologists more or less explicitly propose as the ideal language of their worlds, juxtaposition stands, among other things, for exemplification; which latter, not surprisingly under the circumstances, in those worlds is nothing. Serial order, on the other hand, in my world exists and in its IL is always represented by the expressions for the tuples that ground it. In the conventional notations, however, which are all "linear," serial order, instead of being always represented by expressions for tuples, may, and in some crucial cases does, appear in propria persona as the order of some marks in the series of marks on the line along which all expressions are written, as, e.g., in '$\alpha_1 \in \alpha_2$' vs. '$\alpha_2 \in \alpha_1$'. Such inconsistency in representation not only detracts from the perspicuity of the notation but may be, and in some crucial cases probably was, at least a contributory cause of some grave errors (p. 119). Does that make a nonserially written IL preferable? The matter is worth looking into. So I shall next design such a notation. But let us first smoothen things verbally by taking for granted that each of its primitive marks either is diacritical or stands for either a thing or a function, and by calling every expression of it which is not a primitive mark a *diagram*.

Let α_1 be a determinate which is not a thing and construct "its" diagram, D_1, from a linear but otherwise presumably ideal notation as follows. Represent the parenthesis marking the juxtaposition that corresponds to the canonical step which produces α_1 by a circle, and call this circle the "outermost" one of the D_1 to be constructed. Remember next what we called the narrowness of variation among the canons; make use of some of the conditions the latter specify; and you will see that there are three alternatives. The two expressions whose juxtaposition is now tentatively marked by the outermost circle stand either (a) for two determinates which are both things, or (b) for two determinates at least one of which is not a thing, or (c) for one determinate which is not a thing and for a primitive mark that either is diacritical or stands for a function. In case (a), put inside the outermost circle the two primitive marks for the two things and you have already arrived at D_1. Call such a diagram "elementary." Its α_1 is of course a diad of things. In case (b), if (b1) both determinates are nonthings, draw inside of the outermost circle two circles, mutually exclusive of each other, to represent tentatively the two juxtapositions corresponding to the two canonical steps which produce, respectively, the one and the other of these two nonthings. If (b2) only one of the determinates is a nonthing, draw inside the outermost circle "of D_1" only one circle, to represent tentatively the outermost circle "of" this nonthing, and write into the ring between the two circles the primitive mark for the thing among the two. In case (c), proceed analogously to (b2), so that the result will be one circle within another and in the ring between them a primitive mark that either is diacritical or stands for a function. Carrying out the appropriate one of these alternatives, either you will arrive at an elementary diagram which is the diagram of α_1, the latter being a diad of things; or you will arrive at a pattern with either one or two mutually exclusive "inner" circles inside an "outer" circle. "Fill" now in the same way the inner circle or circles which are not elementary diagrams, repeat the procedure, and you will after a finite number of repetitions arrive at a pattern with one outermost circle and such that its "innermost" circles are all elementary dia-

grams. There being no circle left to be filled, you have come to the
end. The pattern now before you is the diagram D_1 of α_1.

Mathematicians have built elaborate theories about several kinds
of structures they call partial or nonlinear orders. The inclusion-
exclusion patterns of the circles in the diagrams of our nonlinear notation all belong to one such kind. Its details we leave to the mathematicians. But we may, and I shall, take for granted the following
proposition that falls well within the bounds of common sense: The
diagram D_1 of α_1 contains all the cues needed to determine either *the
series,* or, more often than not, *all the alternative series,* of canonical
steps by each of which α_1 can be produced from its ultimate foundation. What now, if anything, in the world does the totality of those series show, or stand for, or correspond to, whatever the proper word
may turn out to be? Or, since the partial order in D_1 contains all the
required cues for those series, what does, at one remove, this partial
order show, or stand for, and so on? Since we undertook to get rid of
serial order in our notation, we must face this question.

If something is to show something else, or stand for it, or what have
you, this something else must be there. In the case at hand it obviously
is the canons; or perhaps, if you would rather put it this way, the alternative serial orders in which they must be "applied" to produce α_1.
Thus we cannot even start answering the question we just discovered
we must face, unless we first ask another. What, if any, is the ontological status of the canons? But, again, one cannot answer this preliminary question without attending to some matters preliminary to it.
That is the cue for the expositional strategy I shall follow. The material in the rest of this subsection is so arranged that the answer to the
question about the partial order in our diagrams will come forth only
at the very end of it.

68* A sufficient reason we need not worry about the details of the
partial order is that all D are finite. Three comments, though, may
help. Consider first the complex linearly represented by '$f_1(a_1) \vee
f_1(a_1)$', and you will see why many diagrams contain several mutually
exclusive circles whose "fillings" are alike in all relevant respects. Consider next a determinate as simple as $f_1(a_1) \vee g_1(b_1)$, and you will appreciate why in most cases there is more than one series of canonical
steps leading from the ultimate foundations of a determinate to the
latter. Compare, finally, '$\bigvee \langle a_1, f_1(a_1) \rangle \vee \bigwedge \langle a_1, f_1(a_1) \rangle$' with '$\bigvee \langle a_1, f_1(a_1) \rangle
\vee \bigwedge \langle b_1, f_1(b_1) \rangle$', and you will see that the availability of "variants" (not:
variants! see p. 219) increases the number of alternative series but
causes no difficulty.

A calculus as such is merely a bit of geometry; say, the collection of all its expressions, each of which is a geometrical design, i.e., as one says, a type rather than a token. To "interpret" a calculus is to "coordinate" to each of its expressions—with the exception of those which are thereby set apart as diacritical—one and only one existent from a domain of being, or, perhaps, from all of it. A coordina*tion*, as I shall here speak, is a class of 2-tuples whose terms are, in this order, an expression of the calculus and an existent of the domain. These classes are there, whether or not there are humans. To *coordinate* a calculus to a domain, however, is to pick out one of these coordinations, which is a human activity. To *interpret* a calculus into a domain is to coordinate it to the latter with the purpose of making the first term of each 2-tuple stand for (or express, or represent) the second; thus turning the calculus into what is called an artificial language. There is no need to go over the familiar. Yet some comments will help; for still others, also about the "picking out," see the next digression.

Reconsider now what the logician-geometrician did when we watched him Goedelizing his calculus (p. 329). He, too, picked a coordination from among those between all expressions of his calculus and some integers in the domain of elementary arithmetic. Yet he did not interpret his calculus into that domain; for his purpose was not to make the former into an artificial language about the latter, but, rather, to use integers, by means of the technique Goedel invented, when talking his own natural language about the former. (E.g., he tells us that an expression has a certain (geometrical) form if and only if the integer he coordinated to it is of a certain arithmetical kind.) That the calculi Goedel studied when he first used his technique can in another step be interpreted into elementary arithmetic is another story. Notice, too, that, characteristically, his coordination does not set aside any expressions which, given a certain interpretation, would turn out to be diacritical.

The IL an ontologist proposes is a calculus he has designed and interpreted. The purpose he pursues we know. His IL is to reflect perspicuously the categorial structure of the world. But we should, and I shall, at this point argue more closely than before that what goes on when he applies this technique, or method, is just that; he applies a technique that is not philosophically problematic and does not commit him to any substantive position in ontology. What, then, does go on? Let us look at two similar situations, one involving an engineer, the other an anthropologist.

An engineer constructing a code of some scope designs and interprets an artificial language. For an up-to-date example, suppose that he builds a computer such that its input comes directly from the atmospheric conditions about which its printouts provide information. The anthropologist, having discovered a tribe whose language as yet no one understands, decides to live with these people until he has learned it. His purpose is to discover the coordinations that make certain (auditory) designs the expressions of a natural language. The differences between the two situations are obvious. Most strikingly, perhaps, while both designs and coordination of the artificial language are very strictly regimented, in the case of the artificial one the regimentation, if that be the word, is so loose that in most contexts speaking of a "calculus" and its "interpretation" will do more harm than good. Yet it will, without doing any harm, help my purpose of the moment, which is to close in quickly on a crucial feature of what goes on, not only in these two situations but also whenever an ontologist builds his IL.

Systematically speaking rather than historically or psychologically, all scientific discourse is always commonsensical and never ontological. Of course we all speak about the same world. Yet no scientist, when about his business, ever asks or answers any of the questions that are the ontologist's exclusive concern. To say the same thing differently, with a phrase I have found suggestive, science is but the long arm of common sense. Still differently, with a phrase just used, scientific discourse is never "philosophically problematic." Now what our ontologist does is, except for two differences that make no difference, the same sort of thing the engineer and the anthropologist do. Yet these two scientists stay clearly within the bounds of common sense. So, therefore, I conclude, does the ontologist when he constructs his ideal language; and that is how I support the claim that this technique is philosophically unproblematic and does not commit him to any substantive position in ontology. One of the two differences that do not affect this conclusion is that, unlike the natural language the anthropologist studies, the IL is not a "language" anyone could speak. The other is that, unlike either the engineer's or the anthropologist's, the domain into which he *must* interpret his calculus is the phenomenological material.

69* (a) A reader is stung by the 'must' just emphasized. Does it, he wonders, commit the practitioner of the method to phenomenology. I first point out to him that the phenomenological material, which is but the innermost core of common sense, and the philosophical movement known as phenomenology are not quite the same. I add that I greatly admire the work of the early Husserl. Next I remind him of the reason, stated at the very beginning of this discourse, why I do not believe that the interpretation of the ideal calculus on which I insist—

if only because any other one would start, as one says, from a universe already constituted—does not commit one to anything. I simply have no notion of an ontology, whatever its specific claims and whatever its method, that does not start from, and does not at all crucial points check back against, the phenomenological jumping-off place and its rock bottom. But, perhaps, I conclude, that is all you mean; if so, we do not disagree. (b) The extremists among those who took the linguistic turn believe that what can be saved from ontology is either logic or linguistics. I believe, and reiterated when these views were mentioned, that logic is a branch of mathematics, that linguistics is a scientific discipline, and that ontology, which is neither, is alive and well. Yet, I added, the ontologist often speaks about logic and at least once must take cognizance of linguistics. The latter we just did. Why we had to do it and what we got out of doing it can be stated in a manner that sounds paradoxical but really isn't. Since the IL is one of the tools of this ontological discourse, we had to take a close look at that tool. What we saw, however, was that, being philosophically unproblematic, the tool does not in any way affect the dialectic. (c) As far as the psychology of discovery is concerned, the ontologist may be, as I in this discourse often was, helped by reflecting on our natural language. Systemically, though, interpreting the ideal calculus "directly" into the phenomenological material, rather than obtaining the ideal language by "schematizing" the natural one, not only unburdens the overall pattern but also sidetracks the tired arguments as to what, if anything, of concern to the ontologist is either lost, or distorted, or prejudged by such schematization. (d) When picking out a coordination one follows 'rules'. But such picking-out is a human activity. Thus I am not, when putting it that way, ignoring the earlier warning that in ontological discourse any use of 'rule' outside of a human context threatens confusion. The "rules" here spoken of are the same kind of thing as the "instructions," spoken of earlier, which we have learned to follow when producing in our minds certain Cartesian chains. (e) How, in detail, does one go about picking a coordination, when, say, interpreting one's ideal calculus into the phenomenological material? (1) One starts by picking out a certain number of 2-tuples, one for each function, such that a design and a function are respectively the first and the second term of each of them.† This way of selecting a primitive mark for each function reflects the uniqueness (p. 114) of the latter. (2) Then one does a similar thing for several *kinds* of designs,

---

† Note, however, that tuples, being diads, are subject to the minimal restriction. Thus there cannot be, as Bergmann here suggests, a tuple one of whose terms is a function, at least in any *literal* sense.—WH

one kind for each ultimate sort, so that each primitive mark thus obtainable "shows" the ultimate sort of the thing to which it is being coordinated. (3) From there on one proceeds by rules, such as, e.g., that, given the two designs coordinated to two determinates, the juxtaposition of the former is to be coordinated to the diad of the latter. Ignoring, safely for the purpose at hand, the familiar complication for n-classes, these rules are such that, each complex being of a certain form (form$_2$ on p. 330), which is *recursively decidable*, one can, given the coordinations (1) and (2), *certifiably* coordinate the complex to "its" design. What complexes exist and what forms they are depends on the canons, which thus "correspond" to the (geometrical) formation rules (form$_1$ on p. 330), which the calculus must have in order to be thus interpretable. It is indeed this correspondence which faces us with the question I left to the end. Two others we had better answer right now. (f) What, first, is the status of those *designs;* and, how, second, does it all fit with the distinction between the recursively decidable and the merely certifiable? Since there are in this world no derived characters, even the design of a string as simple as circle-followed-by-dash-followed-by-square, or, for that matter, still more simply, the wedge design often coordinated to disjunction, does not exist, and, to repeat, what isn't there cannot be coordinated to anything. The obvious substitute for a design, and the only one I can think of, is the class of all multipartite particulars, which, if the design were a character, would exemplify it. (For a comment on the existence of such particulars in this world, see p. 211.) But, alas, making this substitution is to jump from the frying pan into the fire. In this world the mode of a string is in principle inaccessible; yet elementhood in a full-status class is decidable. Hence it is only certifiable whether a certain string is an element of the "class" we wanted to coordinate to a certain complex. Nor is this "class" itself available unless we first add to this world, as in the third Appendix we shall, certain "existents" of merely derived ontological status, such as, e.g., the "class" of all green spots (particulars exemplifying green). All this is as it ought to be, encouraging rather than discouraging. For, otherwise, how could the form$_2$ of a complex be recursively decidable while the form$_1$ of any of the strings (tokens) standing for it is merely certifiable? Only by delving into such "detail" of execution more than just once can one reassure himself that the delicate notion of the modes, on which so much depends in this world, does at least not lead to contradiction. In this discourse, though, once will have to do. I shall go on as before, except for some appeals, at crucial points, to just this detail.

Let us stop for a glance at the map. How far along are we on the way toward answering the question as to (i) *what, if anything, the particular order in our nonlinear notation stands for, or shows, or corresponds to?* I just finished arguing as closely as I can what we have long anticipated. The formation rules of the IL correspond to the canons. A bit earlier we established just as painstakingly that the partial order is a by-product of the formation rules. That leaves no doubt that we must answer the preliminary question we also anticipated. (ii) *Do the canons exist?* Equivalently in this world, can we think them or are they, properly speaking, unthinkable, although we do in fact think them after a fashion? The question is not easily separated from two further ones. (iii) *What goes on when, after a fashion, one thinks what does not exist?* (iv) *Can the canons be stated literally?* Working through this list backward will allow us to cover conveniently a good deal of what must still be said. So I shall start with (iv), proceed to (iii), thence to (ii), interrupt briefly for a probe of the notion of something showing itself, and then, as planned, conclude with (i).

To be literally sayable, we know, is to be expressible in the IL. Can the canons be so expressed? Start once more from a paradigm; take the canon for the simplest sort of atomic fact; state it first in the jargon, influenced by logic, which, although not idiomatic English, is yet close enough to it to pass for a natural language; and try to "transcribe" it into the IL. In the jargon the canon reads; (C1) For any two (things), if one is a particular and the other a universal$^{(0)}$, then there is a third, viz., (the fact of) the former-exemplifying-the latter. We have already argued as closely as we can that 'α_1 is a particular' and 'β_1 is a universal$^{(0)}$' are not transcribable; not to mention that, unless $\alpha_1(\beta_1)$ is a particular (universal$^{(0)}$), what they purport to stand for, not being there, is not even thinkable. Thus we are immediately blocked. But let us explore how far one can get if he replaces the untranscribable by means of the coextensive classes $\overline{Part}$ and $\overline{Univ}^{(0)}$ introduced on p. 00. The expression

$$(6)\ (\alpha_1)(\beta_1)[\overline{Part}(\alpha_1)\ \&\ \overline{Univ}^{(0)}(\beta_1) \equiv$$
$$.(\exists\gamma_1)(\exists a_1)(\exists f_1)\ ((a_1 = \alpha_1)\ \&\ (f_1 = \beta_1)\ \&\ (\gamma_1 = \eta_1(a_1, f_1)))]$$

is, I submit, as close as one can come to transcribing (C1) if one resorts to this expedient. A series of six comments will show, first, why this is so, and, then, why it is not close enough.

1. The notation in (6) is the usual halfway house of convenience. The subscripts are to remind us that upon the new assay of quantification the target letters are constants and that, say, '$(\exists f_1)(\gamma_1 = \eta_1(a_1, f_1))$' abbreviates '$\bigwedge\langle f_1, \gamma_1 = \eta_1(f_1, a_1)\rangle$'. The Greek and Roman letterings will remind us of the differences among the respective ranges, which

latter depend only on what is and what isn't well formed. The "Greek targets" range over all determinates; the two "Roman targets" over all particulars and all universals[(0)], respectively.

2. The two "additional" quantifications, over a_1 and f_1, serve two purposes. (a) They maximize the range of γ_1, or, equivalently, they make the restriction on it, like that on α_1 and β_1, the minimal one. If these three ranges were not all maximal, the distance between (6) and (C1) would be even greater than we shall find it to be. (b) The limited ranges of a_1 and f_1, on the other hand, impress upon us the dependence, which I shall exploit in the fourth of these comments, of '$\eta_1(a_1, f_1)$', which occurs in (6), on the formation rule corresponding to the canon.

3. The material equivalence of (6) does not harm and permits the perspicuous grouping of the quantifiers into an inner and an outer "prefix." Yet there are two reasons why material implication from the left to the right, which is verbally closer to (C1), would do. For one, there are the tautologies of sameness and diversity (p. 197), of which more in the next subsection, by virtue of which (I speak concisely and ignore the often tedious but always innocuous "exception" due to the dummy variables) every determinate is diverse from every other not produced by the same canon from the same argument. For another, since the identity of a determinate which is not a thing (simple) is completely exhausted by its being the product of a certain canon from a certain argument, we cannot even think it except as just that, viz., the product of this canon from this argument.[†] (The misfortunes that befell the relationist when he forgot this have been recorded on p. 129.)

4. The expression '$\eta_1(a_1, f_1)$', which occurs in (6), is well formed by virtue of the formation rule corresponding to (C1). Hence, if it weren't for (C1), (6) wouldn't be well formed either. But an expression cannot stand for what in this blatant sense it "presupposes." I conclude that (6) fails; or, to put it as before, that it doesn't come close enough. Convincing as this argument is to me by itself, it will be supported by, and in turn support, another one which I shall make in due

---

[†] Bergmann speaks here as though *all* nonsimple determinates are values of arguments for functions. This, of course, is not so. Only *facts* are values of a function for an argument; circumstances and classes are not. Bergmann's manner of expressing himself here suggests that circumstances and classes are, so to speak, "functionless values," with the relevant canon itself playing the role of the missing function. Interestingly, in the unpublished paper of which this book is the namesake Bergmann *did* hold that classes are the values of a function for an argument. The argument was held to be the tuple which is here held to be a selector of a class, and the function was to be represented by a symbol which corresponds to the sign 'λ', which is here said to be "diacritical."—WH

course when examining what a canon, if it existed, would have to be. One objection, though, we can meet right now.

5. The objector, having pointed out that (6) and (7) $(\exists a_1)(\exists f_1)(\alpha_1 = \eta_1(a_1, f_1))$ both presuppose (C1) in exactly the same sense, asks me how I can consistently hold that because of this presupposition (6) fails, while (7), which I made the definiens of '$At_0(\alpha_1)$', states literally that α_1 is of the familiar form. I first remind him that what (7) literally states is that something, viz., α_1, shares a certain form with something else, viz., $\eta_1(a_1, f_1)$, and then point out to him that one can of course not say this without mentioning the something else. Nor, I add, do I deny that one can mention only what exists, which, in case the existent mentioned is a determinate but not a thing, "presupposes" indeed all the canons by virtue of which it exists. But I do not see how in this context, which involves the form but not the "existence" of $\eta_1(a_1, f_1)$, presupposing the latter could hurt.

6. '$\eta_1(a_1, f_1)$' is not the only occurrence in (6) that presupposes the canon. Look at the definientia for $\overline{Part}(\alpha_1)$ and $\overline{Univ}^{(0)}(\beta_1)$ on p. 302, and you will see that they are suggested by, and built around, several canons, including (C1). As for these two classes in the paradigm, so for all the others, which, without replacing the untranscribable, take their places in the conditions specified by any canon; such as, e.g., on the side of the expressions, '*Complex*' in the attempt (8) $(\alpha_1)(\beta_1)$ [$Complex(\alpha_1)$ & $Complex(\beta_1) \equiv (\exists \gamma_1)(\exists c_1)(\exists d_1)(\alpha_1 = c_1)$ & $(\beta_1 = d_1)$ & $(\gamma_1 = c_1 \vee d_1)$] to transcribe the canon for disjunction. For the definiens of '*Complex*', see p. 270.

(CNE) *The canons do not exist.* I am ready to argue in support of this proposition. That a canon cannot be literally stated we just established. That, though, does not suffice to establish (CNE). Just remember the grasped ultimate sorts and the transparent modes of the last subsection. To establish (CNE), we must convince ourselves that, properly speaking, a canon cannot be thought, even though when uttering, say, (C1) in earnest, we do think it after a fashion. How, then, can we "convince" ourselves that "something" cannot be thought? I shall consider three cases. In the first case, (a), the answer can stand by itself. In the other two cases, (b) and (c), it is, we shall see, natural to go on answering the question (iii) on p. 344, as to what happens when after a fashion we think what does not exist. Nor is it just natural, it is economical as well; for we shall, by proceeding in this way, also take care of an important item of business that was left unfinished in Section V. (That the questions and answers themselves belong to the third kind of ontological discourse will not, I trust, puzzle you at this late point. So, naturally, does much else in this concluding Section.)

a. "Words we can arbitrarily string together. Sometimes, having made such a string, we cannot, no matter how hard we try, find a thought" or an awareness of which the string would be the text. The completed sentence and the sentence fragment between the quotes are taken from Section II, where the issue of the unthinkable first came up (p. 62). In completing the fragment I took advantage of what we have learned in the meantime. 'Green is red' and 'middle C is louder than', with 'is' both times (I speak concisely) construed as exemplification, are two obvious examples. In such cases we are readily convinced that the futile string does not express anything and soon stop groping for what it might express. That is why I said that in these cases the answer can stand for itself. But perhaps you will agree with all this and yet wonder why on this occasion I am using a new word, 'convince', instead of appealing, as on so many earlier ones, to the phenomenological rock bottom. I can give you two reasons. For one, I am reluctant to make this appeal for something "negative." For another, I want to emphasize that the root—again, I avoid 'ground'—of unthinkability is in this world essentially and unalterably anthropocentric; in a sense in which, in spite of the ultimately anthropocentric jumping-off place for everything in this ontology, transparency is not. Because of this contrast between them, unthinkability and transparency are the two poles of a major axis in the overall dialectic. Of this much more even closer to the end.

In such cases as (a), I just said, one soon stops groping for what the futile string might express. That puts them at one extreme. At the other extreme, (b) and (c) are so chosen that what their strings, with equal futility, purport to stand for "seems" to be transparent. Thus we must eventually account for this "illusion." Trying to do that in Section II would have been merely confusing so I postponed the job. In Section V we could at least fit into a context. Remember the horse, out in the pasture, in our thesis schematized as a M_i & L_i, which, whether schematized or not, is in this world very different from the referent, this-being-a-horse, of an awareness which is, say, a perceiving of it. Thus we were prepared for complications. Yet there was at least the familiar, reassuring connection. The perceiving is, as one says, veridical if and only if M_i & L_i is actual. In such cases as (b) and (c), however, there is in this world nothing that could, even in this broad sense, be connected with the putative referent of the illusion. That is why in Section V I merely said that in these cases, which even in its rather elaborate context are clearly an extreme, we must "scrounge for a surrogate," and then quickly postponed the job once more until we would be ready for it. Now we are.

b. Can one think anything the string (9) 'or is diverse from and' may purport to stand for? In Section III, when distinguishing the ontological notion of separability from the anthropocentric one of independence, we had no difficulty convincing ourselves that a function cannot be intended explicitly (p. 114). Take now a string in which either 'or' or 'and' occurs but does not connect two substrings each of which stands for a complex; make allowance for such idiomatic shortcuts as 'this and that are green'; and you will just as easily convince yourself that one cannot think anything the string might stand for. That in the IL '($\vee$, &)' is ill formed is, loosely speaking, a consequence of this unthinkability but not, as we know, conversely. As for '($\vee$, &)', so for '$\eta_1(rd, gr)$' in (a). The difference between (a) and (b) is that in the case of the latter the illusion of being transparently presented with or-being-diverse-from-and is very strong indeed. How, then, shall we account for it? Take any two complexes, α_1 and α_1, so simple that the forms of (10) α_1-or-α_2 and (11) α_1-and-α_2, and the actuality of their diversity, (11) α_1-or-α_2-being-diverse-from-α_1-and-α_2, are all three, when explicitly intended, either immediately or almost immediately transparent to us. Suppose next that one is in quick succession, perhaps even within a single specious present, presented with the transparencies of (10), (11), (12), in this order; and you will appreciate how easy it is to shoot over the mark, as it were; being, or "seeming" to be, immediately thereafter presented with the transparency of or-being-diverse-from-and. Do I then claim that whenever one is thus deluded, he is living through such a series? Of course I don't. Using 'thesis', 'schematic', and 'speculative' as in Section V, I merely propose the thesis that one's having lived in the past once or several times through such series is, speculatively and schematically, the cause of his present illusion, i.e., to spell it out for once, of his now thinking after a fashion the unthinkable. Past causes of this kind are, I submit, in this case as well as in many others, the primary source of the illusion. A secondary source in all cases is, broadly speaking, language. Less broadly, as we know from Section V, we could not have any of these rather esoteric awarenesses without thinking their texts as a "part" of them. To appreciate how in this case that strengthens the illusion, consider how easy it is to pass, or slip, or slide, from the futile string (9) to the string "'or'-being-diverse-from-'and'", which latter is the text of a visual or auditory fact that is, although its mode is in principle inaccessible, "beyond reasonable doubt."

c. We cannot think anything of which (13) 'pitch is not a relation' might be the text; i.e., more concisely, this string, too, is futile. On the primary material we need not dwell. When explicitly intended, the form shared by midde-D-being-a-pitch and middle-C-being-a-pitch is immediately transparent; so is that of middle-D-being-higher-than-middle-C; and so on. In this respect the illusions of which (9) and (13) are the paradigms are alike. The latter, however, and this is distinctive of them, are the strongest of all; so strong indeed that one couldn't, or at least I couldn't, be convinced of the string's futility without some reflections, and the refinements they produce, on the notion of the thinkable. My thesis is that the extraordinary strength of these illusions is "borrowed." In the paradigm, it is borrowed from another illusion, which, although not the same, amounts to the unexamined belief that (14) 'pitch is a relation' is the text of a thought. As we speak, the intention of this thought would of course be potential and the thought itself, therefore, false. That, though, is beside the point. The point is, rather, that, if one attends, the conviction that the string (14) is futile is almost as readily acquired and, once acquired, as sturdy as in (a). I say "almost" because of the additional strength both illusions draw from (13) and (14) being both grammatically acceptable in the language we speak. ((9), unless one most blatantly confuses words and things, is not!) To balance and overbalance these formidable odds, ask yourself one question. How could one possibly think the negation of the unthinkable? (What would be negated?) The IL does of course perspicuously represent this refinement. Systematically, though, that is a consequence, and not a cause, of our reflections.

Other causes have other twists; but the three we examined will do; we are ready for that of the canons. First, though, let me take out time for five remarks. The first three are obvious; yet they will all help us to steer clear of the style alien to this discourse.

(1) No one but a philosopher, and he only when he does philosophy, has the awarenesses here talked about. That alone puts the ritual appeals to the man on the street out of court, even though asking him how he knows that green is not a relation is a possible opening move of a Socratic dialogue that may afford him a glimpse at the kind of thing philosophers worry about. (2) More often than not, when uttering a string of words in earnest, one either relies on memory or borrows from language. Whenever that happens, whether or not the string is futile, there is nothing to be accounted for. (3) Does accounting for them break the spell of these "esoteric" illusions? In the three cases examined it does and it doesn't. Nor is in these cases what happens to them different from what happens to those "ordinary" ones

which a psychologist knows how to produce in others after he has discovered the "special" conditions under which a certain stimulus pattern causes a perceptual response different from the one it causes under "normal" conditions. If later on this psychologist unwittingly finds himself in those special conditions, he, too, will be deluded, although if immediately thereafter he suspects that they obtain, he may not reach for the fruit that is not there. (4) Since the notion of unthinkability is unalterably anthropocentric, we need not fuss over whether the above "refinement" of it is no more than just that. Quite to the contrary. In view of the dialectical weight the notion is made to bear in this discourse as "one of the poles of a major axis," and, also, in view of the prevalence of epistemology in the post-Cartesian tradition, I would be the first to insist that it must and safely may, without vitiating circularity or what have you, undergo still other refinements. I have already briefly distinguished the unthinkable, the unimaginable, and the indubitable from each other; and we shall review these distinctions, although again but briefly, when taking our farewell look at the overall dialectic. (5) When trying to assay what is there when, after a fashion, we think what isn't, which is the second of the four situations listed in Section V, we must, with a phrase then used of which I reminded you a while ago, "scrounge about for a surrogate." Now we see that for (a), (b), and (c) even this phrase is unduly optimistic. For, everything we found outside of these illusionary awarenesses is either past causes of them or present dispositions, none of which is "connected" with (the referent of) such an awareness as a $\mu_i \lambda_i$, or what it schematizes is "connected" with (the referent of) a perceiving of the horse. In the case of the canons, however, there is, as we are about to see, a surrogate of sorts. (6) Illusion and illumination clash in any world. In this world in particular, the very idea of being transparently presented with what does not exist in either mode is against the grain. Even though it helps to keep in mind that these limiting situations occur only when a philosopher stands at the boundary of thought, it ought to acknowledge that they are most delicate. Yet I do not think of them as signs of failure but, rather, as a reminder that we have once again reached the very boundary, not just of this or that ontology, but of ontological analysis itself; not, in this instance, the boundary between ontology and mere speculation, but that between ontology such as we can do it, on the one hand, and the phenomenological basis from which we must start, if we are to do it at all, on the other.

The canon, if there were such a thing, would have to be a $\bigvee$-generality whose scope is a conditional, such that antecedent and consequent are a certain determinate (actually or potentially) satisfying its condition, and the "existing," or the "existence" (actual or potential), of its product for this determinate, respectively; with existence, or existing, not being assayable in terms of a $\wedge$-generality. But *the unthinkability of such "existence" or "existing" is, I submit, as close to the phenomenological rock bottom as anything merely negative could be.* Nor of course can one think explicitly what requires that, in thinking it, one think the unthinkable implicitly. Thus the canons are unthinkable. Hence, by the fundamental gambit, (CNE) *the canons do not exist.*

70* The last paragraph seems to cover so much of the path on which we started when stating (CNE) on p. 346 that we had better look at the structure of this longish line of thought. (i) Existence (existing) and simplicity (being a simple) do not exist. (ii) What exists can be thought and conversely. Structurally inseparable, (i) and (ii) are probably the two most fundamental gambits of this discourse. Once one accepts the claim as to what a canon, if it existed, would have to be, (CNE) follows immediately from the first half of (i) and (ii). Why, then, the longish preparation? And how about that immediacy? Brief as the last paragraph is, I also registered in it the indispensable near-rock-bottom claim. In the longish preparation, and even earlier by what was said about (6), I supported this claim as carefully as I could; and, of course, indirectly, which we know is the best one can do. As to the immediacy, (CNE) is the most spectacular of the four propositions—the other three corresponding to (a), (b), (c), above—that stop the regress which is the bane of many ontologies. That makes (CNE) one of the cornerstones of the overall dialectic. Such propositions we expect to follow more or less readily from what is most fundamental. Thus everything is as it ought to be.

How, finally, in this case about the illusion? If, instead of clinging to it, you choose to think about the geometrical formation rules of the calculus which we have good reason to believe is the IL, you will find, as I did, that the spell of this particular illusion is broken for good; the reason being that these rules, being neither past causes nor present dispositions, do "correspond," although of course only in the paradoxical way characteristic of some parts of the third kind of ontological discourse, to the canons, which are not there. In this qualified sense they are a "surrogate." Yet there is no surrogate for the seeming transparence. Just remember what has been said about the transparence of the form of a complex, on the one hand, and the capacity of the (geometrical) form of the strings that stand for it.

What, if anything, do the series in the partial order of our nonlinear notation "correspond" to? We are almost ready to answer. Almost, but not quite. It will set the stage for the answer and, at the same time, take care of still another item of unfinished business if we first examine the use that has been made of 'showing itself' in philosophical discourse. The best way to do that is to start from a formula suggested by the *Tractatus:* (F) "What shows itself in the IL does not exist and therefore cannot be expressed in it." Let me first get out of the way what I take to be obvious. Then I shall in five cases tabulate what we have already established. The tabulation will show that (F) greatly oversimplifies the connection between the notions of *showing itself*, of being *expressible*, and of *existing*, or, rather, and equivalently in this world, of being thinkable.

There is, I take it, in all these cases something that does the showing and something that is shown; or, more briefly for the moment, there is the feature and the featured. The former is a feature of the calculus; the latter pertains to what the calculus is about. An uninterpreted calculus, being about nothing, features nothing. In order to know what, if anything, an interpreted calculus features, one must not only attend to its features but also know the interpretation rules. If one must in addition know "something else," one wouldn't, or at least I wouldn't, say that something is showing itself. Attending to a feature may be a perceiving, either immediate or certifiable but always opaque, of a (geometrical) form; it may be an intending of either a sameness or a diversity, whose mode is always either immediately or recursively accessible; or even a coming to know a generality such as either one formation rule or the conjunction of all of them.

(1) With the standard interpretation, where one thing is represented by only one primitive mark, *sameness and diversity* show themselves in propria persona, as it was put; yet they are expressible and are determinates. The sameness or diversity of complexes one cannot decide without making use of the tautologies of sameness and diversity, which are "something else." For things, though, sameness and diversity *show themselves*, are *expressible*, and do *exist*. (2) When it comes to *form*, two distinctions must be kept in mind. The form of a complex (form$_2$) and that of string standing for it (form$_1$) are two and not one. While, say '$At_0(\alpha_1)$' abbreviates the expression for a complex, 'At_0' by itself either with or without abbreviation does not stand for anything. With this proviso, form *shows itself*, is *expressible*, and *exists*. (3) The *ultimate sort* of a thing *shows itself* in the kind of the mark that stands for it; it is *not expressible*, yet it is an entity that *exists*. (4) The *mode* of a complex does *not show itself* and is *not expressible*; yet it, too, is an entity that *exists*. (For the argument that in order to "proceed" from the relevant form of a tautology or contradiction, which does show itself, to its

mode, one must know "something else," see p. 145.) (5). The *canons*, finally, are *not expressible* and *do not exist;* and, since they don't exist, they *show themselves in the formation rules only in a sense that, taken literally, is absurd.* This, as you see, is the only case in which after a fashion (F) holds.

The partial order in one of our nonlinear designs, D_1, and the series within this partial order, can only "correspond" to something that involves the canons which produce the complex α_1, represented by D_1. Hence, since the canons themselves do not exist, the "corresponding" in the case can only be a showing in the style of (5) above. What, then, is being shown? One is tempted to say that the order on paper shows the order in which the canons are applied in producing α_1 out of (the things in) its ultimate foundation. But how can one "apply" what isn't there? Nor must we allow ourselves to be seduced by the suggestion of a temporal order among the several actions of an appli*er*, or produc*er*, or mak*er*. So we had better try again. There is for every maximal series of circles in D_1 a series, S_1, of 2-tuples, such that (a) the first term of the first is a thing, (b) the second term of the last is α_1, (c) the second term of all but the last is the first term of the next, and (d) the second term of each is produced from its first by a single canonical step. S_1 is, in an *attenuated sense* (see 71*), a surrogate for what the serial order on paper purports to show. This, finally, is the answer to the question we left to the end. The attenuation is not a cause for discouragement but, rather, if anything, the opposite. It is a sign that, as a thing being of its ultimate sort, or a tautology whose mode is accessible being one, lies at the exact boundary of the expressible, or, if you please, just beyond it, so the canons and what pertains to them lie at the exact boundary of the thinkable, or, again, just beyond it. And the more accurately we can draw these two boundaries, which mark also the boundaries between the three kinds of ontological discourse, the more confident we may be that all three are worthwhile.

71* I speak of an *attenuation* because, although S_1, unlike the formation rules, has nothing to do with language, I can think of no sense in which it is either "in," or a "part" of, or any other feature of α_1. On the other side of the ledger, though, if S_1 were not there, α_1 would not be there. Nor, speaking concisely, is this particular "being there" an unthinkable "existing." To see that, let α_1 be (a_1, b_1) and consider $(a_1, (a_1, b_1))$ together with $\sim(\exists x)(x = a_1) \supset \sim (\exists y)(y = (a_1, b_2))$. The conditional will do because, as in (7) but not in (6), expressing a canon is not the issue.

Glossary
Index

Glossary

absolutism: 1. The conviction that what we can and cannot think is more than "merely" a "matter of fact." (pp. 66, 67) 2. "One not only sometimes knows something, but when knowing it, he sometimes also knows that he knows it. That, I believe, is the proposition all absolutists must defend." (p. 99)

act (mental): A fact consisting of a particular exemplifying a *thought* and a *species*. (p. 61)

analytic: Any complex which is presented with its mode is analytic. Somewhat more technically, any complex whose mode is either immediately available or recursively accessible. (p. 140)

ascent: Bergmann's term for the "relationship" between a complex and the existential generalization of which it is an instantiation. (see p. 172)

auxiliary act: According to Bergmann one cannot be conscious of certain sorts of existents without also intending (by either perception or imagination) at the same time certain verbal strings which, as we might say, are the linguistic representative of the intention. The act which intends this verbal string, thus enabling one to be conscious of these intentions, is called an "auxiliary act". (p. 208)

awareness: *See* conscious state, below.

"axiom" (note quotation marks): Bergmann's term for those complexes which (i) involve the notion of a class, and (ii) are immediately transparent. Modeled on but explicitly distinguished from *axioms* (no quotes) proposed by axiomatic set theorists (sometimes called 'AST' by Bergmann) as a foundation for their set-theoretical systems. Bergmann's "axioms," unlike the axioms of the AST are selected not for the mathematical elegance their adoption allows but because their modes are 'immediately available', which Bergmann feels is a requirement an ontologist cannot ignore. Bergmann explicitly refuses to adopt as "axioms" the axiom of infinity and the axiom of regularity because, he claims, they are not immediately transparent. (p. 275)

canon: A "rule" or "principle" which specifies which nonsimple determinates exist if certain other determinates and/or makers exist. For example, it is a canon that if a particular, a, and a nonrelational universal of the first type, f, exist, then, if the appropriate type of exemplification, η (meaning, basically, 'nexus'), exists there also exists an atomic fact of that particular exemplifying that universal (perspicuously represented as '$\eta(a, f)$'). Thus a canon is *like* a formation rule which specifies which strings are well formed. But a canon is, if a formation rule, a formation rule of the "ideal language," which means more than a merely conventional rule or stipulation; a canon is somehow based upon a "feature" of

357

reality and so in some, admittedly nonliteral, sense, correct or incorrect. Bergmann eventually claims, though, that a canon cannot be stated *in* the IL and hence does not literally state a fact; nor, as it turns out, does it express something which can be *thought* in a literal sense of this term.

Cartesian progression: "A finite series of awarenesses, each temporally preceding the next, in which transparence spreads from the first to the last." (p. 225; for a more complete definition, see p. 149)

circumstance: A complex whose terms (the proximately "simpler" existents from which the complex is produced) do not require a maker, or function, to bring them together into the complex. Thus the diad, or diversity, (X, Y) [where 'X' and 'Y' range over all determinates] exists given only that X and Y exist. There is no further relation, nexus, or function of *being diverse* required to ground the existence of the diad. This is the force of the claim that if the terms of a circumstance exist then the circumstance eo ipso exists. In addition to diads Bergmann holds that there are two other sorts of circumstances, which he calls 'elementhoods' and 'intentional nexus'. A determinate's being an element of a class is a circumstance which does not require grounding in a separate relation or nexus of being-an-element-of but is simply there (actually or potentially) if the determinate and the class exist. Again, *that* a thought intends its intention is not a complex that requires a tie or connection over and above the thought and its intention but is something which exists (eo ipso) if the thought and its intention exist. Circumstances are thus the "structural counterparts" of internal relationships, relationships grounded in the nature and identity of their relata. (p. 139)

class: A collection of all and only those determinates which satisfy the condition specified by a selector. Collections, as such, have no ontological status; classes owe their ontological status to the "weak togetherness" of their elements' satisfying the selector's condition. (p. 274; on distinction between classes and properties, see pp. 158–63)

clinging: The "relation" between an M-function (maker) and its argument. Clinging is structurally similar to the "relation" between Frege's *saturated* objects and *unsaturated* functions. (see p. 128) The function exemplification *clings* to the diad (f, a); this clinging of the maker to the diad *is* the making of the fact conventionally represented (in the LFC.) as $f(a)$. The term 'relation' is scare-quoted above because clinging in not really a relation; nor is it a "connection" if by that is meant a function. Clinging requires no ontological ground.

cluster: A conjunction of atomic facts, all of the lowest type, some of which may be relational. (see p. 210)

cluster view: The "doctrine, and the inaccurate notion of introspection associated with it, [that] every awareness 'is' nothing but a conjunction of atomic facts, say, $f_1 a_1$ & $f_2 a_2$ & . . . ; $f_1, f_2, . . .$ being such characters as green, hot, . . . but certainly not those . . . which [Bergmann] call[s] thoughts." (p. 82)

collection: A "group" of existents which can be specified by a "mere" list. For Bergmann collections have 'members' while classes have 'elements'. An existent may "occur" more than once in a collection while an element of a class only "occurs" once; in short, an element of a class *is* an element of the class because it satisfies the condition specified by the selector of the class and an existent either does or does not satisfy a condition, while a list may contain the name of an existent several times. Again, collections may have nondeterminates as members but classes can only have determinates as elements. (see p. 48)

complex: Bergmann's general term for any existent which is pervaded by a mode. There are two sorts of complexes, facts and circumstances. (p. 107)

complex I: A complex *every* step in the production of which is an (a)-step (i.e., a *making*, either by exemplification, a connective, or a quantifier), *except* for those (b)-steps which produce standardization diads and order tuples. (p. 139)

complex II: Either a circumstance or a complex *at least one step* in the production of which is the formation of a circumstance which is *not* merely a standardization diad or an order tuple. (p. 139)

cone: The cone of a nonsimple determinate, X, is the class whose elements are all of the determinates that belong to *one of* X's ultimate foundations *and* the intermediate foundations produced from this ultimate foundation by the sequence of steps which produces X. (for technical definition, see p. 181) Note that Bergmann's new assay of general facts allows that general facts may be produced from different ultimate foundations. It follows that general facts (and complexes which contain them) have more than one cone. If a nonsimple can only be produced from one ultimate foundation then it has only one cone.

conscious state (state of awareness):   A general and self-consciously vague term referring to what we would ordinarily call 'mental states'. Strictly speaking, for Bergmann, a mental act is a particular exemplifying (at least) a thought and a species (the particular *may* also exemplify the character of evidence, as well as various temporal relations). A conscious state consists of a *collection* of several such acts. Bergmann distinguishes between, for example, *perceiving* and *perceiving*$_1$, the latter of which is a genuine species (of mental act) but the former of which is a (kind of) collection of mental acts at least one of which must be a perceiving$_1$. Bergmann makes similar distinctions about imagining, doubting, and other conscious states. (see p. 208)

constituent: One determinate is a constituent of another if and only if it is an element of *all* of the latter's cones. (for technical definition, see p. 192)

contextualism: 1. "I emphatically reject all *contextualisms*, linguistic or otherwise, of which [implicit] definitions . . . are the very essence." (p. 50) 2. "The core of *anticontextualism* . . . is that, when presented with a single thing, one can "know" its ultimate sort." (p. 304) 3. Whenever one is implicitly presented with a maker (function) one must also at the same time be presented with at least one analytic complex involving that maker. This is one of the "recoverable cores" of contextualism. (pp. 151)

contingent principle: A "feature" of the world which is so pervasive and deeply rooted phenomenologically that it is more than merely another inductive truth and is, in a sense, such that we cannot seriously believe its denial. Some such "principles" are "anthropological"; that is, they presuppose the existence (at least) of human (or finite) *minds*. An example would be that, for example, no facts except clusters can be perceived without a simultaneous perceiving$_1$ of a *text*. Other contingent principles are not anthropological in this sense. That the world is extensional, and that there are no inhomogeneous relations, are two examples given by Bergmann of contingent principles which are nonanthropological. (p. 225)

core (as in "core of the world"): The *core* of our world is a world otherwise like ours except that it, unlike our world, has no classes. (p. 265; also see p. 313)

criterion: A complex which specifies the conditions in which "two" nonsimple determinates are the same or diverse (i.e., really one or really two). The diversity of *things* is its own ground. The diversity of *nondeterminates* needs no ground (*see* unique, below). But the diversity of nonsimple determinates is grounded, partly, by criterial complexes which specify the conditions which must be satisfied if "two" nonsimples are to be diverse. That "two" diads are diverse unless the first term of the first is the same as either the first or second term of the second, and the second term of the first is the same as the other term of the second, is the criterion "regulating" the diversity of diads. (p. 102)

descent: Bergmann's term for the "relationship" between a universal generalization and a complex which is an instantiation of it. (see p. 172)

determinate: An existent that can be "explicitly intended," or, in other words, can be the whole intention of a thought. According to Bergmann facts, things, circumstances, and classes are the only sorts of existents which are determinates. Makers and entities, since they can only be implicitly intended (something is implicitly intended if it is "contained in" what is explicitly intended), are not determinates. The notion of a determinate is coextensive with that of an existent which "satisfies the minimal restriction." (*see* minimal restriction) Bergmann also characterizes determinates by saying that determinates are all and only those existents which are produced out of *items* by ultimate sorts either with or without makers. (p. 77) In this sense determinates are those existents which contain "matter." (see p. 77)

determinate-I: A determinate which is either a thing or a complex-I. (pp. 313 ff.) (*see* nucleus, below)

determinate-II: Any determinate which is either a class or a complex-II. (p. 313 ff.)

diacritical expression: An expression in the IL that does not represent an existent but directs our attention to the sort of existent that is represented by the larger expression of which the diacritical expression is a part. According to Bergmann his IL contains only four such expressions: (i) "λ" which indicates that the expression of which it is a part represents a class, (ii) "∈" which indicates that the larger expression of which it is a part represents an elementhood, (iii) "(,)" which indicates that the existent represented by the expression formed by filling in the blanks flanking the comma with expressions designating determinates is a diad, and (iv) "M" which indicates that a larger expression formed by flanking the "M" with expressions designating determinates represents the intentional nexus between the determinates represented by the flanking expressions.

diad: The circumstance of two determinates being diverse. If the two determinates are, say, X and Y, then the circumstance of their being, as it were, *really* two and not one is represented (in the IL) as '(X, Y)' and is called a diad. The diad (X, Y) is 'built out of' X and Y, its 'terms'; it is not "made out of" them by a maker. (p. 104 ff.)

entity: Existents which are "totally inseparable" from the existents to which they are "attached." Such existents have the "lowest ontological status," a condition reflected in the fact that there are no signs in the IL representing entities. There are three sorts of entity: (i) items, the individuators in things, (ii) ultimate sorts, which ground the ability of things to be combined with other things into facts by makers (specifically, exemplification), and (iii) the modes, actuality and potentiality. (p. 56)

enumerator: A 2-tuple which is the selector of a finite class. Specifically, any 2-tuple of the general form $\langle c, (c = a_1) \vee (c = a_2) \vee \ldots \vee (c = a_n) \rangle$, such that c is diverse from every a_n. Such a 2-tuple is a selector of the class conventionally represented by '$\{a_1, a_2, \ldots, a_n\}$'.

evidence: A character exemplified by all and only those particulars in mental acts whose intentions are transparent. Every particular which exemplifies the character of *grasping* (that species of act which has a *thing* as its intention) also exemplifies the character of *evidence* (or, if you like, the character of being evident). Every believing to which its intention is presented *with* its mode is also evident (i.e., the particular in the act also exemplifies the character of evidence). (pp. 94 ff.)

explicit presentation: A determinate is said to be "explicitly presented' when it is the sole intention of a mental act (as opposed to being, say, a constituent of something which is the sole intention of a mental act.) (p. 62) According to Bergmann only determinates *can* be explicitly presented.

fact: Any complex the final step in the production of which is an (a)-step. (p. 76) The *value* of a *function* for an *argument*. (p. 126)

foundation: The collection of existents which is specified in the assay of an existent. The '*ultimate foundation*' of an existent is the collection of *simples* specified by such an assay, while the '*intermediate foundation*' of an existent is the collection of *simpler* existents specified by an assay of that existent. Thus, the ultimate foundation of $f(a)$ & $g(a)$ is the collection the members of which are the particular *a*, the two universals *f* and *g*, and the maker &. The intermediate foundation of the same complex is the collection whose members are the two facts *f*(*a*) and *g*(*b*), and the maker &.

form: Bergmann uses the term 'form' in several senses. In Section III he introduces the locution 'form₁' to designate 'any nondeterminate with the one-many feature', a group in which he includes all functions, modes, and ultimate sorts. (pp. 112 ff.) In Section IV he introduces the notion of 'form₂', by which he means the logical form of complexes. To say, for example, that 'this-being-green is an atomic fact' is to ascribe a form₂ to the complex this-being-green. (p. 135) In Section VII, however, Bergmann again introduces a distinction between 'form₁' and 'form₂'. Here he means to distinguish the geometrical shape of a linguistic string, its form₁, and the logical form of a complex that might be represented by a linguistic string, its form₂. (p. 330)

form class: A class such that its elements are all those and only those determinates which share a certain form. (p. 309)

formalists: Those who construe such sentences as 'green is a property', 'universality is diverse from particularity', etc., as referring to the features of a syntactically constructed calculus. (p. 237)

function: Bergmann replaces the anthropomorphic word 'maker' with the word 'function' as a part of his 'standardization', which allows him to construe all facts as values of a function for an argument. (see pp. 125 ff.) *See* standardization, below.

fundamental gambit: Bergmann uses the phrase 'fundamental gambit' in a generic sense to refer to an assumption so "deep" it is beyond argument, or, at least, one for which he will offer no direct argument. In a more specific sense Bergmann's fundamental gambit is his 'Principle of Presentation', which claims that everything thinkable exists and vice versa. This principle presents the ontologist with a task, which is to provide an account or assay for everything (or every important sort of thing) which can be thought.

ideal language (IL):   A collection of primitive marks and certain finite linear strings, with repetition, of primitive marks. These strings are called 'well-formed'. The primitive marks and well-formed strings of them are called 'expressions'. Except for the 'diacritical' expressions, all the expressions of the IL stand for one and only one existent. The purpose of proposing an IL is to perspicuously "reflect" or "display" the fundamental categories of existents in the world as well as the ways in which some are 'produced from' others.

identity: Bergmann's term for the "being and nature" of an existent. The identity of an existent is not anything distinct from the existent itself; rather, when we are presented with an existent, explicitly or implicitly, we are "uno actu" presented with its identity. The identity of something is, in this sense, *what it is*. Needless to say, this sense of identity has nothing directly to do with Bergmann's notion of sameness or the "Russell-Leibniz" conception of identity. (pp. 267 ff.)

immediately available: If a complex is transparent whenever explicitly presented then it is said to be 'immediately available'. (p. 70)

implicit presentation: An existent is said to be 'implicitly presented' when it is *not* the sole intention of a mental act but *is* "in" the intention of something which is the sole intention of a mental act. The term 'in' is ambiguous in the above definition; it may mean 'is-a-constituent-of', but it must also mean something else, since Bergmann claims both that there are existents which *can only* by implicitly presented (entities and functions) and that such existents *can not* be constituents (since they are not determinates). (pp. 62, 63; *see* explicit presentation, above)

independence (dependence): To say that an existent is *independent* is to say that it can be intended explicitly, i.e., that it can be the sole intention of a thought. An existent is said to be *dependent* if it cannot be intended explicitly but only implicitly. According to Bergmann nondeterminates cannot be the sole intention of a thought but must be intended, if at all, as the components of determinates. (pp. 74, 75; see also p. 114)

indubitability: A characteristic of direct awarenesses, or perhaps of certain beliefs about the intentions of direct awarenesses (namely, those simultaneous with the direct awareness). One cannot, Bergmann claims, be directly aware of something and simultaneously doubt it. Indubitability is not the highest "degree of warrant" (= reason for believing), for even though one may not be able to doubt the actuality of an intention of which one is directly aware, one *can think* its negation. The highest degree of warranty is provided by the unthinkability of the negation. (see p. 87)

instrumental awareness: "An awareness, $\mathfrak{A}$, is instrumental for another, $\mathfrak{B}$, if and only if, (1) $\mathfrak{A}$ is among the contributory causes of $\mathfrak{B}$, and (2) the referent of $\mathfrak{A}$, although "linguistic," is not the text of $\mathfrak{B}$." (p. 225) Essentially an awareness is instrumental if it is an awareness of a verbal string that is causally necessary for the process of inference.

internal relationship (relation): If two (or more) elements stand in a relationship that is grounded in the *identity* (the *nature*) of the relata, then this relationship is internal. Bergmann's category of *circumstances* is a "structural counterpart" of the notion of internal relationships, for a circumstance exists eo ipso given the identity and nature of its *terms*. The notion of an internal relation is entirely parasitic on that of an internal relationship: two things are related by an internal relation if and only if they stand in an internal relationship. If would not be inaccurate to say that there really are no internal relations, but rather only internal relationships. (p. 106)

interstitial awareness: An awareness which is a causally necessary link in a sequence of awarenesses the mode of whose referents is transparent. Bergmann does not really make it clear whether this notion is the same as that of an instrumental awareness. (p. 291)

iterator: Arbitrarily chosen determinates which serve as "dummy variables" in the selectors of infinite recursive classes. These iterators, by the manner of their "association with" the first and second element of an infinite recursive class in the selector of such a class, enable a determination of the third fourth, and all subsequent elements of the class. In this way they allow the condition which must be satisfied by all and only the elements of the class to be "encoded" in the selector. (see p. 294)

limiting complex: A complex is a *limiting complex* if and only if it has alternative ultimate foundations which have nothing in common. For example, the (conventionally represented) complex $(f)(x)[f(x) \vee \sim f(x)]$ is a limiting complex. Any and every five-member collection of *a* particular, *a* universal$^{(0)}$, $\vee$, $\bigvee$ and η, each the appropriate number of times, is *an* alternative ultimate foundation of this complex. Another way of saying this is to say that a complex is a limiting complex if and only if it has *no* constituents. (p. 178)

luminous (luminosity):   A characteristic Bergmann ascribes to 'forms': makers, ultimate sorts, modes. Such existents, even though they cannot of course be explicitly presented, often become transparent when they are implicitly presented. In this manner they "stand out" when presented. What "stands out" in this way Bergmann calls "luminous." He opposes and contrasts luminosity with *opacity*, the sheer thisness of *items*. (p. 115) It is clear that Bergmann's use of "transparent" to characterize luminosity is different from, though perhaps related to, his usual and more technical use of the same word to characterize the intentions of certain acts, for forms cannot be transparent in this latter sense.

maker: A nondeterminate existent which grounds the togetherness of a determinate in a *fact*. Facts are either atomic facts, molecular facts, or general facts (generalizations). The makers which account for the togetherness of these sorts of facts are exemplification nexus, connectives, and quantifiers, respectively. Bergmann later replaces the term 'maker' with the equivalent, but less anthropomorphic, term 'function'. (p. 45) (*see* function, above)

material: 1. The "simpler" existents (determinates) out of which a less simple existent is produced in accord with the canons. (p. 45.) 2. The "relationship" between one existent, X, and another existent, Y, that obtains if and only if X is either a *constituent* of Y or X is an *element* of Y. (p. 277)

minimal restriction: The "principle" which places restrictions on which sorts of existent can serve as the terms of a circumstance, or, more specifically, can be intelligibly said (or thought) to be diverse from other existents. According to Bergmann only *things, facts, circumstances,* and *classes* satisfy the minimal restriction; neither makers (functions) nor entities satisfy the restriction and thus cannot be said (thought) to be diverse from (or the same as) other existents. The minimal restriction is coordinated with other significant divisions in Bergmann's ontology. The notion of an existent that satisfies the minimal restriction is coextensive with the notion of an existent that: (i) ir (or can be) a *constituent* of a *fact;* (ii) is (or can be) an *element* of a *class;* (iii) is (or can be) a *term* of a *circumstance* (those circumstances other than diversities). (p. 49) It is also the case that, in Bergmann's terms, any existent which satisfies the minimal restriction is capable of being explicitly intended, for which reason he calls existents which are either things, facts, circumstances, or classes "determinates." (p. 77)

nucleus: The nucleus of a world (or the world) is a world otherwise like that world except (the world) that it "contains" no classes *and* no circumstances other than standardization and order tuples. (p. 313)

opacity: "An item, beyond grounding a One or This, is merely an I-know-not-what. All items, including those of universals, are bare." (p. 116) All items are, in this sense, opaque. All *things,* which are composites of items and ultimate sorts (forms), are thus composites of opaque "matter" and luminous "form."

perceiving$_1$:   An act of perceiving whose intention is a molecular fact such that the particulars "in" the intention are simultaneous with the particulars which are "in" the act of perceiving itself. (see p. 210)

perceptual object: Such "ordinary objects" as tables, chairs, horses, etc. Those "things" which traditionally are held to be substances and/or continuants (though not by Bergmann, who denies the existence of either substances or continuants). Perceptual objects are also not to be confused with "physical objects," which for Bergmann are "theoretical constructs" with which the scientist "replaces" the perceptual object in his attempt to explain their behavior. (see p. 210)

presented$_1$ (as distinguished from presented$_2$):   Often Bergmann will provide an *assay* of something that seems in some manner to conflict with our "ordinary" experience of (or thought and discourse about) that something. In such a case there is 'phenomenological distance' between the *assay* and what one might expect the assay to be if one were guided by this ordinary experience of what is being assayed. To speak of what we are *presented$_2$* with is to speak of the *referents* of our states of awareness (i.e., existents as we ordinarily experience and think about them), while to speak of what we are *presented$_1$* with is to speak of what is *really there,* ontologically speaking. (see p. 214; also see p. 232)

primary class: Any finite class; equivalently, any class whose selector(s) is (are) an enumerator(s). (p. 254)

primary (secondary) perceivings (imaginings):   A perceiving (imagining) which *need not* be accompanied by an auxiliary act whose intention is a *text* appropriate to the intention of the perceiving (imagining) is called 'primary'. A perceiving (imagining) which *must be* accompanied by such an auxiliary act is called 'secondary'. (pp. 217, 218) Bergmann contends that: (i) only perceivings and imaginings can be primary in this sense, (ii) the intentions of primary perceivings (imaginings) are *clusters* (*see* cluster), and thus (iii) any molecular fact which involves any connective besides conjunction *cannot* be primary, no matter how "simple." [note: there are perceivings$_1$ which are primary and those which are secondary]

Principle of Acquaintance: "No act intending a universal, say, f_1, occurs in a life history unless there is a particular, say, a_1, such that $f_1(a_1)$ is also intended, either by this act or by a second act, either simultaneous with or preceding the first, that occurs in the same life history. As for f_1 and a_1, so mutatis mutandis for relations and the higher types." (p. 65)

Principle of Presentation: The claim that whatever is thinkable exists and vice versa. This principle provides the fundamental phenomenological basis of ontology. (p. 61)

pure complex-II: Any complex which has an intermediate foundation such that all of its members are either functions or circumstances. (p. 140)

quantificational I-complex (q-complex-I):   A complex-I such that there is at least one quantification among the steps producing it. (see p. 168) Every generality is a q-complex but not conversely. E.g.: $f(a) \vee \bigvee \langle a, f(a) \rangle$ is a q-complex but not a generality.

quantificational II-complex (q-complex-II):   A complex containing at least one generality the scope of which is a complex-II. (p. 171)

recursively accessible: A complex whose mode is presented (i.e., a complex which becomes transparent) only after a sequence of conscious states called a 'Cartesian progression'. (p. 70; also see p. 149; *see* Cartesian progression, above)

referent: Whatever a conscious state (or, synonymously, an awareness) is a consciousness (or awareness) *of*. Some conscious states may be collections of (simultaneous) mental acts, no one of which has as its intention the referent of the conscious state of which it is a member. If there were a conscious state consisting of only one mental act (there are not, as a matter of fact), then the referent of that mental act *would*, of course, be the referent of that conscious state. (p. 207)

reism: The thesis or belief that all existents are *things*, or, even more specifically, that there are no facts. (p. 129)

relationism: The belief or assumption, not necessarily articulated, that the making of a fact is a relation between its "material" and the fact which is the "product" of this making. Bergmann claims that such a view is suggested by the anthropomorphic term "maker" and so he is led to replace the term with the more ontologically neutral term "function." (p. 125) A fact is no longer to be considered a *product* made by a *maker* from *materials* but rather a "value" of a "function" for an "argument." Thus the fact represented by the string "$\eta(f, a)$" is the value of the function η (exemplification) for the argument (f, a). Bergmann's introduction of the function terminology is closely tied to his "standardization," which involves construing *all* functions (except negation), including exemplifications, connectives, and quantifiers, as monadic and *all* their arguments as single determinates, which are diads. (*see* standardization)

sameness: To say that "two" determinates are the same is to say that they are not diverse; a sameness is thus a fact formed by negating a diversity. This type of "strict" sameness is not to be confused with the more relaxed standards specified by Leibniz' Law. (p. 74 ff.)

scope: The fact or circumstance which serves as the second term of a 2-tuple which a quantifier makes into a generality. This second term must have the first term of the 2-tuple (the target of the generality) as a constituent. A general fact conventionally represented as $(\exists y)f(y)$ is now represented by Bergmann as $\wedge\langle b, f(b)\rangle$ (for some arbitrarily selected particular, b. The expression '$f(b)$' represents the *scope* of the complex. (see p. 168)

secondary class (also called 'Peano class' or 'P-class'):   Denumerably infinite class. (pp. 280–98)

selector: A circumstance *on* which classes are *built*. These circumstances are tuples which specify or "encode" the condition which a determinate must satisfy in order to be an element of the class. According to the canons governing class formation, if a selector exists then, eo ipso, the class of determinates which satisfy the condition it specifies also exists. (pp. 250 ff., 290)

standardization: A systematic way of understanding the ontological content and structure of nonsimple determinates that may conflict, to some extent, with our "naive" phenomenological and linguistic preconceptions but which is nevertheless justified because it allows us to solve certain ontological problems, especially the problem of order. The standardization allows us (or, if you prefer, compels us) to assay all facts, except negations, as the values of *monadic* functions for arguments which are diads (negative facts are the values of a monadic function, negation, for arguments which are complexes). (pp. 120–26)

standardization diads: Those diads which the standardization compels us to "put into" the assay of nonsimples. The diad whose terms are the particular a and the property f, (a, f), for example, is a standardization diad with respect to the assay of the atomic fact of a-exemplifying-f (perspicuously represented by the string '$\eta(a, f)$'). The tuples which the standardization has us place in the assay of certain relational atomic facts, molecular facts, and general facts and, as well, certain sorts of circumstances, are themselves a subsort of standardization diad; these diads are called "order tuples." (pp. 139 ff.)

stratification: A distribution or assignment of existents into strata or "layers" in a way that produces a "type" system for those existents. (p. 140; 323 ff.)

target: In a q-complex-I, the thing serving as the first term in the 2-tuple which a quantifier makes into a generality. The target plays the role, so to speak, which would be played by the bound variables in a generality, *if there were any variables*. Targets are needed because, for Bergmann, there are no variables. E.g., what would be conventionally represented by '$(x)f(x)$' is now to be represented by '$\vee\langle a, f(a)\rangle$' (for some arbitrarily selected particular, a). The target of the complex thus represented is the particular a. Bergmann also allows, in some cases, quantification over complexes and classes; in these cases complexes and classes can also serve as targets. (see p. 168)

tautology: A complex is a tautology if and only if (i) it is transparent, and (ii) so is every instance of at least one of its *forms*. (p. 141)

tertiary class: The "third" sort of full-status class in Bergmann's ontology. There are nonrecursive tertiary classes and recursive tertiary classes.

368 Glossary

Among tertiary classes are the 'form classes', such as the class of all atomic facts (nonrecursive) and the class of all molecular facts (recursive). Also falling within the tertiary classes are recursive classes with iteration steps more complicated than those of standard secondary classes, such as, for example, a 'Zermelo class' whose elements are a determinate, the (unit) class whose only element is the previous determinate, the class whose only element is the previous class, and so on. (pp. 299 ff.)

transparent: Feature of those complex intentions that are presented with their mode (or, more broadly, whose mode is either immediately available or accessible), or of things that are intended as being of their ultimate sorts. (p. 70)

True (False):   Truth is essentially a matter of correspondence, where this is understood in the following way: A *thought* is either true or false depending on whether the fact (or circumstance) it intends is either actual or potential. "$T(g)$" abbreviates "$(\exists p)(gMp \ \& \ p)$" and "$F(g)$" abbreviates "$(\exists p)(gMp \ \& \ {\sim}p)$" (where g is a thought, p its intention). Thus 'T' and 'F', being defined signs, do not appear in the IL and therefore do not stand for anything. (p. 99)

text: A perceived or imagined linguistic string which "represents," so to speak, the referent of an awareness. Bergmann holds that any awareness other than a perceiving or imagining (namely, believing, doubting, etc.) *must be* accompanied by a perceiving or imagining of a *text*. He also holds that any perceiving (or imagining) of anything *but* a cluster requires such auxiliary acts intending texts. (p. 208)

tuple: A diad at least one term of which is itself a diad and the other term of which is a term of that other diad. Thus $(x, (x, y))$ is a 2-tuple for it is a diad one term of which is a diad, (x, y), and the other term of which, x, is term of that first diad. Such a 2-tuple Bergmann represents with the abbreviation '$\langle x, y \rangle$'. The 3-tuple represented by '$\langle x, y, z \rangle$' is $(x, \langle y, z \rangle)$, or $(x, (y, (y, z)))$. In general, the n-tuple represented as '$\langle x_1, \ldots, x_n \rangle$' is the diad $(x_1, \langle x_2, \ldots, x_n \rangle)$. (p. 120)

unique (uniqueness):   Bergmann claims that functions (makers) and entities are *unique*, meaning by this that their diversity needs no ground, that there is nothing "in" or "about," say, one connective which distinguishes it from another. An existent is unique if it fails to satisfy the minimal restriction. (see p. 114)

variant: The value of a quantifier (quantifiers are functions) for an argument. The reason for calling it a "variant" is that, uniquely among the functions, one quantifier can take *different* arguments and, in each case, have as its value determinates which are the same. Thus the function $\bigvee$, taking the determinates $\langle a, f(a) \rangle$ and $\langle b, f(b) \rangle$ as arguments, will have the determinates $\bigvee \langle a, f(g) \rangle$ and $\bigvee \langle b, f(b) \rangle$ as values, but these determinates are the *same;* i.e., the potentiality of their diad is immediately available. (see p. 169)

A consequence of this is that all generalities, indeed, all q-complexes, have *alternative foundations.*

Index